01786

THE
FRYING PAN
OF
SPAIN

THE
FRYING PAN
OF
SPAIN

Sevilla v Real Betis:
Spain's Hottest Football Rivalry

C O L I N   M I L L A R

First published by Pitch Publishing, 2019

Pitch Publishing
A2 Yeoman Gate
Yeoman Way
Worthing
Sussex
BN13 3QZ
www.pitchpublishing.co.uk
info@pitchpublishing.co.uk

A CIP catalogue record is available for this book
from the British Library.

ISBN 978 1 78531 524 4

Typesetting and origination by Pitch Publishing
Printed and bound in Great Britain by TJ International Ltd

Contents

Acknowledgements

THE only fitting way to begin this book is by thanking those people who have made it possible. Firstly, I would like to thank Paul and Jane Camillin at Pitch Publishing for giving me the opportunity to write it, and Duncan Olner, who captured the true spirit of Seville and its passion for football in his eye-catching front cover design.

My family have been instrumental throughout the project. My parents David and Deirdre have offered their unwavering support, my brother Peter kindly volunteered to proofread the text and my brother Christopher compiled an inspirational promotional video.

Further thanks goes to those who have shared their first-hand experiences of reporting on the rivalry, the significance of supporting either club, documenting their histories or who have offered general insights with the project, in alphabetical order: Phil Ball, Andy Brassell, Alfonso Del Castillo, Chris Clements, Dermot Corrigan, Alejandro Delmás, Sara Espeja, José Luis Garrido Peña, Mateo González, Javier Guerra Lamos, Ben Hardman, Sid Lowe, Sarah Martin, Euan McTear, Andy Mitten, Victor Perea, Carlos Pérez Zorrilla, Paul Reidy, Carlos Romero, Javier Terenti, Guillermo Tinoco, Carlos Urbano, Kyle Williams – and many more whom I have spoken to over the course of my research.

Finally, a big thank you to Real Betis Balompié and Sevilla Fútbol Club, who have both kindly lent their support to this project and who have created such a compelling rivalry. To all *Sevillanos* who have helped me establish their wonderful city as my spiritual home, this is for you.

Introduction

SEVILLE is a truly special city, capable not only of taking your breath away at first glance but of continuing to enchant and bedazzle with each passing day. The capital of Spain's Andalusia region is both charming and vibrant but remains fiercely loyal to centuries-old traditions. Few cities are so passionate about religion and none can rival its Moorish architecture, displayed so often under cloudless blue skies. Yet most prominently of all, *Sevillanos* have mastered the art of partying and this is evident on every lively plaza and in each swarming tapas bar.

The Frying Pan of Spain is primarily a football book, but one which also explains the historical, social and cultural relevance which is at the heart of the sport in Seville and within Spain. It is impossible to show what makes its footballing rivalry so revered without first explaining how the clubs and their fans reflect the purity, pride and passion of their city.

Seville is equally split between two footballing institutions: Real Betis Balompié and Sevilla Fútbol Club, but just how equally is a constant source of debate. In 2015, a survey by the Andalusian survey centre found 42.8 per cent of Seville supported Betis, while 36.2 per cent leant their fandom to Sevilla. A year later, the city's Chamber of Commerce produced different results – Sevilla edging out Betis 39.4 per cent to 36.7 per cent. Such a delicate balance of power is exceptionally rare in any sporting city especially when splintering families, siblings and relationships.

These divisions, rather than detracting from a rivalry, add a coating of unity and respect between two fervent sets of fans. That is of course only evident on the rare occasions when they grow tired of winding each other up.

"The average Sevillian will have inherited a very particular sense of humour," Javier Guerra Lamos of the *Peña Bética Escocesa* explained to me. "This is difficult to explain but essentially is a mix going between the absurdly exaggerated and ironic, and this is often translated into ingenious jokes about each other's teams."

Victor Perea, of the *Peña Sevillista El Origen*, echoed similar sentiments when we spoke: "People in Sevilla have a very witty sense of humour, we are very passionate in all we do and having friends and family supporting the other team means that you are always taking the piss. For instance, my father and brother support Betis."

And these splits are common? "Half of my family are Sevilla supporters and it is absolutely normal that there are huge divisions," added Guerra Lamos, the Betis fan. "The majority of my friends in Seville are *Sevillistas!*"

Sevilla fan Guillermo Tinoco told me the city's football rivalry was "polarised" due to intensity and strength of feeling. "The entire family of my sister-in-law and my nephews are Béticos, but of course we still get along. Our *guasa* [sense of humour] is important because we laugh when the other team fails. This is common across families, in workplaces, schools … it's a polarised city and almost nobody names Barcelona or Real Madrid as their team."

This is a city divided in sporting terms but one which is very much united in pride and identity in their home city. "Sevillians have a level of narcissism, there is a popular belief that we are from the most beautiful city in the world," Guerra Lamos added. "This belief that we are the best implicates football too, it pushes the supporters to be passionate to the point of fanaticism."

The conflicting fandom figures are the basis of a fierce rivalry of claims and counterclaims, which go beyond bickering over which club has the larger fanbase within the city's walls. There is often a total absence of consensus on historical claims, including club foundation dates and which team has benefitted more from authorities over the years. I have attempted to critically analyse all these claims, and others, in this journey through the history of Sevillian football. It is important to recognise that historical information is constantly evolving – most notably in the dating of Sevilla's foundation being moved from 1905 to 1890, which has caused predictable controversy elsewhere – and at times, can be contradictory. My aim is to bring clarity to such claims with a balanced and analytical approach and while occasionally there is no wholly satisfactory answer, this only serves to add an extra layer of contention to set this rivalry apart.

And what a rivalry. Both clubs have won the top division title in Spain, both clubs have won multiple Copa trophies, and both have mass bases of support. The two are firmly established in Spain's leading seven clubs and between them have in excess of 90,000 season ticket holders. Between 2006 and 2016, Sevilla won five major European titles – more than any other club on the continent – and built a sporting project which was the envy of competitors across the world. By contrast, Betis have forged a reputation on romanticism and taking pride in their fans' unrivalled loyalty, borne out through their *Manque pierda* philosophy – supporting the team even when they lose, which has been a lot more frequent than a club of their standing deserve. When describing his devotion to the club, famed flamenco dancer Antonio Canales mused: "Supporting Betis is a gift life has given us."

Many fervent football fans will be unaware that Real Betis hail from the city of Seville, and many even ask "Real who?" Yet within Spain, they are a colossus. They have the nation's fourth-largest attendance figures, behind only Real Madrid, Barcelona and Atlético de Madrid. The rivalry they share with Sevilla – officially Spain's second-oldest football club and the first club in the nation to devote itself solely to the sport – is widely acknowledged as being the best in Spain.

"It's unique," European football writer Andy Brassell, who has covered multiple derby matches across the continent, told me. "The fact that it's so big, when both clubs have achieved things during their histories but neither has quite reached the continental elite level, feels like a manifestation of the city's character. It's everything I imagined Spain would be when I was a kid – loud, colourful, outgoing – and that's what the derby is. Noisy. You really feel the claustrophobia of it as well. Having two clubs that can get 50k in their respective stadiums in a city this size is amazing. It's like having Newcastle and Sunderland in the same city."

Both clubs offer true authenticity. *Sevillistas* and *Béticos* hold complete and unwavering devotion to their teams, their loyalty is not to be questioned. Sevilla fans affectionately refer to their club as *Once Barras* – in reference to the 11 vertical red and white stripes on their badge – while Betis supporters are dedicated to the *Trece Barras*, as their shield has an extra two green and white bars.

Their clubs play in true coliseums of the Spanish game – the Estadio Ramón Sánchez-Pizjuán and the Estadio Benito Villamarín, each named after definitive club presidents and situated within 4km of each other. "Both have high, steep sides which gives an intense, almost claustrophobic feel," Chris Clements, who runs the English-language website on Spanish football stadiums, Estadios de España, told me. "Neither have suffered from corporate gentrification and it's worth noting that night matches have a completely different feel to them, adding to the sense of occasion. Within Spain, this match is undoubtedly the most exciting and intense."

On derby days, the 600 travelling fans of either club are marched, via a police escort, along to the den of their fiercest rivals. When celebrating successes, Betis fans congregate in the central Plaza Nueva while Sevilla's support flocks to another of the city's central public squares – the Puerta de Jerez.

Throughout their histories there have been plenty of successes, but plenty of low points too. There have been heroes and villains. There have been tragedies, mass grief and mourning. There has been violence, there has been chaos and there has been controversy. But there have also been a lot of laughs, plenty of good humour and over a century of a fascinating rivalry. The *himno* of Real Betis, belted out by fans before every home game, includes the lyrics: '*Hay una leyenda que recorre el mundo entero*' (There is a legend that travels all over the world). Hopefully this book can do justice to this truly magnificent footballing city.

Colin Millar,
Seville, March 2019

Chapter One

Spain

"Football is an excuse to make us feel happy"
— Jorge Valdano

MY love of football began from such an early age, it feels increasingly impossible to imagine a parallel universe whereby it had no influence on my life. From those endless hours spent kicking a ball about in the garden, watching my local team in Belfast, collecting sticker albums and other fads; it was to prove a passion from which I could not escape, not that I had any desire to.

Football is the only true global sport; encompassing many complex layers within a concept engrained in remarkable simplicity, it encapsulates you from childhood and never relinquishes its grip. No other game is so embedded with politics and identity, nor does any other lend such significance to history or generate such a profound sense of belonging. Football matches can exacerbate wars or grind them to a halt. It is often said that without firstly comprehending politics and history, it is impossible to fully understand the intricacies of many rivalries within the sport but conversely, those subjects cannot be fully grasped without football.

Nowhere does this ring truer than in Spain, where the significance of your football team forms a fundamental part of your identity. It often goes hand in hand with your political outlook, your socioeconomic status and your views on fundamental issues. You aren't a Real Madrid fan or supporter of Barcelona, but a *Madridista* or a *Culé*. In Seville, there are *Béticos* and *Sevillistas* (not to be confused with the term *Sevillanos*, applied to citizens of the city). All are badges of honour. Spaniards often view their association with a club not only in terms of support on the pitch, but also the significance it carries.

The 'beautiful game' does not always live up to its name, of course, but its very existence often brings hope and belief to those whose lives are deprived of such optimism. The resulting off-field tribalism which sometimes manifests itself in the form of violence – as true in Spain as in any other nation – is simply a reflection of society, warts and all, and should football become obsolete, another concept would surely fill the void.

Long before my school days were over – and shortly after I realised my limited playing ability would restrict me from reaching any loftier heights within the sport – my heart was set upon covering football professionally. Yet, my venture into Spanish football came about more by chance than any carefully laid plans. Without any meaningful knowledge of the language or culture, I jetted out to spend three months living in the medieval Spanish city of Cáceres. So remote and isolated was the setting, the experience often felt like being transported back in time.

There was little option but to immerse myself in watching football, with the local bar – as is true with many throughout Spain – showing nothing but La Liga. It was eye opening in part due to the supremely high level of play and technical ability on show, but mainly for the swift realisation that my knowledge was shamefully limited.

It rapidly became apparent that understanding Spanish football and the culture which surrounds it is impossible without a knowledge of the nation's history, geography, socioeconomics and politics. Spain has many guises and faces; the packaged coastal experience frequented by many British holidaymakers is far removed from the reality of daily life within the nation.

There can be a feeling of isolation – particularly acute when on long, tedious bus journeys, travelling through a vast chasm of nothingness – which is often transmitted through the population. Newspapers focus on their locality but little else, simply because there is no great desire, particularly among older generations, to be aware of the goings-on further afield. Fewer than one in ten Spaniards buy a newspaper, a lower rate than 27 other European nations and one of the lowest sales per capita in the developed world.

However, the prominence and significance of Spanish sports newspapers cannot be overestimated. *Marca*, the Madrid-based sports daily, is comfortably the most-read paper in all of Spain. A survey in 2016 found it had over two million readers per day, almost double that of second-placed *El País*, the left-leaning national paper.

Diario AS, the other main sports newspaper based in the capital, ranks third with over a million daily readers while between them, Barcelona-based *El Mundo Deportivo* and *Diario Sport* have just shy of that tally. In total, there are six daily sports papers in the nation with Valencia's *Super Deporte* and *Estadio Deportivo*, based in Seville and focusing on Real Betis and Sevilla, completing the list.

The Madrid-based sports dailies prove so successful in part due to their regional variation and widespread availability, but their existence is down to the fervent interest in football throughout the nation. In many ways, the sport represents everything Spaniards hold dear. A mix of passion, artistry, entertainment, politics, belonging and, of course, controversy and conspiracy theories. The media coverage is often so intense and overwhelming that it becomes incredibly mundane and repetitive. The four main sports dailies devote pages in double figures to Real Madrid and Barcelona. To fill them, not only are matches, press conferences, interviews, analysis, transfer rumours and comment pieces covered, these papers are also bloated with irrelevant details such as players' routines and diets.

Both Madrid and Barça can lay claim to being the biggest club not just within Spain, but also in world football, and for outsiders it is easy to underestimate just how much power and influence they yield. The dynamic of Spanish football culture also stands alone in that it is perfectly common for fans to support multiple clubs within the country.

When I made the city of Seville my home, the first three questions its natives posed were my name, my home city and which football club I supported. If the third answer was neither Real Betis nor Sevilla, I would be quizzed on whether I was a *Bético* or a *Sevillista*. Green or red. Us or them. The concept of uncertainty or disassociation did not exist, nor would it be tolerated. You had to be one or the other.

"We are fiercely proud of our heritage," said Sevilla fan Victor Perea. "In our city you will hardly ever see anyone supporting Real Madrid or Barcelona, this doesn't happen in other parts of Spain. Seville is for Sevilla FC or Real Betis."

Yet small sections of fans from both shades are also fond of either Madrid or Barça – or, in the case of many Betis fans, Atlético de Madrid. It is not uncommon to see tracksuits of one of the Spanish giants at home games of either Seville club, even though both are accustomed to competing against them in Spain's top flight. Many also claim to support local or regional sides, sometimes due to family connections but more relevantly related to a sense of regional pride.

'*Soy Andaluz*' ('I am Andalusian') is a common self-description in the south of Spain. For many it is a way of life and a shared common bond. This interpretation of fandom is unique to Spanish football. In other major European nations, if you do not support the most successful club then you actively wish to see them struggle. Manchester United, Juventus, Bayern Munich, Benfica and Paris Saint-Germain are widely and actively disliked by others. Success breeds contempt and jealousy but the dynamic of fandom ensures that it creates new pockets of support across the nation, often at the expense of local clubs. In Spain, affinity for one club does not rule out similar leanings to several others, often in the same division.

The concept of friendships between sets of Spanish fans is also a running theme. The links are often formed historically and commonly come about as a result of similar ideologies among groups of ultras – many of whom have political leanings, which are not always reflective of the club or its wider fanbase – or of sharing a common enemy. Betis and Atlético fans tend to share a strong friendship while Recreativo de Huelva and Sporting Gijón are other clubs with close links. Sevilla share common ground with Deportivo de La Coruña and Real Oviedo.

Spain is split between 17 proudly autonomous regions, separately ruled under a loose concept of federal self-governance. Each region is distinct with three – the northern Basque Country, Galicia and Catalonia – even speaking their own unique languages. A cultural nuance exists with Spaniards, who usually speak directly, much more than natives of Britain or Latin American nations, and they waste few words.

The football rivalries within each region are marked by pride and local identity, either between cities or within them, with each having its own idiosyncrasies that can, to outsiders at least, seem rather peculiar.

They also have different themes; in Barcelona the rivalry between Barça and Espanyol is generally split along the lines of Catalan independence or retaining loyalty to the Spanish state. In Madrid, distinctions are less clear. Atlético – the club formed by Basque students which would become the club of the Spanish Air Force in subsequent years – have traditionally drawn support from working-class areas of the capital in comparison to Real, who became synonymous with both power and wealth in Spanish football. Rayo Vallecano are based in the Vallecas neighbourhood, an area renowned for its resistance to the Francoist State and belief in social justice, making Rayo the true left-leaning club of the capital. In recent years,

Getafe and Leganés – both based to the south of Madrid but within its metropolitan area – have adapted their long-standing rivalry in the lower divisions to Spain's top flight.

Socioeconomics is the dominant factor in Asturias: Sporting hail from the blue-collar city of Gijón – the most populous settlement in the northern region – while Oviedo, the region's capital, prides itself on architecture and a distinguished, cultured heritage.

Identity is a key theme in Galicia: Deportivo mock Celta de Vigo as 'Portuguese' (some Spaniards look down upon their neighbour's historic economic struggles) while Celta fans respond with jibes of 'Turks', the origins of which are rather less clear. To combat such 'insults', flags of both nations are often flown in each section in an apparent show of defiance.

The Basque derby embodies the inter-city rivalry between Bilbao and San Sebastián (referred to in Basque as Donostia), capitals of the neighbouring Gipuzkoa and Biscay (in Basque: Bizkaia) provinces. This particular rivalry is distinctive in that the clubs share similar ideals of Basque nationalism, with both sets of fans generally mixing amicably and often taking part in shared events surrounding their encounters. The fixture also produced one of Spanish football's most iconic moments in 1976, following the death of General Francisco Franco – the Nationalistic leader who ruled Spain between 1938 and 1973. Captains Inaxio Kortabarria and José Ángel Iribar led their sides on to the pitch carrying the Ikurriña (Basque: Ikurrina) – the flag of the Basque country – which was, at the time, still outlawed in Spain and punishable by a prison sentence.

All of these derbies are fascinating in their own ways and each carries its fair share of baggage in cultural and historical terms. Yet none of these long-standing and enduring rivalries rank as the best local rivalry in Spain. That resides in the heart of Seville itself. No other is contested between two clubs on an equal footing, with the possible exception of Asturias, whose teams have traditionally underperformed and suffered prolonged spells outside the top flight for much of their history.

"The Seville derby is a rarity in Spain," European football writer Andy Mitten explained. "It's a proper two club rivalry in a city between two similar sized clubs. You don't really get that anywhere. Elsewhere, Barcelona are miles bigger than Espanyol, and the same is true with Valencia compared to Levante."

In Andalusia, fans of both Seville clubs are often jibed with '*Vamos a la playa*' by supporters of Málaga, the club of the area's second-most populous city. This references the region's capital not containing a beach. Inter-city matches within Andalusia are generally played against a backdrop of good spirit and cordiality between fans, with light-humoured taunts and ridicule in place of genuine malice or hatred.

Spain's southernmost region is often referred to in unpleasant terms by those based north of its boundaries, with unfounded and stereotypical accusations of its population being workshy and lazy.

Spanish football writer Phil Ball, a long-term resident in the Basque city of San Sebastián, told me there was an element of haughtiness in how Andalusia is viewed in other parts of the country.

"In the north, they kind of look down at it with a slight condescension, as if they're sort of undereducated down there and can't even speak Spanish 'proper'. Then you have the stereotype of gypsy culture, dancing *Sevillanas*, the heat, passion, flamenco ..."

This manifested itself in unsavoury fashion in the 1998/99 season, when Basque Javier Clemente took the reins at Real Betis. His appointment, two months into the season, was greeted with a large deal of scepticism, coming just months after he had led Spain to a disastrous group exit at that year's World Cup. The former midfielder became renowned in coaching circles for implementing a conservative brand of football, one with which fans of *Los Verdiblancos* were unfamiliar and uncomfortable.

However, having won multiple titles at Athletic Club in his native Bilbao, he was a tactician who had an impressive pedigree and more often than not, identity came to the fore as Clemente was an advocate of Basque nationalism. Betis spent most of that season languishing in lower mid-table, having finished two of the previous four seasons in the top four and never below eighth. Fans booed the team off and waved white handkerchiefs, as is customary for underperformance and dissatisfaction. In the midst of this, one rogue home fan near the tunnel spat at the unpopular boss who laid bare his feelings in the aftermath.

"That kind of behaviour is normal down here," fumed Clemente. "I do not want to say it, but this is not the country that I come from." The remarks made national headlines and were met, predictably and understandably, furiously not only by Betis, but the population of Spain's south. They were being called out as second-class citizens; they were unworthy. The comments made Clemente's position untenable and the unhappy marriage of convenience came to a swift conclusion thereafter, but the incident itself is an indicator of fractured underlying feelings held throughout the nation.

In Spain, the idea of localised identity often prevails above all else. Outside of some northern regions seeking greater autonomy, the majority of Spaniards are comfortable with their national tag, yet many would associate first and foremost with their hometown. Each *pueblo* carries a significance and sometimes a stereotype, but such is the variation between each area, generalised assertions are unsatisfactory. These ideas run into football terminology too, with a club's youth system referred to as the *cantera* – 'the quarry', taken from the earth.

When exploring these themes in his book *Morbo*, Phil Ball outlines the significance of a Spaniard's birthplace in the eyes of their compatriots, saying it is not possible for them to be "totally satisfied in their judgement of someone" unless they can find "proof of their hunches". Many natives are fiercely proud of their hometown and region but will freely apply mistruths and generalisations elsewhere.

Speak of Andalusia to the residents of other Spanish territories and it is not uncommon to hear references to its population being *gandules* (a layabout workforce, slackers), comments fuelled by the south's struggling economy but with little basis in fact or reality. A report from Randstad Research in 2018 showed work absenteeism in Andalusia was the lowest in mainland Spain, with northern regions leading the charts.

Andalusia and its provinces are riddled with monetary issues, but its workforce is the victim, rather than the cause, of depressed wages and a general sparsity of jobs. The three poorest neighbourhoods in Spain are all located in Seville, according to a study from the National Institute of Statistics. They are Los Pajaritos-Amate (average household annual income €13,616), Polígono Sur (€14,653) and Torreblanca (€16,433), despite each barrio undergoing a minor improvement from the nadir of Spain's economic hardships.

The Spanish economy is an unbalanced one which relies heavily on tourism, particularly in locations along the Costa del Sol, such as Málaga and Marbella. This in itself leads to internal issues, with Spain's tourist board being the main source of resistance to the concept of bringing the country's clocks back by an hour. In the early part of his premiership, Franco decided Spain should adhere to Central European Time, in a move to bring itself closer to Hitler's Germany. This move was in spite of Madrid being almost directly south of London, with Spain being the westernmost country using CET. In the north-western Galician cities of Vigo, Santiago and A Coruña, the sun does not rise until almost 9am in the depths of winter.

Many Europeans view Spaniards in the same way as those in Spain look at Andalusia – the stereotype of a low work ethic and a tendency towards greater sleep and leisure. Again, the reality is very different. In 2013, a Spanish national commission revealed that Spaniards slept 53 minutes less than the European average. As a result, the study concluded that levels of stress, absenteeism and work-related accidents all increased, with productivity damaged.

There are plenty more myths surrounding Spanish culture which need to be busted. Foreigners may possess a sanitised image of a nation based on relaxation and leisure, but the truth is, the 11-hour working day – typically lasting from 9am to 8pm – is three hours longer than the standard in other Western nations. Whilst long lunches tend to be taken, these do not come close to evening out the disparity, and besides, not arriving home for dinner until 9pm greatly offsets the true sense of a healthy work-life balance.

In late 2016, then Minister for Labour Fátima Báñez introduced proposals to end the working day at 6pm and bring the nation back in line with Greenwich Mean Time – currently only enjoyed by Spain's seven Canary Islands, including Tenerife and Gran Canaria. Ironically, it was tourism boards on the Spanish mainland who offered the main resistance to such plans, arguing – rather flimsily – that a one-hour reduction of evening daylight would deter tourists from visiting. In the time that has elapsed since, Spain has yet to make a decisive stride towards a change in its clocks and thus remains a nation stuck in the wrong time zone.

The fears and uncertainty surrounding Catalonia, the beating heart of the Spanish economy, differ in subtlety but have their roots in similar ideas. Gaining independence would further endanger a precarious national economic situation, which is a key factor – alongside the political and nationalistic ideas of centralism and unity – behind resistance to the north-eastern region's attempts to gain autonomy. Catalan nationalists present an economic argument that their region has the potential to be self-sustaining and is being restrained by Spain. Other Spaniards, many of whom reside in Andalusia, counter with the perfectly reasonable grievance that a break in the Spanish union will disproportionately damage their own living standards. Whilst it is tempting to label such arguments as either politically 'right' or 'left', the situation contains far greater complexity.

The distinct issues which engulf Spain are unavoidable and their waves often engulf the sporting landscape, but when the tide is in, it adds an extra layer of complexity and fascination to matches. Football for many is the ultimate form of escapism. The great Italian manager Arrigo Sacchi once referred to the sport as "the most important of the unimportant things in life". Yet, football equally encompasses and amplifies everything in life in a remarkably simple format. It is for pleasure, incomparable moments of joy and for living. This in part explains why so many are hooked from childhood, locking in nostalgia and a sense of the good old days. There are various complexities behind the popularity of football but at its core, there is a childlike sense of optimism and hope.

Chapter 2

Spanish Football

"People in Andalusia know how to live well,"
– former Real Betis and Sevilla manager
Patrick O'Connell

JUST shy of two million people reside in the province of Seville, with the 2011 census reporting a population of 703,000 within the city – making it the fourth largest in Spain. Yet after Sevilla's Estadio Ramón Sánchez-Pizjuán – which hosted the 1986 European Cup Final between Steaua Bucharest and Barcelona – was renovated in 2018, the combined capacity of the city's two football clubs' stadiums stood at over 107,000. The Estadio Benito Villamarín – the home of Real Betis – had also undergone heavy refurbishment the previous year, with its 60,000 capacity making it the nation's fourth-biggest stadium.

The city itself became only the second city in Europe, after Glasgow, to have three stadiums with capacities in excess of 40,000 when the 60,000-seater Estadio de La Cartuja was constructed for the 1999 Athletics World Championships (London joined this exclusive club in 2006, with the opening of Arsenal's Emirates Stadium). Estadio de La Cartuja, which hosted Porto's victory over Celtic in the 2003 UEFA Cup Final, was one of those included in Seville's unsuccessful bids for the 2004 and 2008 Summer Olympics. Sevilla and Betis own a jointly held three per cent of the stadium ownership rights, with the remainder split between regional governmental departments. Despite initial promises, however, neither team utilised the arena when their own grounds underwent work that temporarily reduced their capacities.

Spanish football has engrained itself in the wider football consciousness in recent years for its success on the European and international stage. The national side won their first World Cup in 2010, sandwiched between consecutive European Championship titles.

La Roja's success preceded the balance of power in European football shifting decisively to clubs in La Liga. Barcelona won the Champions League in 2006, 2009 and 2015 while Real Madrid landed four titles between 2014 and 2018. Atlético de Madrid reached two finals of the competition, only to lose out on both occasions to their city neighbours.

This dominance extended into the Europa League (renamed from the UEFA Cup in 2009) where Sevilla, who had never previously tasted success in Europe, lifted an unprecedented five titles between 2006 and 2016. Three months after their first title, they defeated Barcelona 3-0 in the European Super Cup – the first of four Spanish sides to lift the trophy in eight seasons, while teams from La Liga won nine of the ten trophies between 2009 and 2018.

For a while it appeared that the only clubs who could defeat Spaniards were their domestic rivals. By the end of the 2015/16 campaign, teams from the division had won all nine of the most recent European trophies and had triumphed in 47 of 51 knockout ties against non-Spanish opponents. The only team to knock Atlético de Madrid out of European competitions between 2014 and 2018 were their city rivals Real.

Often derided as a nation with talent and power focused in the hands of a select few, 17 Spanish clubs progressed to at least the last eight of major European competitions between 1998 and 2018, with 12 of those playing in semi-finals. Real Sociedad did not make the list, despite appearing in the Champions League knockout stages. Such a range of clubs is sufficient to form an entire top flight alone.

La Liga clubs and the Spanish national team became the envy of Europe, with others desperately seeking to replicate and overcome the magic formula which had driven such success. The style most closely associated with Spain was one of intricate play, prioritising ball retention and positional territory.

It is logical that such a cohesive and progressive method of play emerged from a nation where basketball – the only activity to occasionally interrupt football's dominance of the front pages – is the second most prominent sport. There is an overlap between basketball and the Spanish ideals of how football should be played: a limited contact sport with strong emphasis on positional and possessive play, passing, close control and intelligent movement, both individually and collectively.

Basketball courts are present throughout Spain, in playgrounds, street corners and public spaces. Active involvement is encouraged, assisted by the country's climate creating alfresco tendencies. It is not unusual for such courts to double up as an area for futsal – another indication of the development on Spanish football style. Effectively a form of five-a-side with a smaller, heavier ball on a hard court, futsal – which is derived from the Spanish *fútbol de salón* and *fútbol sala* – focuses on improvisation, creativity and technique. Playing in tight spaces with a ball you cannot launch up the court forces participants to create space of their own, to build from the back and drag opponents out of their natural position. Such styles are mirrored in the top levels of Spanish football and within the national team.

In September 2017, Real Betis secured a stunning one-goal victory at the Estadio Santiago Bernabéu, home of then-Spanish and European champions Real Madrid. The winning goal arrived in the fourth minute of stoppage time – at 11.51pm local time – as Antonio Barragán clipped in a precise, floated delivery for Paraguayan striker Antonio Sanabria to loop home a header. This was the culmination of a move which lasted a total of 69 seconds, from when Betis goalkeeper Antonio Adán saved a header from Madrid forward Borja Mayoral. Adán played the ball short to deep-lying midfielder Javi García to launch a period of play which included 22 touches, 16 of which were in Madrid's defensive half.

Ahead of the match, Betis captain and club icon Joaquín Sánchez had explained: "We're going to defend with the ball and then we will enjoy having it." In the post-match press conference, when asked about his players' composure and calmness in possession, Betis coach Quique Setién – also a keen chess player – responded: "In these times when people tell you that you have to run, to work, to fight and to compete, I ask my players to think. You have to be clever to have the ball, keep it, make them run, retain some calm in moments of tension."

Setién's style of patient build-up play and value of ball retention are a reflection and consequence of a national psyche regarding how football should be played. Yet the modern style of play in Spain has not always been the prevailing one within the nation, whose ideals of the sport have shifted and adapted markedly since the national side's first outing in the 1920 Summer Olympics.

The Spanish walked away from that tournament with the silver medal – a more-than-respectable outcome considering the lack of precedent on a national level, with La Liga only being formed eight years later. However, the outbreak of the Civil War in 1936 brought football in the nation to a painful standstill and, combined with the global devastation of the Second World War, ensured Spain did not play a match between the 1934 World Cup – eliminated at the quarter-final stage by Italy after defeating Brazil – and the qualifiers for the 1950 edition.

In his article titled *La Roja: The Roots of Soccer's Spanish Fury*, author Jimmy Burns argued that the early editions of the Spanish national side were of "direct, aggressive, spirited style". Indeed, Spain's 1920 side earned the nickname *La Furia Roja* ('The Red Fury') for their physical style of play, which came not only from their physicality but also from having learned the sport from the British. As Burns outlined, it was Athletic Club of Bilbao who provided the yardstick in the early days, with the term *furia* coined to outline their play.

Author and historian David Goldblatt described how *furia* was adapted in a political sense for the gain of General Franco and his new nationalistic state. In his book *The Ball is Round*, Goldblatt noted that in 1939, months after securing victory in the Civil War, Falangist newspaper *Arriba* reported: "The *furia Española* is present in all aspects of Spanish life, to a greater extent than ever. In sport, the *furia* best manifests itself in soccer, a game in which the virility of the Spanish race can find full expression, usually imposing itself, in international contests, over the more technical but less aggressive foreign teams."

Jimmy Burns further explained how Franco politicised the sport to consolidate his own stranglehold on power and emit an image of Spanish strength on to the national stage: "During Franco's dictatorship, between 1939 and 1975, soccer was a pastime that was actively encouraged by the state – that is, as long as it was not exploited by the enemy. And the enemy ranged from communists, Freemasons, and freethinkers to Catalan and Basque nationalists, most of them decent human beings whose clubs were rooted in local cultural identities. It gave Spanish soccer, when I was growing up, its political edge; it separated us soccer lovers into democrats and fascists."

Prominent Spanish football writer and editor of *Diario AS*, Alfredo Relaño, has previously outlined the significance of sport throughout Franco's reign: "Soccer kept growing. Spain began to rebuild itself after the war. It was a time when there was little to do except work as many hours as possible ... pick up the pieces from the ruins, and on Sundays go to the soccer match ... At times there were cycling competitions, boxing fights, and bullfights, but above all soccer, and not much else."

The 1950 World Cup marked Spain's return to the global stage, in a shifting European climate which risked seeing them isolated from the new axis of power. Under boss Guillermo Eizaguirre – a native of Seville who spent his 12-year goalkeeping career at Sevilla – *La Furia Roja* won all three of their first group stage matches, beating Chile and the United States, alongside a historic victory against England in Rio de Janeiro's iconic Maracanã stadium.

The winner over England was netted past Three Lions goalkeeper Bert Williams by legendary Athletic Club striker Telmo Zarra, who won one league title and five Copa del Rey crowns in his record-breaking spell at the club. In the build-up to proceedings, the Basque native had described the match as "the game of the century". Official records put his eventual goal tally for Athletic as 335 in 354 outings, and the Zarra Trophy is still handed out to the top Spanish goalscorer in La Liga in his honour. In her book *Spain 1833–2002: People and State,* historian Mary Vincent highlighted the significance of the tournament, and Zarra's strike in particular, in setting the tone for the sport's influence: "Football – the social drug of Franco's Spain – had genuine inter-class appeal. The Spanish goal that knocked out England was supposedly heard by the entire population."

The dictator recognised the significance of football in portraying Spain as a strong, united nation and he moved to adapt his political ideas of centralised power and uniformity of cultural, ethnical and linguistic aspects across the country. All signs of regional nationalism, including languages, flags (such as the Ikurriña and the Senyera – the respective flags of the Basque Country and Catalonia) and other signs of separatism were to be banned throughout Franco's Spain, with football clubs not exempt from the sweeping changes.

In 1941, the year of Zarra's debut, Athletic were forced to change their name to the Castilian title Atlético Bilbao. In a similar move, Catalan club Espanyol reverted their title back to the original Real Club Deportivo Español. FC Barcelona had to be renamed Club de Fútbol Barcelona and the Catalan flag was removed from their crest.

Oppression of the Basque and Catalan cultures inevitably heightened tensions and sharpened division both within and between regions. Palpable feelings of unease began to dominate and helped provide the backdrop to a culture, and sport, which was increasingly built on a sense of mistrust and assumptions of controversy. This edge plays a huge part in the explanation of the Spanish term *morbo* – which has no direct English translation in this context but encapsulates what drives the rivalry within Spanish football, the fuel that lights the flames.

Politics was not just played out on the national stage but also further afield. The Spanish government forbade the national team from travelling to the Soviet Union for the first leg of their quarter-final in the inaugural European Nations Cup (the precursor to the European Championships) in 1960, thus forcing the nation to withdraw from the competition. The Soviets had backed the Second Spanish Republic in the Civil War and Franco refused to contemplate a trip to the state, instead requesting both matches be played on neutral territory. Unsurprisingly, Moscow rejected this idea.

As Burns wrote: "Franco smelled a communist conspiracy: a Soviet-led propaganda exercise aimed at exposing the Spanish regime's unpopularity among exiles from the Civil War and surviving supporters of the Republic.

"This, combined with a Russian request that the Soviet anthem be played and the Soviet flag be flown in the Real Madrid stadium, proved altogether too much for Franco, and his appointees in the Spanish Football Federation – all Civil War comrades – did as they were ordered and withdrew the Spanish team from the competition."

In sporting terms, *La Furia Roja* struggled to build on their 1950 run, as they failed to qualify for each of the subsequent World Cup tournaments. By the time of the 1964 European Nations' Cup, contested by just four nations, political tensions once again came to the fore. This time Spain were the hosts and unlike four years previously, the Generalissimo sanctioned the team's participation against teams with Soviet-led national governments.

Led by former volunteer Nationalist soldier José Villalonga Llorente – the Córdoba-born boss continuing a strong tradition of Andalusian managers of the national side – Spain required extra time to defeat Hungary. The Magyars, who could no longer lean on the genius of Spanish-based stars Ferenc Puskás, László Kubala and Sándor Kocsis, represented a government who were a satellite state of the Soviets.

So fate would have it, Spain's opponents in the final – held in Real Madrid's Estadio Santiago Bernabéu – were the Soviet Union themselves. Not only did Franco afford the green light to the contest, he attended in a personal capacity. At this stage, he had realised football could be instrumental in helping the nation recover from its global isolation, which was beginning to bite, and wanted his name to be linked to international success. For propaganda purposes, this presented a golden opportunity.

The newspaper *ABC*, viewed contemporarily as being sympathetic to the regime, put their own slant on the event: "Spain is a nation which is every day more orderly, matured and unified, and which is steadfastly moving down the path of economic, social and institutional development." This opportunistic link between the relative success of the Spanish national football team and Spain as a state, and thus Franco's regime itself, is indicative of the significance of the sport.

For the Soviets, the match was also of notable significance, coming within two years of the Cuban Missile Crisis, which threatened catastrophic consequences for world peace. The Spanish were viewed as an ally of the United States and the chance to triumph in their capital, in front of 80,000 fans and Franco himself, was too tempting a possibility to refuse.

Politics dominated the build-up, with Villalonga speaking of the "Hispanic values" of his side. The Generalissimo entered, surrounded by family and cohorts, to chants of his name from the home fans in a display that had a distinctive undercurrent of a political rally. Spain triumphed 2–1, Real Zaragoza striker Marcelino Martínez netting past the great Russian goalkeeper Lev Yashin, then 34, with six minutes remaining.

Spain would not win another tournament for 44 years but despite this, *Marca* journalist Juan Castro later stated that the success swiftly disappeared from the national consciousness: "If you look at that win, the Spanish public don't consider it to be as important as it was.

"It is not in the hearts of the public. That is probably because, although we remember Luis Suárez, it was not a team of superstars. If you ask someone in a Spanish bar who was the coach of the Euro 1964 team, no one would remember Villalonga. It was important at the time, but it has not been kept in the national memory."

Perhaps the tie's potent political undercurrent failed to capture the imagination of the wider public, many of whom remained strongly resentful of what the regime represented. There was an undeniable feeling that the sport had been hijacked for political ends and this was mirrored in the Spanish club scene.

Franco was viewed as holding sympathies for Real Madrid, with allegations that the success of *Los Blancos* was due to them having friends in high places. The truth is not that the club were great because of the dictator's support, but rather his allegiance was because of the club's greatness. Fernando María Castiella y Maíz, the government's Foreign Minister at the time, regarded the club as "the best embassy we ever had". Football is a commodified product in popular culture and is vulnerable to manipulation by ulterior motives.

Madrid lifted six European Cups within the space of a decade, and five in a row between 1956 and 1960. They were Spain's representatives on a global stage – projecting an image of happiness, wealth and unification. Franco's far-right regime may have left the nation isolated in Europe, but they remained wary of how they were perceived outside of their borders. Inward fears over revolts, particularly in the Basque Country and Catalonia, led to paranoia that forced a reactionary response.

Football had thus emerged as the foundation for a tense political situation throughout Spain. By appearing to publicly back Madrid, Franco was aware this was a nod to central power and thus a de facto rejection of regional identity, manifested in the forms of the leading clubs in Barcelona and Bilbao. The Catalan giants had previously pinned the blame on the regime for an 11th-hour U-turn from the mercurial Alfredo Di Stéfano to sign for Madrid rather than move to the Camp Nou. The signing of the Argentine star was era-defining as he established himself as the world's leading player during his time in the Spanish capital.

However, Spanish journalist Manuel Vázquez Montalbán argued Barça and Athletic Club were used as "safety valves" by the regime: they embodied a relatively mild – and crucially, legal – method of expressing anti-regime sentiment which could be managed in such a way that it did not directly threaten the existence of the status quo.

The lack of transparency led to claims and counterclaims, which in turn created a climate of uncertainty and a rivalry which often became poisonous. There is a sense that such a fierce animosity, built primarily on propaganda, mistruths and exaggerations, still holds strong foundations in Spanish football fandom in the modern era.

As recently as 2004, the turbulent waters of Spanish football and politics intertwined in ugly fashion following terror attacks in Madrid. Three days ahead of the national general elections, 192 people lost their lives with thousands more injured after an al-Qaeda terrorist cell bombed four trains within the capital. The immediate aftermath saw the right-wing Popular Party (PP) lay the blame at the door of Basque separatist organisation ETA, with the knowledge that a link to the Middle East would see them blamed for leading the nation into the war in Iraq.

Atlético de Madrid were scheduled to play a match at Real Sociedad that evening, but Frente Atlético – a notorious grouping of the club's ultras with right-wing ideals – staged a sit-in at their Vicente Calderón stadium, insisting the clash in San Sebastián should not proceed. Relations between the sets of fans had already suffered huge fractures due to the murder of one of the Basque club's fans in clashes six years previously. As the weekend turned out, the PP lost the election, but the two sets of players produced a display of togetherness, laying down a Community of Madrid flag prior to the match commencing.

As my bus rolled into Seville's Plaza de Armas bus station during my first visit, I was already acutely aware that this was not a city, nor a rivalry, defined by nationalistic or cultural identity. It did not take long to appreciate that the capital of Andalusia was filled with people fiercely proud of their *Sevillano* origins, regardless of football allegiance. Both Sevilla and Betis fans hail from a region with near total loyalty to the Spanish state, yet which is often met with derision by their northern compatriots. There are allegations that social class has historically differentiated the city's two clubs, but in a rivalry which divides brothers and sisters, fathers and sons, husbands and wives, does this really still hold true? What was it that made this *the* derby of Spain, one which made others seem comparatively tame? What fuelled the *morbo*, and what differentiated two clubs whose homes are separated by a ten-minute car journey? Upon covering the Seville derby, football writer Andy Mitten described the two clubs as being "hopelessly incapable of avoiding controversy" and surmised that much of the rivalry was founded on "half-baked conspiracy theories."

The Frying Pan of Spain attempts to discover the answers, to detail the distinguished football culture in the city and capture the unique sense of fandom within its jurisdiction. Home to two of the nation's most illustrious football institutions, Seville effortlessly radiates charm and history, at the same time providing the backdrop of conditions for a wicked storm of *morbo*, intense passion and fierce loyalty. '*Sevilla tiene un color especial*' is the title of the emblematic song of local pop group Los del Río and those with the privilege of visiting the Andalusian capital can testify this sentiment. My hope is that this book can do justice to the truly magnificent city, which I can proudly call my adopted home, and to its wonderful football fans.

Chapter 3

Seville City

"You are no city, you are a universe," – Fernando de Herrera, 'divine' poet from Seville

THE first thing that strikes you is the heat. During the summer months it becomes engulfing and often overpowering. White sheets are erected around the city centre, stretched across the rooftops of shops and offices to protect those below from the piercing glare of the sun. Water vapour systems are installed outside bars and cafés, offering sweet, cooling relief to those lounging in the shade. The air is so parched and stagnant that it sticks in your nose and mouth, offering a taste of suffocation.

Many residents escape south – to the beaches of Cádiz, Málaga, Almería and Huelva – while others flock to Portugal's Algarve. Businesses shut for months, streets become vacant and an almost eerie silence descends upon the city's cobbled alleys and pathways. Blinds are slammed shut and uncovered balconies are abandoned.

The climate in Seville is cruel over the summer months and the locals are forced to adapt with little option but to rise early and stay up late. Coffees are ordered before midday and beer is consumed after sunset. Between times, shelter is sought, and air conditioning turned up full. There is no alternative for those in pursuit of anything approaching comfort.

Between June and early September, the temperature often sits comfortably over 40 degrees Celsius, leading many to dub Andalusia's capital as the hottest city (of over 100,000 inhabitants) in western Europe. Some studies suggest Córdoba – two hours to the east – takes that crown, but even so, the truth is inescapable: it is really, really hot.

At times it feels like the sun is perched inches above your head, blurring your surroundings into a melting maze. Yet to wander the streets of Seville, mirages are never far from the surface. Moorish-style architecture dominates the city with most buildings high-rise and painted vibrantly to combat the determined, constant waves of sunshine. The Old Town – the largest of its kind on the continent – is peppered with stunning, mesmerising landmarks which fit the ideals of paradise.

The Real Alcázar – an enormous former Moorish royal palace – with its vast encompassing gardens, is planted in the middle of the city. The idyllic location is a reminder of the city's past significance, built by Castilians on the site of an Abbadid Muslim residential fortress that had been abolished after the Christian conquest of Seville.

The adjoining Seville Cathedral – the world's largest Gothic cathedral and once Europe's largest building – was constructed in place of the Mosque, which had acted as the centrepiece of the former Islamic Andalus empire. It is among the grandest of its kind in the Western world, with its iconic Giralda bell tower offering spectacular views across the city. Such grand religious buildings are as much about power and symbolism as about faith, leading historian Hugh Thomas to argue in his book *Rivers of Gold: The Rise of the Spanish Empire:* "Men built churches to inspire, to overpower, and also to impress, for they were works of propaganda as well as spiritual comfort."

Laurie Lee, the English writer and Hispanophile, wrote of his visit to the city in 1951: "Seville remains, favoured and sensual, exuding from the banks of its golden river a miasma of perpetual excitement, compounded of those appetites that are most particularly Spanish – chivalry, bloodshed, poetry and religious mortification."

Only from the Giralda's elevated position can you appreciate the true sprawling beauty of the centre of this metropolis. The city follows the Guadalquivir river, as it weaves its way past the leafy and vibrant Alameda de Hércules before flowing south, alongside the neighbourhood of Triana – the cultural significance of which will be examined in Chapter 6 – before heading to the Heliópolis district, home of Real Betis. The bird's-eye view lays bare just how the layout has been designed to combat the sunlight: white buildings dominate the landscape, reflecting the glare of the sun and providing an uplifting sense of carefreeness. In contrast to the often-dreary Georgian-style architecture which dominates so many British cities, the Andalusian capital positively glows in the sunshine.

Seville pulls at the heartstrings of its visitors, who are forever losing their bearings in the winding streets, leading through to hidden squares and mysterious courtyards. Maps are rendered useless when navigating the intertwining pathways which flow seamlessly from one neighbourhood to the next. Only once entangled in the city's web can the ambience and charm truly take hold as you stumble upon the finest eateries and flamenco bars.

The city's gastronomy is well renowned, and it hosts many of the nation's best tapas restaurants. Dishes are relatively simple to prepare with local specialities including *gazpacho* (cold tomato-based soup), *huevos a la flamenca* (eggs baked with chorizo and tomato sauce) and *espinacas con garbanzos* (spinach with chickpeas). But, as with many other aspects of Andalusian life, it is less about 'what' you eat and more 'how', 'where' and 'when' you eat it.

Seville's climate and the nation's general eating habits mean that lunch is often the biggest meal of the day, with dinner not being consumed until after 9pm. Spotting beleaguered tourists in the early evening is an easy task as they file into restaurants, tentatively enquiring if the kitchen is open only to be met with confused looks and requests to return later.

Spaniards typically eat little and often, but this is particularly pronounced in the south, where the climate allows for regular alfresco dining at affordable prices. Most restaurants are comprised of pokey interiors with a sprawling outdoor area, with rainy days usually grinding business to a halt. Eating and drinking out is a crucial cultural concept for *Sevillanos*, with large open spaces – such as the Alameda de Hércules – lined with bars, restaurants and cafés, often visited by groups of parents while their children enjoy kicking a football about nearby.

Andalusia's capital is self-aware and has refused to rest on its laurels, with the proactive city council making great strides to overturn a once traffic-congested centre into a pedestrian-friendly zone. Between 2007 and 2012, a tram system (with stops outside each main tourist attraction), an underground metro service (with a stop in Nervión, directly beside Sevilla's Ramón Sánchez-Pizjuán stadium) and a community bike-sharing scheme were all introduced. In Sanlúcar la Mayor, 20km to the west, Europe's first commercial solar power plant opened. The protected bike lane network within Seville is a success which reflects the city's characteristics: the flat terrain, the relatively compact centre, the politics and the prevailing progressive mindset. It dominates the city, providing quick, accessible and affordable transport to those travelling within it.

In 2003, bike-advocating politician Paula Garvín – leading Seville's local United Left party – was elected deputy mayor, entering a coalition with left-leaning PSOE (Spanish Socialist Workers' Party). Three years later, Garvín persuaded mayor Alfredo Sánchez Monteseirín to run a poll asking the population, "Do you think cycling infrastructure would be good for Seville?" A resounding 90 per cent of respondents answered 'yes', and plans were accelerated to implement the lanes by the time of the next election – which was subsequently won. Close to 5,000 parking spots were abolished, while Seville's transportation department was awash with money in the wake of the recent economic boom and funds collected from the mass construction of new housing.

Such incentives ensure that the historical significance of the city is fused with a sense of modernity ideal for maintaining contemporary relevance – reflected in its *Lonely Planet* award for being the world's best city to visit in 2018. As you make your way down Avenida de la Constitución – the main central street – there is no hint of fumes, with the only aroma coming from the ripe oranges that line the city's pathways. In 2006, the arterial route was closed with the estimated 21,000 vehicles which passed along it daily forced to look at alternative methods of transport. Even central parking zones have been abolished, with the nearby Metropol Parasol – an eye-catching wooden structure offering a central vantage point – built on a former car park in Plaza de la Encarnación.

Seville is a metropolis which draws upon all that typifies Spain in the eyes of foreigners. Few nations offer quite the level of regional variation or diversity as this one. Splintered into 17 regions, your experience of Spain will be influenced almost entirely by your location within it. Not only do the autonomous communities differ by their weather and geographical features but there are tangible contrasts in culture, socioeconomics and wealth.

Seville is the capital of Andalusia – the most populous and southern of Spain's regions, stretching west from Huelva, bordering Portugal, to the eastern Almería, overlooking the Mediterranean Sea. The region's name is derived from the Arabic 'Al-Andalus', reflecting the Islamic empire which, at its 8th-century height, controlled most of the Iberian Peninsula. The subsequent Christian Reconquista was an ultimately successful but slow process, with the Moors controlling the territory between 711 and 1492 but being steadily shrunk as they were pushed back south to contemporary Andalusia.

Originally recognised under the name *Spal* (translated as 'lowland' in the Phoenician language), Seville was Latinised to *Hispalis* when under Roman rule before becoming *Ishbiliya* after the

Moorish conquest in 712. Following similar conquests of nearby Jaén and Córdoba, the city fell under the Christian Kingdom of Castile, ruled by Ferdinand III, in 1248 – ending five centuries of Islamic rule. The city's complex religious history and heritage are never far from the surface; a monument in Puerta de Jerez reads: "Hercules built me, Julius Caesar surrounded me with walls and high towers, and the Holy King won me with Garci Pérez de Vargas." This was referencing Vargas, a Castilian knight of the 13th century who was considered a hero of the Reconquista. The municipality of Dos Hermanas, in the province of Seville, has a street named after him, as does Alcalá de Guadaíra, whose surrender took place in 1246. The city of Seville also has a street labelled with Garci Pérez in the Casco Antiguo District.

Moorish influences are still prominent in modern-day Seville and across Andalusia, particularly in relation to architecture. Seville's Giralda bell tower ranks alongside Granada's stunning Alhambra palace and the Mezquita de Córdoba in being among the most accomplished monuments in Spain. Each Andalusian city is awash with Moorish-inspired designs driven by Mudéjar – Moors who remained after the Reconquista but did not convert to Christianity. These styles led to the colourful courtyards throughout the region.

It is impossible to recognise the significance of football within Seville before first understanding the role of the city itself and its importance in shaping Spain as we know it today. Not only was Andalusia fundamental to the formation of the nation itself, it is also the area that gave birth to Spanish football. But what do we know of Spain? What themes do we associate with the country? The more these ideas are explored, the more persuasive the idea of the Andalusian capital encapsulating Spain becomes.

It is impossible to ignore the significance of the typical weather conditions in the city and the ever-growing worth of tourism, but Seville is much more than just sunshine and historic landmarks. It gave birth to Flamenco dancing and few Spaniards are so enthralled with the concept of bullfighting as *Sevillanos*, even if the controversial sport does not sit comfortably with everyone. The city's bull ring – given the long-winded title of Plaza de Toros de la Real Maestranza de Caballería de Sevilla – is strategically located in the heart of the city, opposite the Torre del Oro (a former military watchtower) and alongside the Guadalquivir. The 12,000-seater stadium is routinely sold out, with events typically held between March and September.

The Feria de Sevilla (Seville Fair) is one of the most illuminating spectrums from which to view the city, typically taking place annually in the middle of April. Seville grinds to a standstill with many of its leading citizens dressing in their finery and renting out horse-drawn carriages – usually confined solely to tourists – to transport them to their destinations.

To an outsider looking in, there is a distinct feel of being transported back to the 1800s. Men traditionally dress in their figure-hugging *traje corto* (short jacket, tight trousers and boots) with fancy hats perched upon their heads while females are adorned in their *trajes de flamenca* (a typical flamenco-style dress).

The fairground itself feels surreal: it is surrounded by such a traditional dress sense and upwards of 1,000 *casetas* (decorated marquee tents) divided into rows, with only the horse-drawn carriages allowed into the complex. Aside from the strong stench of horse manure – which becomes increasingly prominent and uncomfortable throughout the week – the event itself essentially formalises the preconception of the laid-back and fun-loving Andalusian way of life.

Each *caseta* is home to a prominent grouping within the city: usually families, political movements, friendship groups, clubs or, perhaps most strikingly of all, *peñas* of Real Betis and Sevilla fans. *Peñas* – the strict English translation is 'a group of friends' – are a tradition particularly significant in Spanish football, with the groups sitting together at home games and often gathering in a set location to watch away matches and other events. It is an idea which revisits the Spanish significance of socialising and feeling a unique sense of identity, often in a sporting or political sense.

Peñas can be given an official stamp by the clubs themselves, with those located in other cities afforded priority for away tickets in the region when the club comes to visit. Many have banners within their own stadium, while others erect flags outside their designated bar on matchdays. There is a unique sense of togetherness and belonging felt within such groups.

While Seville incorporates much of what foreigners envisage as 'typically Spanish', it is also thought that the city has been strongly shaped by Latin American influences. After all, the Latin American cultural image of openness, inclusivity, colour and noise chimes with that of southern Spain. So too are there similarities in accents: just like Andalusians and unlike the rest of Spain, Spanish-speaking Latin Americans generally do not pronounce the letter 'c' as '*th*' – this is known grammatically as *seseo*.

This influence stems from the 16th century, when mass emigration from Spain towards America began and, due to originating from the poorest part of the nation which had also been inflicted by the most instability and political upheaval, Andalusians filled many of the ships. After all, the possibility of a dangerous emigration carried fewer risks for southern Spaniards and with them they brought their dialect. Between 1492 and 1519, one in three emigrants to the New World were Andalusian and two thirds of those were from the city of Seville.

Despite the exodus from the nation's south, it was during this time that Seville grew into one of the richest, biggest and most cosmopolitan cities on the planet thanks to being granted control of Spanish trade with the American continent. Migration losses were also offset by mass immigration into the city, with notably high numbers of Genoese and Florentine merchants becoming fully Hispanicised.

The Guadalquivir river was navigable to the Atlantic Ocean, 100km away, allowing Seville to become the *puerto y puerta de Indias* (port and gateway of the Indies). Rapid development saw the city become a centre of commerce, trade and science with its population growing greater than 100,000, migration turning it into Spain's most populous urban area. It built the conditions for many contributors to Spain's Golden Age to emerge from the city through painting, sculpture and literature. Diego Velázquez, Bartolomé Esteban Murillo and Francisco de Zurbarán – three of the nation's most influential artists – all grew up in the Andalusian capital.

However, tragedy would later hit the city and derail its importance on both a Spanish and European scale. Half the city perished in a plague in 1649, before another epidemic in 1800 killed approximately 13,000. Sandwiched in between, the governmental offices which oversaw business with the Americas were transferred to the nearby coastal city of Cádiz in 1717 due to increasing difficulty in navigating the congested Guadalquivir.

The city's significance continued to dwindle due to its relative geographical isolation in European terms and, whilst industry helped bring growth later in the 19th century, Seville's heyday could not be matched.

The world fair Ibero-American Exposition was held in the city for 13 months between 1929–30 and promised to place the city back on the map. Preparations spanned over two decades with exhibition buildings – many of which would provide a lasting legacy – constructed in the central María Luisa Park along the Guadalquivir.

The fair's centrepiece was the picturesque Plaza de España, which today consists of governmental buildings and remains a fundamental tourist attraction, providing the setting for scenes in the *Lawrence of Arabia* and *Star Wars: Episode II – Attack of the Clones* films. Its grandeur is breathtaking with carefully designed *azulejos* (ceramic tiles) visible throughout. A 500m canal, crossed by four bridges, bends around the complex. Along the base of the exterior sit 48 alcoves, each consisting of a map of each province of Spain and region of Andalusia.

The Exposition was viewed as a massive step towards modernising Seville, with the national government injecting funds to widen cobbled streets and build hotels in anticipation of the crowds. Ten of the visiting nations constructed elegant pavilions to display their exhibition, with many still visible along the Avenida de la Palmera, a key route of transportation which runs parallel to the Guadalquivir river and bypasses the Estadio Benito Villamarín, home of Real Betis. Five years after the Exposition closed, Betis won their first and only Spanish league title, while across town, Sevilla triumphed in the Copa del Rey. The city's football clubs mirrored the increasing status of Seville and promised to create a legacy of success and longevity.

However, these years proved to be yet another false dawn for the city as the Spanish Civil War broke out in 1936, with Seville swiftly falling to the Nationalist forces led by General Francisco Franco. Five years earlier, the left-leaning Republican Socialists had won 57 per cent of the Seville vote in the national elections, with just 39 per cent behind the Monarchist coalition. This had led to the proclamation of the Second Republic and King Alfonso XIII's flight into exile.

The precarious situation eventually caved in in July 1936 when, led by the Francoist General Gonzalo Queipo de Llano, 4,000 troops staged a military coup in Andalusia's capital. A number of other officers were arrested as he gained control of the 2a División Orgánica and sharp upheaval began. Resistance started with the inner-city working-class neighbourhoods of Triana and Macarena mobilising alongside unions and left-leaning political groups, but they were no match for the army's weaponry and swift, brutal decisiveness. The quick victory for Nationalist forces came as little surprise. Geographically, Seville was relatively isolated and was far removed from the feelings of nationalism which existed to the north. Furthermore, it was already the main Spanish city for the arms industry and many of its most wealthy citizens threw their weight behind Franco's forces.

Neither Seville club could escape the clutches of the Falangists. To this day, both sets of fans argue as to which club stood to benefit from links to the regime and many claims are fiercely contested on both sides. There is compelling evidence to suggest that key figures at both clubs either helped or benefitted from the regime, while both clubs accommodated their methods – even if they did not do so through choice. The Betis stadium, then named El Heliópolis, became a parking zone for military tanks, while there have also been suggestions that Republican prisoners were tortured inside its jurisdiction. Due to its location in the centre of the city, Sevilla's Nervión doubled up as an administrative hub for the regime.

Repression in the city lasted six months, with 3,028 lives lost including key political figures – Horacio Hermoso Araujo (incumbent mayor), José González Fernández de la Bandera (former Republican mayor) and José Manuel Puelles de los Santos (president of the Provincial Council) among them. De Llano was officially made commander of the Nationalist Army of the South, who were responsible for 8,000 deaths in Seville throughout the three-year Civil War.

Historian Paul Preston believes the total number of fatalities sanctioned by the General throughout Andalusia stands at a staggering 45,000 (although the real figure could be significantly higher), with the Spanish Civil War expert describing his nature as "erratic, unreliable, unstable and volatile, irascible and always ready to resort to violence. He was both a bully and a sneak." British writer and Andalusian resident Gerald Brenan described the General as a "born sadist".

De Llano remains a hugely divisive figure almost seven decades after his death. Buried in the city's Basílica de la Macarena – which he helped build – debate raged over whether his body should be exhumed. The dispute is one of several such controversies across Spain, with the General viewed either as a fascist criminal or a fierce protector of Catholicism who helped to fight the 'evil' of communism in his nation.

The basilica is one of the city's most famed landmarks – standing behind the fortified walls used by firing squads during the conflict – and De Llano's plaque has sat modestly alongside that of his wife since his death in 1951. All the original fascist symbols and Civil War references have been wiped from the memorial, which now refers to the General only as an "honorary senior brother", but the ire is directed more so at the personality of he who lies within rather than any description.

De Llano helped build the basilica for the Virgin of the Macarena – which opened two years prior to his death – to house the religious relic which was saved in 1936 from a nearby church that had been burnt down by left-wing militants.

Authorities in Andalusia want his body exhumed in line with Spain's 2007 'Historical Memory Law', which ensured the state would offer support for families wanting to unearth the bodies of relatives who had suffered during the Civil War, but which also included a section on removing public figures loyal to Franco during the war. The PSOE government of the time wanted to push through this law but the conservative Partido Popular, upon their election into power in 2011, killed the move with the explanation that they did not wish to "reopen old wounds" in the country. (At the time of writing, the exhumation of Franco from the Valley of the Fallen mausoleum near Madrid has been approved but due to its controversy and the ongoing unstable political situation in Spain, whether it will happen remains unclear.)

This has led to inconsistent and localised enforcement of the ruling, with areas run by left-leaning councils pushing ahead with exhumations. In 2016, the northern city of Pamplona decided to exhume the bodies of Franco loyalists Emilio Mola and José Sanjurjo, but the added intricacy in Seville is that while the authorities wished to remove De Llano's body, it is the Macarena brotherhood who own the building in which he is held.

The organisation holds sway in the city: over 400 years old and possessing 13,000 members, they are renowned for their charity work and their prominence in Semana Santa – the Holy Week of events across Seville at Easter. Reluctant to conform to the demands of the elected politicians, this standstill is indicative of rifts within society in Spain's deeply religious south.

Like in the rest of the nation, economic growth remained relatively stagnant during Franco's rule, although development became tangible from the mid-1950s. The Virgen del Rocío hospital was opened in 1955 next to the Avenida de la Palmera and quickly grew into one of the most important in the south of Spain. A large-scale urbanisation project took place, exemplified in the barrio of Los Remedios – to the south of Triana, along the western bank of the Guadalquivir – becoming the city's first planned neighbourhood, attracting many middle-class residents.

Franco's death in 1979 brought about the return of democratic elections and three years later, Spain had a *Sevillano* prime minister:

Felipe González of the PSOE. His term spanned 14 years – to this day, the nation's longest-serving elected leader – and it included the Universal Exposition of 1992 taking place in his home city.

As is the way in Seville, any public figure feels obliged to declare their football team – and thus by default, turns half of the population against them – and González nailed his colours to Real Betis, pointing to his time at the Colegio San Antonio Claret, a stone's throw from the Estadio Benito Villamarín. As is customary, this provoked derision among fans across the Seville divide who derided the prime minister for opportunism and pointed to his lack of attendance at matches. Retorting *Béticos* argued his membership of the club commenced in 1979, while evidence emerged of his attendance at the Copa del Rey final two years earlier as Betis defeated Athletic Club of Bilbao.

González's main legacy was one of modernisation and in his home city, highways were constructed and a new runway at Seville Airport opened to complement the newly built Santa Justa train station, which provided the Andalusian capital with the high-speed AVE train system to Madrid. A new sense of optimism and inclusivity was sweeping across Spain and this was epitomised in Seville, which had refound its confidence and self-belief. Tourism, technology, commerce and industry are all growing in the city, despite the economic uncertainty of the nation and Andalusia in particular.

Civil War scars remain throughout a country which continues to be divided politically, economically and culturally, in chasms which exist in and between regions, social classes and age demographics. Spain is increasingly politically aware and engaged, with its population unafraid of forming opinions and adopting political stances.

Yet overriding this layer of sincerity and mindfulness is a sense of fun and warmth, with the cordiality often more prevalent in Andalusia and Seville than any other region. The endless sunshine is conducive to eating out and socialising. Siestas and fiestas are fundamental pillars of everyday life, with festivals and merriment engrained into society.

Famed flamenco singer and composer Rafael del Estad, a native *Sevillano*, wrote his song 'Las Dos Orillas' (The Two Shores) as an ode to his hometown. A section of the piece goes:

Seville is Triana, and the Guadalquivir.
Seville is the land where I was born.
Seville is the palace, of the Moorish kings
The shore that has the Torre del Oro.

Who will I thank, for my birth in Seville?
In the city of dreams, in the corner where they shine
The sun, the moon and the sky.
Seville brandishes its cathedrals
And the bells that ring in its towers.

* * * * *

These attitudes, with such pride in their roots, are carried into
football fan culture: matchdays are a sea of colour, played to a
backdrop of constant, rhythmic chanting. The expressive nature of
supporters within Seville mirrors the life and soul of the city. Speak
to any football supporter in the city and within minutes they will
refer to *sentimiento* – feeling. That one thing which encompasses the
joy, the pain, the suffering and the emotional turmoil that come with
supporting their clubs. They live and breathe their clubs; they take
the rough with the smooth and share an unbreakable bond.

Irishman Patrick O'Connell managed both teams in Seville,
making it a home from home. "He used to say that he loved Seville
because the people here live life like it is their last day on earth," said
the Betis public relations officer, Julio Jiménez Heras. Naturally, it
is important to understand and appreciate the culture and history
of how it all started. But overriding that is the importance of having
fun, valuing a sense of well-being and enjoying all that life has to
offer. In Seville, they know how to maximise those things more than
anywhere else.

Chapter 4

The Birth of Football in Seville

"For more than 100 years my team has been fighting, and carrying the name of our city." – Sevilla FC's Centennial Anthem, composed in 2005 by singer Francisco Javier Labandón Pérez (more commonly known as El Arrebato)

ON 25 February 1890, Isaías White Junior penned a letter which would decades later be considered the catalyst for Spain's first-ever documented football match. The previous month, White had assumed the role of secretary at the newly formed Sevilla FC. The club's foundation was fuelled by the growing number of British workers in the city and the region of Andalusia.

This was a time when many British mining companies set up camp around the Río Tinto: a river which flows in the south-west of Andalusia, from the Sierra Morena mountains down to the city of Huelva. The Industrial Revolution and subsequent expansion of European trade had seen a sharp rise in importing and exporting, with the succulent oranges which grew across the city of Seville being the main export from the south of Spain.

Tons of the fruit were plucked and shipped across the world, with a high demand in the United Kingdom, where the oranges were also used for producing marmalade. Inevitably, companies began to spring up across the Spanish city to gain a share of the market and direct operations back home.

The growing British expatriate population within Seville, mainly comprised of managers and directors of companies within the city, were said to be keen to start a local football team. The sport itself was beginning to blossom back in the United Kingdom, following the formation of Notts County – the nation's first football club – in 1862. In the three decades that followed, dozens of clubs across Britain sprung up and attracted great interest across the social divides, uniting both factory workers and managers.

Seville's strong British contingent was largely made up of Scotsmen and, as was tradition, they celebrated Burns Night – along with a group of Spanish friends – on 25 January 1890 in a café in the heart of the city. Amongst this party were Edward Farquharson Johnston from Elgin, Glaswegian Hugh MacColl (for linguistic reasons, known as Hugo in Spain) and Isaías White Junior, of English heritage on his father's side but a native of Seville with a Spanish mother.

On the final day of the following month, a letter printed in *La Provincia de Huelva* was cited under the heading 'Huelva Recreation Club' – whose significance is tied in directly to the birth of football in Seville – with a brief introduction explaining that a letter had been received 'from the secretary of the Sevilla Football Club'.

> "As probably you have heard we have recently started a football club here," read the letter. "It has been proposed to ask the members of your Club to visit Sevilla and take part in a friendly match with us under association rules. If it would be convenient for you to come on Saturday 8th March, that date would suit us.
>
> "We would propose that the match commence about 5pm so as to take advantage of the cool of the evening and that afterwards your team should dine and spend the evening with us." The letter was signed off with, "Yours faithfully, Isaías White J."

It was White, a resident of Calle Bailén in the centre of Seville, who evidently engineered not only the birth of Sevilla Football Club but also the first reported football match in the entire nation.

Spanish football tends to attract controversy at every turn and debate rages over issues relating to the formative dates of clubs. Age and longevity are understandably a source of pride with a continuous temptation for oneupmanship to generate some sense of superiority and triumph. Such suspicions are held towards Athletic Club of Bilbao's claims that they were formed in 1898 despite the absence of any firm evidence, with the oldest surviving documents relating to their club dated 1901. The Basque giants were undoubtedly a trendsetting club in Spanish football, winning the first two editions of the Copa del Rey and being one of only three clubs, alongside Real Madrid and Barcelona, to have been founding members of Spain's top flight in 1929 never to suffer relegation. This has not prevented reservations over their date of conception, which could be an attempt to outdo the longevity of Barcelona, a club conclusively formed in 1899.

Sevilla have not escaped contention over their official age and the club did not register their articles of association with the Civil Government of Seville until 1905, despite White's claims 15 years earlier of playing by the 'Association rules' in line with British football. However, an article in the *Dundee Courier and Argus*, dated 17 March 1890 and unearthed in 2012, outlines the club's original formation and participation in the first organised match in the country earlier that year.

In 2005, *ABC de Sevilla* released the encyclopaedic *Sevilla F.C. Cien Años de Historia* to commemorate the club's 100th birthday. At that time it was thought they were formed on 14 October 1905, with the book itself detailing how the 'pioneers' – José Luis Gallegos, Paco Alba, Joaquín Valenzuela and Carlos García Martínez – had brought the club into existence due to being "excited about the practice of a sport born in England and that was beginning to break through in Spain".

With this foundation date in mind, Sevilla were recorded as the 15th football club in Spain, but the emergence of the report in the *Dundee Courier and Argus* has rewritten the history books. In December 2015, three years after the article came to light, a meeting of club shareholders voted to formally adopt 25 January 1890 as the official date of foundation in Sevilla's articles of association.

"There had previously been pieces of evidence which had suggested the possibility of the club being formed in 1890 but only now can we know for sure that we are the oldest Spanish club specifically devoted to football," said Javier Terenti, from the history department at Sevilla FC. "This is all thanks to the British people. In 2007, Sevilla visited Glasgow, in a sort of tribute to our club's first captain [Hugo MacColl], and we won our second UEFA Cup [a victory over Espanyol]. Everyone here feels really proud of our origins."

Carlos Romero, director of Sevilla FC's history department, added: "We would be honoured to let the city of Glasgow know about the fact that the first captain and one of the founders of the oldest club in Spain specifically devoted to football practice was from Glasgow – Hugo MacColl."

The connection between the Andalusian city and Dundee almost certainly carries even deeper significance due to the strong Scottish influence on the club's formation. There is a possibility that two of the founding members, D. Thomson (there is no record of his Christian name) and Robert Thomson, were related to the general manager of the *Dundee Courier* at the time – David Coupar Thomson – who would himself found major publicist D. C. Thomson & Company. (Coincidentally, there was also a Robert Duncan Thom(p)son involved in the 'foundation' of the Sociedad de Football in 1905, before the starting year was later changed to 1890.)

Perhaps either of the Thomsons or another of Sevilla's Scottish contingent sent reports to the *Courier* outlining developments at the club. This is based on pure conjecture and may be impossible to prove, with the article in question merely containing the byline "From a Seville correspondent". The article itself is displayed below, with revealing information into the events which led to the birth of the Sevilla FC we know today.

"Some six weeks ago a few enthusiastic young residents of British origin met in one of the cafés for the purpose of considering a proposal that we should start an Athletic Association, the want of exercise being greatly felt by the majority of us, who are chiefly engaged in mercantile pursuits. After a deal of talk and a limited consumption of small beer, the Club de Football de Sevilla was duly formed and office-bearers elected. It was decided we should play Association rules and so that no time might be lost we determined to have a practice game next (Sunday) morning ..."

The good-humoured recollection of "a limited consumption of small beer" may have been referencing *cañas* (the smallest beer measurement sold in Spanish bars) but more interesting is the motivation behind forming a club: "the want of exercise" among those whose lives were devoted to working. The idea of forming a football club – one which would go on to be a major player on not only the Spanish but the European stage – to provide a sense of escapism from the monotony of daily life, is eye-opening. It is also telling that Sunday was the earliest opportunity for these souls to get together and have a kickabout, such was the demanding nature of their own work schedules.

Edward Farquharson Johnston, the British vice-consul for the city and owner of prestigious company McAndrew & Co. that shipped oranges and minerals back to various locations in the UK, had been elected club president following the Burns Night meeting. MacColl was sworn in as club captain, having moved to Spain as a marine engineer before becoming a manager at Portilla White, one of the most notable foundries in Spain, jointly owned by Isaías White. It was the Glaswegian's decision for the club to participate in "Association rules" football as the best way to combat the concerns regarding their physical health.

The report relates how training consisted of rowing "about a mile and a half" down the Guadalquivir river, before having "a very pleasant" match of five-a-side football. It details how the participants "were about half and half Spanish and British". This practice led the group to think "we were something of ourselves" before outlining how this led to an invitation to a similar grouping, from a nearby city.

"There being a Recreation Club amongst our compatriots in Huelva, we wrote asking them if they could form an eleven and come to Seville and try their strength against us, and in a few days got a wire that they would meet us on Saturday 8th March ...

"... unfortunately, with the arrival of our friends from Huelva came rain. However, they had come eighty miles to play us, and play we had to. The ground was in good condition not withstanding the heavy downpour, and at 4.45 a start was made, before about twelve dozen spectators."

This contest took place, Sevilla club records state, at the Hipódromo de Tablada – the local racecourse which had granted permission for the 70-minute-long event. Located along the banks of the Guadalquivir, the venue could house 3,000 spectators but indications suggest only about 150 were present, perhaps on account of the weather. Interestingly, the Hipódromo was contemporarily the standout sports venue in Seville but it was demolished in 1915 to make way for a military airfield.

The opponents being referred to were Huelva Recreation Club, now known as Recreativo de Huelva – the oldest football club in Spain. Recre's foundation date predates Sevilla's by just over a month, although the first club of Andalusia's capital can lay claim to being the first Spanish club who were solely dedicated to football. The city of Huelva (pronounced Well-ba in English) is located along the Gulf of Cádiz coast, around 90km west of Seville.

The club, like Sevilla, was the brainchild of two Scots – Alexander Mackay and Robert Russell Ross, both doctors. Formed officially on 23 December 1889, its purpose was to provide the workers at the Rio Tinto mines, who fell under their care, with physical recreation via a variety of sporting activities including football, cricket and tennis. The significance of their formation is recognised in their nickname: *El Decano*, the Dean of Spanish football. The title of Spain's oldest football club will always be their badge of honour, one no other club can claim.

It carries even greater weight with the hindsight of the travails Recre have faced since their formation. They have been in existence for comfortably over a century yet have spent only five of those years in Spain's top flight and their 2006–09 stint in La Liga was not only their most recent time dining at the top table, but their only spell which has not been met with relegation at the first attempt.

Unsurprisingly, not everyone is satisfied with Recreativo's status as Spain's first club. Gimnàstic de Tarragona, a Catalan club based south of Barcelona, point to their records showing a foundation date of 1886 – predating the Andalusians by three years. However, Gimnàstic's name itself is an indicator of why such an argument is flawed. The club may predate the Recreation Club formed in Huelva but the sports it practised included gymnastics, athletics, basketball and tennis but not, crucially, football. Indeed, there is no record of the club having played a game before the outbreak of the First World War in 1914, by which date 28 Spanish sides had already participated in football.

There are claims that Recre themselves were an entity before their official formation in 1889 and had in fact been playing matches five years before this date. In recent years, documentation held by the descendants of Ildefonso Martínez has come to light to throw fresh light upon the club's roots. Martínez was the son of Madrid native Eduardo, who had helped construct the railway between Huelva and Seville having been hired by William Sundheim, referred to as the "father of Recre".

Sundheim, an Anglo-German who took up residence in the province in the early 1870s, is said to have been the man who convinced the Bank of London to invest in the mining of the Rio Tinto region and to have organised the meeting to officialise Recre's status on 23 December 1889, thus steadfastening the link between the British migrant workforce, the city and the sport, again reflected by the 'Recreation Club' title.

Ildefonso Martínez was a worker in Huelva's gas factory, which is fittingly the site of Recreativo's Nuevo Colombino home, a 21,000-seater stadium built in 2001 to replace its predecessor. He worked alongside the club's founder Dr Mackay and his family held documents dated 1 March 1888, under the name of Mackay himself.

The documents include a letter of invitation to Martínez to participate in a match for "Club de Recreo", a literal translation of Recreation Club, against a group of sailors from a ship named *Jean Cory*, which had arrived at the port of Huelva. Another interesting piece of information from the letter was that "Club de Recreo" had already been playing for "some years".

Alfredo Moreno Bolaños documents in the historical archive of the Rio Tinto Foundation how Mackay arrived in the city in 1884 and immediately set up the "Sociedad de Juego de Pelota" (Ball Game Society), who proceeded to participate in football matches in successive years in a time period overlapping with the claims of "Club de Recreo" participating in football matches.

Author Phil Ball devoted a chapter to Recreativo in *Morbo* and he cites 1994 publication *Historia del Fútbol España* as claiming that the club was founded as early as 1880, although the *Historia* fails to present any compelling evidence. Perhaps this was a reference towards the matches between groups of British miners at the time, although such kickabouts would surely have predated this year and, in any case, there is no information to suggest any organised clubs or societies were involved. Perhaps locals helped supplement the teams, no doubt more accustomed to the fierce heat which can engulf the region, but this is an indication of the motivating factors behind forming clubs rather than any hard evidence itself.

In a separate development, fresh evidence has emerged that Exiles Cable Club were formed in the Galician city of Vigo in 1873. Local historian José Ramón Cabanelas presented his findings in 2018, claiming the club – made up of English cable and telegraph workers – played matches against other groups of English workers in the region. Indeed, *Eco Republicano de Compostela* reported on a match in the nearby port of Vilagarcía in the same year. The Exiles name is said to have come from the workers' origins in Cornwall, England, which had the reputation of isolation – as did the nature of a cable worker. While such evidence appears compelling, no clubs were officially registered and – partly due to no sustained effort for historical correction – there is no recognition in the record books. Most information surrounding this entity is shrouded in mystery, with it being assumed that they disappeared in the early decades of the 20th century.

It is a fact that Recreativo are Spain's oldest football club, while it is also true to say that Sevilla FC are Spain's oldest club to be solely devoted to football. This has not stopped fans debating the intricacies of dates of documents being lodged and the legitimacy of reports. Following Sevilla's decision to adopt 1890 as their official birth year in late 2015, fans of Recreativo held up a banner reading: "In 2005, SFC said they were founded in 1905. In 2015, they said it was 1890. In 2025, they will say that they founded the Catholic church. Sevilla do not have any shame nor dignity."

UEFA, European football's governing body, has recognised 1890 as the club's foundation date and their clash with Recreativo as Spain's first documented football match. This is despite the club not having their articles of association (the legalisation of their formation) officially ratified until 1905. These dates are sources of pride for many fans and disagreement leads to ill-feeling and mistrust. This in part is to be expected due to the nature of the evidence – which at times is unsatisfactory due to either its uncomprehensive detail or that it may be inherently slanted by bias – and by the constant emergence of new documents which may conflict with established information.

It is fair to say Sevilla FC were a dormant club in the immediate years leading up to 1905 – in part due to their main founders leaving the city for business purposes – but it is important to allow historical facts to be altered based on the emerge of fresh evidence.

* * * * *

Huelva is an Andalusian city in name but it feels a world away from the region's capital. The city has a backdrop of greyness, reflecting an industrial heritage and containing a skyline at points dominated by smoke billowing out of factory chimneys. Unlike Seville, the streets are not alive with flamenco music or bustling with tourists. In fact, here lies one of the quietest cities in Spain, one which contains a different, more relaxing allure. The locals share the warmth and helpfulness of their Andalusian neighbours but with a tangible sense of modesty, perhaps tinged with an acute sense of surprise to encounter a tourist in their city.

Their hometown is both charming and efficient – terminology that cannot be contemporarily applied to their football club. Recre have fallen on hard times in recent years and have faced the ongoing threat of extinction since 2016, with debts spiralling and fan unrest palpable. Having fallen into Spain's regionalised third tier, the team have battled to avoid further relegation on the pitch, while off it financial woes have continued to cast a shadow over proceedings.

Upon my first visit to the city in 2014, I was keen to find out more about *El Decano* yet the task would not prove straightforward. A vacated building in the heart of the centre displayed sufficient hints that this had previously housed the club shop, with a blue-and-white banner emblazoned with the club badge and several iconic moments from their history, including images of those early Recreation Club sides.

Further along the reel was a shot from the 2003 Copa del Rey final – Recre's only cup final appearance which culminated in a 3–0 defeat to Real Mallorca – and from three years later when arguably the club's darkest and finest moments came within hours of each other in Madrid. The 2006/07 campaign was the best in *El Decano*'s distinguished history: they recorded an eighth-place finish in La Liga and narrowly missed out on European football, with young playmaker Santi Cazorla enjoying a spellbinding run of form. The crowning moment came five days before Christmas, with a 3–0 victory at the Galácticos of Real Madrid.

However, 20 December 2006 has primarily been remembered for tragedy. Four fans of Recreativo lost their lives earlier that day in a bus crash en route to the Spanish capital. An emotionally charged game went ahead with Florent Sinama-Pongolle, Ikechuckwu Uche and Emilio Viqueira securing a stunning victory.

Within a decade of the Bernabéu success, hard times had once again befallen both the city and the club. Huelva had been hit particularly hard by the economic downturn; industries that had provided the bedrock of the city began to depart and Recreativo, once the only club in Spain to be owned by its city hall, had fallen into monetary hardship under private ownership. Around 10,000 people took to the streets of Huelva in mass protests against the running of the club – double the average attendance.

Despite a precarious situation, the club has continued to fight. With the loyal backing of fan groups and with a debt of over €8m recently wiped from its books, it appears once again to be moving towards local government ownership. Almost 120 years previously, it had all been a tad more jovial, when Recreation Club had met Sevilla for Spain's first (documented) football clash.

"The players presented a motley appearance," continued the Scottish newspaper's report. "... all kinds of costumes being in requisition, and our left wing, never before having the honour of belonging to any athletic club, appeared on the scene in night dress, in the shape of a fantastically-patterned snit of pyjamas. He was hailed with shouts of derisive laughter, and dubbed by the natives as the Clown Yugles.

"The game was a most pleasant one of two thirty-fives, resulting in a win for Seville by 2 to 0, Ritson drawing first blood, followed shortly after by the Clown Yugles, unexpectedly by all, not less so by himself.

"It is only fair to state that the Huelva Club had never played together before, and had also that morning a railway journey of four hours, and consequently played under great disadvantages. Our English doctor acted as an umpire for Seville, the Secretary of the Recreation Club acting in a similar capacity for Huelva, the British Vice Consul discharging the duty of referee to everyone's satisfaction."

The light-hearted events described outlined the spirit of fair play in which the event took place with the emphasis on Recre's "great disadvantages" for a trip which nowadays would be a de facto local derby in the context of Spanish football and the vast distances between its participants. The report explains how the two groups "pleasantly spent [the evening] with toast, song and sentiment" in the Suizo restaurant – one of Seville's most distinguished eateries, described as part-Spanish, part-French. This evening of merriment was a concept referred to as "the third half", when both clubs would come together to celebrate a day of hard work and good football.

Sevilla's left-wing – whose good spirits could clearly not be dampened by the jibes relating to his choice of appearance – perhaps had even made use of the restaurant's supply of small beers. "The non-success of the 'Clown Yugles' in endeavouring to balance himself on a vacant chair not even harming the harmony of the meeting." The most satisfactory explanation of the "Clown Yugles" nickname appears to be in connection with a juggler in a circus, with his "patterned snit of pyjamas" likely to have drawn parallels with the familiar act of the time. Despite attempts to discover the identity of the individual, history has so far retained his anonymity.

In finishing, the hope of a return game in Huelva was mentioned in an effort to continue the cordial relationship between the two formative clubs. Only in recent years has it come to light that such ambitions were successful and meetings between the two Andalusian clubs were "now regarded as an annual event", according to an article published on 10 January, 1891.

Oddly, the snippet was found within a copy of *The Field, the Farm, the Garden, newspaper for the Gentlemen of the Country*, a publication running between 1857 and 1933, publishing a variety of work including letters from Charles Darwin and encompassing a range of sports. Under the banner "FOOTBALL IN SPAIN" in edition 1,985, a correspondent outlined how "wherever Englishmen are settled, they never rest content until they have introduced their national customs and games".

Interestingly, the report does not correspond exactly to that published in the *Dundee Courier* ten months previously, instead suggesting that football "had formed a part of activities in Seville for some years" rather than as recently as the previous year. Perhaps such an inconsistency was due to the piece being translated when it was typed up, or perhaps the reporter himself was misinformed.

Sevilla played Recreation Club on Saturday, 27 December 1890 at a ground referenced as "the racecourse", presumably meaning the Hipódromo de Tablada, which held the first encounter. All of the exiled English population were said to be among a healthy crowd alongside Spaniards "eager to be initiated into the mysteries of football". The sport at this point had yet to catch on in the wider public consciousness, "as the local papers described it, it is played without sticks or baskets for protection".

The Huelva-based club had clearly improved from their first primitive encounter and held the hosts to a scoreless draw thanks to a "fine defence", while the forwards of both clubs were "most conspicuous". We can also conclude that Geddes, of Sevilla, was not the subtlest player "as he was dangerous to friend and foe alike." Indeed, such was the absence of genuine goalmouth action, the most excitement on the touchlines was said to be had by the females in attendance who "had reference to the legs and attitudes of the players rather than to their play".

Perhaps the sight of the players in tight-fitting shorts was more revealing than had been intended.

As was customary, the two teams spent the evening wining and dining, this time at the luxurious Hotel de Paris, organised at the behest of Johnston, referred to throughout the report by his vice-consul title. The piece concluded by revealing the Scot as the referee in the tie – presumably vetted by Recreation Club as being of good character – while confirming the two line-ups:

Sevilla: E. Plews (goal), H. MacColl (captain), G.T. Charlesworth (backs), D. Thomson, H. Stroneger, W. Logan (half-backs), H. Welton, J. White, J. Poppy, P. Merry, T. Geddes (forwards).

Huelva: E. Wakelin (goal), Thomson, Jones (backs), Norman, Oliver, Hodge (half-backs), Hopper, Mundell, Birchall (captain), Garcia, Birchall (forwards).

Umpires: Dr Langdon (Sevilla), Mr Bower (Huelva).

The sparsity of Spaniards within the squads is perhaps the most interesting angle of the XIs. We already know of White's *Sevilliano* roots whilst it is suggested that Welton and Merry had also both been born in the city. The only Hispanic name on Huelva's team sheet was Garcia, although it is possible Oliver was also a Spaniard.

In 1894, Sevilla's first captain MacColl returned to the United Kingdom after spending seven years in the Andalusian capital. Later that year he set up engine building company MacColl and Pollock Ltd. along with Gilbert Pollock, whom he had worked with at Portilla and White foundry and played alongside at Sevilla. Based in Sunderland, it is thought that the two sourced the red-and-white stripes of Sunderland AFC, the local English team, to match their newlyformed Spanish club.

A match was arranged between Sevilla and Recreativo on 31 January 1909 at the Tablada racetrack – which had hosted their infamous first clash – to raise funds for the victims of the Messina earthquake, which had struck the previous month. Historical accounts suggest that Sunderland's striped red-and-white kit had been sent specifically by MacColl for the match. However, a delay in the shipment ensured that Sevilla had to once more use white kit and an executive decision ensured from that point onwards it would be the club's principal kit.

Sevilla's badge still holds the red and white stripes and whilst their kit did not adopt the same design, the red-and-white colours – occasionally with a dash of black – have been the club's main colours since and have resulted in the nickname of *Los Rojiblancos* (red-and-whites). The red and white Sunderland-style stripes were the club's secondary kit between 1913 and 1945, before a change to just red. Red and white stripes were used for away kits in the 1972/73 and 2015/16 campaigns but have never since been a permanent fixture.

Born as Sevilla Football Club, their original name lasted 51 years before General Franco's government issued a decree forcing all companies with a 'foreign title' to be changed to Castilian Spanish. Whilst this was primarily targeted at those in the Basque Country and

Catalonia, consistency ensured the Anglicised 'Football' was removed from the title and the club were subsequently known as Sevilla Club de Fútbol. The decree was orchestrated by General José Moscardó, placed in charge of the newlyformed La Delegación Nacional de Deportes (DND) which had total control over Spanish football's governing body, the REFE.

Football was said to be Moscardó's strongest passion and the position ensured he would have a disproportionate level of control over the sport across Spain. Athletic Bilbao became Atlético de Bilbao, while FC Barcelona became Barcelona Club de Fútbol. Athletic Club de Madrid merged with the airforce team of Aviación Nacional of Zaragoza to become Athletic Aviación de Madrid, who immediately won the league titles in 1941 and 1942. The regime directly meddled with clubs at boardroom level, elevating into power Falangists such as Eduardo Lastaragay at Atlético de Bilbao. Moscardó himself was viewed favourably by Franco and the former military governor was appointed coach of the Spanish national team for the Olympic Games in both 1948 and 1952.

The decree banning foreign titles in company names was not overturned until 1972 and three years later, Sevilla's *socios* voted for a name change. However, it was not to return the club to its purified British roots but instead met history halfway, with the new name being Sevilla Fútbol Club. In 1992, SAD was subsequently added to the title to reflect the club's becoming a *Sociedad Anónima Deportiva* – Public Limited Sports Company, as part of a change in the nation's sporting laws.

MacColl died suddenly, aged 54, at Glasgow's Central Station Hotel on 31 August 1915 whilst on holiday. Following a lifetime of various business ventures and innovation, he was said to have left a fortune of just shy of £15,000. In late 2015 Sevilla historian Javier Terenti located his gravestone in the Cathcart Cemetery, on the outskirts of Glasgow. Johnston, the first president, was buried in his Scottish hometown of Elgin while Pollock – MacColl's business partner and fellow Sevilla founding member – was laid to rest in the Isle of Man.

The club and football within the city have come a long way since those formative years, but the influence of these men cannot be underestimated and their legacy continues to grow annually with their brainchild now a major force in both Spanish and European football.

Chapter 5
Football Spreading Roots

SPAIN'S first recorded football match between Sevilla and Recreativo did not lead to an explosion of the sport across the nation, not immediately anyway. It was to be another eight years before the nation officially had its third club (although as already discussed, the formation date of Bilbao's Athletic Club remains contentious) while no other club was formed in Andalusia until 1907, by which stage 16 other Spanish clubs had sprung up.

Perhaps it should come as no great surprise that the sport took so long to spread its roots throughout the nation. The players of Sevilla and Recreativo endured notable hardships in finding time away from work to compete in matches, never mind attend training sessions. Spain is a vast nation and cities were poorly connected. This lack of infrastructure restricted the growth of ideas and the early clubs which sprung up did so as a direct result of British influence.

The Basque city of Bilbao became home to miners from across England's north-east and shipyard workers from Southampton, Portsmouth and Sunderland. Together they formed Bilbao Football Club in 1900 but two years earlier the story goes that students – upon their return from courses in England – formed Athletic Club, with a notably English spelling. By 1903, the two clubs merged to create Athletic Club of Bilbao.

Grabbing the initiative, it was the Basque club who set the benchmark for the formative years of competitive football across Spain. They racked up 13 Copa del Rey titles in the competition's first three decades and four of the first seven league titles. Their playing style offered the blueprint for the early days of Spanish football – a physical and direct approach with a heavy British influence, leading to the early *La Furia Roja* of the national side. Despite Athletic Club adopting a policy, in 1912, of signing players native to or trained in the Basque Country, the club's links to English football have provided a strong undercurrent to their existence with a total of nine English managers, including five of their first six.

Yet just as the contrasting fortunes of Sevilla and Recreativo have shown, longevity alone does not guarantee success. On Catalonia's Costa Brava lies the fishing port of Palamós; primarily famed for its prawns, the town is also home to Spain's fourth-oldest club and the first in the region. Formed in 1898 by local merchant Gaspar Matas i Danés, it is believed his studies in England gave him a thirst for football and his hometown its very own team.

The port has withstood the waves of gentrification and commercialisation which have engulfed the region, but its football club has also been immune to any notable success. The glory days of Palamós were confined to the early 1990s in which they reached the Spanish second tier for the first time ever and won the Copa Catalunya in 1992 before losing the decider two years later to Espanyol.

Spanish football writer Jimmy Burns outlined the "intensification of political and class divisions" as a fundamental reason for strangling the growth of sport across the nation, but particularly in Catalonia, at the turn of the century.

In *La Roja: A Journey Through Spanish Football* he wrote that the city of Barcelona "became embroiled in a seemingly endless cycle of repression and violence that left little time to watch, let alone learn, an innovative sport."

One year prior to FC Barcelona's formation in 1899, the Spanish Empire lost its grip on power in Cuba as ideas of anarchy and nationalism continued to trump the idea of devoting serious energy to sport. The working classes felt energised and those in cushier surroundings felt threatened by the changing winds within society.

The successful attempts to gain independence from Spain across Central and South America led to nationalistic ideas within Catalonia, with many of its inhabitants not associating with the rest of the nation culturally, socially, politically or indeed linguistically.

The growth of such ideas coincided with the foundation of FC Barcelona, who have acted as a de facto sporting wing for the Catalan state. The club's famed motto *Més que un club* (more than a club) is an attempt to reflect this. Formed by Joan Gamper – a Swiss national so enthralled by the region that he changed his birth name Hans Max Gamper-Haessig to a Catalan one – to carry a movement, which swiftly grew into one of the world's leading clubs.

Just as with the Anglicisation present in Athletic Club and Sevilla Fútbol Club (named FC rather than the Hispanicised Club de Fútbol), Barcelona have retained their FC rather than CF in acknowledgement of their founding figures.

Gamper led a mixed group of Swiss, English and Catalan to form a club who have provided a focal point for Catalan identity ever since. In 1925, then Spanish prime minister, General Miguel Primo de Rivera, accused Barça and the club of promoting Catalan nationalism. The dictator's main slogan of 'Country, Religion, Monarchy' was in direct contrast to the nationalistic spirit of FC Barcelona. Two years earlier, the General – founder of the Falange, Spain's fascist-inspired political party – orchestrated a coup which overthrew Spain's parliamentary government of Spain. Among his first steps were to suspend the nation's constitution, establish martial law and impose strict censorship to suppress regional and cultural expression.

The events of 14 June 1925 reflected the increasing political angst and tension across Spain and Catalonia, with Barcelona playing a prominent role in reflecting society due to their success on the pitch and growing support base off it. The club took part in a contentious match against CE Júpiter in honour of the Orfeó Català, a long-running choral society who had become institutionalised in Catalan culture. The clash had initially been blocked by the central Spanish government, but the decision was changed under growing public disaffection.

A band from a visiting British Royal Navy ship docked in Barcelona provided the pre-match music but the events did not go to plan. The playing of *Marcha Real*, Spain's national anthem, was roundly greeted with boos and jeers from the supporters in attendance, forcing the band to break into an impromptu version of *God Save the King*, which was met with widespread applause.

As a punishment, General Rivera forced the closure of the club's Les Corts grounds for six months – reduced to three upon appeal – and crucially, forced Gamper's resignation and ordered his expulsion from Spain. Upon his return to Switzerland, Gamper spiralled into money problems and depression which culminated in tragic circumstances five years later, as he committed suicide. In 1929, the previous year, his brainchild won the first league title in Spanish football after the Spanish Football Federation had agreed upon ten teams to form a top flight.

To the west of Catalonia lies the Basque Country, home to Athletic Club. The region is another hotbed of regionalist nationalism but its strand is more insulated and separatist. In part, this relates to the Basque language having no apparent relative and thus being more difficult to understand. Assimilation is more welcomed by Catalan nationalists, whose romance language shares similarities with Castilian Spanish and who historically have been more open to inclusivity in their movement.

Whereas FC Barcelona's history has been one of internationalism, Athletic Club's policy of signing players either from or trained in their region is a form of moderately expressing the ideas of Basque nationalism. The club's motto of *Con cantera y afición, no hace falta importación* (with home-grown talent and local support, foreigners are not needed) is reflective of the nationalist consensus within the region. In their co-edited publication *Identity*, Brian Michael Goss and Christopher Chávez argued that "setting ethnic limits on membership of its playing roster mimics the essentialism which underpins Basque nationalism". In 1937, Athletic's political awareness came into the spotlight as they formally supported the Basque campaign for independence and encouraged their players to represent the region's 'national team'.

Real Sociedad, Athletic's main regional rivals, imposed a similar policy for two decades from the late 1960s and despite the self-imposed restriction, enjoyed their golden days during the early 1980s, winning back-to-back league titles. The eventual abandoning of this approach was due to La Real's need to broaden their player recruitment due to the greater political and financial muscle flexed by their rivals in Bilbao. After all, the area is home to a mere 2.19 million inhabitants. However, both clubs are well renowned for their productive youth systems, with an ethos of nurturing youth players and development through coaching.

Nationalism, politics and identity have formed part of Spanish football's framework since its inception and the early years of its clubs indicate how these concepts swiftly used football as an embodiment of such ideas. The formation of these clubs reinforced and, in some cases, fostered allegiances to non-sporting causes, which naturally became intensified during the Civil War in the 1930s. Almost a century later, football fans and clubs reflecting society still rings true.

Yet society in Andalusia – wonderfully varied and diverse in itself – did not house nationalistic ideas and as such did not seek to divide itself from the rest of the Spanish state. But that is not to say that splinters did not exist within the region and the city of Seville in particular. Still relatively cut off from the rest of Spain – and particularly the economic powerhouse cities in the nation's north – it would take its footballing representatives some time to establish themselves and forge identities. Unlike other cities of a similar standing, Seville was to become divided from within.

Chapter Six

Triana

"In the streets of Triana, those who cannot sing, follow the rhythm of clapping" – lyrics of Soleá por Triana, written by Demófilo (Antonio Machado Álvarez)

PERCHED along the west bank of the Guadalquivir river lies the neighbourhood of Triana, a district entrenched in history and significance yet also riddled with contradictions and often a lack of historical clarity, not that any of that really matters. In many ways this is the cultural heart of the city, yet in others it does not really feel part of the city at all. Where Seville is effortlessly stylish and elegant, Triana offers the region's mythical aura and its soul, warts and all.

Triana prides itself on representing 'otherness' and 'another way of seeing Seville'. Historically, it has been situated outside the city walls, along the riverbank and staring across to the city. Calle Betis runs parallel to the river, buzzing with liveliness and of course shares the name with one half of the city's football allegiance. The street itself is home to a selection of picturesque riverfront restaurant terraces directly facing the Torre del Oro along with many of the finest bars and nightclubs in the city. Further along, public vantage points allow clear views of the bullring and the Giralda. This one truly gentrified street of the barrio does not paint an accurate picture of what lies within.

Meander further into Triana and you will find yourself in a maze of narrow, cobbled streets much like the Santa Cruz area, home to the centre's main tourist attractions. There are notably fewer sightseers here, gone too are the grand buildings and designated areas of greenery. Triana has retained its historical charm and distinctive sense of cultural identity. There is an authentic feel, expressed through life on the streets, through the shared use of public spaces and belonging. It feels real.

The closer to Triana's heart you venture, the more striking it becomes why this particular part of Seville is not the chosen area for honeymoons and romantic getaways. The streets are bland, reflecting the blue-collar nature of the district – humbler than any other in the centre of the city. An absurd reflection of the class divide is evident in the street names, which translate directly into 'work', 'prosperity', 'desire', 'virtue' and 'loyalty'. General Franco's belief in generating unwavering dedication among the apparent working class is evident. Whatever intentions the dictator had, Triana never shared them and resisted his forces throughout the Civil War, which in part explains the absence of aesthetical charm throughout its streets today.

The oldest historical records of the area date back to the 11th century, when it was definitively a small community of workers' cottages and farmhouses. In that period of Al-Andalus, the area was referred to as *Atrayana* – Arabic for 'the area along the river'. In 1711, the Moors then constructed a floating bridge, to be built upon a line of boats, to connect the two sides of the river. The contemporary author, Ibn Sahib al-Sala, wrote: "The building of the bridge beautified Seville and Triana, and the ease with which people could cross brought them prosperity, unity, security and wealth." Remarkably, this floating bridge remained in place for seven centuries before eventually being replaced by the Puente de Triana which stands today. Due to the location along the Guadalquivir, the area frequently fell victim to torrential flooding – historically forcing residents into refuge in the Castillo de San Jorge (now the location of the Mercado de Triana) – before the river was eventually reconstructed to minimise such hazards.

However, despite the lack of archaeological evidence to support a theory, it seems highly reasonable that Triana was populated as early as Roman times. This is intertwined in the confusion regarding the origin of the name Triana. A hypothesis exists – proposed by Justino Matute Gavira in his work *Aparato para describir la historia de Triana y de su iglesia parroquial* in which he agrees with fellow Seville historian Rodrigo Caro – that the derivation of Triana is from the Latin expression *Trans amnem*, meaning 'those beyond the river'. Another theory suggests that it comes from the patronymic form Traius or Traianus plus the suffix 'ana' to mean 'the city of Trajan' – the Roman emperor from AD 98–117, who may have authorised the colonisation of land around Seville. This explanation seems particularly plausible as Trajan was born in Italica – lying five miles to the north of the city. Nowadays a protected area of Roman ruins (including the old 25,000-seated amphitheatre, one of the largest in the Roman Empire), the site was the hometown of at least two Roman emperors – Trajan and Hadrian, while records are conflicting that Theodosius was also born there.

Triana would later become famed as the home of Seville's world-renowned tile workshops. Romans introduced grapevine and olive farming in the 2nd century and as a result, potteries sprung up to produce the pots and jars needed to store the produce. The strong tradition intensified under later Arab rule with many innovative techniques born in Calle Alfarería (which directly translates as 'pottery street'). Virtually all the tiles used in the construction of Seville's churches, hotels, bars and private houses, as well as all the main sites, were produced and manufactured in the district with the clay itself sourced from the nearby La Cartuja area, lying to the north. None of the glamorous tourist attractions are located within Triana, but they exist due to the graft of the barrio's population.

Niculoso Francisco 'Pisano' became one of the many Tuscans to migrate to Triana in the late 15th century and he began the practice of painting scenes like a canvas upon tiles, thus driving business further. He is also said to have played a major part in the development of the much-famed 'arista' tile. At its height, there were said to be 50 ovens in the district producing bricks, tiles and dishes daily. The Ibero-American Exhibition of 1929 gave a new impetus to the ceramics industry in Triana, as both the Plaza de España and Plaza de América, along with numerous Ibero-American pavilions, made use of the local ceramics in their decoration.

Triana has many varying claims to fame. Two docks existed at either end of Calle Betis – situated along the arterial Rio Guadalquivir route – Los Camarones (shrimp trawler) and the Mulas dock, where boats were repaired. It was from here that the first voyage around the world in human history, the Magellan-Elcano circumnavigation, set off. Under the command of Ferdinand Magellan and Spanish navigator Juan Sebastián Elcano, the 19 survivors became the first men to circumnavigate the globe in a single expedition.

The cultural origins of the art of flamenco have deep roots in the neighbourhood too, originating from the melting pot of ethnicities and communities which resided side by side. The music has been heavily influenced by and associated with the Romani people in Spain, who initially did not live in Triana by choice. They were not allowed inside the main city walls and this separation, in part, gave way to the long-term feelings of resentment, mistrust, and rebellion. Indeed, they were originally forced to settle in Cava de los Gitanos (the 'gypsy' area, now along Calle Pagés del Corro), which was separated from the Cava de los Civiles (civilian area). The Romani were not allowed inside the main city walls. This separation between the *Cavas* was only ended in 1893 and the *gitano* (gypsy) quarter remained until the 1950s.

The Romani population devoted themselves to trades such as blacksmithing, metalwork, basketmaking and farming. They lived and worked alongside those from the colonies, from black communities and within the framework of the former Jewish and Moorish communities which held prominence within the region.

This blending and fusion of cultural legacies led to the mixing of differing ideas and forms of expression which manifested themselves in the form of flamenco. At its soul, this is the expression of an idea of 'otherness', of belonging to a minority who had inbuilt qualities of resistance and who had become accustomed to a nomadic existence. Flamenco is a hybrid culture, intending to be flexible and all-encompassing, representing a counterculture whilst also remaining aware of its heritage and spirit. Flamenco was far from unique to Triana itself and it exploded with the increased movement between the area and the rest of Seville, Cádiz and other neighbouring towns and cities, including Jerez de la Frontera, Utrera and Lebrija.

In the 1960s a new musical form of expression also took off with the growth of Andalusian rock, which attempted to fuse flamenco soul with English-speaking progressive rock. An example of the avant-garde in music, it reflected a movement which was self-aware and forward-thinking, attempting to maintain and renew the relevance of its culture within an evolving world.

Tradition runs through the veins of Triana, evident in the design of its buildings and layout of its streets but also in its frequent festivals and celebrations, which usually carry religious overtones. The Esperanza de Triana is arguably Catholic Seville's most adored statue of the Virgin Mary, with its local *hermandad* (brotherhood) one of the most powerful in the city, with over 12,500 members and dating back to 1418. It is viewed daily by many locals in the district and is a key component of the city's annual Semana Santa.

Like many fellow *Sevillanos* and indeed, those across the nation, bullfighting is afforded notable significance in Triana. One famous bullfighter was Joaquín Rodríguez Ortega, known as Cagancho and referred to as 'the gypsy with green eyes'. Newspaper archives show

how Ortega's love of Betis often trumped his own career. In 1942, he failed to turn up at a scheduled appearance in favour of watching *Los Verdiblancos*, leading to him being disqualified from events for three years. He was one of a notably high proportion of matadors from Triana and if they perform particularly well at Seville's bullring – on the opposite bank of the river – they are carried, shoulder-high and still adorned in their metallic suit, along the Guadalquivir and across the Puente de Triana to the backdrop of great fanfare. This ritual will pass the statue of Juan Belmonte, the Triana local who became one of Spain's most adored matadors. Belmonte's gaze looks inward towards his barrio and not across to the Giralda, evident in the background. Many locals insist this symbolism captures the local pride of Triana: nobody here forgets their roots. Others swear they have never crossed the river and whilst these claims sound more than a tad dubious, such is the conviction with which it is said, it is hard to be quite sure.

Laurie Lee summed up the raw experience of visiting Triana in the 1955 publication *A Rose for Winter: Travels in Andalusia*. Whilst walking around the district, he "saw a girl of five dancing solemnly under an old wall (and) a boy fighting a dog with goat horns tied to its head." Had Lee travelled to the area two decades later he may have found a different experience, or so Franco may have hoped. In 1968 the city council voted to build a new housing estate to the south of the city. The bluntly titled Las Tres Mil Viviendas (The Three Thousand Homes) was a project designed to ethnically cleanse Triana – which was increasingly being incorporated into modern Seville – of its gypsy population.

Comprised of ugly tower blocks, the entire project reflected the disdain in which the Spanish establishment held the Romani population. Unsurprisingly, the newly built area swiftly developed a notoriety for crime and substandard living conditions. The poverty-stricken area became a no-go zone for *payos* (a term used for non-Romani Spaniards) as the dividing lines in Spanish society were once again redrawn. However, with the transfer of the gypsy population came the movement of its cultural heart and soul. From the impoverished Las Tres Mil Viviendas came the hugely successful music act Pata Negra who founded 'blueslería' – a fusion of contemporary flamenco expression and blues, while critically acclaimed flamenco dancer Farruquito also grew up in the barrio.

The evolution of Triana through the decades is indicative of its continued significance to Seville and how, despite governmental attempts to mould it into an area of conformity, it remains distinctive and authoritative.

An area often frowned upon from the outside by aristocrats looking down their noses, such sneering at its working-class roots and ethnic diversity has only served to heighten the pride and siege mentality. Full of meaning and history, Triana's distinctive identity and character offers a fascinating insight for those visiting the city. A neighbourhood both linked to and separate from Seville, it is quintessentially the most important suburb and the critical conscience of the Andalusian capital. The river running through the city does not just serve as a geographical divide. A bastion of resistance weathered by centuries of marginalisation, understanding the historical significance of Triana is fundamental when speaking of the city.

Seville-based football journalist Carlos Urbano, author of Betis-based book *La Década Perdida*, told me: "Triana is the most iconic neighbourhood in the city, for sure. Its people suffered the most after the Spanish Civil War broke out." Speaking of the penchant for producing matadors, singers, dancers and musicians, the attention then turned to football and the association with his beloved Betis.

"Triana has been the birthplace of so many footballers who have played a big part in the history of Betis," Urbano continued. "Francisco 'Paco' Telechia, Quino Sierra, Alejandro Pozuelo and Dani, the hero of 2005 [referencing the winning goalscorer of the club's second Copa del Rey title, and its most recent major trophy, see Chapter 30]. They were all born and raised in Triana.

"But there are other significant figures in the club's history: Alfonso Jaramillo, who saved the club once, and Pedro Buenaventura Gil, who performed a number of roles at Betis."

Buenaventura Gil really was 'Mr Betis' – devoting four decades of his life to serving the club in a variety of capacities. Initially a coach of the youth team, he later became co-ordinator of the club's academy, the technical secretary, the club's representative on the Andalusia Football Federation and on the Spanish FA's Escuela de Entrenadores (coaching school). He even had four different spells as interim manager in 1977, 1982, 1988 and 1989. His son Pedro became head of youth development at the club in 2014 while his other son, Lorenzo, became a fitness coach loyal to Pep Guardiola across spells at Barcelona, Bayern Munich and Manchester City.

In an interview with the journalist Manuel Fernández de Córdoba that *ABC* published in October 2000, 17 years before his death, Buenaventura Gil said: "The 'manquepierda' [see Chapter 10] was never a conformism, but a cry of the wounded heart, a cry of rage, the 'musho' Betis is the pride of a race: the Bética. We are born Béticos and that is how we live." The raw passion and emotive nature of Buenaventura Gil's words are striking. His love for Betis surpassed the idea of just a football match, a sporting event. These feelings encompass much greater significance and speaking to *Sevillano* natives, regardless of club association, it became increasingly clear that this fervour was the norm.

Alfonso Jaramillo – born in the heart of Cava de los Gitanos – was another influential figure in the history of the club, helping them at their darkest hour. Between 1947 and 1954, *Los Verdiblancos* spent seven successive seasons in Spain's third tier – the only time in their history they have been outside the top two flights – with Jaramillo assuming the position of treasurer.

The club's second *socio*, (partner) he famously spent hours at home cooking meals for the players to eat for the long journeys between matches. In 1961, whilst working for the Seville city council, he proved influential in helping the club purchase its Estadio Benito Villamarín of which they had been lead tenants since 1939 (see Chapter 14). Shortly before his death in 2012, aged 98, Jaramillo's memoirs were published and authored by Rafael Medina. The publication was entitled *Entre Triana y el Betis* (between Triana and Betis), reflecting the significance of his barrio and football club upon his life.

Triana and Betis go almost hand in hand. The word Betis is derived from the Roman *baetis*, used for the Guadalquivir river. The club's Benito Villamarín stadium lies a short walk from the river and south-east of the Triana barrio. There are many figures from within its boundaries who have represented Sevilla with distinction but its close ties with Betis are much more than solely geographic. When Betis won promotion back to the top tier of Spanish football in 2015, huge parties were held across the barrio and the Puente de Triana bridge over the Guadalquivir was filled with celebrating fans, each holding a green flare to create an iconic image.

The neighbourhood is also a source of great controversy. It is cited by many *Béticos* as the cause of an internal split at city rivals Sevilla which led to the formation of their own club in a dispute contested by their neighbours. It's a debate which many believe started a rivalry and its dispute has provided a backdrop for claims and counterclaims over a century. It is time to separate the facts from the myths.

Chapter 7

And Then There Were Two

ON 12 September 1907, and almost 18 years after MacColl, Johnston and White had started football in the city, Sevilla FC were to be handed a crosstown rival. Whereas the Andalusian capital's first club began after a meeting of business owners and the city's vice-consul, the roots of Seville's second team were rather humbler. Unlike *Los Rojiblancos*, the newly formed club would undergo numerous fundamental changes before finally emerging as Real Betis Balompié.

The one constant throughout the club's history has been the word *Balompié*: the literal Spanish translation of foot-ball, rather than the fútbol used by virtually all other major forces in Spain (and football, as used contemporarily by city rivals Sevilla FC). Formed in 15 Calle Cervantes, in the heart of the city, España Balompié was started by a group of students at the polytechnic school. The majority studied medicine, but all were preparing to be enrolled in the army due to their familys' military backgrounds.

This group were said to have been playing football in their spare time and had wished to formalise this interest and form their own club. It was the España en Sevilla festival which helped to kickstart such aspirations. The event was one of national pride and intended to mark the 100-year anniversary of the Guerra de la Independencia Española (Spanish War of Independence), which overlapped with the 1807–14 Peninsular War.

The conflict held significance for Seville, as it caused the city to hold temporary but real political power in Spain for the first time in its existence. Events had started when the allied Spanish and Napoleon's French forces invaded Portugal in 1807, before France turned on Spain the following year and led to chaos across the peninsula.

Former Spanish prime minister and *Sevillano,* Francisco Saavedra, declared war on Napoleon's troops and helped re-establish links with

Great Britain. The city became the capital of 'free Spain' and became the administrative centre for military operations, regularly hosting renowned British military figures including Arthur Wellesley, the first Duke of Wellington. Seville had previously been Europe's most significant city in terms of economics but between December 1808 and January 1810 it held genuine political power for the first time.

This period was sweet, but it was also particularly short, as the city surrendered to French forces who had surrounded it without a shot being fired. Spain's political capital moved further south to the safe haven of Cádiz, which housed the first national assembly and became instrumental in modernising and liberalising the nation. The history department of *ABC* describes Seville as contemporarily becoming "the most Frenchified city in Spain" during this flux and reasons that this drove the underplaying of this period by historians.

Instead, the city prefers to focus on the role of Spanish artillery officer Luis Daoíz y Torres, who led the Dos de Mayo Uprising. Daoíz directed the resistance against the French forces who were attempting to topple the Spanish monarchy but died in the fighting and has been remembered as a national hero for his self-sacrificial role. A monument stands in his honour in Seville's Plaza de la Gavidia – the street in which he was born – to reflect his image of a frontrunner in the fight for an independent Spanish state.

It was in this context that the polytechnic students decided to patriotically name their venture España Balompié after attending the centennial parade in Seville. Yet a fundamental reasoning for the delay in forming the club was the construct of the name itself. The English term 'Football' had no satisfactory direct translation into Spanish, due to its combination of two separate nouns. So, the students sought the advice of journalist and Spanish language academic Mariano de Cavia to assist them.

De Cavia responded via the newspaper *El Liberal* (which ceased to exist after 1936 following raids from Franco's Nationalist forces) to suggest "pPiebalón" would sound ugly in Spanish, and he instead recommended the use of "balompié" to meet the "purity and richness of the Spanish language". The journalist pointed to existing Spanish words "buscapié", "hincapié", "rodapié", "tirapié", "traspié" and "volapié" as reasoning for his choice. De Cavia complained that the term "fútbol" was used "clumsily" by his compatriots, who "had no understanding of what they are saying".

Such insistence upon this terminology can be regarded as an attempt to convey their pride in their Spanish roots – undoubtedly fuelled by the celebration of their nation's independence from France – and a deliberate attempt to avoid using Spain's Anglicised 'fútbol' or simply 'football'. Few other professional clubs use the term and even Albacete Balompié started life in 1940 under the name Albacete Football Association, before the Falangist government's decree banning foreign words in titles came into force the following year (see Chapter 4).

Within months, the Seville-based students had altered the title of the club to Sevilla Balompié to distinctively reflect the club's origins in the Andalusian capital, although it has been suggested – with no documented proof – that such a change was not universally accepted among the founders. By 1 February 1909 the club was registered at the government offices – thus formalising their existence in the eyes of authorities – and the initial kit colours (after a provisional spell of using white shirts, like Sevilla FC, which we can assume was due to their widespread availability) consisted of a light-blue top, white shorts and black socks. These colours may have been chosen as they were the colour of the Spanish infantry at the time, although there is no documentation to support such a theory. Las Tablas Verdes, a blog run by a group of Real Betis historians, argues this is a "biased interpretation" which wrongfully portrays the club's foundation as "militaristic, conservative and reactionary." The badge too was also a light-blue shade with 'Sociedad Sevilla Balompié' (Sevilla Football Society) emblazoned upon the rounded crest.

The first use of the famous green and white stripes used by their Real Betis Balompié successors did not come until 1910. Manuel Ramos Asencio, the Sevilla Balompié captain at the time, had spent a year of his studies in Dumfries, Scotland, and his first association with football had been to watch Celtic in Glasgow. Andrew Kerins, known by his religious name Brother Walfrid, was an Irish Marist Brother at the same school and was the founder of Celtic. In 1910, an article in Málaga-based magazine *La Unión Ilustrada* displayed team photos of Balompié and Betis FC – who we will examine in closer detail in Chapter 8 – on 27 October. Balompié are playing in green and white vertical stripes (a tweak from the Scottish club's horizontal hoops) while Betis played solely in white.

Sevilla Balompié began life with just shy of two dozen members with over half their initial number dominated by brothers. There were the Hermosa brothers (Luis, José, Andrés and Pedro), the Wesolouski brothers (Edmundo, Guillermo, José and Jacinto), the Cascales brothers (Juan and Francisco), the Gutiérrez brothers

(José, Manuel and Antonio) and the Castillo brothers (Juan and Alfonso).

The parents of the Gutiérrez brothers had relocated from Huelva – their father was a decorated army lieutenant – while the Wesolouskis had moved from Jerez de la Frontera, due to Seville's strategic position and their military backgrounds. José Gutiérrez and Jacinto Wesolouski, the eldest brothers of their respective families, became close friends on their medicine course.

The club may have had intentionally Spanish beginnings but of their 15 statutes written upon their formation, the eighth stated: "All foreigners who wish to play for this society will be able to do so." It was Alfonso de Castillo Ochoa who was appointed as the first chairman with the club registered to his home address – 29 Calle Alfonso XII. Vicente Peris Mencheta was given the role of club secretary, assisted by Salvador Morales, while Roberto Vicente was appointed vice-president and Manuel Ramos Asencio handed the role as the first-team's trainer and captain. Other names from the initial documents include Manuel Moreno Calvo, Tomás Cuesta Moñereo and José Fernández Zúñiga.

In 1936, José Gutiérrez – one of the club's founders – wrote a piece titled 'A Brief History of Betis Balompié' in Madrid-based newspaper *El Siglo Futuro* which may help us draw further conclusions about the club's birth. "Back in 1906 several Sevillian youth kicked a ball, following the simplistic rules that they could deduce from a collection of postcards that the father of one of them had sent back from France," wrote Gutiérrez. Another suggestion is that Gutiérrez discovered football in the Cantabrian municipality of Herrerías, where the mining company, The Betal Metal & Chemical, Ltd. was located, and he subsequently passed on the game, played by the foreign workforce, to fellow students.

The piece continued that their initial kickabouts took place at Tiro de Línea, which is now a neighbourhood within brief walking distance of the club's Benito Villamarín stadium. The area received its name as it was initially used by the military to test-fire cannons manufactured at San Bernardo, once again highlighting the martial links of the club's founders. In 1906, the area was predominantly land grazed by cattle during the city's *feria* celebrations, making it a feasible, if short-term, solution for organising matches in a convenient location.

There were still few areas within the city suitable for hosting football matches, with Sevilla Balompié playing their first match at the Campo Huerto de la Mariana, which is nowadays in the area known as Plaza de America – within the central Parque de María Luisa. Interestingly, this is the same area where Sevilla FC played in between 1905 and 1908, before switching to the centrally located Campo del Prado de San Sebastián. Despite the clubs playing in such close proximity to each other, the formative years produced little animosity between them. It is said the two clashed in unofficial friendly matches, although these are undocumented with little firm evidence that any were organised by either club.

The first recorded match between the two took place in 1909 and somewhat ironically, came on 14 February – St Valentine's Day. Love is not usually in the air when these two teams meet, and the first clash may not have been much different. Sevilla FC ran out 4–0 victors in a match held at their Prado de San Sebastián home, which would in 1911 become temporarily shared with Sevilla Balompié. It is notable how Balompié's early nomadic days mirrored their city predecessors and historical indications suggest that as interest swelled in the sport, both clubs outgrew their former homes and required more spectator-friendly venues.

A report in *El Correo de Andalucía* the following day outlined how the game was played out "in front of a sizable crowd" but somewhat controversially began by clarifying that it was Sevilla's third team against the strongest team of Sevilla Balompié. No further details of goalscorers were provided in the brief report, perhaps an indication as to the lack of significance in which the game was held. After all, this was no more than a friendly match and whether it was even publicised is unclear.

However, this does appear to mark the beginning of football genuinely taking off in the city and the following year, the Copa de Sevilla took place for the first time. Held between the teams of the city, Sevilla Balompié won the inaugural edition in 1910 before recording further victories in 1911, 1912 and 1915, when the competition was then discontinued. Whilst these triumphs would no doubt have claimed local bragging rights, the trophy itself was not recognised in an official capacity and would not become formalised until the creation of the Federación Andaluza de Fútbol in 1915.

The newly formed governing body of the sport across the region subsequently started the Campeonato Regional Sur – also referred to as the Copa de Andalucía, but into which teams from the Extremadura region occasionally entered – which was held in each season thereafter. Whilst this was viewed as a trophy and tangible glory, it also ensured the winners qualified for the national Copa del

Rey. The formation of a Spanish league system would not happen for well over a decade and the national cup competition was the one true opportunity for a club to assert early claims of authority across Spanish football.

Andalusia's Campeonato had been running unofficially since 1909 with Seville clubs failing to win any of the initial six editions. Recreativo de Huelva won each of the first three tournaments including two final victories over Sevilla FC, while Español de Cádiz – the short-lived major player within the coastal city – won the following three tournaments.

It was a scramble for power across Andalusia and within Seville itself. There were notable financial incentives attached to winning these tournaments while the prestige which arrived with victory was significant. Victories heightened attention and this subsequently increased support bases, business interest and the possibility for growth. Yet somewhat inevitably this also brought with it internal power struggles and historical controversy.

Chapter 8

Conflicting Accounts

BY the end of the first decade of the 1900s, Sevilla FC and Sevilla Balompié had established themselves as the powerhouses of football in Andalusia's capital. The sport was gaining traction and the formalisation of sporting governing bodies and organised regional cup competitions was well underway. What comes next is a subject of controversy within the city which still leads to squabbles among historians and sets of fans. If there is one thing *Sevillanos* love it is the ability to wind up – and conversely, regularly wade in to debates with – their rivals from the other half of the city. Conflicting accounts of history lead us today to choose which version of the past is closer to the truth.

What we can say with certainty is that Betis Football Club became the third club in Seville. Furthermore, it is fact that on 6 December 1914 the board of directors of Sevilla Balompié approved a proposed merger between the two clubs. Betis is derived from Baetis, the Roman name for the city's Guadalquivir river which flows through Seville and after which the Roman province was subsequently named. The individuals involved in the emergence of Betis and the precise year of formation – either 1909 or 1910 – are elements that are up for question.

Such ambiguity has arisen from a combination of factors. Firstly, there is often a lack of documented evidence from this period with many of the emerging clubs failing to maintain recorded dates, events and names. Whilst there was press coverage of the sport, this was somewhat limited, often written under pseudonyms and with limited consistency. Many of these reports may have been penned by officials of the clubs involved and potentially with an ulterior motive, so it is not always clear how much weight should be afforded to them. The formation of Betis has often been based on tales passed down through the years and thus there are versions which have deviated from the truth. Thorough examination is required to reach greater clarity.

In his 1958 publication *Medio Siglo De Fútbol Sevillano* – described as covering the "victories, anecdotes and ventures" of Real Betis Balompié – author César del Arco writes that Betis FC were formed following a split within Sevilla FC, with director Eladio García de la Borbolla walking out of *Los Rojiblancos*. Del Arco does not describe the events with incisiveness, going so far as to exercise a word of caution on the accuracy of events by also stating "whatever the truth ..."

This version is also verified by the official club website of Real Betis Balompié. As with Del Arco, the club are not willing to comment with complete authority on the birth of Betis FC, as the website says: "We should be cautious of the veracity of this information." They too say that García de la Borbolla, along with his brothers Francisco and Rafael, was responsible for the club's formation in 1909 and its offices were registered in Calle Mariscal.

There are clear gaps missing in the information provided which have fuelled historical doubt and indecision. Firstly, Betis FC did not appear to form a team until 1910 with the website referencing a newspaper report from that year commenting on the "inexperience of the recently created team". Furthermore, the club was dissolved three years later in 1913 and would not merge with Sevilla Balompié until December 1914. The website surmises that Eladio García de la Borbolla was indeed influential in the merger with Betis FC having been reborn from the ashes alongside help from José Gutiérrez – one of the brothers involved in the formation of Sevilla Balompié – and Miguel Folgado.

In 2007, Leonardo Rodríguez de la Borbolla – a descendant of Eladio – wrote an article in *ABC* to outline the version of events which had been passed down his family through the years. He wrote that Betis FC were born in the house of Rafael García de la Borbolla and Rodríguez de la Borbolla – Eladio's father – and that the table where the documents were signed remains treasured in their home.

Each García de la Borbolla was a member of Sevilla FC and decided to split to form their own club, along with Eladio's uncle Pedro Rodríguez de la Borbolla – a liberal politician with power in Cazalla de la Sierra, a small town in Seville's province – and three of his cousins. The account lists several other names involved in the split: Antonio Domínguez Henke Zerezos, Guillermo Comesaña y Arahal, Tomás de Haro García, Alarcón de la Lastra, Otero Bravo and Manuel Puig de la Lama.

What was the reason for such a split? According to Leonardo, those who walked out on Sevilla FC did so because of a board decision against signing a player who "worked in pyrotechnics" and was then playing for a local side named Recreativo de la Calzada (a team representing roadworkers). Such a decision, says this account, was taken on the basis that the individual in question was from a working-class background. The board of directors at Sevilla was contemporarily comprised from landowning classes and, it is alleged, believed football "had to belong to families of certain social relevance".

The story goes that the factory worker had been housed in Triana and such a background was enough for three Sevilla directors to veto any move to bring him to the club. We have already examined the significance of the Triana district in relation to Seville (Chapter 6) and this version of history speaks of a manifestation of the social divisions which have historically separated the area in a sporting sense. But this is anecdotal and cannot be relied upon for a forensic deconstruction of the event. Indeed, Leonardo does not make mention of Triana, or indeed any other area, with reference only to the player's factory job. Linking the neighbourhood to the formation of Betis FC has gained traction in the years since but without any firm evidence, this may be viewed as somewhat opportunistic.

Leonardo himself writes of the reaction of then Sevilla FC president Paco Alba on hearing the news of the split: "Man, Eladio, are you going to leave me here alone?" The problem with this piece of information is, contrary to Leonardo's account, Sevilla FC do not record Alba as assuming the club presidency until 1914. It is logical to assume the club were correct on this count due to documented evidence and that in 1909, Sevilla-born Alba would still have been a teenager. Indeed, he is only said to have gained the presidential position following a long-running disagreement with José Luis Gallegos. Alba's argument that Sevilla FC should remain a football club first and foremost (with other sports included, but not prominent) triumphed over Gallegos, who wished for the institution to be multi-faceted by nature. Alba would oversee the construction of the club's new Campo de Sport del Sevilla FC stadium but died suddenly aged just 31.

Research from historian Juan Castro Prieto directly contradicts the recollections of Del Arco, the Betis website and Leonardo Rodríguez de la Borbolla. Castro authored the detailed book *Primeros pasos del foot-ball Sevillano* – in which there is a section outlining the "crisis of birth" of Betis FC – and wrote the article 'The Huelva origins of Real Betis Balompié', published by *ABC* in 2011. He writes of a stark contrast between his research and the other accounts, stating that the birth of Betis FC followed a split in an existing club within the city, but that was at Sevilla Balompié and not Sevilla FC, as previously thought.

Castro details how the split occurred in January 1910 (not in 1909 as other records suggest), back in the unofficial days of the Campeonato Regional Sur, which was at the time known as the Copa Mackay, in honour of the Huelvan club's founder and president. It was the first edition of the tournament and it was held in Huelva, with hosts Recreativo defeating Sevilla Balompié 4–0 before overcoming Sevilla FC 2–0 in the deciding game. Gutiérrez brothers Antonio and Manuel – both of Huelva origin – were said to be frustrated at their lack of participation and walked out of Balompié, whom they had helped create.

This version appears to be supported by an article which appears in *El Liberal* on New Year's Eve 1909. This details a meeting between the second teams of Sevilla Balompié and Sevilla FC, in which José and Manuel were both playing in the centre of midfield for Balompié with Antonio not featuring at all. José was the only brother to travel with Balompié to the tournament in Huelva the following month and such discord may have led to a split within the club.

The author continues that the two Gutiérrez brothers were followed by fellow students from the polytechnic including Manuel Domínguez Anillo, Manuel Folgado, Diego Otero, Alberto Henke and Guillermo Comesalla in forming Betis FC, although he does confirm Eladio and Francisco de Asís de la Borbolla later joined their ranks from Sevilla FC. So perhaps it is possible that whilst a splinter in the city's first football team did occur, certain strands of the legend have become warped by time, hearsay and exaggeration.

* * * * *

Betis FC started life by using the same white shirts as Sevilla FC – perhaps a move which helped fuel accounts that it was the same individuals who had begun each club, although it is most likely this was due to ease of access to white shirts – before deciding permanently on green-and-black striped shirts. Their badge was circular with a green background, with a prominent **B** emboldened in black over FC, to fit cohesively alongside their kit.

Castro's account continues that Manuel was the first president of the newly created Betis FC with Antonio also enjoying prominence in the new set-up. Indeed, in 1911 the *Official Guide of Trade and*

Industry in Seville documented that two of Seville's three clubs were run concurrently by the Gutiérrez brothers, as the elder José was elected president of Sevilla Balompié. This publication – commonly referenced as the Guide of Gómez Zarzuela, in honour of the famed Seville musician Vicente – also verifies the ideas of Betis being started in 1910 and playing their first game on 27 February of that year against Sevilla Balompié, as opposed to 1909. Castro continues that the following year all three brothers were playing at Betis FC and, in 1913, they all represented a new Seville-based team named Andalucía FC.

This was a period when football's popularity had exploded and clubs were springing up across the Andalusian capital. Recreativo FC officially became the fourth club when they lodged their relevant documents with the civil government on 17 September 1911, although evidence suggests they had been in existence previously and were indeed the side referred to as Recreativo de la Calzada by Leonardo Rodríguez de la Borbolla, when detailing events in 1909. Playing in black-and-white halved shirts, their standout player was Hilario Navarro Hurtado, who would go on to star for Real Betis Balompié.

Recreativo FC were founded by Luís Molini Briasco – head of the Seville Tramways Company and who would go on in future years to publicly confess his affection for Sevilla FC. His curiously varied career would lead in 1915 to creating the Andalusian School of Referees, while he officiated many of the first matches between Sevilla FC and Real Betis Balompié. Interestingly, it was his lofty power-wielding position at the head of public transport within the city – rather than his role as a match official – which would provide one of the building blocks for the bitterness between rival fans in Seville.

The city's fifth club were Andalucía FC when they officially registered their documents on 1 February 1913, leading to a plethora more coming into existence in the period that followed: Español FC, Híspalis FC, Athletic Club, Torre del Oro FC, Sociedad Gimnástica, Ideal FC, Estrella FC, Sociedad Ibérica FC, Giralda FC, Infantil FC, Industrial FC, Club Deportivo de Football, Triana FC. There truly was something for everyone and this was particularly notable in light of the city's passion for bullfighting – which was in danger of becoming the second 'sport' of the Andalusian capital.

The bloating of the football scene in Seville would inevitably have stretched resources and it was in this year of the sport's mass participation that Betis FC were to disband shortly before summer. Among those to leave was Manuel Domínguez, appointed as Sevilla FC secretary in October, while others jumped ship to Balompié.

Castro's research does not focus on the reasoning behind the split – although referencing the Gutiérrez brothers and president Miguel Folgado (who was said to enjoy a greater passion for cycling than football) temporarily representing Andalucía FC, in an era where multiple representation occurred commonly – but it does find that this hiatus was short-lived and, led by Eladio's uncle and politician Pedro Rodríguez de la Borbolla, Betis re-emerged in 1914 with the added 'Real' (Spanish for 'royal') title.

This stemmed from the formation of the Copa del Ayuntamiento de Madrid – a national Spanish Cup in 1902 – which would then develop into the Copa del Rey (King's Cup). Spain's monarchy began a campaign of greater integration into the sporting world and particularly football. The 'Real' term was sought by many clubs with the oft-used mechanism of clubs agreeing to appoint the King as an honorary president of their institution. Upon the monarch's acceptance, the 'Real' would be inserted into the club's title and a crown added to the badge.

The reigning King – Alfonso XIII – subsequently became the patron of sporting institutions across the country. Many of those clubs still reference 'Real' as a fundamental element of their title – Real Madrid, Real Sociedad, Real Betis, Real Zaragoza, Real Oviedo – while others such as Celta de Vigo, Deportivo de La Coruña, Espanyol, Racing Club de Santander, Sporting de Gijón and Recreativo de Huelva no longer do. This in itself is an insight into the conservatism that remained deep-rooted in Spanish society, where the monarchy's 'badge of approval' was seen as carrying significant weight.

Betis FC acquired the title on 17 August 1914 thanks to the role of the Marquis of Mochales (Miguel López de Carrizosa y de Giles), according to historical accounts. In 2014, *Diario de Sevilla* ran an article written by Leonardo Rodríguez de la Borbolla which detailed the chain of events which led to the formation of Real Betis Balompié in 1914. The account details how the Marquis – the butler of King Alfonso XIII – was close friends with Pedro Rodríguez de la Borbolla, who Leonardo previously claimed quit Sevilla FC to originally form Betis FC. The report claims the friendship was linked to their heritage, with their fathers both born in Jerez de la Frontera in 1825. The two were classmates and were said to have spent a great deal of time together, going into adulthood.

Real Betis have maintained a close association with Spain's monarchy in the years since. Infante Juan was the designated heir of King Alfonso XIII but never took the post due to the establishment of the Second Spanish Republic in 1931, followed by Civil War and Franco's dictatorship. He married María de las Mercedes, the Countess of Barcelona, a confessed Betis fan. Her son Juan Carlos I and grandson Felipe XI – the two subsequent monarchs following on from Franco – are honorary socios of Betis, despite Felipe's declared support of Atlético de Madrid.

In February 2009, five years before his abdication, Juan Carlos I spoke anecdotally of his mother's devotion to Betis. The club were heading towards relegation from the top flight and the King was attending an event alongside Sevillian lawyer Jose Luis Escañuela, who had just been appointed president of the Spanish Tennis Federation.

Referencing Escañuela's love of Betis, the King said: "Thank goodness my mother [who died nine years previously] is not around to see them like this, she would not have taken it well. Every time Betis lost, she phoned me and asked 'how is this possible'?"

Escañuela added: "The only thing we can say with certainty is that *Béticos* will always stay with the club, regardless of what league we are in, and Juan Carlos has told me that his mother thought the same."

Yet it appears a strange anomaly that Betis FC would be granted the title of Real when not only were they not one of the two major football institutions in the city but were not even registered with the civil government in 1913 and did not compete in the following Copa de Sevilla tournaments. Indeed, there is no record of them returning to action until taking on Sevilla FC in October 1914, while it was only the previous month that a new set-up had been brought into place.

Records indicate Pedro Rodríguez de la Borbolla was the effective president with the Marquis of Mochales as honorary president, José Gutiérrez elected vice-president, Eladio García de la Borbolla was secretary and Guillermo Comesaña the treasurer.

The first indication that they would gain the title appears in an article dated 1 February 1914 in *El Correo de Andalucía*. The somewhat ambiguous piece, without a byline, was lacking in firm details but promised "news very soon" regarding "a 'royal' and pleasant surprise" which had been prepared for "some time".

Historians suggest this casts great doubt upon the Borbolla account of the derivation of the title and that Betis FC only returned into being with the promise of the monarch's approval. In December of that year, Real Betis FC were to merge with Sevilla Balompié to form Real Betis Balompié and suspicion arises that such a move was linked to the granting of patronage. After all, Balompié were created by students whose parents were high-ranking offers in the Spanish army, commanded by King Alfonso XIII. Whether this was a highly coincidental sequence of events or otherwise remains up for debate and, just as with the birth of Betis FC, their eventual unification with Sevilla Balompié is an issue riddled with contradiction.

Chapter 9

Unification of
Real Betis Balompié

SEVILLA Balompié and Real Betis met twice in the lead-up to the amalgamation, on 25 October and 15 November, with Balompié emerging victorious on both occasions. It is thought that these two games were strategically planned by club officials, with the results an afterthought considering the meetings planned between the senior figureheads.

On 6 December 1914, Sevilla Balompié's board of directors approved plans for a merger with Real Betis FC, whose board also sanctioned the move two days later. An article in *El Liberal* on 17 December confirmed the news: "The two clubs Betis FC and Sevilla Balompié have agreed a union to form a single club with the name of Real Betis Balompié."

According to the history section of Real Betis Balompié – who officially came into existence on 23 December – Betis FC had promised to carry their newly acquired 'Real' title into the merger, following royal approval, although it appears Balompié offered the more appealing half of the deal. They would provide the players, the trophies (the Copa de Sevilla titles) and the stadium – El Campo de las Tablas Verdes (The Ground with the Green Boards), located in Prado de San Sebastián. Indeed, the club was still referred to as Balompié in the immediate period following the merger to reflect the context in which the move was conceived. It was not until the 1930s and the club's first appearance in Spanish top-flight football that the club would be referenced as Betis with the fans known as *Béticos*, rather than the previously used *Balompedistas*.

The first appearance of the newly evolved institution was on 27 December 1914: a 3–1 loss against Recreativo de Huelva, wearing their green-and-white kit, which would earn them a nickname of *Los Verdiblancos*. The newly formed club lined up with: José Fernández Zúñiga, Antonio Gutiérrez, Hilario Navarro, Antonio Palacios, Herbert Jones, Andrés Hermosa, Enrique Añino, Carmelo Navarro, José Hermosa, Santana, Carrión.

There would be no luck either in their back-to-back matches against Britannia FC of Gibraltar on 3 and 4 January, with 4–0 and 6–2 losses respectively in games played at the Hipódromo de Tablada. The games were played back to back due to atrocious weather making the pitch unplayable and forcing the postponement of the first meeting.

Interestingly, they had reverted to yellow-and-black shirts with white shorts for these clashes, before then switching to a solely green shirt – described in local reports as a darker, bottle-green – with white shorts (the green and white stripes would be exclusively used from 1919 onwards). There is little indication as to why the club wore yellow and black for these two matches, with the club only using this kit in one season since – as a secondary kit in their 2014/15 campaign, when they won the second tier.

Britannia had a reputation for being a formidable outfit and Real Betis Balompié fielded two players from Sevilla FC: Manolo Pérez and 16-year-old Enrique Gómez Muñoz. A year earlier, Gómez Muñoz had signed for his boyhood club Sevilla FC against the wishes of his father, who saw football as an unbecoming sport and wished for his son to carry on with his medical studies. By the age of 17, he was a regular in Sevilla's starting line-ups and he came to an agreement with the club to be named as Spencer on team sheets and announcements, thus to avoid the wrath of his father. He thought of the name from Thomas Spencer Reiman, a worker from Williams & Humbert winery, who setup Xerez FC (Jerez is Spanish for sherry, and the city Jerez de la Frontera is famed for its wine production) in 1907 and subsequently gained fame as their captain, coach and president.

In 1920, Sevilla FC's Spencer temporarily switched to Real Oviedo as he carried out his military service, but it was with Sevilla where he gained cult-hero status. He was the club's first scorer in the Campeonato de España (which was later renamed the Copa del Rey) against Real Madrid, then known as Madrid CF, and helped the club to semi-finals in the competition, before eventual losses to Barcelona and Athletic Club of Bilbao in 1919 and 1921 respectively. Spencer also featured in a total of nine Copa de Andalucía titles for Sevilla in an era when they asserted genuine hegemony in the southern region.

Upon his return from Oviedo, his father addressed him over his deception but the two came to the agreement that he would continue in the sport due to his success.

Spencer was known as a supreme creative talent, dazzling opponents with his natural technique and ability to create chances for team-mates. He became the club's first player to win an international cap, along with his team-mate Herminio Martinez Alvarez. Both featured in Spain's 3–0 victory over Portugal in 1923 at El Campo de la Victoria (the Field of Victory), then the home of his club side.

Tragically, like many players of his era, his life was to be taken early, as he died aged just 27 after suffering complications following appendix surgery. Such was Spencer's enthusiasm for football he was reportedly rushed back to compete in a Copa del Rey clash against Real Madrid. Historian Alberto Cosín wrote: "His ambition was to play but it was a decision taken too hastily. He was not fully recovered." Spencer passed away on 14 March 1926, with players from both Sevilla and Madrid carrying his coffin to the cemetery. Today there stands a statue in honour of the forward at Sevilla's Estadio Ramón Sánchez-Pizjuán.

However, Spencer was not the first player connected to Sevilla to pass away at a tragically young age. In the summer of 1917, Juan Tornero de Orta – a 23-year-old who was born in Seville but spent only one season at the club after moving to Italy – died after contracting typhoid fever. Following his death, the sports journalist Antonio Olmedo wrote a column commemorating the player, whom he called a "dear friend" who had "helped his side to great triumphs". Tornero's greatest moment was in Sevilla's 2–1 Campeonato de España triumph over Madrid (see Chapter 11) where he left the stadium "on the shoulders of his admirers".

* * * * *

Two days later Real Betis Balompié would pick up their first victory and it was a most significant one, overcoming Sevilla FC 1–0 with the Copa de Plata (Silver Cup) trophy donated by the local Sociedad Artística Sevillana. Alberto Henke Montero de Espinosa scored the only goal of the game on a "splendid afternoon", according to a report in *El Correo*. A month later, on 7 February, the two met again in the Prado de San Sebastián but this time at Sevilla FC's Mercantil playing fields – their home from 1913 to 1918. This time it was the Copa de Oro (Gold Cup) up for grabs, with Sevilla triumphing 4–3. Henke was once again on the scoresheet for Real Betis Balompié along with

Carmelo Navarro and Pepe Hermos, but Alfonso Mata's hat-trick and a Gregorio Navarro goal were enough for *Los Rojiblancos* to triumph.

Betis FC may have been the first entity to disappear (temporarily, and then via a merger) as the city's football scene dramatically began to narrow down, as it did across the country. Recreativo FC and Andalucía FC, two of the most prominent, merged into Unión Andalucía-Recreativo the week after Real Betis Balompié played their first games. With Juan Gómez as president and Enrique Machuca as secretary they wore a red-and-black shirt but like many others in the city, the project proved unsustainable and swiftly tailed off.

The first match in an official competition for Real Betis Balompié came on 21 November 1915 as they played out a 2–2 draw with Club Athletic de Sevilla in the first Andalusia-wide Campeonato Regional Sur. Carmelo Navarro was the first scorer for the club with the occasion taking place at Sevilla FC's Campo del Mercantil – which was the chosen venue for all matches of the competition's first edition, due to the public interest. A newspaper clipping from the time speaks of a "strong attendance" while action shots show a crowd three lines deep around the pitch. The reporter notes Navarro, Ramos and Hermosa as the strongest Betis players, while there was also "a very good referee, with the necessary energy".

The Campeonato format was split into two sections prior to the semi-final stage: Sevilla and Cádiz, with a tie-breaker replay required in the event of a draw. A club could enter the tournament at a cost of five pesetas, with the reward of winning including a coveted spot in the national Copa del Rey.

Real Betis Balompié overcame Club Athletic de Sevilla 5–0 in their replay on 8 December and 11 days later they eliminated Español FC Sevilla 2–1 following a draw. Sevilla FC were next up, having defeated Híspalis FC 8–0 in the previous round. The first clash between the two powerhouses ended in a 2–2 draw on New Year's Day, before Sevilla won 5–0 the following day.

However, the inaugural competition was not to be won by a Seville-based team, despite Sevilla overcoming Recreativo de Huelva 2–1, following a replay, at the semi-final stage. On 23 January they fell to a 2–1 defeat in the showpiece against Español de Cádiz, who clinched the victory following a ten-minute spell of extra time. The coastal-based club celebrated their historic achievement at Sevilla's Hotel Inglaterra before returning to Cádiz by train, where thousands of adulating fans awaited at the station and street parties were held throughout the city. However, in a sign of administrative problems to dog the club throughout their existence, they did not take up their position in the following year's Copa del Rey due to costs.

Remarkably the club, which became known as The Invincibles during its early years, was to fold in 1929 with local historians citing a lack of an appropriate stadium in the city. Coinciding with the introduction of organised national league football in Spain for the first time, a series of unfortunate events spiralled into their early demise. At the beginning of that season, they were eliminated from the first level of the ever-expanding Campeonato and they would not be among the selected group of clubs included in Spain's new two-tier league system.

Having already seen their requests for a new, modern stadium rejected by the city council, who instead prioritised the construction of a bullring, the cocktail of misfortune was completed when a storm hit the city and virtually destroyed the club's Campo Ana de Viya home. Three months later, on 25 June 1929, *Diario de Cádiz* published an unsigned article which read: "Last Saturday the General Meeting of Español de Cádiz was held. The ten partners agreed that, given the inconveniences that exist for the development of the club, it was best to dissolve it." The amateur club Mirandilla FC still existed in the region and they would later develop into Cádiz Club de Fútbol, who became the major force in the city.

* * * * *

Thanks to the work of historian Manuel Carmona Rodríguez in *Enciclopedia Del Real Betis Balompié*, it is now possible to fully detail Englishman Herbert Richard Jones: the first president of Real Betis Balompié. Born in Ceylon – now Sri Lanka – he first moved to Spain as a 24-year-old, meeting his future wife in Cádiz. He was a founder of Español FC in the coastal city in 1911 before moving to Seville the following year, where he joined Sevilla Balompié and was swiftly installed as club captain. He became affectionately known as "Papa Jones" and was also known as "alma mater" due to his authority.

It was an odd quirk of these early days that players doubled up with senior positions on the club's board of directors, in a similar vein to Carlos García Martínez – the second president of Sevilla FC (beginning the role at the tender age of just 22) who served across two spells whilst also representing the club in a playing capacity. There were no rules in place to prevent such occurrences and the most unusual example appears to be that of Sevilla FC goalkeeper

Paco Diaz, who surprisingly doubled up his role with treasurer at rival club Betis FC.

Jones remained a crucial figure at Real Betis Balompié until September 1918, when he was called by the British army to fight in France during the First World War. This information was relayed by Seville-based historian Pepe Melero as published on website La Palangana Mecánica, sympathetic to Sevilla FC, which cites a report in contemporary *Madrid Sport*. "Mr. Herbert Richard Jones, soul of Real Betis Balompié and notable referee of the southern region, has had to join the English army that fights in France," read the Madrid-based weekly paper. "We wish you good luck." Real Betis historian Alfonso Del Castillo told me Jones was "a crucial character" in the merger and subsequent existence of Real Betis Balompié and despite suggestions he perished during the war, later records show he died in Streatham, London, in 1950, aged 65.

Indeed, Jones appeared to have been one of the most popular sporting figureheads within the city of Seville. Accounts place him as even more popular than Sevilla Balompié's president Juan del Castillo, whom he would replace in the position following the merger. He was said to share a very healthy relationship with his counterpart Paco Alba at Sevilla FC, so much so that there was speculation that it would be those two clubs who would be the merger in the city.

A post in *El Noticiero Sevillano* on 1 August 1914 said the intention of such a proposal was to "wrestle the Copa del Campeonato Regional Sur from Huelva, as Recreativo have been the major force in the region for four years". However, underlying antagonism between the two clubs – who by this stage had built up a strong sporting rivalry due to regularly competing for the same titles – ruled out such a possibility.

Real Betis Balompié started their existence with a bang, carrying on Sevilla Balompié's dominance in the Copa de Sevilla with a 3–0 victory over Español FC in the 4 April 1915 decider. The outbreak of the war shaped football in the city with players of British origin dragged away and financial difficulties beginning to manifest themselves. As we evaluate, it was Sevilla FC who asserted near total dominance on the Campeonato Regional Sur over the following 15 years while Betis struggled to maintain their existence.

In November 1918, they attempted to revive their fortunes by relocating to the 19,000-capacity Campo del Patronato Obrero, which would provide their home until moving into the Estadio Benito Villamarín – which remains their stadium – until the early 1930s. Located in the Porvenir district – in the south of the city's centre – beside the Parque de María Luisa, the Patronato Obrero was inaugurated with a memorable 9–1 victory over Español FC from Cádiz. It was located beside many factories and on the doorstep of swathes of the working population, which may in itself have given roots to the club's perceived working-class support at the time.

As for the Gutiérrez brothers, José returned to his Puebla de Guzmán hometown in the province of Huelva where he spent the rest of his life as a qualified doctor, Manuel decided to follow his father's footsteps and join the military but lost his life in Spain's colonial war after being transferred to Africa, while Antonio became a teacher in the small Roman city of Sigüenza, north-east of Madrid. The work of Castro has detailed their significance in shaping football in Seville and their legacy – should we assume this account to hold the closest accuracy to the truth – is Spain's hottest football rivalry.

Chapter 10

Tensions Boil Over

THE idea of the merger between Sevilla Balompié and Real Betis had been to create a team capable of dominating football in the south of Spain. Paradoxically, the medium-term results of the move saw Sevilla FC establish themselves as the supreme power not just within Seville, but in the entirety of Andalusia.

Following the initial success of Español de Cádiz, *Los Rojiblancos* were to triumph in 18 of the next 20 editions of the Campeonato Regional Sur while they reached the final in every one of the 21 seasons for which the competition ran. This period of success was critical for the narrative which was to provide the backdrop for how the rivalry between Seville's two clubs would develop in subsequent years. Sevilla FC became synonymous with success and subsequently with power and wealth. By contrast, Real Betis were developing the status of the city's underdog and would learn how to wear this as a badge of honour.

Yet while many from outside the city interpret this as representing a societal divide, between uptown Sevilla and downtown Betis, there is little firm evidence to suggest this was ever the case in the purest definitions. Just as with Franco's later public backing of Real Madrid, it is logical to assume that prominent politicians and businessmen would seek to use football to heighten their own public standing. It is not outlandish to assume that a similar power play was occurring in Seville, with resources becoming increasingly concentrated in fewer hands. But in terms of ideological differences or social discrepancies, the differences may not have been significant.

"Sevilla FC is constituted under the following premise," read president José Luis Gallegos in a 1905 speech following the club registering its official documents with the civil government. "It is a club to which any person can belong without distinction of social level, religious or political ideas. All will be welcome here."

Gallegos was born in Jerez de la Frontera but he represented a continuation, of sorts, of the club's British roots. He had been sent to England as a young child to study and he grew up surrounded by football, which he participated in regularly. He returned to Seville in 1903 and was taken aback by social attitudes to the sport, which had yet to attract mainstream attention in his native country.

According to the Sevilla FC website, football at this point was deemed an "unseemly activity in the Sevillian society and was even persecuted by the authorities". Indeed, after meeting like-minded individuals, they began to meet but only practised the sport behind closed doors so as to not attract attention. A year after his return, Gallegos kickstarted the process of formalising the club with the authorities to end the secrecy and legitimise the venture.

Another individual involved in this gesture provided a clear link between the early British founders of Sevilla FC and those who brought the club back to life, in an official form, 15 years later. Carlos Gustavo Langdon was just three years old when Sevilla FC were formed in 1890. His father John Sydney was an English doctor who had settled in Seville with his French wife and had assisted the founders of the city's first football club.

The Langdon family – who Spanish historians Juan Castro and Agustín Rodríguez claim arrived in Andalusia from Gibraltar "in the last quarter of the nineteenth century" – played a hugely influential role in the birth of Spanish football. John Sydney's brother William – who became referred to as Guillermo in Spain – had moved to Huelva as executive of the Rio Tinto Company, and was involved in the creation of Recreativo de Huelva in 1889. John had not only volunteered to be Sevilla FC's club doctor but records now show he was the linesman in Spain's first football match against Recre (see Chapter 4).

He resided in 9 Calle Don Remondo, in a building which is still preserved today and within which Carlos Gustavo was born. Both he and his father were to die tragically young – John perished, aged 45, in 1899 while Carlos passed away in Dos Hermanos (the city neighbouring Seville) at the tender age of 25 in 1913, before his second son Nathaniel was born.

Charles Langdon was born two years before the death of his father Carlos and in 2005, upon their centennial celebrations – prior to the emergence of information dating Sevilla FC back to 1890 – his son Christian, a dentist who at this point was living in Gibraltar, was contacted by the club to take part in the celebrations. As he later explained, he was totally unaware of his ancestors' links to Sevilla FC as this information had never been passed down through the years.

"Until 2005, and on the occasion of the centennial of Sevilla FC, our family were not aware of the founding work of my grandfather and my great-grandfather," Christian explained in an interview with *ABC de Sevilla*.

"Football, a century ago, was frowned upon as a sport and not viewed in the manner it is nowadays, which is why, I suppose, we were not told of anything. Prior to this I did not feel a predilection for any team. Some of my friends are supporters of Madrid, others support Barcelona and there are others who associate with English clubs.

"Now my entire family are proud to be descendants of a founder of Sevilla FC, a club who have achieved remarkable successes in recent years. The club already has lots of fans in Gibraltar and now it has more, so we will try and make our own *Sevillista Peña!*"

Upon the inauguration of the club's new ground at Campo del Mercantil on New Year's Day, 1913, then Sevilla FC president José María Miró Trepat echoed the early comments of Gallegos: "In our meetings we do not talk about politics," he told the assembled crowd. "In the heart of our sporting society there is no difference between the rich and the poor, our passion and hobby is united by our love of this club. People here of all social classes rub shoulders together. Our aspiration is to win and our prize is the admiration of others."

Miró Trepat's words were viewed as significant. Born in the Uruguayan capital Montevideo before moving to Barcelona, he became renowned as a wealthy businessman, setting up a successful chain of cafés throughout Spain. A man of many talents, he co-founded Espanyol de Barcelona (the club only altered to Catalan from the Castilian Español spelling in 1995) and became their second president, whilst also representing the club as a player. In 1903 his brainchild Velódromo de la Calle Aragón was the first Catalan stadium which charged spectators for admission to matches. It was Miró Trepat who bought the land and his family's business who constructed the stadium.

His move to Seville in 1907 was born from necessity, as he was recovering from a lung disease. His attempts to return to normality saw him head the city's Café Tupinamba before linking up with Sevilla. Five years later, and having proved influential in the club's off-field growth and business plan, he was appointed as Sevilla president. While his spell at the helm spanned just 18 months, it was he who instigated the construction of the Campo del Mercantil.

This was already the fifth ground in the club's history but unlike the others, the Campo del Mercantil was required to accommodate the club's growing popularity. Its predecessor, the Campo del Prado de San Sebastián, was simply a roped area of land on the periphery of the Parque de María Luisa. Often their 'home' overlapped with their city rivals and could only be distinguished by the colours erected on matchdays, moving location in the fields from match to match.

Built due to Miró Trepat's business contacts, the Campo del Mercantil was named in recognition of the chief benefactors. A permanent setting, there was no entrance fee due to the absence of an external wall – although a wooden fence surrounded the pitch – but Miró Trepat proposed the club charged rent for use of seats and the wooden terrace. The ground was located directly to the north of the Prado de San Sebastián, parallel to where Calle José Maria Osborne stands today. It was the president's entrepreneurial spirit which laid the foundations for Sevilla to build commercial contacts, a portfolio of wealth and ultimately sustainable growth.

Just as with Espanyol, Miró Trepat's focus was on laying long-term foundations and less than a year after opening Sevilla's new stadium, he moved to Madrid and became president of Gimnástica de Madrid and of Racing de Madrid. In doing so, he became the first individual to have led four different Spanish clubs, and he retained his association with the Andalusian heavyweights due to being awarded the position of honorary president.

Not content with his lofty positions in the worlds of business and football, the Uruguayan-born innovator competed in the 1920 Olympics in shooting sports before being elected deputy mayor of Madrid in 1927 following election on to the capital city's council.

* * * * *

Miró Trepat had laid the foundations for Sevilla's professional growth and the club continued to evolve in the period following his absence. On 21 October 1918, the club opened the Campo Reina Victoria – located on the current Calle Chaves Rey, adjacent to Avenida de la Palmera and, interestingly, near the Heliópolis district which Real Betis would later make their home. It was a move fuelled by necessity, with the city council carrying out extensive renovation works at Prado de San Sebastián – the land where the Campo del Mercantil stood.

Events earlier that year defined the period and early rivalry between the two teams, with the usual controversy, claims and counterclaims all attempting to distort the situation. Just like so many other aspects of Sevillian football of this time, there is more than one version of events.

What we know for sure is that on 10 March 1918, Sevilla beat Real Betis 22–0 at the Mercantil in a play-off match to determine who advanced from the city's category in that year's Campeonato Regional Sur. It is a result which stands out as the biggest victory in the derby, by a notable distance, and juxtaposed against other results of that time. In many ways, the incidents and context surrounding the game provide the most compelling catalyst for the intense rivalry within Seville.

The two teams were streets ahead of their group opponents – Español FC of the city and Unión Andalucía Recreativo – with the two established powers racking up a combined eight victories from eight over their opposition, scoring 52 goals and conceding just three. By this stage, the balance of power in the city had been firmly established with the myriad of smaller clubs struggling to attract players, run training sessions and eventually ceasing to exist.

The decisive meetings in the group were between Sevilla and Real Betis, who at the time were referred to in reports as *El Balompié* and, on occasion, *La Real*. They had not tasted victory in a derby match in three years, despite the meetings tending to be relatively well-matched and consistently full-blooded. Sevilla triumphed 3–2 in their home group game at the Mercantil in January in an encounter which was not loaded with controversy.

The return game was played at the nearby Campo de la Enramadilla – the home of Betis, which had gained a definitive enclosed space within the Prado San Sebastián that season – on 24 February and it was a clash that would gain infamy. The hosts were to end their winless run in the fixture as they triumphed 3–1 but the game is remembered for events which saw players from Sevilla attacked by those in attendance. The match coincided with general elections that day and the security present at the match was lower than usual as a result. It is said that Sevilla had regularly protested the venue's suitability for hosting such clashes, arguing that the pitch and goal sizes were outside the regulations, but such claims fell on deaf ears.

The two teams for the clash were:

Real Betis Balompié: Portillo; Canda, Barzanallana; Salvador, Balbino, Barragán; Puig, Carmelo, Artola, Cabeza, León.

Sevilla FC: Diaz; Alcocer, Trujillo; Ismael, Ramírez; Pérez, Cruz, Armet, Spencer, Ramos, Escobar.

Betis raced into a two-goal lead, in front of a reported 3,000-strong crowd, before Sevilla then pulled a goal back, which is when the controversy really began. As *El Correo de Andalucía* reported: "Near the end of the game a dispute arose between some players that spread among the others like wildfire.

"Sevilla began to attack repeatedly and in these climactic moments a spectator threw himself at a Sevilla player, assaulting him cowardly and brutally in the back." The player who was stabbed, which the report omitted to say, was Sevilla's Manuel Perez 'The Terrible'. The report continued: "Real Betis Balompié's board has told us the aggressors are not socios of their club and they regret all events."

El Noticiero Sevillano's match reporter stated: "A player of Sevilla was slapped reportedly by a large group of fans … another spectator, whom we are told is a Pyrotechnics worker, ran onto the pitch with an object in his hand, assaulting the left-half of Sevilla." *El Liberal* called the attack "cowardly and brutal". The *Madrid Sport*'s report confirmed the incidents occurred five minutes before the scheduled end of the game before suggesting "those who say that soccer is a more noble sport than cycling" could do well to re-evaluate their opinions, while referencing how the Spanish Civil Guard had recently been required for matches in the Basque Country. Images of the stadium at the time show that there was no barrier or rope between the fans and the pitch.

Despite the reported violence, the remainder of the game was played and, perhaps unsurprisingly, Sevilla's players could not find an equaliser and indeed Real Betis scored another goal to seal victory. Betis fans took to the streets surrounding the Paseo de las Delicias to celebrate their triumph, perhaps believing that the victory indicated a power shift in the city. The result stood and despite Real Betis topping the group on goal difference – and the head-to-head record with Sevilla – the rules of the competition stated that a tie-breaker was required in the event of the group winners finishing level on points.

At this juncture facts become blurred with anecdotes and assumptions required to decipher the following sequence of events. The Federación Andaluza de Fútbol drew Sevilla's Campo del Mercantil from a raffle to determine the venue of the tie-breaker on 10 March.

As their results suggest, Real Betis had been boosted during this season by the arrivals of a series of players who were completing their military service in the city. We have already established the club's roots as having fundamental links with the Spanish military, and this was still evident during their formative years. Two of their stars included Canda and Artola, who had arrived from Sporting de Vigo and Real Sociedad respectively. Other notable arrivals included Balbino from successful Vigo side Real Fortuna FC (who won the Galician Championship nine times between 1906 and 1922), Barzanallana joined from Español de Cádiz, while goalkeeper Portillo and forward Reina had arrived mid-season.

It is within this context that the figure of General José Ximénez de Sandoval takes centre stage. Considered a war hero in Spain due to his killing of Cuban revolutionary leader and independence martyr José Martí, the Málaga-born militant became Andalusia's General Captain in 1914 when moving to Seville. Sandoval took the unusual decision of intervening in footballing matters as he insisted, upon hearing of the events at the Enramadilla the previous month, that nobody within his ranks should take part in such a sport. "It is not good that men who wear the military uniform are involved in events as scandalous as those that occurred in the last Real Betis-Sevilla match," Sandoval is reported to have remarked.

The decision infuriated Real Betis, for whom this decision would disproportionately impact as it ruled out a number of their star players from competing. Many of their fans screamed of a *Sevillista* conspiracy, as it would effectively render the decisive game meaningless due to their team being stripped of many stars. There is no evidence to suggest this was anything beyond a military decision but, for one team, the decision stunk of an unfair manoeuvre and proved their suspicions of favouritism amongst the city's authorities. Reflecting upon Sandoval's decision a century on, Canal Sur's Manuel Ladrón de Guevara said the General had "unknowingly ignited a fire that even today, 100 years later, is still burning."

As a protest, Real Betis made the decision not to send any of their first-team squad and instead played a team of children. Upon receiving this information, Sevilla reportedly pondered whether to participate themselves before deciding that they would treat the game as normal. It is likely that had they decided not to take part, the authorities would have viewed this as a forfeit and thus they would have been eliminated from the competition.

The result was a record 22−0 victory, in a game which swiftly descended into farcical levels. The youthful Real Betis team finished with just six players on the pitch after five were shown red cards. Reports of the time suggest that they were under instruction not to attempt to play football but instead to rough up their opponents, with the *Madrid Sport* describing: "The kids of Betis were instructed not to aim for the ball and one after another, they were sent-off."

Historians debate the validity of the Real Betis line-up that day being comprised of 'children'. A photo later emerged that was published in 1958 by *Marca*, which claimed to show the young team which participated in the match.

There are a variety of claims questioning the accuracy of the photo; the first argument is that the background is not the Campo del Mercantil and so the picture is unlikely to have been taken on the day of the match. However, as there were a number of pitches within close proximity of the Prado San Sebastián, it is within the realms of possibility that it was taken on the same day. And what of the shirts? The photo is in black and white and the team shirt is white, while reports from the day say Real Betis played in their traditional light-blue. Again, it is far from conclusive that the photo was inaccurate, as light-blue could feasibly have been displayed as white in such photos.

Perhaps the argument with greatest weight is that of the actual player ages. The individuals appear to be within the 13–16 age bracket, yet the Real Betis team from that day was recorded as: Zúñiga, Alonso, Montaño, Justito, Tobi Iglesias, Arjona, Cueli, Matarredona, Barroso, Jiménez, Cruz. Iglesias went on to play for Sevilla FC and if their club records are accurate, he would have been 18 at the time of the match.

Whereas Real Betis fans cried of a conspiracy back in 1918, many *Sevillistas'* claims of a hoaxed photo appear to be somewhat fanciful. Such a dramatic scoreline and evidence of a fully changed Betis line-up point strongly to a totally unrecognisable team who had no ambition of making the match competitive. What we do know for sure is that this is a record result but, equally, the match was played in circumstances which remove its context beyond the realms of local bragging rights – those which are so dearly-loved by *Sevillanos* of both shades.

The outcome benefitted neither side in that campaign. Betis were heavily fined by the regional federation with their president removed from the board. Sevilla did not end up lifting that season's trophy, with Recreativo de Huelva topping the final group which also comprised Español de Cádiz.

* * * * *

General Sandoval's decision to interfere in football was the first instance of Real Betis fans believing foul play from the authorities was undermining their club. There have been accusations that the cutting of a regular tram service from the Triana district to Heliópolis in 1960 was a cynical move by those in power to further marginalise their club.

The Estadio Benito Villamarín – still the home of Real Betis today – was originally constructed in 1929 for that year's Ibero-American Exposition in the city, with the Heliópolis neighbourhood which surrounds it subsequently taking off amid the city's population boom. Luís Molíni Briasco, who had previously founded the city's Recreativo FC and became a referee (see Chapter 8), was head of the Seville Tramways Company – responsible for the city's tram routes and services. Molíni was a fan of Sevilla and his close friendship with the club's president Ramón Sánchez-Pizjuán was well known and, perhaps naturally, led to suspicions over his partiality in decision making.

However, a passage from author Nicolás Salas in his Seville-transport focused book *El Tranvía, Crónica de Costumbres de la Ciudad de Sevilla* casts plenty of doubt over such suspicions. Salas claims a tram service had run to the Heliópolis area from the beginning of the 20th century until its final tram stopped in 1960. This was the year that the city's trams went into public ownership with the city council subsequently replacing them altogether with a bus route.

Records show that Molíni occupied his position from the early 1940s until 1957, while in 1944 a new tram route was introduced to link Heliópolis to the centre. A matchday poster from 1949, when Real Betis hosted Algeciras, stated there would be "a double tram service to the stadium", while Salas wrote that the Seville Tramways Company "organised special services to facilitate the presence of fans" at both Real Betis and Sevilla matches.

The shutting down of the tram route to Heliópolis left Betis fans "with just a precarious bus service as means of transport" to watch their team, according to Salas. "Their followers suffered and whilst their team struggled on the pitch [the club were contemporarily in Spain's third tier] so too did fans. They had the difficulties of having to walk on foot long distances to attend matches of their team." There can be little doubt that the isolation of the club's stadium on the city's transport grid would impact potential for growth, although there is little evidence to suggest Molíni was responsible for such an outcome.

Spanish football journalist Carlos Urbano told me: "I'm not quite sure the tramways decision had anything to do with the rivalry. Besides, since then there have been many mayors of Seville who are Béticos – such as the current incumbent, Juan Espadas – and they did not propose any tram or other form of transport to the stadium."

It was during this period that the Real Betis motto 'Viva el Betis manqué pierda!' ('Long live Betis even when they lose!') was first used. This is a cry of defiance, of taking pride in having to go the extra mile – in this instance, quite literally – to support their club. Spanish cartoonist Andrés Martínez de León (an honorary member of the club) coined the phrase through his alter ego Oselito – a character in a series named 'Oselito and Betis', which had begun as early as 1918 in *El Noticiero Sevillano*.

Usually pronounced in a thick Andalusian accent, the phrase sounds more like 'Viva er Beti manqué pierda' with regional locals tending to drop final consonants and *l*s blending into *r*s while in standard Spanish it should read *anqué* rather than *manqué*. The core message remains the same: clarity of unwavering support regardless of fortunes on the pitch. It is a realisation that they are not Barcelona or Real Madrid and that, in terms of tangible trophies or success, they are not even Sevilla. But they are Betis, and for them the *sentimiento* is raw, and they would not have it any other way. The large numbers who continued to attend matches both home and away gave rise to the term 'Green March'. Many Béticos cite this period of turmoil as the defining period in moulding the club's character, identity and fighting spirit.

How can it best be defined? "It is an expression of unconditional love and faithfulness," Carlos Urbano explained when I spoke with him. "Most football fans often declare it to their teams, but there are not many clubs who can express this 'way of life' in words. These clubs are, in my point of view, the most special, but it is the fans who make them special!" The fans are the essence of football in the city.

Chapter 11

Jostling for Power

IT was at the Reina Victoria from 1918 onwards that Sevilla genuinely grew into the region's dominant force, leaving Betis, Recreativo and Español de Cádiz in their wake. Their fans referred contemporarily to the ground as El Campo de la Victoria (The Field of Victory) and it is said that visiting players were often beaten psychologically before setting foot on the pitch due to the home comforts it provided Sevilla.

Featuring wooden terraces and a short pavilion, it was one of the most modern stadia in Spain and provided proof of the vastly superior resources the club enjoyed over their city and provincial rivals at that time. The original idea from the club's board of directors was to relocate to the central Nervión district – which would eventually provide their long-term home – which at the time housed the city's slaughterhouse.

However, the plans were changed thanks to the intervention of Manuel de Medina y Carvajal – a Sevilla fan and son of the Marquesa de Esquivel, a member of the local aristocracy. Manuel persuaded his mother to rent out an area of farmland to the club at a reasonable annual rate of 2,000 pesetas. The move was relatively affordable as the club improvised to keep prices down, including transporting the old 'red boards' from the Mercantil to identify the stadium, while advertisements of local companies were included for the first time at sporting events in the city.

Within five years of its construction, the stadium hosted its first international match as Spain triumphed 3–0 over Portugal. The match was also the first international featuring Seville-based players: Herminio Martinez Alvarez and 'Spencer' Enrique Gómez Muñoz (see Chapter 9).

Not unusually in these years leading up to the Spanish Republic and Civil War, there was the interweaving of power, politics and football. Manuel and his mother fled to Gibraltar following their implication in the failed 1932 monarchical coup orchestrated by General José Sanjurjo (who four years later was a leading figure, along with Franco, in the Nationalist uprising to start the Spanish Civil War). They would return to Seville two years later after Alejandro Lerroux's government issued an amnesty to those involved. Manuel would later become part of the Diputación Provincial de Sevilla (the Provincial Council of the city which contemporarily was a wing of the Falangist-run state) having previously served as a director at Sevilla.

It was under the presidency of Enrique Balbontín Orta, another politically significant individual, when the Marqués de Esquivel formed part of Sevilla's boardroom. Balbontín was a prominent businessman in the city, inheriting his family's foundry – one of the longest-running companies in Seville – from an early age. He served as the club's president for just one year after succeeding Paco Alba, with his long-term future residing in politics.

Balbontín was a member of the Sevillian Provincial Council between 1925 and 1930 before becoming the city's mayor in 1939. His appointment coincided with Franco's arrival to oversee the city's planned celebrations of Civil War victory. During this period following the General's ascent to power, political appointments were not coincidental, with the regime ensuring those sympathetic to their ideals were elevated into positions of influence. Balbontín held the mayoral position for less than a year but, as reports from *ABC* at the time show, he was at the head of events celebrating the fascist and totalitarian regime in Italy and Nazism in Germany.

Enrique Balbontín would preside over the Diputación Provincial de Sevilla between 1940 and 1943, again crossing paths with the Marqués de Esquivel. When Balbontín left his post, he was replaced by Ramón de Carranza y Gómez-Pablos, whose career took place almost in reverse. Ramón de Carranza would preside as Sevilla president between 1957 and 1961, overseeing their move into the Estadio Ramón Sánchez-Pizjuán, which remains their home to this very day (it is important to note the Estadio Ramón de Carranza, in which Cádiz CF play, is named not after him but his father – another Nationalistic figure who was appointed mayor and civil governor of Cádiz by General Queipo de Llano).

Ramón de Carranza – who gained the title of Marquis of Soto Hermoso – was a staunch monarchical conservative, supporting Queipo de Llano's military coup in 1936 and was subsequently appointed to a variety of influential positions in the new regime. He did not exit the political arena until his late 50s, when he opted to formalise his interest in football and gain prominence at Sevilla.

El Liberal, in their reporting of the 1918 Campeonato Regional Sur, speak of "aristocratic" Sevilla FC taking on "plebeian" Real Betis. The talk of football in the paper frequently referenced a class divide between the clubs. As a retort, Sevilla fans point to their counterparts' links to the military and even that the Spanish king was an honorary president of the club (although we have already examined how this, in gaining of the 'Real' title, had little relevance).

Sevilla historians have since highlighted a report from newspaper *La Unión* in 1915, shortly after Real Betis Balompié came to fruition. The article references a number of "Honorary members" of the club including Eduardo Dato (Spain's Conservative prime minister, who ironically has a street named after him running alongside Sevilla FC's Estadio Ramón Sánchez-Pizjuán) along with his successor, Antonio Maura and various governors, counts, presidents and ministers. The significance or weight which should be afforded to any of this information is questionable as such titles are relatively meaningless, even if the links provide a level of interest.

The trajectories of Marquesa de Esquivel, Enrique Balbontín and Ramón de Carranza all provide greater relevance for examining how the development of football in the city – as a case study for the general trend across the nation – was intertwined with business, money and political power. It would be lazy, and historically incorrect, to assume that the political stance of these individuals in any way represented Sevilla as a club or the consensus of their fanbase. Contemporary reports may hint at such a divide, but the motives of anonymous reporters are questionable, and no further details are provided. Indeed, both Sevilla and Real Betis were comprised of individuals sympathetic to the Falangist regime. Furthermore, it is logical to assume all clubs in this period would be open to governmental support – regardless of whether this was nationalist or republican – to further their own position. Unlike elsewhere in Spain, this was not a dividing line with which to fuel a rivalry but rather another vehicle in the race for power and prestige.

The rise of individuals to lofty positions within clubs and political positions was propelled by inherited affluence and social status. This demonstrates football's growing status within Sevillian society. At the start of the century, the sport was frowned upon and often played secretively due to the social stigma attached to it. Within a handful of decades, powerful individuals were using their status within the sport to exert political power and vice versa.

* * * * *

Seville native Carlos Piñar y Pickman succeeded Balbontín as Sevilla's president in 1921 and oversaw the club's continued local and regional dominance as they extended their Campeonato Regional Sur winning streak. Football was gradually beginning to modernise and Spanish sides, in honour of their roots, continued to follow where British sides led.

The concept of a professional first-team manager began to seep its way into British football around the turn of the century but the first examples of this within the Spanish game did not arrive for another decade or so. Until that point, the 'manager' was essentially an extension of the role of the on-field captain. Sevilla's website documents the all-encompassing role including "selecting and instructing players" and "assisting in the refereeing of the match". These players were typically defenders – those who could see the game in front of them and who possessed a notable understanding of where players should be positioned.

Hugh MacColl was the inaugural captain of the club and subsequently was their first manager, not that such a title had any genuine significance at the time. Joaquín Valenzuela, Eugenio Eizaguirre and Arturo Ostos all followed, as did José González 'Pepe' Brand, a skilful forward who spent the entirety of his 16-year playing career at the club before stints as 'manager', in the modern sense, between 1939 and 1942.

Throughout the first decades of the 20th century, Spanish teams used their British equivalents as the benchmark for success. The links went beyond many Iberian clubs having strong British roots, but this practice indicated a recognition that tactically, technically and physically they were several stages down the evolutionary process.

Four of Barcelona's first five managers were English: John Barrow, Jack Greenwell, Alf Spencer and Ralph Kirby, the latter of whom went on to coach Athletic Club in Bilbao. At the San Mamés, Kirby had temporarily replaced the legendary Fred Pentland, who enjoyed a fine playing career as a forward with Blackburn and Middlesbrough in England. Pentland became renowned in Bilbao for introducing the pass-and-move playing philosophy, while he is largely credited with ensuring the club were one of Spain's dominant forces throughout the 1920s–30s. He had already managed at Racing Club de Santander while he would go on to have three spells with Athletic Club de Madrid (the precursor to Atlético de Madrid) and one with Real Oviedo.

Elsewhere, Dublin-born Arthur Johnson was the first recognised manager of Real Madrid, in a continuation of his career as a centre-forward. Such a tradition of contemporary British influence has been carried into modern-day football terminology in the nation, with many Spaniards referring to their coach as 'Mister'.

Like so many other characters and stories of this time, the story of Sevilla's first full-time manager is packed with intrigue and, somewhat infuriatingly, provides as many questions as it does answers. The son of a well-known grocer in Donegal, roving Irishman Charles O'Hagan led a fascinating existence which, flying in the face of any clear logic, led him to become the first man in Sevilla's hot seat.

His playing career began in the Irish League with St Columb's Court and their successors Derry Celtic, before moving to Merseyside where he represented Old Xaverians before signing for Everton. During his time in Liverpool he supplemented playing football with work at the local Spanish fruit merchant, whose most popular goods were Sevillian oranges. At this juncture we must move outside recorded evidence and delve into educated guesswork, but potentially O'Hagan's arduous job at the fruit merchant could have eventually formed contacts which would see him relocate to the Andalusian capital two decades later.

O'Hagan went on to enjoy spells at Tottenham Hotspur and Aberdeen, while he won 11 caps for Ireland. It appears he gained notoriety for unpredictability and lack of commitment to one firm project. He retired from playing aged 31 – in an era when many outfield players continued into their 40s – while in 1915, reports emerged of him serving as a Second-Lieutenant of the Leinster Regiment in the First World War. Stationed in France and Belgium, he would have been exposed to mass loss of life and for years it had been feared O'Hagan was included in those unparalleled numbers.

However, in 1920 he reappeared at the centre of a match-fixing allegation – claiming his former Aberdeen team-mates had, 12 years previously, accepted a £15 bribe to throw a match against Celtic in the Scottish Cup. Within a month, he retracted these assertions and wrote, in a newspaper ad, that any such remarks made in his name were "entirely false, malicious and slanderous." Whether O'Hagan had been pressurised into withdrawing the accusations or whether another individual had acted in his name previously, remains unclear.

Following on from that bizarre episode, the Buncrana native was appointed as Norwich City boss but after just four wins from a possible 21 in the dugout, he was relieved of his duties. It was not until 1923 that Charles O'Hagan would once again resurface, with *El Liberal* reporting on "the wonderful news" that Sevilla had secured a managerial appointment.

> "After a lengthy search, Sevilla FC have succeeded in signing a new trainer to coach our players," the piece began. "The man in question is Mr Charles O'Hogan, an experienced Irish footballer who played with such important British clubs as Tottenham Hotspur, Everton and Huddersfield, the first of which he played with in last season's FA Cup final.
>
> "O'Hogan arrives with glowing references and we believe that under the experienced management of this trainer, Sevilla FC will reach the highest standard of football in the shortest time possible now that all these elements have been installed.
>
> "The board of directors at Sevilla FC deserve the most cordial and sincerest of congratulations for their astuteness in this area, for as with the current development of football in Seville such an improvement was required.
>
> "Now all that remains is for our players, while capitalising on this sacrifice the club has made, to respond with the required enthusiasm to the methods of Mr O'Hogan so that the manager's work may bear abundant fruit in the shortest possible time."

The article itself is filled with inaccuracies: referencing a non-existent playing spell with Huddersfield and an FA Cup final appearance with Tottenham – whose only cup final had arrived 14 years after O'Hagan left the club. His name was even misspelled as 'O'Hogan', although this was perhaps more understandable given the language barrier. Whether these other errors were a result of facts being lost in translation or were actively encouraged by O'Hagan himself – such as "glowing references" and "experienced management" – is unclear.

This was, somewhat remarkably, not the first appointment of an Irishman at a top Spanish club. Arthur Johnson was the first at Real Madrid, even if he was referred to throughout his career as 'English' (it is important to note that Ireland was still one nation and part of Britain during this period). A year before O'Hagan's move to the sun-soaked Andalusian capital, fellow countryman

Patrick O'Connell had succeeded Fred Pentland in the hot seat at Racing Club de Santander. As we discover, Dubliner O'Connell was to become the manager with arguably the greatest significance in Sevillian football in later years.

O'Hagan was to last just one season at Sevilla but his spell was a successful one, winning all seven matches in the Campeonato Regional Sur as the club notched their sixth successive title. There was less success on the national stage with a Copa del Rey quarter-final exit to Basque club Real Unión de Irún – a powerhouse at the time. Real Unión won the competition that season while their fourth and final title came in 1927. A founding member of La Liga, they were to be relegated from the second tier in 1942 and have only appeared in the top two divisions in three campaigns since.

Sevilla had failed to make serious inroads in the Copa del Rey. Comprised of winners of Spain's regional tournaments, their Campeonato Regional Sur successes ensured they were regular competitors. They first appeared in 1917, playing Madrid CF on three occasions. Despite triumphing 2–1 in Seville, 4–0 and 8–1 defeats ensured an early exit. The latter defeat is said by historians to have triggered a change in philosophy at the club.

Forward Juan Armet, nicknamed 'Kinké', was known in his playing days for having a sharp tactical brain and understanding of the sport. He would later go on to have a successful management career spanning Valencia, Real Betis and Real Madrid but at the time was part of a fearsome Sevilla attack which also consisted of Pepe Brand, Spencer, Escobar and León. The club's participation in the national tournament is said to have given Kinké a brainwave. The greener, softer pitches present throughout the rest of Spain would be conducive to playing shorter passes and retaining possession. Until that point, Sevilla had been used to the hard, dry pitches of southern Spain, often starved of rain, which was the basis of a more direct playing style.

Sevilla reached the Copa semi-final stage twice. In 1919 they were afforded a bye but lost 7–3 over two legs and withdrew the following year after failing to meet Barça's request to play their meetings in Madrid. In 1921 the change of direction brought its results, and the Andalusian champions defeated RS Levante de Murcia 2–0 and 3–0 to advance to the semi-finals to face Athletic Club and controversy.

The Spanish authorities had agreed in advance of the tournament that the final would be held in Seville, before later switching the venue to Bilbao. A report from Madrid said "the decision was not explained" but it was thought that for economic reasons "and a more favourable climate" the event would be switched to the Basque Country. Journeys between cities were lengthy and tiresome with poor transport infrastructure across Spain, with home advantage often proving decisive in national matches. Yet the sense of injustice for Sevilla was to grow further when their semi-final victory over Athletic Club was declared void. Their expulsion was due to the fielding of four players who had participated in other regional championships that year – against competition rules of the time.

Historian and Sevilla fan Agustín Rodríguez later wrote: "Athletic were so sure they would win the tie that they preferred to accept the undue line-ups before playing against a team with only seven players. Then the situation changed, and they retracted upon what was agreed and they won in the offices what they could not win in the field."

Sevilla – wearing black armbands in memory of former chairman Paco Alba, who had passed away the previous month – won the first encounter 4–2 before a 1–1 draw with both legs staged in Madrid. The match reports raved of the Andalusian side's display against their Basque opponents, using phrases like "they played liked angels", "what a way to play", "dominating like no other" and a "display of great skill". The report also stated Sevilla received a standing ovation from the Madrid-based fans upon the full-time whistle, as an appreciation of their authority.

Athletic Club ran out comfortable 4–1 victors in the final over Athletic de Madrid in their San Mamés home. A subsequent report stated Sevilla were the true "champions of Spain" (as no league system was yet in place) and were the strongest team in the "collective conscience" of fans.

However, Sevilla could not push on from this apparent position of strength to establish a dynasty on a national basis as they had done in Andalusia. In 1922 they suffered a heavy quarter-final loss to FC Barcelona and the following year were outdone by CE Europa of the Catalan capital at the same stage. O'Hagan could not break the last-eight curse, but the 3–1 loss to eventual champions Real Unión de Irún was respectable.

It was not only national circles within which Sevilla were impressing; they were now competing in friendly matches against clubs from England, Portugal, Poland and Czechoslovakia. O'Hagan oversaw encouraging results and was said to be popular with his squad but after one year he was gone. No official reasoning is on record with one unverified guess, as mooted by one unofficial Sevilla fan site, claiming "fans of the time say his love of wine was incompatible with his position as manager."

* * * * *

In 1925, Sevilla's Reina Victoria played host to the Copa del Rey final with FC Barcelona racking up their sixth triumph with a 2–0 victory over Basque club Arenas Club de Getxo. Sevilla had once again fallen at the first hurdle, losing a tiebreak 3–2 to Athletic de Madrid at Valencia's Mestalla Stadium after one win apiece. It would be another 74 years before the final of Spain's only national cup competition returned to Seville, when it was hosted at the newly built La Cartuja stadium, which was utilised again two years later. The home stadiums of Sevilla and Real Betis were then not used for the cup final, despite being among the largest in the nation, until 2019, when it was confirmed that the Benito Villamarín, home of Betis, would host that season's showpiece.

The so-called 'Sevillian School' with Kinké, Spencer and Brand at the head, was Sevilla's defining playing style in the 1920s – they were known as the 'line of fear' for opponents – and whilst it brought further Campeonato Regional Sur titles, their stranglehold on the trophy was eventually ended by Real Betis in 1928. Balompié had been runners-up in seven of the competition's previous eight editions but their progress had stagnated in the intervening years. Many of their leading figures departed with some jumping ship for sporting reasons and others leaving the city altogether.

In 1924, official club records show original founders Castillo, Wesolowski, Hermosa, Fernández, Zúñiga and Cascales all returned to the Betis board with a rejuvenation in terms of results, even if a power shift in the city did not take place. They did lift one piece of silverware in 1926, defeating their city rivals in La Copa Spencer – a one-off match to commemorate the death of the Sevilla forward, who had died from his appendicitis earlier that year (see Chapter 9).

The player had passed away in March but due to the economic hardships of his mother, Andalusia's Federación Regional Sur de Football organised an October encounter with all funds to go to the family. Real Betis were the opponents for Sevilla, partly due to their presence guaranteeing the largest possible crowd at the Reina Victoria but primarily because the premature death of the player served to unite a city in grief. Tragic premature bereavements continued to mould the intense rivalry over the decades that followed, underlining the mutual sense of respect and togetherness that both clubs share but which is rarely on show. Betis triumphed 3–1 at the home of their city rivals, which triggered a rare run of victories in the rivalry. Betis captain José Estévez was not to receive the trophy itself for a further three weeks due to a delay in its production by the council. However, it was worth the wait and the piece of silverware – which holds significant sentimental value for both clubs in the city – still holds pride of place in the Betis museum.

Betis won both group encounters against Sevilla in the following year's Campeonato Regional Sur but results elsewhere in their group ensured progression went to a tie-breaker in which *Los Rojiblancos* triumphed 3–0. Twelve months later, Real Betis Balompié finally got their hands on the trophy – the first officially recognised piece of silverware in their history. Again, they got the upper hand over Sevilla, triumphing twice at the Victoria before winning the showpiece 3–1 in Córdoba.

Winds of change were sweeping across the city and due to construction work for the upcoming Ibero-Americana Exhibition, Sevilla were forced to vacate their Reina Victoria home, migrating instead to the Nervión district which at the time was largely vacant. After several renovations, the stadium would hold 30,000 by the 1950s but upon its opening it was less than half that. Unbeknown to the club at the time, the neighbourhood would provide their permanent home.

This move coincided with the formation, for the first time, of a Spanish league system. It was decided that there would be three top divisions formed with ten clubs in each. The entry process for the top flight would be guaranteed for any side who had either won the Copa (Arenas, Athletic Bilbao, Barcelona, Real Madrid, Real Sociedad and Real Unión) or reached the final (Athletic Madrid, Español and Europa). Other sides who had lost in the decider – Español de Madrid, Real Vigo Sporting and Gimnástica – had already been dissolved. That left one remaining spot in the first edition of Spain's Primera.

Ten teams, including Real Betis and Sevilla, applied for the final spot and they were subsequently entered into a knockout competition to determine the participant. Betis defeated Alavés in a Christmas Day clash in Madrid before eliminating Real Oviedo 1–0 in Valencia at the quarter-final stage but their return to the capital saw their run ended with a 2–1 defeat to Racing de Santander. Sevilla went one round better – eliminating Deportivo de La Coruña 4–1 in Madrid (having received a bye) and conquering Depor's Galician rivals Celta de Vigo 2–1 in the last four, to face Racing Club de Santander.

Under the guidance of Hungarian boss Lippo Hertzka, Sevilla came within a whisker of sealing their spot at Spanish football's top table. The 'promotion final' ended 1–1 on 3 February, with a replay three days later producing another stalemate – this time 2–2. It was the Cantabrian side, coached by Irishman Patrick O'Connell, who edged their way to victory three days later with a 2–1 triumph. The man in Racing Club's dugout would later atone for the heartbreak he caused Seville's leading lights in a sparkling managerial career.

Sevilla's first match at their newly built Campo de Nervión was a 12,000 sell-out with fate dictating the fixture list produced Real Betis as the first visitors. The visitors continued their improved form in the derby with a 2–1 triumph on 7 October 1928. The land where the stadium stood had been rented from the Marquis de Nervión, with the ground surrounded by a large uncovered tribuna alongside three smaller terraces.

Despite the opening defeat, Sevilla bounced back to win the ten-team second tier as they edged out Iberia SC on goal difference. The league was competitive – Sevilla won just eight of their 18 fixtures – with two points awarded for a win and one for draws. Betis failed to generate any true momentum throughout the campaign and finished sixth, with Sevilla exacting revenge with a 3–0 victory at the Campo del Patronato Obrero. However, they would once again be denied a spot in the top flight by Racing in a promotion/relegation play-off. Despite triumphing 2–1 in Nervión, a 2–0 loss in Cantabria dashed Sevilla's top flight hopes once more.

* * * * *

Those near misses would prove costly for football in Seville, which was not represented at the top level of Spanish football for the first four years of its formalised existence. The trend which took hold saw Sevilla as perennial bridesmaids in the promotion race, always present but consistently falling just shy with Betis failing to make the top half in their first three attempts.

As well as attempting to fulfil sporting obligations, the two clubs remained socially conscious and in 1931 a special friendly match was arranged to help combat the rising unemployment in the city. 'An extraordinary service of trams will leave the Plaza San Francisco, at reduced prices," read a clipping from *El Liberal*, under the title "To Benefit the Unemployed Workers'. "The full proceeds will be donated to those without work in the city. The two teams will compete for the magnificent trophy of the Ayuntamiento de Sevilla."

The event was the brainchild of the Seville city hall with Mayor José González Fernández de la Bandera delegating councillor Isacio Contreras to arrange proceedings. "The unemployed beg us to make an application to the transport companies," added the report, "so that on Sunday they do everything in their power to facilitate access to Seville for people from the villages to come to witness the interesting meeting. We welcome the request, for believing the opportunity. We hope for rapid transport to the stadium."

The match was held on 6 September at the Estadio de la Exposición, which, as its title suggests, was built for the Ibero-American Exposition two years earlier and was used sporadically for sporting and political events. Unbeknown to the club at the time, this was to become the permanent home for Real Betis the following decade after being renamed Estadio de Heliópolis, to carry the title of the rapidly expanding area which had rarely held any notable significance before the Exposition. Heliópolis was transformed into an area of relative affluence, connected to the city centre by avenues lined with pavilions and home to grand residential houses, notably modern and spacious in comparison to those in the more central barrios.

The stadium itself instantly became the most significant in the city, a grand design holding 18,000 spectators. It was officially inaugurated on 17 March 1929 when Spain ran out 5–0 victors over Portugal while two days later it played host to a 'select' match between players from Seville against those from Portuguese capital Lisbon. The 'home' team were comprised of players from both clubs of the city but predominantly Sevilla, including goalkeeper Guillermo Eizaguirre and José González 'Pepe' Brand.

Heliópolis was also the ground used by Uruguayan club Rampla Juniors, who had included Seville in their European tour. On 27 May, Sevilla took on the South Americans in a 'friendly' clash which ended in a 2–2 draw but was remembered by those in attendance as a violent spectacle. A report of the clash described how the visiting team reacted angrily to the awarding of a Sevilla penalty, with tempers spilling over and a player subsequently receiving a red card. The decisions of official "Señor Trujillano" led to chaotic scenes with the Uruguayan side "showing aggression" towards him before Sevilla fans invaded the pitch amid mass confusion.

The fundraiser between Seville's two great rivals in 1931 was played in notably better spirits. Sevilla ran out 3–2 victors, although Real Betis historian Alfonso Del Castillo argued the green-and-white half of the city split their squad to also participate in a friendly against Portuguese side FC Barreirense. Besides, the result was academic in comparison to the admirable intentions of the events for the benefit of the city's unemployed. A sold-out stadium suggested this show of unity across both clubs and city authorities was a tremendous success.

Chapter 12

Breaking the Elite

FOR all the frustration and near misses as Seville's clubs tried to win a place amongst Spain's elite in the late 1920s, the decade that followed saw both clubs establish themselves among the nation's most revered. It was a period of intense flux for Spain at an institutional level: the Second Spanish Republic was established in 1931, five years later Civil War broke out and before the decade was out Franco was in power. Football had largely been an act of escapism in its early years and whilst this aspect intensified for many, its course was defined in large parts by the ever-changing constitutional crisis.

The latter half of the 1920s had seen a sharp increase in professionalism: managers with the sole task of running first-team affairs, footballers becoming full-time and playing for wages with professionalism regularised in 1926 by the Spanish FA. Both Real Betis and Sevilla began to incorporate other sports into their institutions, as was common across the Iberian Peninsula. Athletics, cycling and hockey were among the sports brought into the fold with clubs looking to increase membership and strive towards greater influence.

By the 1930s, football's blossoming in the city could be marked by a new wave of clubs such as Calavera CF, Triana FC, Osario CD, Triaca FC and Jupiter FC forming to represent their own barrios following the upturn in fortunes for the two superpower clubs in Seville. As Sevilla historian José Melero reflected, football had "integrated into the social fabric of the city" and had become both a major activity and form of popular entertainment, rivalling the success of cinema and theatre. It became the custom for fans of both Betis and Sevilla to welcome their team back to the city following an impressive away triumph by greeting them at the Plaza de Armas – the main bus station in the city, which is still prominent today.

Bustling areas within Seville such as the Alameda de Hércules are said to have displayed fixtures, results and league tables.

Betis – who like all Spanish sporting institutions, were stripped of their Real title after the Republic was declared – were embarking upon their true golden age and despite remaining mired in the second tier, conspired, against all the odds, to reach the final of the Copa del Rey in 1931. At the time under the presidency of José Ignacio Mantecón Navasal – a Republican who proudly identified as a politically left-leaning figure and later migrated to Mexico – the club found unparalleled success.

However, the prelude to this remarkable feat began with a bizarre sequence of events the previous season, when the club only avoided relegation to the third tier by the skin of their teeth. With just three matches of the 1929/30 season remaining, it became apparent that it would either be Balompié – the title by which they were still known – or Cultural y Deportiva Leonesa who would suffer the indignity of relegation.

With three matches remaining, the situation was tense and a 4–1 defeat for Betis at Real Oviedo set alarm bells ringing at the Seville-based club. The same day, Deportivo de La Coruña were Cultural Leonesa's opponents but with ten minutes remaining and the game tantalisingly poised at 2–2, the referee was forced to temporarily delay proceedings. Reports of the time say this was due to alleged intimidation from the Leonesa fans. The *Heraldo de Madrid* reported players of Deportivo were attacked amid a pitch invasion and when the official attempted to resume the final segment of the tie, the visiting team refused to take to the field.

Reportedly fearing for his safety, the referee returned to his hotel where he was "forced to write", according to the newspaper report, that Leonesa had won the match 3–2 despite the game being level when it was abandoned. Intimidation against officials was commonplace during this period but the extent to which the result had been manipulated by instilling such fear was notable. The referee union lodged an official complaint to the local León police force and to the Spanish FA. However, the football authorities would only be able to act upon the result following an investigation which meant that, initially, Leonesa were awarded the two points – as was the way at the time – to move them one clear of Betis.

On the penultimate day of the season, the two would go head to head at the Patronato Obrero in Seville in a crucial clash. Despite the visitors taking an early lead, two goals from Betis striker Ramón

Herrera were enough to clinch victory. However, reports credited the victory to goalkeeper Jesús Bernáldez – a native of Seville – whose nickname became 'hard hands' due to his shot-stopping ability.

Despite no longer sitting at the foot of the table going into the final day, Betis were not yet safe. They had to travel to Deportivo Alavés who needed a win to clinch the title while Leonesa travelled to Real Murcia, who had nothing to play for. Betis crashed to a two-goal defeat which saw them fall below Leonesa – who triumphed 4–3 at Murcia – once more. However, the Spanish FA's outcome for Leonesa's indiscretions was still pending and *ABC* wrote upon the conclusion of the league on 1 April that "it is probable" that Leonesa would be deducted two points, and thus would be relegated.

It was to take another two weeks before anxious fans of both clubs discovered their fate. Perhaps surprisingly, Deportivo were not automatically awarded the victory, but the FA decided that the scoreline of the match should be recorded as 2–2. Thus, both Leonesa and Betis finished on 14 points with the Andalusians earning a reprieve courtesy of having a one-goal better goal difference.

Former Sevilla playing legend Kinké was replaced in the hot seat by the Catalan Emilio Sampere, who had previously been at the helm of Real Murcia. Sampere arrived in Seville for the first time on 6 December 1930, just one day ahead of hosting Zaragoza-based Iberia SC (who the following year would merge with Zaragoza Club Deportivo to form the current Real Zaragoza) in the league opener. Betis shook off the apathy of their previous campaign to win their first five league games, but their form nosedived with just two wins from their remaining 13 outings, leaving them languishing in sixth.

The Copa only commenced in April upon the conclusion of the league games, but hopes were not high for Betis – whose final league game before cup action saw them thrashed 6–0 by champions Valencia. The luck of the draw had pitted the out-of-form Segunda side against Real Sociedad. The Basque side had finished third in the top flight, level on points with second-placed Racing de Santander and champions Athletic Club.

Incredibly, Betis won the first leg in Seville 5–1 as José Altuna, Rosendo Romero and Andrés Aranda Gutiérrez all found the net while Rafael Sanz netted a brace. It was arguably the best individual result in the club's history within the context of both team's form, although the clash still had one more meeting to come. The first leg was played on 12 April and two days later the Second Republic was proclaimed, ensuring the names and badges of both clubs changed halfway through the tie. Both sides would lose the 'Real' from their titles while 'Sociedad de San Sebastián' would swiftly change their name to Donostia Club de Fútbol (they reverted to Real Sociedad after the Civil War in 1939).

The return game at the Basque club's Atotxa Stadium was always going to prove a massive test for Sampere's side. Before the tie, Betis had been forced to complete a rearranged, yet ultimately meaningless, league clash against Sporting Gijon which had previously been postponed by rain. Despite resting many of their star names, the 5–0 loss suggested that the first leg Copa victory would prove the exception rather than the norm. Despite a crucial goal from striker Sanz, the Basque side took a 4–1 second leg lead with just 50 minutes on the clock. Despite waves of pressure from the hosts, Betis remarkably held out for the final 40 minutes with 'hard hands' Jesus along with defenders Lorenzo Tondo Gil and Jesusín coming in for special praise.

Progression saw them handed a last 16 draw which appeared relatively kind – Catalan side FC Badalona of the third tier. However, they needed a second leg home victory courtesy of Adolfo Martín González and José Suárez González, otherwise known as Peral, to gain a 2–1 aggregate triumph. By this stage, Betis sensed a rare opportunity for glory. They were the only Andalusian team remaining in the competition after Sevilla's exit to CD Castellón and they were paired with Madrid CF – the predecessors to Real Madrid.

Reports say the first leg at the Patronato Obrero was a 19,000 sell-out and Betis put on a show for their fans. Madrid's Antonio Bonet inadvertently netted into his own goal before Enrique Soladrero Arbide and Enrique Garrido Reguera added to the Betis tally. Indeed, press reports of the time heap praise upon Madrid's great goalkeeper Ricardo Zamora for keeping the score as low as three, frequently referring to his fine saves. This was to prove an unassailable lead going into the second leg, with Madrid managing just a 1–0 victory in the Chamartín.

Basque side Arenas Club de Getxo lay in wait in the semi-finals and were favourites after finishing first in the Primera that season. The top-flight side had home advantage in the first leg and ran out 2–1 victors, with future Betis legend Angel Martin Saro among their scorers. In an interview published in *El Liberal* on 12 June, between the legs, Betis boss Sampere was adamant he was confident in his side's ability to turn around the tie in Seville. "I have full trust in my players. We will have a full-strength team and with our fans behind us, I have no doubt we can reach a score sufficient to overcome the Basques."

Sampere was right; two days later Betis won 1–0 thanks to an own goal from Arrieta and on 16 June a tie-breaker was played at the Chamartín in the Spanish capital. Enrique and Sanz both scored in a 2–0 win for Betis and thus a remarkable spot in the Copa final was reached – it was the first time this feat was achieved by a club outside Spain's top flight.

The final was played against league champions Athletic Club Bilbao in front of a recorded 20,000 fans at the Chamartín, and in unseasonably wet conditions. The Betis team that took to the field that day was: Jesus 'Hard Hands', Andrés Aranda, Jesusín, Peral, Soladrero, Adolfito, Timimi, Adolfo II, Romero, Enrique, Sanz. Goalkeeper Jesus had to be replaced in the second half by substitute goalkeeper Pedrosa due to an injury.

It was to prove one step too far for Betis against Athletic with goals from Ignacio Aguirrezabala, Roberto Etxebarria and Agustín Sauto Arana, better known as 'Bata', putting the Basques in control before Sanz pulled a consolation goal back. Athletic secured their 11th Copa title to make it a league and cup 'double', but upon their return to Seville's Plaza de Armas bus station the returning Betis players were given a rousing reception. Two bands played at the festivities with players lofted upon shoulders in a display of great pride.

An Andalusian club had finally reached the final of Spain's national cup competition but the challenge of breaking into – and conquering – the top flight was yet to come.

* * * * *

By the early 1930s, there was growing uncertainty surrounding Spain's political situation, but football continued to provide a welcome form of normality and alternative discourse. The 1931/32 season began in the usual format, with Sevilla winning the Campeonato Regional Sur. Unlike previous seasons, the competition was decided by a league format rather than the previous knockout ties. For the fourth consecutive campaign Betis were the runners-up – losing 4–2 in Nervión before winning 3–1 in the return at the Patronato Obrero. The most notable game, however, was an abandoned match in Huelva; with Betis leading the hosts 2–1, the referee called a halt to proceedings due to alleged attacks on the visiting players. Upon his decision, the home fans stormed the pitch and attacked the official, leading to Recre's disqualification from the competition and a heavy fine.

The first three seasons of the Segunda had seen Sevilla continue their superiority in the regional Andalusian tournaments, finishing above their city rivals on each occasion and the previous year finishing second, behind only Valencia. *Los Rojiblancos* were now being coached by José Quirante – the first man to play for both Barcelona and Real Madrid. Yet despite carrying on with their Campeonato dominance, Sevilla's league form plummeted under his management. The perennial promotion challengers endured two of their three worst campaigns historically in back-to-back seasons under Quirante, finishing eighth and then ninth.

As Phil Ball detailed in *Morbo*, the coexistence of both Seville clubs has been played to a backdrop of one's fortunes being in direct contrast to the other. Ball referenced Spanish football writer Juan José Castillo's somewhat convoluted description of the rivalry as "*cal y arena*" (lime and sand). When one was gaining momentum, the other entered a seeming period of decline and it is important to place this in the context of both clubs being similar in stature. Both have long since been established comfortably within the nation's top eight clubs, yet neither are comparable in stature to either of Madrid's established powers or Barcelona. Yet the bragging rights are usually definitive and in the immediate period after the Second Spanish Republic was declared, it was Betis who carried the flag for the city.

Los Verdiblancos carried on the momentum gained from the previous season's run in the Copa to establish themselves as serious promotion contenders in the Segunda. From the season's fledgling matches it became apparent that Betis and Real Oviedo would likely go toe to toe to secure a place in the Primera. Seville proved to be a fortress for Sampere's side – they did not lose at their Patronato Obrero throughout the campaign. A curious statistic thrown up from their league campaign was that they won every match at the stadium except for the derby against Sevilla – a 1–1 draw – while a 3–2 win in Nervión against their city rivals was their only victory on their travels (they did win 1–0 at Catalonia FC, but due to their opponents folding before the close of the season all of their previous results were declared null and void). This is a useful indicator of the contemporary significance of home advantage in Spain, with away teams often burdened with lengthy, gruelling journeys on substandard forms of transport with comfort very much an afterthought.

The season was marked with eye-catching victories for Betis in their home stadium including a 5–1 victory over Athletic de Madrid and a 4–0 triumph against Sporting de Gijón. However, dreadful away form kept threatening to undermine the Sevillian club. An early 1–0 defeat at Oviedo threatened to be decisive as did a 4–1 defeat in

Gijón – with Sporting alongside Deportivo de La Coruña and Real Murcia threatening to join the title race.

With four matches remaining, Oviedo took top spot on a remarkable day when the Asturians defeated Deportivo 6–0 and Sampere's side fell to a remarkable 10–1 defeat to Athletic de Madrid at the Metropolitano in the capital. All roads then led to the Patronato Obrero on March 20, with Oviedo the visitors. *ABC* noted that for Betis the title clash could be defined as their "to be, or not to be" moment, but that their impregnable home form made them "the favourites". Despite going two goals down and with the Asturians looking to have one foot in the top flight, Betis roared back with four unanswered goals to storm to victory. A 1–1 draw in Vigo at Celta kept the Andalusians on course for promotion going into the final day. And they delivered it, once again recovering from an early setback to defeat Deportivo 3–1 at their fortress.

The *Heraldo de Madrid* counted the "extraordinary support" who chanted the name of their team and Sampere after falling a goal behind, while upon the final whistle Betis fans passed celebratory glasses of sherry amongst themselves to toast the achievement. Fans then gathered in the city centre to celebrate the success with the players. Levels of Betis support had significantly increased since their Copa run the previous season, rocketing from 786 *socios* to 2,321 within the space of a year.

Betis players, perhaps still revelling in their promotion, could not replicate their previous Copa form and were eliminated from the round of 16 with a defeat by CD Español with Sevilla falling to Donostia at the previous stage. Nobody was aware at the time but the Copa defeat was to be Emilio Sampere's last at the helm of Betis, with the news of his departure such a surprise that *ABC* printed it in three separate editions – 14, 16 and 22 July. It was met with surprise and even anger by many fans, with the supporters group Peña Bética del Bar Jerezano printing a letter in *ABC* voicing their "deep disapproval" and confirming they would challenge the club's ownership on the issue at the next meeting.

Sampere's replacement was Patrick O'Connell, the second Irishman to coach in the city following the reign of O'Hagan at Sevilla the previous decade. The Dubliner arrived with a modest coaching reputation: it was he who had denied Sevilla a spot in Spain's top flight four years earlier with Racing de Santander. He had guided the Cantabrian club to five regional titles in his seven years before going on to enjoy an unremarkable two-year stint at

Real Oviedo in the Segunda, then falling out of managerial work for a year. These were big shoes to fill and only in hindsight can this be considered a shrewd appointment, as at the time it was met with great scepticism.

However, any fears of an immediate struggle in the top flight were put to bed by O'Connell's side and the first two campaigns saw impressive fifth- and fourth-placed finishes respectively. In a trend carried on from previous campaigns, *Los Verdiblancos* struggled on the road with just three victories from 18 attempts outside Seville across these two campaigns. One could say they even missed their city rivals in the division. After all, the closest club in geographical terms were Real Madrid, over 500km to the north. Seven of the league's ten teams were based in the north across these two campaigns, with Valencia the only other exception.

In football terms, the area south of Madrid had been out of sight and out of mind for most Spaniards but the situation was changing. In 1932, Juan Domínguez Osborne left his position as Sevilla president after seven seasons to be replaced by Ramón Sánchez-Pizjuán y Muñoz – viewed by many *Sevillistas* today as the most influential figure in the club's illustrious history. The club had faced multiple challenges under his predecessor, finding it tough to replace the feared forward line of the 'Sevillista School'. Following the promotion of Betis and the continued struggles of Sevilla on a national level, the Sevillista Association was formed with Emilio Gayoso at its head. This was essentially a fan pressure group to force the club from its dormant spell.

Sánchez Pizjuán, the son of liberal politician Eduardo Sánchez-Pizjuán, played for Sevilla's second team as a 17-year-old but his greatest contribution did not come on the field. He studied law and philosophy before, aged 23, he was ushered on to the club's board. An influential figure within the city, by the time he was appointed president he was tasked with elevating the club into the top flight and re-establishing their status as the city's top dogs. His political background was key, employing a diplomatic approach to quell unsatisfied fans.

Strong investment was overseen to reverse the club's ailing fortunes. In 1932, Fede, Segura, Silvosa and Torróntegui were all signed and the following year, Euskalduna, Pepe López, and Tache arrived. Sevilla now had a team with the backing and aspiration to follow their eternal city rivals into the top flight. They were handed a significant boost ahead of the 1933/34 campaign, when authorities confirmed the number of spots in the top flight would increase by two to 12.

As a result, there was no relegation across the top two divisions that year while there were two automatic promotion spots from the second tier. As it turned out, Sevilla only needed one spot as they went up as champions. Undefeated through their first ten outings and never once dipping out of an automatic promotion slot, Ramón Encinas's side secured the Segunda title. Having previously won the Tercera division with Celta de Vigo and having coached Deportivo Alavés in the top flight, he was an experienced appointment and maintained his impressive track record in Nervión.

Promotion was secured on 18 February with a two-goal victory in the Madrid barrio of Vallecas against nearest rivals Athletic de Madrid, who also earned promotion that campaign. It was the first promotion in Sevilla's history and predictably led to jubilation in the Andalusian capital with fans taking to the streets to celebrate the achievement.

Almost immediately, the mood changed with alarming news reaching Seville regarding a train crash between the stations of Villanueva de la Reina and Andújar, in the province of Jaén.

More than 1,000 Sevilla fans were returning on a special train from Madrid, having witnessed their team's historic victory, when their vehicle collided with an express service carrying goods between the capital city and Seville. Eleven Sevilla fans lost their lives in the tragedy, which saw upwards of 100 more injured. The joyous mood in the city turned to horror and a week of mourning was declared.

Dozens of medics and railmen swiftly mobilised to provide resources while many concerned relatives travelled to Jaén, waiting to receive news about their loved ones. They suffered a nerve-shredding wait to discover the extent of the crash, which many feared would be much worse, particularly due to the overcrowding which tended to happen on such vehicles. The vast number of travelling fans would have been unthinkable the previous decade, but such was the improvement in transport and infrastructure alongside the increasing affordability of match tickets, away followings began to notably grow.

In 2014 – 80 years after the catastrophe which remains the worst football-related tragedy in Spain – Sevilla FC organised a tribute to those who lost their lives and all those injured in the accident. Club president José Castro Carmona placed a commemorative plaque to the victims near the home dressing room at the club's stadium. "It is right at the door of the dressing room and will act as an encouragement to our team and to our fans," Castro explained. "It is here where you enter our dressing room and you must give everything you have in each game for this club, because this is what those who lost their lives demanded."

Six months after the Madrid tragedy there was another news story that brought great sorrow to Seville. Former Betis president Ignacio Sánchez Mejías, a native of the city who later became one of the most famed matadors in Spain, was gored in the Manzanares bullring and the subsequent gangrene killed him, aged 43. Sánchez Mejías had broken free of bullfighting's tendency to side with conservative, traditional views and instead forged close bonds with the Generación del 27 group of poets. This left-leaning movement challenged long-held views on the Catholic Church in Spain and the role of the military.

Sánchez Mejías was a man of many talents, combining his love of football, bullfighting and politics with poetry, acting and business interests. A visionary in many fields who accumulated the financial means to fund his interests, including Betis, he was credited with assembling the majority of the squad who would secure the club's greatest triumph less than a year after his untimely death in Madrid.

"Ignacio was kind of a hero, he was popular, had modern views and money," a Seville-based journalist, who did not wish to be named, told me. "He put things in order at Betis and positioned them to sign great players. When he died, his heirs at Betis did not rise to the occasion."

Granada-born poet Federico García Lorca eulogised his friend in 'Weeping for the Death of Ignacio Sánchez Mejías'. Within two years of this piece, García Lorca was shot dead by the Guardia Civil due to the expressive, uncensored nature of his poetry. His body has never been found.

Tragedy was a theme which became interwoven with the city and its clubs over the years but, just as in 1934, Seville and its powerhouses would not let it break them.

Chapter 13

Kings of Spain

THE 1934/35 campaign promised to be significant for football in the south of Spain with both Betis and Sevilla now among Spain's elite for the first time. Nobody could have foreseen just how glorious it would be, nor how the increasingly precarious political situation in the nation would subsequently define the situation in the seasons thereafter.

The names of each first-team squad member are forever etched into the folklore of each of Seville's clubs. For Betis, they are Urquiaga, Areso, Aedo, Peral, Gómez, Larrinoa, Adolfo, Lecue, Unamuno, Timimi, Saro, Caballero, Rancel, Valera, Espinosa, O'Connell. Six Basques, three Sevillians, three Canarians and an Almería native, coached by an Irishman – 'Don Patricio', as he was affectionately known. They would become champions of Spain's top flight, against the odds. For Sevilla fans, the players' names also roll off the tongue: Eizaguirre, Euskalduna, Deva, Alcázar, Segura, Fede, López, Torrontegui, Campanal, Tache, Bracero, coached by Galician Ramón Encinas. They would also end the season with a landmark triumph, lifting the Copa de la República – as Spain's national cup competition was temporarily known.

The core of the side that won Betis the Primera title was comprised of Basques whose parents had migrated to Andalusia when the nation's changing economic situation saw the north temporarily begin to wane. These six players are fundamental not only to explaining the title triumph but also the events that followed. This was the penultimate league season before Civil War broke out and all were forced to abandon ship. Defenders Serafín Aedo and Pedro Areso played for Euskadi – the Basque country's national team – which toured Europe and the Americas over the Civil War years, but others migrated.

Until 1935, the Primera title had been shared among the 'big three' of Real Madrid (contemporarily Madrid CF), Barcelona and Athletic Club from Bilbao, with players from these clubs dominating the Spanish national team and individual awards. One of the Betis stalwarts throughout the campaign was goalkeeper Joaquín Urquiaga – a native of the Basque capital who spent the remainder of his career in Mexico after 1936 – who conceded just 19 goals in 21 league outings (he is historically noted as winning the division's Zamora award that season for the lowest goals-to-games ratio, but this gong was only officially awarded for the first time in 1958). Under Patrick O'Connell, *Los Verdiblancos* gained a reputation as a pragmatic side who valued organisation and defensive structure. They conceded 15 goals fewer than the second-best defence (Real Madrid) yet were outscored by six other sides in the table.

Much of their goal output relied on two players. Víctor Unamuno had been signed the previous summer from Athletic Club and such was his efficiency in front of goal, he netted 101 times in 144 top flight appearances. Thirteen of those arrived in this title-winning campaign, while attacking midfielder Simón Lecue scored nine goals. Renowned for his ability to time his runs into the box, Lecue's performances earned him a spot in the Spanish national side – he became the first Betis player to win an international cap – and widespread acclaim, with many insisting there was no better attacking midfielder in Europe at the time.

It was a season punctuated by unusual results: Betis won all but two of their home games, a scoreless draw against Arenas Getxo (who went down without a win on the road all season) and a pulsating draw with Sevilla on the penultimate day of the campaign. Going into that game, the stage was set for a thrilling, climactic end to the campaign with Betis and Real Madrid tied on points. With just two rounds of games remaining, Betis were hosting their city rivals – who finished a respectable fifth in their first top-flight campaign – while Madrid were away to Barcelona.

The Catalan giants had suffered an 8–2 reverse by their *El Clásico* rivals earlier in the campaign and, despite enduring an underwhelming mid-table campaign, were out for revenge. Their emphatic 5–0 victory opened the door for Betis, but they had to claw their way back from behind twice in the derby with a hungry Sevilla – keen to spoil any party – to rescue a point. Lecue's penalty before the break had levelled the score and this strike would ultimately prove highly significant.

It was still the case that league positioning was decided by goal difference rather than the head-to-head record between the teams, so despite Betis winning 1–0 in both clashes against Madrid, the superior goal difference of the capital team ensured the Andalusian side had to finish above them on points. Leading the way by a solitary point on the last day, Madrid were to host already-relegated Arenas while for Patrick O'Connell it was to be a meeting that was written in the stars as he took his side to his former club Racing de Santander.

Inevitably, what happened next has had its share of *polémica*, as controversy engulfed the events of the final day. Officials from Madrid protested that the Irish boss had visited the hotel where his opponents were staying the night before the game in an alleged attempt to convince them to throw the match. Twenty years earlier, O'Connell had been the captain of Manchester United in a clash against Liverpool which later saw seven players banned for their involvement in rigging the match. Liverpool, comfortably mid-table, hosted United with the visitors needing a win to escape relegation, which they duly managed with a 2–0 triumph. It soon emerged that large sums of cash had been placed on that exact result at odds of 7-1. Supporters were immediately suspicious of the performances of several players, while O'Connell himself – not known for his goalscoring ability – demanded to take a penalty with the score at 1–0, before blasting it well wide of goal.

O'Connell was never found guilty of wrongdoing that day and there is an argument that his deliberately missing the chance to complete the 2–0 scoreline suggests he was not involved. But in his role as captain it seems unlikely that he had no knowledge, and his grandson Mike O'Connell later confessed: "I don't know if he was involved or not, but he would have had it in him, he would have enjoyed the intrigue."

While Madrid called foul play on O'Connell's actions the night before the decisive league game, Betis retorted that it was *Los Blancos* who were using underhand tactics. There was no denial of the Dubliner's visit to Santander players from Betis, but they claimed the boss was informed that their club chairman José María de Cossio was a Real Madrid fan and had offered them a substantial bonus to beat Betis.

Racing, managed by Englishman Randolph Galloway, had nothing meaningful to play for but their El Sardinero home was packed with 16,000 fans expecting them to end their season on a high. Within five minutes the game was as good as over with 18-year-old José González Caballero and Unamuno netting quickfire goals to put the visitors in total control. The home fans were immediately critical of their side's effort, or lack of it. "The crowd quickly turned on Racing by accusing them of fixing the match and of defeating Cantabria's sportsmanship," read newspaper *La Voz*, while *ABC* reported chants of "Rigged, rigged!"

The Betis hurricane on the banks of the Bay of Biscay was unrelenting – Unamuno grabbed a third before the break, Caballero made it four just after the hour mark before Unamuno completed his hat-trick. For the best part of two hours Betis knew they were the champions before the final whistle confirmed the news, and the celebrations began. The scale of this achievement should not be underestimated. Ahead of the league campaign starting, Madrid magazine *Blanco y Negro* wrote that Betis had the weakest squad in the top flight and would likely rank last of its 12 participants. This was the first genuine shock in Spain's top division and it rocked the foundations of football on the peninsula.

Fittingly, Saturday, 28 April coincided with that year's *feria* within Seville with the full-time result reportedly 'running like wildfire through the booths' at the party. Many chalked up the score outside the tents to let others know the good news so the celebrations could be stepped up a notch. Up north in Santander, the party was reported to have gone on into the small hours of the morning before the champions, led by president Antonio Moreno Sevillano, took off for Bilbao – where the league trophy was still situated from the previous campaign.

The Primera trophy was thus handed over to Betis captain Unamuno, whose hat-trick the previous day had propelled his side to such a glorious finale. The squad then returned to Seville on the team bus which was nicknamed the Green Arrow. Arriving in the Andalusian capital at 8pm, they were met by adoring fans before travelling to the City Hall to meet mayor Isacio Contreras before a gala lunch the following day at the Hotel Colón.

Almost two decades after the success, Patrick O'Connell was interviewed by newspaper *Sevilla* and was asked the secret behind the triumph. "Not having too many injuries," he responded. "I did not have many players, but I knew they were always ready so they could not suffer muscular injuries. For this I prepared them as I understand that a player must be trained for avoiding these."

And how did he go about it? "By ensuring that in training, a player never reached his full physical capacity, leaving at least a margin of 10 per cent compared to his effort level in games. Players can burn out; they sustain muscular injuries from excess training and we needed to avoid this at all costs. My experience was crucial for this, you had to know the players and what they were capable of. The mistake football clubs make now is by sacking managers after just one season, by dispensing with them at the first sign of difficulty. Clubs need continuity and a coach who knows his players inside out. This was the situation for me at Betis."

The interview was conducted in O'Connell's final year living in the city, before he passed away five years later in London. "I am a lover of Seville. I like to be here; that's why I have not left. Seville is the only place in the world where I can always learn something."

The achievement ensured that Betis had become the first Andalusian team to appear in the top flight, to reach a Copa final and to win the top league. In April 1935, no Andalusian club had yet won the Copa but two months to the day after *Béticos* had brought the city to a near standstill with their celebrations, their city rivals would have a notable triumph of their own.

Due to the mass expansion of professionalism in football across Spain, the 1935 Copa del Presidente de la República – as it was known throughout Spain's Second Republic – included 50 clubs, with Sevilla not entering the tournament until the round of 16 due to their pedigree in previous years. The title of the tournament was related to Spain's political situation at the time and *Los Rojiblancos* were one of only three clubs – alongside Real Madrid and Athletic Club of Bilbao – to win the tournament in its three forms: the Copa Presidente de la República, del Generalísimo and the Copa del Rey.

Their most impressive result came straight away, eliminating Madrid CF thanks to a 1–0 victory at Nervión, followed by a defensive display of resilience at the Chamartín which saw them withstand a barrage of pressure to earn a scoreless draw. The competition significantly opened up with Madrid's elimination whilst Betis saw off Athletic Club, ensuring the Copa's two most successful teams – who had shared the trophy in each of the past five seasons – were eliminated ahead of the quarter-final stage. Fancied Oviedo, who had finished the league campaign in third, were defeated by Zaragoza.

League champions Betis were the next giants to fall, eliminated in the last eight by Catalan side Sabadell. They had fallen to defeat in the Segunda promotion play-offs as they chased a first-ever promotion to the top flight but, despite coming up short in the league, Sabadell's exploits in the Copa saw them reach the only final in their history.

The upsets kept coming as Levante eliminated Barcelona while Sevilla edged out Athletic de Madrid with a 2–2 draw at the Campo de Vallecas – the scene of their promotion triumph the previous campaign – before edging a thrilling five-goal encounter in Seville.

The semi-final proved a rather less nerve-wracking affair for *Sevillistas*, who by this stage of the competition were the only top-tier side remaining in the competition. Their opponents, Osasuna, had won that year's Segunda title but were clear underdogs going into the tie and a 4–1 victory for the home side in Nervión killed off any hopes of a comeback, but progress to the showpiece was ensured with a 1–0 victory in Pamplona. Sabadell's run continued with a fine 4–1 aggregate victory over Levante to set up the final in Madrid's Chamartín stadium.

More than 5,000 Sevilla fans made the trip to the capital on 30 June with a fleet of buses departing the Plaza del Salvador the previous evening. Many fans were left disappointed upon arriving in Madrid, with signs outside the stadium explaining that all 15,000 tickets had been snapped up. It was a special day for Sevilla, whose amateur team, coached by famed former forward Pepe Brand, triumphed 1–0 over Ciosvin de Vigo in their own cup final – traditionally played in the same stadium ahead of the main event.

Just as with Betis, players of Basque descent were crucial in Sevilla's success with defender Pedro Aurrecoechea Echeandía, known as Euskalduna, opening the scoring before Asturian forward Guillermo González del Río García, Campanal, struck twice to make it a convincing triumph. Campanal had joined Sevilla aged 17 from Real Sporting de Gijón and spent 17 years as a player at the club, scoring an official total of 218 goals, including over 100 in the Primera. He would be the star man in a number of the club's most famed results, including netting five goals in a remarkable 11–1 victory over Barcelona in 1940. It was an extraordinary career which no doubt would have led to more goals had he not missed most of the 1932/33 season to complete his military service. Campanal gained international recognition, scoring twice in three appearances for Spain, whom he represented at the 1934 World Cup.

Without doubt one of the greatest figures in the club's illustrious history, Campanal would later go on to manage the club across two spells in the 1950s. His most influential signing whilst manager was his nephew, Marcelino Campanal – with Guillermo hence being known as Campanal I, while the younger player, an imposing defender, was nicknamed Campanal II. The nickname is said to have derived from his family's business in his hometown of Avilés. Travelling to the Andalusian capital took Marcelino four days by boat. "I'm the only player in the history of the club to arrive by sea," he joked decades later in an interview with *Revista Líbero*. It proved to be worth the wait as the defender spent 16 seasons at *Los Rojiblancos* and surpassed 400 appearances with the club (to this day, he is one of only four players to do so).

"Today I have seen the archetype of *La Furia Española* in action," said famed Spanish sports broadcaster Matias Prats amid a particularly energetic performance from Campanal II, who earned the nickname 'the hurricane of Avilés'. Vicente Del Bosque, who would go on to manage Real Madrid and Spain to great success, recalled Campanal II as "being more than an athlete" and, "his strength was in exploiting his physique, he was outstanding."

Like his uncle, Campanal II was capped by Spain and at 23 became the nation's second-youngest ever captain (only behind Ricardo Zamora) and the first from Asturias to earn the honour. So revered was his playing style, a documentary film entitled *Campanal, la leyenda de La Roja* was released in his honour in 2012. Despite his reputation for physicality, he was only sent off on two occasions, whilst he conceded two penalties throughout his career, hinting that he was rarely rash with decision making and could channel his *furia* into his performances if not his personality.

However, he was involved in a particularly infamous incident in a 1961 'friendly' against FC Porto in which he later admitted "there was a terrible atmosphere". In an incredible turn of events, the defender would spend two nights in a Portuguese jail cell after he reacted to an incident that saw team-mate and close friend Curro Romero suffer a broken nose.

"I went there in his honour then they [Porto players] all came for me," he explained, years later. "The police beat me after, but if it were not for them then I may have been killed! I had to pay 200,000 pesetas to be released." Upon hearing the news, thousands of Sevilla fans took to the Parque de María Luisa to help fund the compensation package. Three years earlier, in the pre-season Trofeo Ramón de Carranza final, Real Madrid president Santiago Bernabéu reportedly told his Cádiz counterpart Ramón de Carranza that his side would refuse to play the second half if Campanal II was still playing, due to the manner of his performance. Subsequently, Sevilla substituted him off at half-time. Quite clearly, 'friendlies' meant little to the defender.

"Besides being a footballer, I was an athlete," Campanal II recalled. "Above all, I wonder what would have happened if I had dedicated myself to athletics. I ran the 100 metres in 10.8 seconds when it was very unusual to run below 11 seconds. I competed in the high jump, the long jump, discus, the hurdles and weight-lifting. I always took good care of myself because my passion was sport and so I did not drink nor smoke, and I still do not." He met his wife playing tennis in Seville, and they had six children. Fittingly, his granddaughter became a youth tennis champion in Spain.

Campanal II was resilient and played through the pain barrier on more than one occasion. "All my life I have been very competitive." His team-mates reported how he played on with an injured back and would urinate blood after matches. He once completed a game in Gijón with a broken fibula and on another occasion, following a head collision in a match at Valencia, he had to ask those around him which colours his team-mates were playing in. It is no surprise he is remembered so fondly at Sevilla and, just like his uncle, he would later be inducted into the club's hall of fame.

Back in 1935, many in the capital did not appear too happy with Sevilla triumphing in the Copa del Presidente de la República decider, with the club's website recalling: "The only negatives were the comments against Sevilla from the Madrid-based press, who still had not forgiven the eventual winners for having knocked out Real Madrid and Atlético de Madrid along the way." The team were welcomed back to the city the following day at the Plaza de Andalucía with mayor Isacio Contreras once again involved in the trophy handover. Both the first team and amateur sides were celebrating following their double success, with both attending a banquet that evening at the Hotel Andalucía Palace, nowadays known as the Hotel Alfonso XIII. It capped a glorious season for the city and its clubs, who now held both of the nation's most prestigious trophies, breaking the stranglehold of Madrid and Spain's north over football.

* * * * *

It is often said that timing is everything. Just as everything had fallen into place for both Seville clubs, the following years were to provide a reality check, particularly for Betis. There were certain elements that the club could control and which, perhaps, would have impacted on their fortunes regardless of the commencement of Spain's Civil War. The club's finances were not healthy despite the recent league title, with economic mismanagement becoming an unwanted running theme across the club's existence. What cannot be denied is that fate and the outbreak of national flux rocked the city of Seville and notably shaped the paths of its clubs.

Season 1935/36, the final season of Spanish football before a three-year break due to the events across the nation, saw both Seville clubs fail to make the top half of La Liga. Betis ranked seventh, two places above Sevilla, with a hangover impact seeming to take hold over the city. For Betis the drop-off was inevitable as their overachievement had brought the attention of Spain's wealthiest clubs. Defender Pedro Areso departed to Ciudad Condal while Lecue – "the star player of the Betis title-winning side without a doubt", as the club's website recalled – joined Madrid CF in a notable transfer worth 60,000 pesetas. The death of former president Ignacio Sánchez Mejías (see Chapter 12) has been cited as causing a reduced wage budget and fall in sporting standards.

One player who did stand out for Betis was forward Francisco González, Paquirri. Having grown up in the Alameda de Hércules area of Seville, Paquirri played for the club's youth team in 1932 before earning his first-team debut, aged 20, the following year. A backup player in the title campaign, it was not until 1935/36 that he began to make his mark on the first team and was often selected in preference to the prolific Víctor Unamuno. He would spend a decade – interrupted by the Spanish Civil War – in the first-team squad before joining Deportivo de La Coruña then Cádiz CF. He returned to Betis in in 1949, when they were in the third division. Despite being aged 36, he netted 14 times in 13 appearances and ensured he was one of only six players to represent the club in each of the top three divisions.

It was during the period after the Civil War, when Betis would fall into notable decline, that Paquirri would become the side's most valued player. Indeed, he became the club's top scorer with a total of 109 goals in official competition (he also scored 36 times in 39 friendly matches), a record that would remain intact until the following century when Rubén Castro eventually eclipsed him. However, considering the disrupted nature of his Betis career, his goal output was incredible, particularly his league record of 72 goals in just 81 games.

Betis participated in the first edition of the Iberian Cup, a trophy designed to pit the champions of Spain against their Portuguese counterparts – FC Porto. The one-off match, which was not recognised by either FA, saw the Portuguese champions granted home advantage at the Campo da Constituição in a game which they won

4–2, with teenager José González Caballero netting both goals for Betis.

Following this clash, boss Patrick O'Connell would depart the club, joining Barcelona. Betis would once again turn their attention to English football to find his replacement with Howard Charles Slade, a former midfielder who was then a coach at Aston Villa, chosen. The appointment was ill-fated and abandoned after a matter of months, before the league campaign even got underway.

Slade would manage *Los Verdiblancos* for a friendly encounter against Italian giants Internazionale, who at the time were operating under the title Ambrossiana-Inter. The situation in Italy under fascist dictator Mussolini foreshadowed what would soon unfold in Franco's Spain, with Internazionale forced to change their name because of the reference to internationalism which, in the eyes of the authorities, was the equivalent of championing communism. Inter had merged with Associazione Sportiva Ambrosiana, in honour of San Ambrosio – the patron saint of Milan.

Just as the Madrid press had upset Sevilla earlier that summer, they were to infuriate the green-and-white half of the city with an article published in September ahead of Slade's side travelling to Inter. Legendary Spanish goalkeeper Ricardo Zamora penned an article in Madrid publication *YA* saying that Betis should not have taken part in the encounter as it had damaged the image of Spanish football. Historians of Betis conclude this was a result of the "deep malaise" in the capital following their club pipping Madrid CF to the league title just months before. However, the Seville club could not replicate this form in Italy, losing 6–1.

Slade was replaced in the dugout by former player Andrés Aranda, who had debuted for the club as a player in 1921 before helping them reach the Copa final and promotion the following decade. By 1925 Aranda had been a first-team regular and during a three-week-long tour of Germany that year, earned the nickname *El Científico*, the scientist. As a player, he was famed for playing across the pitch including as an emergency goalkeeper, such was his adaptability.

Now aged 30, he was considered by some as an appointment rooted in practicality and indicative of the club not being willing to risk bringing in another manager from abroad. Aranda would enjoy a distinguished coaching career which included a stint at Recreativo de Huelva, while 1935 was the first of four spells at the helm of Betis. His fourth and final spell was to end in tragedy, as he passed away just days after his appointment in March 1965 while preparing for his side's clash with Real Zaragoza.

* * * * *

In his first season at the helm, Aranda could not match the unprecedented success of his predecessor Patrick O'Connell with the most significant moment for the club arriving at the end of the campaign. They reached an agreement with the Seville city council to become tenants of the Estadio de Heliópolis, constructed for the Ibero-American Exposition (see Chapter 11). In return, they would hand over the grounds of the Patronato – their home turf which had formed the basis of winning the top two leagues and their 1931 cup run – to the authorities. The contracts were signed by both parties on 15 July 1936 but within 48 hours the switch was instantly dropped from the public consciousness. A military coup was launched on the streets of Seville as the nation descended into Civil War, changing the course of history.

* * * * *

The years that followed marked a period that many would rather forget, with misery and untold suffering as a fierce conflict blazed throughout Spain. Organised league and cup football was abandoned with players of all colours caught up in proceedings and with the country deeply divided.

Franco's troops took control of areas including Andalusia and the north-western region of Galicia, ensuring various notable clubs, including Real Betis and Sevilla, could not compete. The Republicans held early power in Madrid, Barcelona and Valencia along with swathes of the surrounding countryside, whilst also controlling much of the Levante coast. As a result, regional cup competitions such as the Campeonato Levante and Campionat de Catalunya went ahead.

Alongside the emerging football powers in Seville, the nation's two most successful clubs in the years preceding the Civil War – Madrid CF and Athletic Club de Bilbao – did not take part in matches. The Basques' omission was logical, many of their players and fans were either combatting Franco's forces on the front line or had fled across the border to France. The club were said to have had an application for the Campionat de Catalunya rejected by Barcelona, whilst navigating elsewhere in the nation would have entailed too high a degree of risk.

Madrid's absence is more curious. History often indicates the club as one of central power and on the right of the political spectrum, with club legend Santiago Bernabéu personifying this stance. Then the manager of the club, Bernabéu was arrested during the conflict for membership of CEDA (a far right-wing political grouping). He later fled and fought for the Nationalist forces under the command of general Agustín Muñoz Grandes, subsequently being rewarded for his military efforts in Catalonia by Franco himself.

Bernabéu did not represent Madrid CF as a club – his own strand of political opinion was not shared by many others possessing power within the club – and whilst he became president following the Civil War, his predecessor Rafael Sánchez Guerra was a staunch Republican and left-wing militia Antonio Ortega was reportedly acting president over the Civil War period, although this is not recognised by the club.

Neither Madrid CF nor Athletic de Madrid were admitted to the newly formed Mediterranean League – the eight-team de facto replacement for the Primera. The reasons behind this are debated, with internal divisions over the definition of a Republican club a persistent theory behind their exemption.

Therefore, it was FC Barcelona who were the most successful club to compete in the division, led by former Betis boss Patrick O'Connell. Soon after, the Irishman and his players set sail away from the conflict to take part in a tour of Mexico and the United States which was to significantly boost the club's finances and place them on a stable financial footing for the seasons which followed, despite the reason for their visit being to raise money for the Republican cause. The whopping $12,500 profit was deposited in a Paris bank account, although only five of the 16-man playing squad returned to the club following the conclusion of the conflict.

By 1939 Franco's troops had claimed victory and despite the outbreak of the Second World War grinding football to a halt across most of Europe, it was to recommence in Spain. For one of Seville's clubs it was to provide continued success but for the other a dark period in their history was about to begin.

Chapter 14

Civil War Aftermath

BEFORE the Civil War, it was Betis who held the balance of power in the city. After decades of Sevilla hegemony in the Andalusian Campeonatos, *Los Verdiblancos* had roared back following a period when they flirted with the possibility of going into the abyss. The spell in the limelight was brief and the Civil War hit Betis hard: the club's offices were bombed, membership dipped into double figures, the spine of their title-winning team had fled, and the club were out of money.

Football resumed in Spain after the Nationalists' triumph with the 1939/40 campaign, strangely coinciding with the commencement of the Second World War and football elsewhere in Europe grinding to a halt. Following the end of the Spanish conflict that spring, there was uncertainty over which clubs would be able to scramble together a squad to continue. Barcelona's future had been partly stabilised by their North American tour, under Patrick O'Connell, and there were doubts over the continuity of Betis, though they eventually reaffirmed their status.

This was a decision which ultimately backfired as, along with Racing de Santander, Betis were relegated with just six wins in 22 league outings. In hindsight, they should have taken the route of Oviedo – another club hit hard by the Civil War and whose Estadio de Buenavista had been badly damaged. The Spanish FA granted the Asturians a moratorium to allow them to sit out the campaign and rebuild their club, before being reinstated the following year. The Betis club website acknowledges that not going down a similar route was a "grave mistake" by their club. Whilst the league season was to prove painful for Betis, it was Oviedo's sabbatical which triggered a series of events that ultimately caused heartache for Sevilla too.

It was a strange twist of fate that had started three years prior, in the final campaign before league football was abandoned. On the last day of that campaign, Athletic Madrid hosted Sevilla in a basement battle to avoid relegation. The capital-based club needed only a draw but fell to a 3–2 home defeat, with Chacho missing a penalty in the dying moments. Along with Osasuna, Athletic were relegated while Sevilla, dramatically, survived.

However, the withdrawal of Oviedo created a spot in the top tier and both previously relegated sides had demanded to be reinstated. Reports of the time suggest the Pamplona-based club had an agreement in place with the Spanish FA in 1938, a year before the Civil War ended, allegedly due to the area's assistance in the Nationalist triumph.

Meanwhile, Athletic had amalgamated with Aviación Nacional – the team of the Spanish Air Force, based in Zaragoza, which had been created during the civil war to assist the Nationalists – to become Athletic Aviación. The situation for Athletic was like Betis: facilities had been damaged, their team had been decimated (losing eight players to the Civil War), their membership plummeted, and they were effectively broke. Madrid had been the final city to fall to Franco's troops and the regime initially held strong misgivings about the city. The decision was taken that such a sporting partnership with 'liberators of the Fatherland' would be the perfect way to assimilate the capital with the new ruling elite.

With both clubs demanding the final spot in the top flight, the Spanish FA decided to hold a one-off play-off in November 1939 at a neutral venue to determine the league's 12th team. Athletic Aviación triumphed 3–1 in Valencia's Mestalla – which had been repaired following damage – to claim their place back among Spain's elite.

Earlier that month, the final Campeonato Regional Sur was played out and, rather predictably, it was won by Sevilla. Oddly, that season's tournament began in January and was played out across three months, whilst the conflict was still ongoing, indicating how Andalusia's early fall to the Nationalists provided the chance to return to normality swifter than the rest of war-torn Spain. *Los Rojiblancos* topped an eight-team group to seal their 18th, and final, Andalusian title. (There was previously an element of doubt over the club's 1932/33 title, with research recently revealing a tournament had taken place alongside the temporary Centro-Sur championship. This had pitted Andalusian clubs against those based in Madrid and Castilla-León, and was won in both its seasons by Madrid CF.) This brought a chapter of

Andalusian football to a close with its clubs now competing on an exclusively national basis.

The newly formed Athletic Aviación were managed by former legendary goalkeeper Ricardo Zamora, who had proved the subject of much controversy during the conflict. Playing for Madrid CF when fighting broke out, he became a propaganda tool for Nationalists during the Civil War. Newspaper *ABC*, which leant their support to Franco's troops, falsely reported that Zamora had been shot dead by Republicans. He would later be arrested and imprisoned by Republican militia before being freed. He escaped to France to take up a player-manager role with Nice – the link being his former Barça and Madrid team-mate Josep Samitier – before returning to Madrid in 1938. To end any doubt over his political leanings, he took part in a benefit match for Nationalist soldiers, featuring for a Spain select side against Real Sociedad.

As fate would have it not only would Athletic Madrid's 1936 relegation be overturned but they enjoyed revenge over Sevilla by pipping them by a solitary point in that season's title race. Damage to their Metropolitano home meant they were forced to temporarily play at their old Vallecas base and then Madrid's Estadio Chamartín, but ironically it was their home form – 10 wins from 11, with Betis being the only team to earn a draw – propelling their league success.

The Civil War had undoubtedly changed the football landscape in Spain with Barcelona and Athletic Club Bilbao the two major institutions to be hit hard, while emerging clubs Oviedo and Betis also saw their mid-1930s progress majorly derailed. Athletic Aviación and Sevilla – both of whom had spent more time in the Segunda in the league's first seven seasons – were vying to fill the gap. The Madrid-based side won back-to-back league titles immediately after the Civil War and claimed a top-three spot in ten of the subsequent twelve campaigns. Sevilla too cemented themselves as prime title candidates, itching to equal the title won by their fierce city rivals, whilst also continuing their ascendancy in cup competitions.

A fundamental reason for the club's continued growth was the foresight of president Ramón Sánchez-Pizjuán. It is undeniable that the club benefited from events which had unfolded during the Civil War. Their Nervión stadium became the Nationalist headquarters during the conflict and whilst the stadium of rivals Betis was bombed, the Nervión became a hub of importance. In April 1938, Sánchez-Pizjuán struck a deal to not only buy the land on which the previously rented stadium stood, but also the 42,000 square metres which surrounded it. Whilst this set the president back a reported 429,000 pesetas, the area's subsequent evolution into a swanky district open to business over the following decades saw the club make a notable profit.

"There is no evidence that this was underhand, but to pull off such a purchase at the height of the Civil War was unusual," noted Chris Clements, who runs the English-language website on Spanish football stadiums, Estadios de España. "Sevilla's directors either had links to or were sympathisers of the Nationalist Party. It was not unusual for people that had money to see the Republic as a threat to their status."

Sevilla's intertwined fate with Athletic Aviación had begun ahead of the league campaign, with the nation's football authorities staging the Copa del Generalísimo the previous summer. Commencing just one month after the end of the Civil War, only 14 clubs competed in the tournament with Athletic Club Bilbao, Barcelona and holders Madrid CF among the absentees. Sevilla eliminated Aviación Nacional (in the final outing ahead of their merger with Athletic Madrid) who had themselves knocked out Betis in the previous round.

A semi-final victory over Alavés, which included a remarkable 6–5 first-leg victory in Seville, saw Pepe Brand's Sevilla advance through to the final. The famed forward had ended his playing career six years earlier and would secure his first piece of managerial silverware on 25 June 1939. Sevilla faced Galician club Racing de Ferrol in the final, the hometown club of the Generalísimo himself. The final took place in Barcelona's Montjuic stadium, partly as many other stadia had been left unplayable due to damage and partly for the regime's propaganda purposes. Throughout Franco's reign, a key strategy was to include – or to be seen to include – areas which diametrically opposed his ideas, as a signal that his rule would include those of all backgrounds.

Sevilla's forward line became famed as *La Delantera Stuka,* after the Luftwaffe's bomber plane which had first appeared in the Spanish Civil War to assist Franco's forces – despite later suggestions that such a reference may have been in some way linked to the regime at the time, there is no evidence that this was the case and in all likelihood was simply a contemporary reference for destruction. What is clear is that the potent attack was a worthy successor to the Sevillista School – headed by Kinké, Spencer and Brand – who had become so feared 15 years prior.

Sevilla's *Los Stukas* were López, Torrontegui, Campanal, Raimundo, Berrocal and Pepillo with records indicating that across four seasons they netted 216 goals between them. Six of them arrived in the 1939 Copa del Generalísimo showpiece as the Andalusians thrashed Ferrol. Campanal was the hat-trick hero for Brand's side with Raimundo grabbing two and Torrontegui the other. The trophy was handed over by General Moscardó, a high-ranking Franco officer propelled into the role of Sports Minister (see Chapter 4).

As the history section on Sevilla's club website recalls, the players were informed by Sánchez-Pizjuán that they would each be awarded a 500-peseta bonus for their success, while they dined in Barcelona's Hotel Ritz with General Moscardó, also invited by the club president. Sánchez-Pizjuán was arguably the most influential figure in Sevilla's history with fans lauding his role in guiding the club into Spanish football's elite. However, due to the club's successes coinciding with Civil War victory, doubts have emerged over the club's motivations and its president's liberal credentials.

Historian Agustín Rodríguez has since recalled: "Ramón Sánchez-Pizjuan did a great job when Civil War broke out in Spain. Apart from preserving the entire squad to prevent them from going to the front line, with the help of Antonio Sánchez Ramos and coach Pepe Brand they assembled a large squad of players. This included the most important attack in the history of Sevilla, the *Stuka* with López, Pepillo, Campanal, Torrontegui, Raimundo and Berrocal."

In May 1939, a month after hostilities had ended, *El Correo de Andalucía* ran the following piece outlining those war casualties associated with the club: "Sevilla FC, so deeply rooted in Sevillian life, has had its share of the fallen, its dead, for the cause of Spain. There were 18 casualties, of which seven were players, either old or contemporary. They have shown their contribution to the nation and the heroism of the club.

"Here are the names of the boys: Manuel Del Camino Parladé, Alfonso Tristán López, José Del Camino Parladé, Luis González de la Vega, Proyecto Ros Albert, Manuel Iglesias García, Rafael Gallardo Díaz, Ernesto Guzmán Revuelto, Alfredo Moreno Suárez, Pedro Santos Monge, Manuel Romero Encinas, Miguel Alfaro Pérez, Isidro López Martínez, Francisco Fernández Palacios y Velasco, Enrique López López, José Pérez Falcón, Pedro Llorca y Llorca, José María Osborne y Vázquez."

That summer, a friendly match was arranged by Sevilla which pitted a select team of players from the city against that of their Lisbon counterparts. *ABC* wrote of the decision: "The Sevilla FC board of directors were in unanimous agreement to arrange a fixture to pay homage to the Spanish troops." Portugal's prime minister at the time was far-right authoritarian, António de Oliveira Salazar, while contemporary reports referred to "our Portuguese brothers".

Of the Seville team that started the match, ten were from Sevilla (Bueno, Joaquín, Villalonga, Torróntegui, Segura, López, Pepillo, Campanal, Raimundo and Berrocal) alongside Aviación Nacional's Germán. Pepe Brand was the manager of the side. *El Correo de Andalucía* described how the Andalusian team would present "a beautiful pennant" to their opponents, emblazoned with "The Year of Victory" and "with the Falangist flag on the back".

There is enough evidence to suggest that Ramón Sánchez-Pizjuan was comfortable in aligning himself and his club with high-ranking figures in the Spanish regime, but this is a far cry from believing he was a Falangist himself. Before and after the national conflict his main skill was acting diplomatically, forging allegiances with those in high places and winning popular support. It is important too to recognise the context of contemporary Spain, and that by 'adhering to the cause', the president was protecting his club and the players.

"Do not believe the talk about Betis being the 'people's team' or Sevilla being a club aligned to the fascists, it was not like that at all," a Seville-based journalist who wished to remain anonymous told me, when asked about how the Civil War had impacted the clubs. "Both clubs had a lot of people on the Nationalist side and both had many on the Republican side too. It's true Sevilla had many middle-class supporters, good people, who were punished by execution over their beliefs, as did Betis. But they both attracted a great deal of fascists in their ranks. Take Francisco Bohórquez Vecina; he was a high-ranking commander of Queipo de Llano who signed numerous execution orders. In 1936, he was president of the Tertulia Bética." But it was true Betis suffered the most? "Yes, of course," added the reporter, "but that was mainly due to bad internal organisation. Many of their stars had left by 1936 and there was no succession planning."

As with their city rivals and many clubs across Spain, both clubs had employees who fell on both sides of the Civil War divide. Such media reports glorifying those who had 'sacrificed their lives' for their nation were written in an environment in which such commemorations were common. Republican-leaning media outlets swiftly became extinct and the war casualties on their side became a statistic, whereas the Nationalist deaths were personalised as martyrs.

One such individual whose death was not widely reported was that of José Manuel Puelles de los Santos, who holds a special place in the history of Spanish football. He was the first club doctor within the sport when he was hired by Sevilla and worked as a doctor of the Press Association. A man of many talents, Puelles de los Santos also wrote poetry, newspaper columns and gave lectures in university, before joining political grouping Partido Republicano Radical. He rose up the ranks to become deputy mayor in Seville by 1933. As with so many of his political persuasion at the time, he was to meet an untimely end after the military coup of Queipo de Llano (see Chapter 3) within Seville. In July 1936, Puelles de los Santos was offered the opportunity to leave Spain by plane but opted to stay, believing he had nothing to fear. A day later he was arrested by the military and two weeks later he was executed, even though his death was not recorded until September 1937.

Aged just 42, Puelles de los Santos was an individual who played a significant part in daily life in Seville, working in hospitals, universities, newspapers and the city's football club. His work exemplifies the profound change which the Civil War brought across Spain, signifying the loss of talent and contribution to society. It is important to remember his story, and those of thousands of others, whilst acknowledging the loss and hurt inflicted upon vast swathes of Sevillian society.

Back on the football pitch, the 1939 Copa victory and subsequent runners-up spot was just the start for a period of Sevilla successes as city rivals Betis entered a period of notable decline.

Chapter 15

A Tale of Two Cities

THE two decades that followed saw the widest gap open up between both Seville clubs in their existence. Sevilla successfully established themselves as one of the nation's leading sides with 15 top-six finishes in the first 18 campaigns following the Civil War, while Betis went into freefall. There were hopes that the club's 1940 relegation would prove to be a blip and within two seasons they were back up after winning the Segunda, with the 'Real' patronage returning to their title. This season merely masked the long-term decline of the club as they finished bottom of an expanded 14-team top flight in 1943.

By this stage, *Los Verdiblancos* had been overtaken as Andalusia's second club by Granada, who spent four years in the top flight between 1941 and 1945. It would take Betis 15 years to return to the Primera and their situation hit rock bottom on 13 April 1947. The stage was Racing de Santander's El Sardinero home, which had 12 years prior seen Betis's greatest triumph as they lifted the Primera title with a 5–0 victory. In a cruel twist of fate, the Cantabrian venue also saw the club's lowest moment as a 4–1 defeat condemned them to relegation to the Tercera – the name for Spain's third tier at the time (it is now known as the fourth tier, with Segunda B being used to reference the third level from 1977 onwards).

At a time when the immediate future of football clubs across Spain was called into question by financial difficulties and when disappearing to the third level – which also meant the end of professional football – often ensured lengthy spells in the wilderness, it was hard to envisage a reverse for the club. It never rains but it pours, in this instance quite literally. A year after they fell to the Tercera, heavy rainfall saw the Tamarguillo – a subsidiary of the Guadalquivir river – break its banks and flood the Estadio de Heliópolis. As *ABC* later recalled, the floods "would have made Noah pale" and caused havoc in the barrios of Tiro de Línea, La Corza and Heliópolis. Betis were sunk both in terms of results and circumstances outside their control. Miraculously, only one match was forced to be postponed but it further damaged the economic situation of the club.

This was a test for Betis and it is no exaggeration to note that many other clubs of lesser resolve would have crumbled under such adversity. This coincided with the cancellation of a tram service linking the stadium to the city centre and Triana district, hitting hard the legions of fans and giving birth to the motto 'Viva el Betis manqué pierda!' (see Chapter 10).

What made things worse for Betis fans was the prolonged successes and stabilisation of their city rivals. The woes of *Los Verdiblancos* led to the darkest days in their history while, in contrast, Sevilla enjoyed their most successful spell of the 20th century. Led by their devastating *Los Stukas* forward line, Sevilla emerged as Spanish title candidates in consecutive years. Following their near miss in 1940, the club led the way at the halfway stage of the following campaign before a mid-season slump saw them finish fifth. Their strength was in their famed attack and they remarkably managed a club record 25 goals in three consecutive games: defeating Barcelona 11–1, Real Oviedo 4–0 and Valencia 10–3, while a 5–4 triumph over Real Madrid soon followed. They ended their 1940/41 campaign with 70 goals in their 22 outings – almost a goal per game better than runners-up Atlético Bilbao, who had recently been forced to change their name to Castillian Spanish by the regime.

Two significant blows, of different severity, failed to derail the prolific Sevilla's ascendancy. Firstly, Ramón Sánchez-Pizjuán was to step down from his position as club president after accepting the vice-president role at the Spanish FA. He left the club in a strong financial position and with the platform for continued success, while he believed his new-found position in Madrid could continue to influence the club's fortunes.

Spanish football continued to be shaped by Franco's regime with the newly founded National Sports Delegation, chaired by General Moscardó, hand-picking club presidents and representatives on federations at both a regional and national level. The state was intent on forming ideological coherence throughout its clubs while individuals who did not fall in line were purged.

Antonio Sánchez Ramos was initially appointed as Sánchez-Pizjuán's replacement but within a year he was replaced by Jerónimo Domínguez y Pérez de Vargas – the Marqués de Contadero. Oddly,

22 years earlier he had been appointed president at Betis and thus became the first man to hold the position within both clubs. Perhaps Pérez de Vargas was more loyal to power than any one concept, as he would later serve as the city's mayor between 1952 and 1959, having built his initial reputation as a Franco loyalist during the Civil War. As previously analysed, the relationship between lofty positions within football clubs and political power was intertwined.

In the dugout for Sevilla, Pepe Brand was initially replaced by coach Victoriano de Santos during the 1941/42 campaign, but tragedy again was not far away. De Santos had starred as a midfielder for Athletic Madrid, Barcelona and Valencia before finishing his playing career at Granada, a year before his step into management. However, within months of his first coaching role he fell ill, and Sevilla were forced into recalling Brand to see out the season. The following February, de Santos passed away, aged 43.

Pérez de Vargas would sanction strong financial investment in Sevilla's playing staff as they continued to pursue national glory. A year before his arrival Spanish internationals Andrés Mateo, a left-half, and midfielder Pedro Alconero, who would go on to become club captain, arrived. Alconcero cost a not inconsiderable 60,000 pesetas but would turn out to represent excellent value, playing 272 top-flight matches for the club across 11 seasons – a club record at the time of his retirement – and later becoming a youth team coach.

However, it was the investment from Pérez de Vargas which truly elevated Sevilla into a position of greatness. His first move was to appoint Patrick O'Connell, who had guided Real Betis back to the top flight the previous season. It was the Irishman's second stint at *Los Verdiblancos*, to whom he would return for the ill-fated 1946/47 campaign, which marked their relegation to the third tier.

Betis fan and historian Alfonso del Castillo wrote: "Sevilla fans are very suspicious of the coach from the start due to his background with Betis. He was even accused of continuing to frequent Betis meetings while managing Sevilla."

Having landed the city's only Primera title eight years earlier (along with two Segunda titles and a Copa runners-up medal), and with a highly talented Sevilla squad at his disposal, his task was simple: win the league.

It would not be possible to label O'Connell's Sevilla as an underperforming side – in his first season they finished second, behind only Atlético Bilbao, before ranking third the following campaign. However, such doubts over the Dubliner's loyalties within the city may have made his departure inevitable when results on the pitch did not match expectations. In O'Connell's third and final season in Nervión, Sevilla finished tenth and the Irishman was relieved of his duties.

The 1946/47 return to the green-and-white half of the city was his final spell in Seville before he returned to Racing de Santander, also by this stage in the third tier, for two seasons as his managerial career in Spain came full circle. On 5 September 1954, five years before O'Connell's death in London, Real Betis hosted an Andalusia Select side in Heliópolis as an honorary match for the man who had achieved so much success in the city and earned the adored nickname Don Patricio.

A report from *ABC* two days later detailed events:

"With his famed hat in hand, akin to a well-known bullfighter, Patricio O'Connell stormed onto the green pitch at Heliópolis. Alongside him were the captains and current managers of both teams. He shook hands with all players and retired to the presidential box, waving his hat to large cheers from the crowd. The tributes came from both Betis and Sevilla, who provided not only players but a donation of 1,000 pesetas to the Irish coach."

* * * * *

Sevilla had not won a title by the time of Patrick O'Connell's departure in 1945, but despite the aberration of his final season, this was an upwardly mobile club who were assembling a squad for which Spain's ultimate crown was inevitable. Two years before O'Connell left the club, *Los Rojiblancos* signed a fresh-faced 20-year-old striker who many fans believe is the finest player to ever wear their shirt.

"It is not easy or fair to compare players of different eras," prominent *Estadio Deportivo* journalist Carlos Pérez told me, when posed this question. "But those who saw him play live and watched generations of Sevilla would argue he was [the best]. He did something too that was almost unimaginable today: he rejected approaches from Barcelona and Real Madrid. He always stayed loyal to the club. He won a league title, a Copa trophy and was Sevilla's only *Pichichi* [the annual award for the top scorer in the top flight]. It is no surprise the club made him their first *Dorsal de Leyenda* [club legend]."

O'Connell coined his nickname *El Niño de Oro*, Golden Boy, when Juan Arza joined Sevilla in the summer of 1943 from rivals Málaga. The Costa del Sol club had been relegated to the third tier that year and were forced into selling. Born in Estella, south-west of Pamplona in Navarra, Arza had begun his career at Alavés before moving to Andalusia. He never lost his love of bullfighting, so important in his hometown, and regularly showed the grace and elegance on the football pitch that would have seen him equally at home in a range of other activities.

Sevilla fought off interest from several rivals, including Real Madrid, to land the sought-after striker. His sister Jesusa already lived in the city while the club decided to break their transfer record to complete his signing for 90,000 pesetas, along with arranging two friendly matches against Málaga. Doubts may have been cast that this youngster could break into the feared *Los Stukas* front-line, but such reservations were blown away by a debut hat-trick against Sabadell.

Arza's record speaks for itself. In 349 league games across 16 seasons he scored 182 goals, along with 24 in the Copa and five in European competition. However, there was criticism that he only won two caps for the Spanish national team, with his exclusion from further squads something of a mystery that was a source of controversy at the time. Speaking affectionately of 'Juanito', Sevilla club media recalls: "His limited participation with the national team simply did not make sense." As Pérez alluded to, Arza was also one of only two Seville-based players – the other being Betis striker Poli Rincón in 1983 – to win the *Trofeo Pichichi*, awarded to the top league scorer of that year. With 28 strikes in 29 appearances during that campaign, Arza disrupted a four-year spell which was being dominated by Real Madrid's majestic Alfredo Di Stéfano.

While Arza's arrival alone could not quite nudge Sevilla toward their coveted league crown, the incorporation of fellow striker Juan Araujo, two years his elder, into the side in 1945 was another massive moment. It was no surprise that his first season in Sevilla's first-team squad brought about their ultimate glory – the Primera title. Araujo had come through the youth ranks at the club before a two-year loan spell at nearby Xerez to gain first-team experience. Across 11 seasons with Sevilla he found the net 158 times, including the crucial goal in Barcelona which clinched the title in his first season, and he is third on the list of the club's highest-ever scorers. He trails only former strike partner Arza (207) and Guillermo Campanal (218), the latter of whom was, during the title campaign, in his final season before retirement and was used primarily from the bench.

* * * * *

Despite all the star arrivals at Sevilla in the early 1940s there was to be one loaded with more controversy within the city: Francisco Antúnez, who took the unprecedented step of swapping the green half of Seville for its red side. Tensions were understandably still high across Spain with suspicion and misgivings present across those of all colours and political persuasions. As cited by Phil Ball in *Morbo*, Radio Moscow carried the transfer news as follows: "Sevilla, the capitalist team of the city, have trampled upon their noble proletarian neighbours Betis, abusing the power handed to them by the fascist Francoist regime."

Such allegations are dubious at best. While several individuals across both clubs undoubtedly cosied up to the regime, this was in a personal capacity. Nuance and contradictions are constant throughout the Seville derby. Sure, Sevilla were founded by 'bourgeoise' businessmen and for the majority of their existence enjoyed a stronger financial footing, while Betis were the team founded by military members. At varying points in their history, they were flush with money and friends in high places, just like their city rivals. In a historical context, the Betis support appears to have generally been derived from leftish areas within the city, most notably Triana, while Sevilla's fanbase was a better reflection of the well-to-do *señorito* culture. All of this has become blurred by time and social changes but perhaps in the 1940s, there was a strand of truth behind Radio Moscow's claims. But the team of the fascist regime?

There is plenty that does not add up, with both clubs being home to high-ranking and influential individuals on both sides of the political divide. Manuel Blasco Garzón, the Sevilla president between 1923 and 1925, was a member of the Radical Republican Party and after his participation in the Civil War fled to Argentina, where he wrote his book *Evocaciones Andaluzas*. Across town at Betis was José Ignacio Mantecón, president between 1931 and 1933 as they won promotion to the top flight. Mantecón too fled after the Republican defeat, moving to Mexico and helping with the subsequent refugee crisis before joining the Spanish Communist Party. On the flipside, staunch Falangists Ramón de Carranza (Sevilla) and Eduardo Benjumena (Betis) have occupied the same posts at the clubs. In any case, nobody could have ascended into a true position of power at clubs during this period without the approval of the regime.

The one club during this period whose success can notably be linked to a helping hand from the authorities are Atlético Aviación (see Chapter 14). Following on from the Allied victory in the Second World War, their name reverted to Atlético de Madrid as the Spanish regime began an attempted shift in its perception to the outside world, ending official ties between the military and sporting outfits.

Francisco Antúnez – who had played in the youth teams of both Seville clubs – was a highly sought-after player and with the struggles of Betis outside the top flight, a move away had appeared inevitable. A report in *Marca* in June 1945 spoke of Real Madrid's interest in his signature while the first reports of Sevilla's interest emerged three months later, as detailed by the Madrid-based daily and local Seville media. Both clubs' advances were rejected by Betis, who saw Antúnez as an invaluable asset.

The controversy began four months later, when on 24 January Sevilla renewed their interest and lodged a bid, said to be 80,000 pesetas, which was accepted by Betis. However, it swiftly emerged that the offer was accepted on behalf of the club by vice-president Carlos Hernández Nalda and treasurer Alfonso de la Torre Quesada with the rest of the board, led by Eduardo Benjumea, in disagreement. Both Hernández Nalda and Quesada resigned, claiming they had been given tacit approval by the president and arguing that in any case, Betis were in urgent need of funds.

By 26 January, the transfer had been confirmed by the press while the following day Antúnez debuted for Sevilla in a 1–1 draw at Real Madrid, on the same day Betis beat Gimnàstic 6–1 in Seville in the Segunda. The result was almost an afterthought for the home fans, who were outraged that their star player had been sold to their rivals and that those responsible did not appear to signal their intentions to others. So enraged were the *Béticos* that they raised 60,000 pesetas to reverse the deal, according to historian Alfonso del Castillo. Betis technical secretary Manuel Simó had reportedly travelled to Córdoba train station on the day of the games to stop the player travelling with his new team-mates to Madrid, after Antúnez had not reported to Betis training, but was left stumped by Antúnez unexpectedly boarding at the San Jerónimo stop.

Marca then ran a headline detailing the mess as the "Spanish FA declined all responsibility" to deal with the issue. The green light had instead been given to Sevilla by the Federación Regional Sur, with Betis fans pointing to former Sevilla secretary Antonio Calderón Hernández wielding the decision-making power. Two days on from Antúnez debuting with Sevilla, Betis lodged a complaint that the signatures of the two directors – who had both now left their roles – were not legitimate as they had not received the president's signature nor consulted with the board of directors. The secretary of the Spanish FA then travelled to Seville to speak with both clubs but with no resolution found, the case was passed to the top of the federation – led by president Javier Barroso and his number two, Ramón Sánchez-Pizjuán.

A decision was not reached until 14 February, after several lengthy meetings. The verdict was that Antúnez was now a Sevilla player but both clubs would be fined: Sevilla because they had fielded the player in three matches without passing all the relevant documentation and Betis for publicising their written complaint. Betis were infuriated by the outcome and decided to take their complaint to the Delegación Nacional de Deportes, the highest level for judicial-based sporting decisions. On 11 April, the committee decided to cancel the transfer but uphold the results of all games in the 1945/46 campaign which for Sevilla would prove hugely significant. The Spanish FA was criticised in the ruling for not adhering to its own regulatory guidelines for the transfer and its 'lack of rigour', leading to a series of resignations.

The transfer debacle had clearly strained relations between Betis and the Federación Regional Sur governing body, now headed by former Sevilla director Antonio Leal Castaño. *El Correo de Andalucía* reported how the club refused to take part in the annual Copa Primavera in protest and decided to instead arrange their own friendlies against Real Córdoba, Cacereño and Recreativo de Huelva, in which Antúnez played.

The summer of 1946 saw a renewed effort from Sevilla to sign the player, although newspaper *Sevilla* (not connected to the club) ran a headline saying Betis had "3,000 reasons not to sell", chief among them, the report stated, the "sporting and economic improvement of the club". But by August Betis were once again destabilised by president Eduardo Benjumea's resignation and the Federación Regional Sur appointed Alfonso de la Torre Quesada – the treasurer who had resigned from the club over the 'sale' of Antúnez – as his successor.

The outlet *Sevilla* immediately reported the likely chain of events which did, ultimately, occur: "It is said that the first important decision that Mr De la Torre will take as president of Real Betis Balompié will be the transfer of the player Antúnez, the great midfielder, to Sevilla FC, in whose ranks he contributed to the success of last season. It should be remembered that Mr De la Torre was the one who negotiated last season the transfer of the aforementioned player to the current Primera champion, later being disallowed by the Board of Directors that Mr Benjumea presided over."

On 28 August, the media outlet reported that Betis had called an emergency meeting at which it was unanimously agreed not to recognise de la Torre (who was not the beneficiary of "favourable atmosphere") as club president and that they would be willing to take the extreme step of "dissolving the club" should "the series of obstacles being imposed upon the club be continued". By 4 September, de la Torre was gone while *Marca* and *ABC* both reported "a substantial rise" in the number of *socios* of the club during this period, hinting that his removal had garnered popular support among the fanbase along with the directors.

The most protracted transfer within the city of Seville was finally formalised on 14 September 1946 for a fee of 115,000 pesetas, confirmed the Federación Regional Sur. The deal was to include Sevilla's backup goalkeeper Francisco Carmona Reina, known as 'Paquillo', moving the other way alongside two friendlies between the clubs – but neither of these aspects of the deal came about.

Francisco Antúnez remained at *Los Rojiblancos* until 1952 and kept a low media profile over the years that followed, but in 1973 he spoke to *Marca* about the saga: "Here [in Seville], there is a belief that you need to either be a fan of Sevilla or Betis, and in either case, want the death and struggles for your rivals," he said. "I do not conform to that and I will never accept that view. I have always been a professional in how I have conducted myself and you do not need to manifest your support for one or the other. For the record, it was Betis who offered me the most money at the time. I swear that the reason I changed club was to prosper in a sporting sense, and not because I was guided by economic interest."

Antúnez died on 16 August 1994 and, curiously, Betis played Sevilla in a pre-season Trofeo Ciudad de Sevilla encounter the same day. However, such was the strength of animosity still resonating from his transfer five decades on, Betis board member Manuel Ruiz de Lopera moved to block a minute's silence being held in his honour.

* * * * *

Ramón Encinas had returned to the Sevilla dugout in the summer of 1945 to replace Patrick O'Connell and despite the tenth-place finish of the previous campaign, his side was tipped to challenge for honours. Encinas had occupied the position in the three seasons preceding Civil War and had engineered the club's promotion and subsequent Copa title. The previous campaign he had missed out on the league title with Real Madrid by a solitary point to Barcelona.

One year on from narrowly missing out on glory with Madrid, Encinas had his shot at revenge over Barça. Sevilla travelled to the Catalan club's Campo de Les Corts stadium on the final matchday of the campaign, leading the hosts by one point – the slender margin which had denied Encinas last time out. They knew a draw would clinch the club's first-ever league title but faced their toughest fixture of the campaign. Three of Sevilla's four defeats that year had come away from Nervión while the other was a 3–2 home reverse against Barcelona.

The title challenge had once more been propelled by *Los Stukas* with Sevilla averaging over two goals per game throughout the campaign. It had been an open league season, with six of the 14 participants at one point leading the way while Atlético Bilbao were on top with two games to go but defeat to relegation-threatened Alcoyano in their penultimate match blew their chances. The Sevilla team for the match in Catalonia was as follows: Busto, Joaquín, Villalonga, Alconero, Antúnez, Eguiluz, López, Arza, Araujo, Herrera, Campos.

The reported 500 Sevilla fans were sent into raptures in the seventh minute when Juan 'Pato' Araujo headed home López's cross to give the visitors the lead. The onslaught from the hosts, needing two goals without conceding, was relentless. Bravo levelled the scores three minutes after the hour mark to once more put the tie back in the balance but, despite persistent pressure, Sevilla defended resolutely and held on for their required point to win their first-ever Primera title.

Celebrations were understandably extravagant with the team bus making stops at several cities en route back to Seville. They were welcomed in Córdoba with a crate of champagne from the local team while in Alcalá de Guadaíra, the hometown of defender Joaquín, the mayor declared a public holiday due to the partying. As Sevilla FC's history section recalls, the red and white colours of the team decorated "all the balconies from Puerta de Jerez to Plaza Nueva" in the city upon their return with Seville's mayor awarding each player a gold watch with the city's coat of arms engraved on it. The trophy was paraded in front of the club's adoring fans in a friendly match at Campo de Nervión the following week, in which the champions defeated their opponents from Granada 4–0. Eleven years on from Betis bringing the trophy to Seville for the first time, Sevilla had equalled their achievement.

* * * * *

Ramón Sánchez-Pizjuán was re-elected Sevilla president in May 1948, after the regime had relaxed its level of influence in the appointment of club officials. Comprehensively defeating his predecessor Antonio Sánchez Ramos on the ballot paper, Sánchez Pizjuán's task was simple: to continue Sevilla's success on the national stage. He rejoined during a lull in league performances; following the 1946 triumph the club finished sixth, fifth, eighth and tenth in the Primera with the side which had brought them so much success in the first half of the 1940s beginning to age.

However, the magic touch of Sánchez Pizjuán became evident within six weeks of his return with the club triumphing in the 1948 Copa del Generalísimo. The Andalusian club had eliminated Basque duo Atlético Bilbao and Real Sociedad on their way to the showpiece in Madrid, which pitted them against a strong Celta de Vigo side – in their first-ever Copa final after finishing a club-record fourth in the league that season.

Held at the Estadio Chamartín in Madrid – the scene of Sevilla's first Copa triumph 13 years earlier – the final pitted Patricio Caicedo's Sevilla against a Galician side now coached by legendary goalkeeper Ricardo Zamora. Of the reported 60,000 in attendance, 5,000 had travelled from Seville while 3,000 had made the rather more arduous trip from Vigo, in the north-west. The vast majority of the crowd were Madrid-based natives, who were said to have favoured Celta. Partly this may be explained by their underdog status, the fact Zamora was their manager or that their side contained Spanish internationals Miguel Muñoz and Pahiño, who would both sign for Real Madrid that summer.

Muñoz gave Celta a sixth-minute lead but the evergreen Juan Arza restored parity 13 minutes later. However, the star of the game was undoubtedly Mariano Uceda. The forward had arrived from Real Zaragoza the previous year and had already made a significant impact in that season's Copa run, netting five goals in an 8–1 quarter-final victory over CD Castellón. His first goal, on the hour mark, was the most important not only in separating the sides but as it also injured Celta goalkeeper Francisco Simón with outfield player Gabriel Alonso forced to replace him. Mariano netted two more for *Los Rojiblancos* as Pahiño was dismissed for Celta, whose numbers were depleted further by injuries to Yayo and Aretio.

As was tradition following recent successes, Sevilla's return to the Andalusian capital was delayed by a series of stops along the way to gain the adoration of fans and be honoured at various town halls.

Seville's mayor Bermúdez Barrera laid on a lavish reception at the city hall with each player and boss Patricio Caicedo rewarded with a specially engraved watch and cigarette case. The following day, local press reported the squad as celebrating their success at the Jesús del Gran Poder hospital – in the centre of the city – as they spent time with the children there.

The Copa victory was Sevilla's third such title, all achieved under the presidency of Ramón Sánchez-Pizjuán, continuing their remarkable level of success. The club has successfully adapted their success in regional Andalusian competitions – lifting 18 of a possible 21 titles – to a national level, lifting four major titles in a 13-year spell. They would go on to reach a further two finals, in 1955 and 1962, but lost on both occasions in Real Madrid's newly constructed Santiago Bernabéu stadium, going down to Atlético Bilbao and Real Madrid respectively. Nobody could have predicted in 1948 that it would take another 29 years for a Seville club to lift the trophy and that it would be 59 seasons before Sevilla themselves would regain the title.

Chapter 16

The Rivalry Returns

THE greatest rivalries in football are within cities, whether it be Buenos Aires, Glasgow, Rome, Milan or Madrid. Inter-city rivalries may be an intriguing fight for regional power, for the pride of their birthplace and a sense of local identity but their inner-city equivalents hold all that and more. These are the games which divide families, stadiums are within walking distance and fans are surrounded by the divisions; there is no motorway separating them.

Between 1940 and 1958, only two Seville derbies were held as Betis hit their nadir with just one season in the Primera. As if to prove the demonstrable gap in quality between the two teams in that period, Sevilla comfortably won both games by an aggregate score of 10–2. Few other rivalries could endure such a lengthy dormant period without losing an edge, or at least being fundamentally diluted in the eyes of a generation. On the contrary, this spell of inactivity was the foundation for the derby to be elevated on to another level as it was decisive in forming the image and spirit of both clubs.

For Sevilla, they had become a multiple Copa winner, a Primera champion and regular contenders for the top prizes. They had built on their early Campeonato Regional Sur dominance to become southern Spain's Real Madrid, Barcelona or Athletic Club. This was the club with the stars, with the trophies and with a mentality of winning. In normal circumstances, this would lead to a clear power structure, with them pulling away from their rivals off the pitch, as well as on it.

Had Betis transformed into a middling club between the top two divisions without ever garnering any genuine successes nor any total catastrophes, they would likely not have grown into the social institution they did throughout the post-Civil War era. This was a club who swiftly fell from their position as champions, then fell from the top flight before falling from the Segunda. As if to clarify their on-field underperformance, they spent seven seasons in the third tier. As they celebrated their Golden Jubilee in 1958, they had spent more of their existence in the Tercera than the Primera. They were the underdog and their fans were so accustomed to losing that their spirit became hardened and unbreakable. "Betis was a thousand times speared, but never died," as honorary club member and cartoonist Andrés Martínez de León (see Chapter 10) wrote.

Six decades on, Mateo González, the head of sports at *ABC de Sevilla*, agreed with Martínez de León's sentiments: "This period is at the core of Betis's history. The club's scars are like titles. People remember the club travelling to small villages close to Seville to play league games, which brought them closer to fans. There are also stories of how the team used raffles to get money to pay for the players' food and even their clothes. That's why Betis saw a huge expansion in support within the lower classes, linked with popular folk, and why they now seem to be closer to the people."

The 'Green March' became integrated into Spanish terminology referencing their growing following on matchdays. The worse their team's results became, the more fans turned up. A report in 1954 in *ABC* entitled 'The invasion of Córdoba by Betis fans', said that among the sizable number of travelling fans for a third division fixture were "a group of true Betis enthusiasts who undertook the journey by cycling." By way of contextualising this fandom, a round trip from Seville to Córdoba is just shy of 300km.

Writer and poet Joaquín Romero Murube – a member of the Generación del 27 group (see Chapter 12) – attempted to analyse the situation in his 1958 piece 'Why I am a Bético', published in *ABC* to help mark the golden jubilee celebrations. In the lengthy piece, Murube drew upon the themes of romanticism, tenacity and pride in his Sevillian heritage. "Even a lunatic like the one who writes this alludes to football without knowing a word of it," he wrote, in a nod to the logic-defying hold the sport casts over billions, before focusing on the reasoning behind his own devotion.

> "Betis achieved an unsinkable morale, unscathed by defeat. But instead of assuming that inexplicable resignation in response to so much adversity – unfortunately for us – we shrugged our shoulders instead of feeling elation in our hearts. After this catastrophe, Betis charged onward every matchday afternoon with ever greater enthusiasm searching to conquer glory."

By 1954 the worst of the misery was over as Betis, after several near misses, lifted the third division title and were promoted back into the second tier. They were led by manager Francisco Gómez who had, 19 years earlier, been a key team member of the Primera title victory. He had arrived as a midfielder from Athlétic de Madrid the previous summer, but the then boss Patrick O'Connell had converted him into a central defender – a position where he thrived.

His commitment to the cause was summed up by an anecdote of a match against Real Oviedo, when O'Connell had instructed him to man-mark the revered international striker Isidro Lángara. Midway through the first half, Lángara jogged to the sidelines during a break in play to take a drink of water. He almost choked on his drink when he noticed Gómez's proximity to him. "What are you doing here, kid?" quizzed Lángara. "The boss has told me to follow you everywhere," the Betis defender replied.

Betis lifting the Tercera was another cornerstone in the formation of their identity, as it ensured they became the first club to win the top three divisions in Spain. This record stood until 2000 when Deportivo de La Coruña won the top flight for the first time, but no other club has achieved this feat in Spain and it is doubtful any ever will. Perhaps more remarkably, Gómez was involved in all three achievements – winning titles as a player in 1935 and 1942 before his role from the dugout in 1954. Portu, a Betis player who remained at the club throughout their rise from the third tier back to the top flight, said of his boss: "It was always very funny to see that man pick up all the cigars, before placing them in a small basket that he was carrying in his hand." Gómez subsequently earned the nickname among his players *El de los puros* (the one with the cigars).

The Tercera campaign – at this point regionalised into six groupings – was a gruelling 36 games but Betis romped to promotion with 25 victories and just four losses. Just as with their Primera title, their defensive organisation and discipline – perhaps no surprise with Gómez at the helm –was the key factor, as they conceded exactly half (28) the number of goals runners-up San Fernando had let in.

A triumphant dinner gala was held at Hotel La Rábida on Calle Castelar with the squad assembling to celebrate the end of their hiatus from professional football. One of those players present was Luis del Sol, a 19-year-old who had broken into the team that season and displayed outrageous ability, standing out as a star player. Having been born on 6 April 1935, 22 days before Betis lifted their Primera title, perhaps del Sol was always destined for greatness. His family were from Soria, in the Castile and León region, but relocated to Seville two months after Luis was born as his father's work was moved to the Andalusian capital.

Del Sol first began playing football for his work team after joining his local aviation company aged 14, and was capable of playing against those twice his age. Betis signed him two years later and, still a teenager, he became a fixture in their starting line-up. He swiftly developed into the team's most valuable player with his all-energy, relentless style of play earning him the nickname 'Seven Lungs'. The Betis youth system would form a pattern of developing at least one star performer per generation and del Sol started this trend, becoming a symbol of the club over the course of his illustrious career.

Despite interest from more illustrious clubs he spent the first seven seasons of his career, five of which were outside the top flight, in Heliópolis. Del Sol was a complete midfielder, offering all the physical and technical attributes required for true greatness. Alongside his stamina, pace and strength, he was renowned for his fleetness of foot and passing accuracy. He was often cited throughout his career as offering strong leadership skills, showing the temperament and mentality of a champion, which explained his future roles as a captain and manager.

Renowned for chasing lost causes, turning over possession and launching attacks in transition phases, del Sol defined the rejuvenation of Betis on the pitch, reflecting the passion and intensity of its loyal fanbase. His first boss, Francisco Gómez, known for his no-nonsense approach, was influential in the early stages of his development. Del Sol later recalled, "In my first season, I twisted my ankle chasing the ball and was paralysed with the pain. It was agony. Then I noticed the coach looming over me, shouting at me to get up and return to the game. You could not say no in those situations."

Having been influential in steering Betis back to the top flight, del Sol joined Real Madrid in the summer of 1960 for a landmark 6.5 million pesetas. The deal at first was said to have deeply saddened him, having only discovered it when the wife of then Betis president Benito Villamarín expressed her best wishes for his new venture. He adapted to his new surroundings with ease, earning the nickname of 'The Postman' from Madrid legend Alfredo Di Stéfano, due to always delivering the perfect assists. Aged 37 and following stints at Juventus – where he spent eight seasons and is now commemorated on the Walk of Fame at the Juventus Stadium – and Roma, del Sol returned to Betis for the swansong of his playing career before retiring the following year.

He has occupied the positions of coach and technical secretary since retirement, while he is fondly remembered as one of the greatest players of his generation. *Los Verdiblancos* have honoured del Sol by renaming their training complex Ciudad Deportiva Luis del Sol while its 1,500-capacity stadium, in which reserve team Betis Deportivo Balompié play, is now Estadio Luis del Sol.

* * * * *

The 1950s had seen the restoration of Betis's ability to get results on the pitch and by the end of the decade the Seville derby would return to the Primera. The absence of their city neighbours had had no adverse impact on Sevilla, who recorded two runners-up spots in 1951 and 1957 respectively, each time being thwarted by Madrid. In 1951 they missed out by two points to Atlético de Madrid despite winning all but one of their 15 matches at their Campo de Nervión home, a run in which they kept nine clean sheets. Six years later their home form was even better, defeating each of their 15 league rivals in Seville but winning just two of the reverse games, which ultimately cost them a second title.

Between 1953 and 1957 *Los Rojiblancos* were coached by Helenio Herrera, the Argentine was the first non-European manager at the club. He had previously guided Atlético de Madrid to two league titles and would later lead Barcelona to multiple Primera trophies whilst building his ultimate legacy in Italy, with his 'Grande Inter' side winning seven trophies including two European Cups.

Under his stewardship, Sevilla never finished below fifth and continued to improve their league position, culminating in the runners-up spot in his final season – a placing which the club has failed to duplicate in six decades since. Renowned as a strict disciplinarian and visionary of the era, the official history section of Sevilla media describes Herrera as "eccentric and controversial" but his ability to guarantee results was never in doubt.

The 1956/57 campaign proved to be one of the most painful in the club's history, following the death of Ramón Sánchez-Pizjuán on 28 October 1956. The land purchase deal struck by the president 18 years earlier (see Chapter 14) had been critical in securing the club's finances over the years and the club were proposing to use their stockpile of money to construct a new state-of-the-art stadium in Nervión. *Los Rojiblancos* had specifically saved 50 million pesetas for the project, which would be designed by revered architect Manuel Muñoz Monasterio.

The development in many ways mirrored what Real Madrid had pulled off with their new Estadio Santiago Bernabéu opening in 1947 (named the Nuevo Chamartín until 1955). That project produced a state-of-the-art building capable of housing more than 75,000 fans and so impressed was Sánchez-Pizjuán by his counterpart's vision that he hoped to replicate such a ground in the heart of the land which he owned. Similarities between the stadiums upon opening were clear with the same architect behind each.

Sánchez-Pizjuán had been the visionary for the scheme and it was swiftly decided following his passing to dedicate the stadium in his honour. "He wanted to build a great stadium for his Sevilla," said future club president Ramón de Carranza in the aftermath of the news. "On his inert body, I promise that this stadium will be built. Ramón, go quietly to heaven, your wishes will be fulfilled."

Yet a string of misfortunes was to befall the club following his death. As Spanish football writer Chris Clements noted: "Progress was hampered by the quality of the subsoil. Over 800 concrete piles had to be sunk before construction of the main body of the stadium could commence, and it soon became obvious that their war chest would only cover a third of the costs."

The entire project had to be modified and the power void left by Sánchez-Pizjuán made the situation more precarious. The original plan had been to build a landmark 70,000-seater stadium but the total outlay of proceedings meant that this had to be downgraded by 17,000 as the corners of the stadium were left unfilled and the upper tiers incomplete. As with Betis two decades earlier, a desire for a brand-new stadium was intended to elevate the club to greatness but, mainly influenced by misfortune and bad timing, was to lead directly to a notable decline.

Few could have foreseen just how severe the deterioration in results would be. In September 1957 Sevilla had played their first game of European football, beating Portuguese champions Benfica 3–1 at Nervión in the European Champions Cup. Vicente Pascual Sebastián – better known as Pahuet – opened the scoring and despite Francisco Palmeiro equalising for the visitors, strikes from Antonio Iborra and 'Pepillo' (José García Castro) secured the victory. "That day was great," Pahuet, who passed away in 2018, later recalled in an interview with UEFA. "I'm not a handsome individual but the club directors were all coming up to me saying, 'Oh, Pahuet, you are just beautiful!'"

The following week Sevilla secured progression with a scoreless draw in the Portuguese capital. With the match played in the afternoon due to the absence of floodlights at the stadium (somewhat ironically named Estádio da Luz), visiting goalkeeper José María Busto was the star performer as Pahuet saw an effort ruled out for offside. The Andalusian club's run took them past Danish club AGF Aarhus in the last 16 with a 4–2 aggregate victory before a quarter-final exit to Real Madrid. The capital club had ousted them in the battle for the league title the previous year and were too strong this time round, with an inspired Alfredo Di Stéfano netting four goals in an 8–0 first leg rout. The second leg was almost void but early goals from Ismael Payá and Pahuet briefly threatened to dampen Madrid's procession before a double from Jesús María Pereda ensured it ended 2–2 on the night. *Los Blancos* would win the tournament, their third in succession in a dominant period in that competition, which saw them win the first five editions. For Sevilla, it would take another 60 years before they reached the same stage of the competition.

Thirty years earlier, Sevilla's Campo de Nervión had been inaugurated with a 2–1 defeat to Real Betis in a quirk of the fixture list. By 1958, Sevilla had their shot at revenge at the newly constructed Estadio Ramón Sánchez-Pizjuán, with the fixture list manipulated to ensure Betis – who were back in the top tier after a 16-year absence – were once more the visitors for the first competitive match on 21 September.

A fortnight prior, Sevilla had played out a 3–3 friendly draw against Andalusian neighbours Real Jaén to open the stadium. The goalscorers that day were indicative of the changing times in European football and the creeping modernisation. Austrian-Czechoslovakian Tibor Szalay, a summer signing from Austria Vienna, was the first Sevilla scorer in the stadium while Antonio Oviedo and Argentine José Carlos Diéguez were also on the scoresheet for the hosts. There was also a Portuguese and three Paraguayans in the Sevilla first-team squad that season, under the guidance of Hungarian boss Jenő Kalmár – who had joined from Austrian side FC Admira Wacker. Kalmár arrived in Spain following the Hungarian Revolution of 1956, with star players Ferenc Puskás, Sándor Kocsis and László Kubala also moving to the Iberian Peninsula.

The first competitive game at the Estadio Ramón Sánchez-Pizjuán, played out in front of a full 40,000 capacity, foreshadowed the waning of Sevilla's dominance both within the context of their own city and the national stage. Luis del Sol opened the scoring for the visitors in the second minute but an eight-minute spell before the break saw Tibor Szalay level from the penalty spot before José Carlos Diéguez gave the hosts the lead on the stroke of half-time. However, it was another of the Hungarian imports who stole the show in the second half: Janos Kuszmann. The 20-year-old levelled the scores six minutes after the break before Esteban Areta restored the lead midway through the half and Kuszmann then added a fourth.

Another footnote to this match was that it saw the Betis debut of Basque defender Eusebio Ríos, a summer signing from Indautxu, who would prove to be a star for the side over the next decade and gain international recognition. Ríos would later have a short-term stint in charge of *Los Verdiblancos* in 1988 while his son Roberto would spend five years at Betis, before joining Athletic Club Bilbao in 1997 for 2 billion pesetas, a then-record for a national player. Roberto, who was frequently linked to Manchester United during his career, was forced into retirement, aged 30, following a series of injuries. Upon hanging up his boots, he became long-term assistant to future Betis manager Pepe Mel.

FIRST FOOTBALL MATCH IN SPAIN.

[FROM A SEVILLE CORRESPONDENT.]

Some six weeks ago a few enthusiastic young residents of British origin met in one of the cafés for the purpose of considering a proposal that we should start an Athletic Association, the want of exercise being greatly felt by the majority of us, who are chiefly engaged in mercantile pursuits. After a deal of talk and a limited consumption of small beer, the "Club de 'Football' de Sevilla" was duly formed and officebearers elected. It was decided we should play Association rules, and so that no time might be lost we determined to have a practice game next (Sunday) morning. Accordingly next

Dundee Courier, *report of Spain's first football match between Sevilla and Recreativo de Huelva, 17 March 1890*

26.

FOOTBALL.

NOTES BY FORWARD.

It will be news to many that the game of football has a sound footing in Spain. It has been said (writes a correspondent of the Field) that wherever Englishmen are settled, they never rest content until they have introduced their national customs and games; and Englishmen in Spain are no exception. Football has for some years formed a part of the Christmas festivities at Seville, and the club, under the presidency of the genial vice-consul, Mr E. F. Johnston, is in a flourishing condition. On Saturday, December 27, the match with Huelva, which is now regarded as an annual event, came off on the racecourse, where an excellent ground has been obtained —thanks to the kindness of the authorities. Almost all the English residents were present, and a fair mustering of Spaniards, eager to be initiated into the mysteries of football, which, as the local papers described it, is played without sticks or baskets for protection. The company had no right to complain of the amusement afforded them, as a fast game resulted in a tie, neither side succeeding in scoring; and, indeed, the only words of adverse criticism were those of the Spanish ladies, and had reference to the legs and attitudes of the players rather than to their play. The backs on both sides played well, and to their fine defence the Huelva team owed their escape from disaster, whilst of the forwards Welton and White for Seville, and Birchall for Huelva were most conspicuous. To Geddes, of Seville, the doubtful compliment is paid that he deserved mention, as he was dangerous alike to friend and foe.

The Otago Witness *report on Sevilla v Recreativo, Christmas Day 1891*

Report from the first ever Sevilla derby, Real Betis v Sevilla, 15 February 1909, El Correo de Andalucia

Match poster for first match of Real Betis Balompie, following merger between Betis FC and Sevilla Balompie

Sevilla: Equipo del Real Betis Balompié que tomó parte en el partido

Sevilla: Equipo del Club Atletic, que jugó contra el Betis

Sevilla: Dos detalles interesantes del partido jugado el día 2.º entre el Real Betis y el Club Atletic
Fot. S. del Pando

21 November 1915: First ever official game for Real Betis. 2-2 against Athletic de Sevilla in the Campeonato de Andalucia. Carmelo Navarro was the club's first scorer

Sevilla players with the club's first trophy– the 1917 Campeonato Regional Sur title (Sevilla FC history department)

A vintage postcard featuring footballer Enrique Gomez Munoz, known as Spencer, 1922

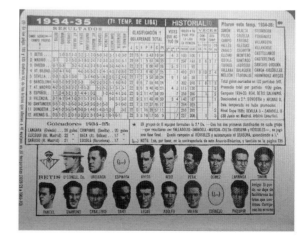

Real Betis 1934/35 La Liga winning squad

Pedro Berruezo memorial match,
Sevilla FC v Romania

Real Betis v Chelsea,
Cup Winners' Cup
matchday programme,
March 1998

Sevilla badge evolution

Real Betis badge evolution

Betis FC badge/kit

Real Betis kit evolution

Sevilla kit evolution

Diego Maradona
at Sevilla

Diego Maradona in action for Sevilla in introductory friendly match against Bayern Munich

Sevilla's Sanchez Pizjuan stadium front

Lorenzo Serra Ferrer at Real Betis

Real Betis winger Denilson scores a penalty against Sevilla, February 2000

Real Betis fans

Joaquin celebrates his winning goal in the Seville derby against Sevilla, 2005

Real Betis win the Copa del Rey, 2005

Real Betis players celebrating their 2005 Copa del Rey Final triumph

Sevilla's 2006 UEFA Cup win

Navas and Adriano with the Super Cup

Antonio Puerta in action for Sevilla

Sevilla v Real Betis in Sanchez Pizjuan

Antonio Puerta mural

Sevilla lift the 2016 Europa League title

Ben Yedder scores at Old Trafford against Manchester United

Two icons – Jesus Navas versus Joaquin

Seville's picturesque Plaza de Espaca

Aerial view of central Seville

Seville's Torre del Oro by night

Chapter 17

Betis Bounce Back

THE 1958/59 season saw newly promoted Betis thrive on their return to top tier football as they finished sixth – just one point off a top four spot. The return derby in Heliópolis saw the hosts triumph 2–0, with goals from Brazilian midfielder Wilson Faria Moreira and Heliodoro Castaño as Betis completed their first-ever league double over their city rivals, who finished six places below them in the final standings.

The man in the home dugout was Antonio Barrios, who had guided *Los Verdiblancos* to the Segunda title the previous campaign – fittingly, amid the golden jubilee celebrations. He was a distinguished figure in Spanish football, coaching a variety of clubs across three decades. This was the first of his three stints in charge of Betis, while between these spells he twice took the helm at Sevilla. (In doing so, Barrios became the first man to manage both clubs, before later being followed by Luis Cid, Luis Aragonés, Vicente Cantatore and Juande Ramos.) Barrios is more fondly remembered within the green-and-white half of the city, following up the 1958 promotion with the same feat nine years later when recalled by the club. He was also the best-performing coach of Sevilla during the 1960s, with a decade-high sixth-place finish in 1962 coupled with progression to that season's Copa final.

Yet history perhaps gives Barrios less credit than he merits at both clubs. Sevilla were a club in decline during his first spell; the fans at the time could not have known that their cup final would be their last for 45 years and that they would suffer their first-ever relegation before replicating such a lofty league finish again. Whilst he will ultimately be remembered for two promotions with Betis, the man most linked to their change in fortunes was president Benito Villamarín.

Originally from the Galician province of Ourense, Villamarín was a savvy businessman who took the helm at the club in May 1955 when Manuel Ruiz Rodríguez – who himself steered the club through its most difficult years, forging strong relationships with other teams to stabilise the financial situation – resigned from his position. The club had just finished fifth in their return to the second tier and five months after assuming his position, Villamarín told the newspaper *Sevilla*: "The task of strengthening a team is very important, but it is also important to ensure the club's economic prosperity. That is my job." It was financial mismanagement and a lack of coherence off the pitch across the previous two decades which had derailed the club, and this rhetoric was long overdue.

His first season saw the club narrowly miss out on their aim of promotion with a play-off loss, but two years later they returned by winning the second-tier title, topping the 18-team southern section. "The important thing is to consolidate the triumph and continue our progression," Villamarín said at the promotion celebrations. "Until then, our task cannot be considered successful." Understandably, there existed a clear air of optimism following decades of misery. "The important thing is that Seville now has two teams in the First Division, this will benefit everyone," said vice-president Guillermo Gómez while vice-secretary Pascual Aparicio added: "Betis, within Spain, is potentially in the top ten. Our desire is that this promotion will develop the club further."

Villamarín is undoubtedly one of the most influential figures in the history of Real Betis and is credited with stabilising their finances, even if that meant taking unpopular decisions, such as the sale of Luis del Sol to Real Madrid. The president's true legacy was the purchase of the Estadio de Heliópolis, ensuring Betis would now own the stadium which they had been tenants of since the commencement of the Civil War. As with Ramón Sánchez-Pizjuán across the city, the vision and foresight in such a move not only led to both men being rightly revered by their clubs, but the stadium itself being christened with their names.

The purchase of the stadium at Heliópolis was celebrated the following week as 500 Betis members attended a tribute evening to thank Villamarín. Among the distinguished guest speakers were Alfonso Jaramillo (see Chapter 6), on behalf of the Peña Bética de Triana, and Juan del Castillo, one of the founders of Sevilla Balompié.

By the time of the purchase, the club had already ensured major upgrades to the stadium to meet their refound top-flight status, including the installation of floodlights by June 1959, celebrated with a friendly match against Sporting Clube de Portugal. Just as their old Campo del Patronato Obrero had proven so important in their Primera title over two decades prior, their Heliópolis form provided the backbone to their success upon returning to the division. Betis won 11 of their 15 home matches in the 1958/59 campaign as it became a fortress.

Home advantage proved to be a decisive factor in derbies between the Seville clubs over these years. Sevilla won just twice at the Villamarín in 18 meetings between 1958 and 1980 while, conversely, Betis triumphed just three times in 26 trips across town at the Pizjuán between 1959 and 1986.

A defining figure in the derby games between the two in the early 1960s was Luis Aragonés, who had joined Real Betis in 1961 as part of the deal which took full-back Isidro Sánchez to Real Madrid. It was reported that Madrid president Santiago Bernabéu was infuriated at the club's decision to allow Aragonés to depart and his worst fears were realised when the player later went on to establish himself across the capital at Atlético.

The Betis manager at the time was Fernando Daučík, another who had fled Hungary the previous decade, and who, just like Antonio Barrios before him, would have multiple spells at the club with a brief move to Sevilla, among others, sandwiched in between. One of his first moves was to sign his son Yanko Daučík from Salamanca, with the transfer much more than just a gimmick as after two highly productive seasons, he would be transferred to Real Madrid.

The manager's son struck up a profitable attacking understanding with Aragonés, who debuted in a friendly against Fiorentina on 12 August 1961 – when Villamarín was to conclude his purchase of the stadium. Aragonés was to find the net 41 times in 93 official appearances for the club, swiftly showing his ability to score various types of goal. He was said to be a playing disciple of the great Alfredo di Stéfano, whom he attempted to mirror during his time in the Spanish capital, and alongside his vast array of natural talent, was credited for his football intelligence which would later develop into a highly successful coaching career.

The first two years of Aragonés at Betis saw the rivalry with Sevilla intensify with the clubs pitted against each other in consecutive seasons in the Copa del Generalísimo, ensuring the pair met on eight occasions in the space of 17 months – unprecedented since the Civil War. Aragonés scored six goals against Sevilla while Betis won six of the 10 derbies in which he played. In his final derby at the Villamarín, in September 1963, he opened the scoring in a 3–1 Betis victory before later being sent off for his part in a mass brawl. By this stage, the two groups of players had become familiar with their meetings and predictably this led to heightened tensions and increased incidents of on-field conflict.

Aragonés was to join Atlético de Madrid in the summer of 1964 in a landmark 11 million pesetas move, which also included defender Colo and midfielder José Miguel Martinez. These moves highlighted the increasing disparity in finances between both clubs in Seville and the elite within Spanish football. Betis – in Catalan coach Domènec Balmanya's solitary campaign in charge – had finished that season in third, four places above Atlético, yet the differential in economic power ensured that prolonged periods of success increasingly became a rarity.

Alongside those who left for Atlético, the summer departures list included János Kuszmann – who was still remembered for his impact at the Ramón Sánchez-Pizjuán six years earlier – Campos, Portilla, Senekowitsch, Areta, Liert and Castro. Yet their third-placed finish the previous campaign ensured their first-ever participation in Europe: the 1964/65 Inter-Cities Fairs Cup, the precursor to the UEFA Cup and, eventually, the Europa League.

The most notable arrival for Betis that summer was striker Enrique Mateos, who had risen to prominence in the late 1950s with Real Madrid. Despite mainly being a backup forward, he scored 50 times in 93 matches, netting nine goals in 16 European Cup appearances and featuring in four of the campaigns in which *Los Blancos* lifted the famed trophy. He was capped internationally for Spain and in 1961 joined Sevilla. His first campaign in Andalusia proved fruitful, as he scored 14 goals and helped his side to that year's Copa final. But his form then waned, and he didn't manage to take his goalscoring in a single season to double figures again. He joined Recreativo three years later and subsequently moved back to Seville, this time to play for Betis. He would go on to manage across Spain's top divisions in a two-decade coaching career, with his most notable achievement leading Cádiz CF to their first-ever promotion to the top flight in 1977.

With Mateos unable to rekindle his earlier form, it was Fernando Ansola who was the main source of goals for Betis, netting 59 times in 114 top flight appearances for the club before switching to Valencia in 1966, a year after he debuted for Spain. Ansola was the club's top scorer in the Primera until being ousted by Hipólito 'Poli' Rincón two decades later, but by this stage Ansola had sadly passed away following a brain tumour, aged just 46.

The emerging star of the team was Rogelio Sosa Ramírez, who spent the entirety of his 16-year professional career at the club. As the Betis website recalled, he is a player who came close to defining the club itself: "different and unpredictable". Born in the small town of Coria del Río, on the shores of the Guadalquivir river, he began his football career at Acción Católica CF, started by a local priest, and joined Betis as a teenager following spells at Tomelloso CF and Ponferradina.

Well-known football agent Luis Guijarro described Rogelio as a "Mercedes footballer" and attempted to bring him to Barcelona for a 12 million pesetas transfer fee. When Betis rejected this approach, Barça winger and Spain international Carles Rexach was included, plus the transfer fee, but again this was not accepted. The sale of Luis del Sol had proven traumatic, and the club were keen to avoid a repeat at all costs. The loyalty of Betis to Rogelio was reciprocated with the player never seeking to play anywhere else. His playing style was certainly unique, with an ability to score directly from a corner – 10 of his goals for the club are thought to have come via this unusual manner, known as an 'Olympic goal'. It is believed this is the highest number for any player in the history of professional football, with Uruguayan set-piece specialist Álvaro Recoba said to be the second highest with six. (Future Real Betis icon Joaquín Sánchez Rodríguez, see Chapter 27, scored an Olympic goal in the 2019 Copa del Rey semi-final against Valencia.)

Rogelio's left foot was such a weapon that he developed the 'Mahogany Left' nickname while his dribbling technique became known as *la tostá* and his toe-influenced shooting was *la rosca*. His work rate was questioned by Betis coach Ferenc Szusza, who demanded he covered more miles on the pitch, to which he famously responded: "Mister, running is for cowards." With a distinctive playing style, Rogelio dazzled Betis fans across his career and became a true club icon.

The season had begun promisingly for Betis, winning the annual Ramón de Carranza Trophy – a prestigious pre-season tournament hosted by Cádiz CF. Sevilla had won the first three editions from 1955 through to 1957, defeating Atlético de Portugal in the inaugural tournament before relinquishing their grip to Real Madrid in 1958. The invitational tournament swiftly developed to include four contestants, with Betis joined by the illustrious line-up of Real Madrid, Benfica and Boca Juniors (Cádiz would not become regular participants themselves until the late 1970s).

Rogelio's free kick defeated Benfica before his stoppage-time goal ensured a victory over Argentinian club Boca Juniors as Betis secured the trophy. That is where the success ended for *Los Verdiblancos*, whose weakened squad was exposed as soon as competitive action got underway. They dropped nine places from the previous campaign's top-three finish and avoided relegation only courtesy of having scored more goals than Real Murcia. They exited the Copa at the round of 32 and their first European campaign lasted just two matches, proving hugely anticlimactic.

The Andalusian side's opponents were Stade Français FC, part of the multisport Paris-based club whose most successful entity is rugby club Stade Français Paris. It was a quirk of the draw as Betis manager Louis Hon – appointed that summer to replace Balmanya who had left for CD Málaga (who became Málaga CF in 1992) – had previously played for the Parisians before a move to Real Madrid, becoming their first-ever French player. Betis had been favourites for the tie as their opponents had only survived relegation in the French Division 1 the previous year by one point. Indeed, Stade Français were only in the tournament courtesy of the unusual requirement of the French capital holding a major fair that year and as the city's highest-ranking team they were assured a place.

As the title Inter-Cities Fairs Cup suggests, the competition was an idea to promote international trade fairs and generate economic growth between cities following the devastation of the Second World War. Betis earned their place in the competition due to the work of technical secretary José María de la Concha, who had been chosen by Benito Villamarín to put forward the club's case. He held meetings in Bologna with president of the Italian Federation, Ottorino Barrasi, who held an influential role in sanctioning entrance to the tournament. On-pitch performance was not a defining criterion, yet the club were confident that their third-placed league finish would boost their chances. Seville had hosted the Feria Nacional de Muestras from 1958, and thus its clubs met the qualification criteria.

The problem was that multiple Spanish teams met the criteria, and each put forward separate arguments for taking part. With Real Madrid qualifying for that season's European Cup, Barcelona, Valencia, Athletic Bilbao, Real Zaragoza and Atlético de Madrid all wanted to be awarded a place. Villamarín was desperate for his club's inclusion and he subsequently struck up an amicable relationship with FIFA president Stanley Rous. Due to the growing pressure, the governing body decided to expand the competition from 32 teams to 48, thus allowing all of the Spanish applicants to enter.

The Betis team that day against Stade Français was Pepín, Paquito, Ríos, Aparicio, Suárez, López Hidalgo, Frasco, Breval, Rogelio, Azcárate and Ansola. After a scoreless first half, José López Hidalgo opened the scoring for Betis with a low shot flying into the corner of the net. It was the first goal the club had ever scored in European football and it sent the packed Benito Villamarín into euphoria. But with 12 minutes left on the clock and the home side visibly tiring, Stade Français forward Portier left three defenders for dead before firing the crucial away goal past legendary goalkeeper José Casas Gris, known as Pepín.

The Valencia-born goalkeeper was one of Spanish football's most iconic shot-stoppers across the 1950s and 60s, spending eight years at Las Palmas in the top flight before transferring to Betis in 1960 following the Gran Canarian side's relegation. However, it would not just be at club level that Pepín gained fame as he played a major role in Spain's sole major 20th century international title, the 1964 European Championship. Pepín earned the nickname 'The Hero of Belfast' for a stellar display against Northern Ireland in the play-off to qualify for the tournament. In October 1963, he kept a clean sheet at Windsor Park in Belfast as *La Roja* ground out a 1–0 victory before securing a 1–1 draw at the San Mamés in Bilbao to progress to the finals and subsequent glory.

There would be no such European glory for Betis, who lost the return leg 2–0 at the Parc des Princes three weeks later as Philippe Pottier and François Stasiak found the net. It was a poor result for the Andalusian side against a team who had little or no expectations. Perennial domestic strugglers, the hosts had lost three matches in a row going into the clash and the game was played in front of just 6,000 spectators. So low was the profile of the game, it was only mentioned once in that day's French printed press – a small corner on page eight of *L'Equipe*.

The Sevillian press had named *Los Verdiblancos* 'EuroBetis' ahead of the tie, but after the defeat it was journalist Luis Carlos Peris who renamed them "Currobetis", after bullfighter 'Curro' Romero. The Seville local gained notoriety for his unpredictable performances, alternating fantastic displays of triumph alongside frequent flirtations with catastrophe. It is perhaps fitting that Romero – who is sculpted outside the city's bullring – is a *socio* of Betis, with the "Currobetis" reference applied sparingly in the decades of club instability since.

There was an extra element of regret attached to the defeat, as the winners of the tie had been paired to meet the winners of Juventus, for whom Luis del Sol was now starring, against Belgian club Royale Union Saint-Gilloise. As predicted, the Italian giants progressed but Betis could not meet their end of the deal and there was to be no reunion.

The defeat to Stade Français summed up a failure of regression for Betis; Louis Hon was gone soon after – moving to Real Zaragoza, the emerging Spanish power in the 1960s, who earned the nickname *Los Magníficos* – while his replacement Rosendo Hernández saw no immediate upturn in results. Club legend Andrés Aranda was then called upon for a remarkable fifth spell in the dugout, but tragedy was to strike as he suddenly passed away in the aftermath of his appointment (see Chapter 13). Ernesto Pons would see out the final few months of the season amid the increasing realisation that this era was coming to its conclusion.

Already grief-stricken by Aranda's death, fresh concern was directed at the rapidly declining health of club president Benito Villamarín, who was forced to abandon his position within the club in 1965, four years after being diagnosed with advanced lung cancer. "I always have to surrender the arms of my unconditional affection and devotion to you," Villamarín wrote in an open letter upon announcing his decision. "I would have liked to have overcome [the illness] before leaving but God has not wanted it that way and here I am forced to walk away at a time when the ship of Betis needs more than ever the energies and hopes of a good helmsman. This is a decision that hurts my soul.

"Beticismo is an unbeatable flag of Sevillanism and enthusiasm, and I will always remain faithful to the ideas of the club. I am always ready to serve the club as it wants me, and I will always love them."

Villamarín was replaced in the position by his brother and vice-president Puga Avelino Villamarín on an interim basis before Andrés Gaviño Gordillo was appointed permanently. However, such was the period of flux there would be another three presidential appointments before the end of the decade: Julio de la Puerta, José León and José Núñez Naranjo, the latter of whom finally brought stability with a decade-long premiership.

Benito Villamarín passed away eight months after he resigned from his position, on 16 August 1966, with newspaper *Sevilla* reporting on his funeral the following day. Speaking of his "painful illness" which he "carried with exemplary integrity", the events were then detailed. "Because of the popularity he enjoyed, the act of interment was a great and heartfelt expression of mourning," the report read, before noting the entirety of Betis directors, players and coaching staff were all present. As ever, a prominent death impacting either club brought great unity and strength to the city of Seville, as the account continued: "The representation of Sevilla Club de Fútbol was headed by its president, Manuel Zafra, and secretary general, Angel Díaz."

Bad news often comes in threes and a year after manager Aranda's passing *in situ* and four months prior to Villamarín's death, Betis were relegated. Catalan-based *El Mundo Deportivo* perhaps sums up the situation best, describing the sequence of events as Betis being "faithful to its DNA of peaks and chasms". The manner of the relegation was particularly painful, with a goal in the final minute of the final game condemning *Los Verdiblancos* to their fate. Travelling to Málaga's La Rosaleda on the final day of the season, Betis knew only a win could save them from demotion while such an outcome would condemn the hosts. Ansola gave Betis the lead midway through the first half and that is how the game remained until the final minute, when Luis María Otiñano – who died 31 years later in a motorbike accident in the city, aged 54 – broke Betis hearts with a leveller. The Seville-based club finished bottom of the 16-team league, but just one point behind 12th-placed Español and safety while Málaga, in 13th, ultimately joined them in the Segunda following a play-off loss.

Yet Betis's penchant for unpredictability was to strike once more before the season was out. The Spanish football season was still formatted so that the Copa del Generalísimo did not commence until the conclusion of the league campaign. Betis eliminated Real Oviedo and then Español, but nobody gave them a chance in their quarter-final tie with Real Madrid. This was during a decade of domestic dominance for *Los Blancos*, who would win eight of the ten Primera titles on offer.

The first leg was played in Seville on 8 May 1966, three days prior to Madrid's European Cup final against Partizan Belgrade in Brussels. As predicted, Madrid fielded a much-changed starting line-up, although regular goalkeeper Antonio Rodrigo Betancort, Uruguayan defender José Emilio Santamaría, midfielder Félix Ruiz and the great Ferenc Puskás, now 39 and in his final competitive outing, all played. Rogelio was the star of the show, netting two goals in a 3–2 victory for the hosts.

The other goalscorer for *Los Verdiblancos* that day was Joaquín Sierra Vallejo, more commonly known as 'Quino'. The son of poet

Juan Sierra, a member of the Generación del 27 group, and hailing from Triana (see Chapter 6), it was no surprise that he developed a reputation as a free-thinker, possessing a rebellious spirit. He was the youngest of three brothers, all of whom were highly educated and all three possessing tremendous football ability – a rare combination. The eldest brother Juan played for the youth teams of Sevilla while Ignacio and Joaquín both represented Betis. It was Ignacio who was said to possess the most natural talent, but a broken leg whilst playing with the Andalusian youth team derailed his huge promise.

Quino openly referenced his leftist politics and became one of Spanish football's most outspoken characters. This identity was amplified when Betis promoted him to their first-team squad in 1963 following his success with their Triana Balompié reserve side. Aged 18, he was told by the club that he must sign a professional form to debut in the first team. Not only did he soon discover this form was not necessary for his participation but by signing it he was activating the *derecho de retención* (right of retention) clause, which would not be abolished until 1979. This gave almost exclusive power to clubs in negotiating terms with new players as it allowed them to automatically trigger a contract extension for existing players by adding 10 per cent to their wage packet. Due to his informed and grounded upbringing along with his desire for social justice, Quino was outraged and defiant. The groundwork for his later role as the president of the Spanish Player Union (AFE) was in place.

Yet Quino was also a fine forward and made his mark across eight seasons in Seville. His first prolonged run in the team came in the 1965/66 campaign with his peak coming three seasons later when he netted 32 goals in the Segunda for Betis and became one of the few players from outside the top flight to earn international recognition for Spain, scoring on his debut – the final goal in a 6–0 drubbing of Finland. The player was a Betis fan, of this there is little doubt; he remained at the club through two relegations with an unwavering level of performance and work rate. Arguably, it was such strength of feeling that led to him becoming so critical of the club which ultimately led to his protracted departure.

Real Madrid attempted to sign him in the summer of 1970, but Betis rejected these advances and invoked their *derecho de retención* over the player, which escalated tensions that had long been bubbling under the surface. He argued the clause was "enslaving" players and he stopped attending training sessions, making himself unavailable for selection. When confronted by Betis vice-president Pepe León, he responded: "You are the one who has no shame! How can you come down here to insult some professionals? Get out now!"

Quino was forcing an exit which was duly granted the following summer as an 18 million peseta offer from Valencia was accepted. He was an iconic figure who ended his spell in Heliópolis on a sour note, but his desire for greater players' rights went beyond any other contemporary. It was no surprise that he was an attendee of the formative meetings of the AFE, before being elected as their first president to represent the interests of players. In a reflective piece on his impact on Spanish football, *El País* mused: "Today, as he looks out into the sea in his Cádiz residence he will believe that, after everything, it was all worth it."

His goal against Madrid in the 1966 Copa quarter-final was one of the most significant moments of his career on the pitch. Despite the slender advantage, there was a sense Betis had missed a golden opportunity to put the two-legged tie to bed. Rogelio had spurned the opportunity to complete his hat-trick from the penalty spot and three days later Madrid secured their sixth European Cup title. Four days after their triumph in Belgium, *Los Blancos* hosted Ernesto Pons's relegated outsiders in the second leg at the Santiago Bernabéu. On 15 May 1966, a gruelling, epic encounter which few had foreseen took place.

There had always been the distinct possibility that Madrid would win by one goal during the 90 minutes and take the game into extra time (away goals were not a factor in this era). Considering their exploits half a week earlier, this was always going to be a scenario which favoured the Andalusian side and so it came to pass. Famed winger Francisco Gento opened the scoring in the 21st minute for Madrid, who were fielding all their stars, but they could not find a decisive second in regulation time. After the game, Quino confessed: "[Madrid midfielder] Manolo Velázquez told me that they were worn out."

The fate of the visitors had appeared to be sealed when Gento turned provider to feed Pirri to open a two-goal advantage six minutes into added time but in the 118th minute, just before the full-time whistle, Betis forward Jesús Landa equalised. "I saw Quino carrying the ball forward then Pedro de Felipe slipped and then it was just instinct," Landa later recalled. "Quino found my run and I did not have to think to score."

After two hours of punishing football, the teams could still not be separated but, in a time before penalty shoot-outs were widely used, the only way to separate the sides was to continue playing extra time in 20-minute instalments. Betis were reduced to 10 men as Francisco 'Frasco' Ortiz was dismissed for dissent but in the ninth minute of extra time's third section (the 149th minute of the encounter), Landa scored again for 2-2. Betis, down and out a month before, were eliminating the European champions at the Bernabéu. "I was ice-cool, and they were broken, I saw the gap and I knew before I received it that it was a goal," Landa added. "It was the feat of my life."

The Basque native had joined from Real Valladolid the previous summer and would spend five seasons at the club, only two of which were in the Primera, before moving to Deportivo de La Coruña. In many ways, he epitomised the Betis team of the latter half of the 1960s: full of spirit and endeavour, capable of stunning the most illustrious of opponents but ultimately short of the star quality needed to replicate the glory days or indeed maintain top-flight status. Bouncing between the top two seasons, it would be a further decade before *Los Verdiblancos* challenged for major honours once more.

Chapter 18
Sevilla Sales
Signal Stagnation

THE date of 21 April 1968 was a day the city of Seville would rather forget. On the penultimate weekend of La Liga action, the relegation of both Real Betis and Sevilla was confirmed. For the former it was their fourth demotion in their history and second in three years but for *Los Rojiblancos* this was a first – their 34-year uninterrupted stay in the Primera was over. The fact it was Juan Arza in the dugout underlined the fall in playing standards from the heyday of El Niño de Oro's Sevilla.

The previous campaign Sevilla avoided relegation courtesy of defeating Real Gijón (later renamed Sporting de Gijón) in a promotion/relegation play-off. Indeed, they had recorded just one top-seven finish that decade – the fall did not come as a great surprise. This was the third of Arza's four spells at the helm, having replaced Antonio Barrios after just three wins in the opening 18 games. Under the former striker, results modestly improved but not enough to prevent the inevitable.

Sevilla's status had suffered since the death of president Ramón Sánchez-Pizjuán 12 years earlier, with cutbacks in budgets having a significant impact on the quality of the squad. Unlike in previous years, they were no longer able to retain their playing talent.

Manuel Ruiz Sosa was one such star, a local boy from the Sevillian town Coria del Río, who would no doubt have helped his side to domestic glory in a different era. The midfielder soon earned the nickname the 'Pearl of Coria', due to his tremendous talent. Promoted to Sevilla's first-team squad as a teenager in the 1956/57 campaign, he helped the side to a second-placed spot, the European Cup quarter-final the following year and, in 1962, the final of the Copa del

Generalísimo. On each occasion, the club who stopped Ruiz Sosa and Sevilla was Real Madrid.

Known as a player of high technical ability, he was able to run a game from the middle of the pitch and had no shortage of physical strength. Indeed, the one drawback he suffered from, as often detailed, was his lack of height. "I have had to do without some very good players, for example Ruiz Sosa from Andalucía," said Spain youth boss Ramón Melcón in 1954, when explaining the player's exclusion for a game against Germany. "He displays great intuition with his play, shows fantastic temperament and an extraordinary backbone. In short, his only disadvantage is his height, and since in this position there are other very good players of equal quality, I have selected those who are taller."

After eight seasons in the first team at Sevilla, in which he won international recognition, Ruiz Sosa was sold to Atlético de Madrid in the summer of 1964. He had been en route to true greatness at Sevilla and in 1959 he won the Trofeo Patricio Arabolaza (referred to as the Trofeo a la Furia Española) – a trophy set up by *Marca*, running between 1953 and 1968, awarded to the Spanish player who had displayed the most *furia*, in reference to the roots of football in Spain (see Chapter 2), that campaign.

The only thing missing for the midfielder at Sevilla were trophies, yet in his first season at Atlético he won the Copa and the following year he won the league. This was one of the great Atléti teams, formed by plucking talents from both of Seville's powerhouses (for Betis's departures to Atlético in 1964, see Chapter 17). It was only an injury which cruelly denied Ruiz Sosa a spot in Spain's 1966 World Cup squad.

Almost three decades after leaving the club, Ruiz Sosa returned to Sevilla in 1993 to be assistant to former Atléti team-mate Luis Aragonés until 1995. He continued to work at the club in a variety of capacities, mainly as technical secretary and with the club's youth teams, with whom he was influential in the rise of future stars José Antonio Reyes, Sergio Ramos and Antonio Puerta. Many tears would be shed over the fate of the latter, but it was Puerta's actions on the pitch which led to Ruiz Sosa weeping.

The full-back's crucial goal against Schalke in the semi-finals of the UEFA Cup brought the club a first-ever European final and Ruiz Sosa, watching on, broke down in tears. His Sevilla were finally great again, and he had played his part with the development of these protégés.

* * * * *

A year after Ruiz Sosa joined Atlético, more stars would exit Sevilla. Central defender Francisco Fernández Rodríguez, known as Paco Gallego, joined Barcelona, while Paraguayan striker Juan Bautista Agüero – signed from Olimpia in 1958 and spending seven seasons in Andalusia – switched to Real Madrid.

It was Gallego's departure which again signalled the sign of the times, as Sevilla were once more robbed of the prime years of a superb talent. As early as his teenage years, Gallego was earmarked as a future Sevilla captain and promised a huge future within the game. He joined the club aged 14 and within three years became part of the first-team squad.

The oldest of ten brothers, Gallego was physically imposing, becoming renowned for showing composure on the ball and being an excellent reader of the game. When Gallego was later called up by the Spanish national team, coach Ladislao Kubala commented: "He is a player who has everything you could want in that position. He knows how to suffer, does not waver and can be counted on during difficult matches."

By 1965, aged just 21, he was the first name on Sevilla's team sheet and widely regarded as one of the league's best defenders, with the potential for significant improvement. He had been included in the Spanish squad for the successful European Championships and would win 36 international caps. With team performances middling and Sevilla in need of money, an exit was inevitable and that summer he joined Barcelona in a deal worth 7 million pesetas. "I wanted to continue improving, but I did not have any desire to leave Sevilla," Gallego recalled in an interview with *ABC* in 2014. "But Barcelona wanted to sign me and there was not much choice, I left and ended up enjoying great years in Catalonia."

Gallego certainly enjoyed great success at the Camp Nou, winning six major titles including two league trophies and two Copas across a decade which saw him amass just shy of 250 Primera appearances. By 1975, the defender was 31 and as he still had energy left in the tank, specifically requested that he be allowed to return to Sevilla. "I wanted to spend the remainder of my career at Sevilla," Gallego explained. "My contract at Barcelona had one more year but I wanted to return and they did not deny me that opportunity. I still have special affection for Barcelona, those were ten special years and they showed me lots of love. For me, it was a perfect career."

He would spend five further seasons at *Los Rojiblancos*, with a match in his honour held against Barcelona on 30 August 1979 at the Estadio Ramón Sánchez-Pizjuán, although he would play a further three matches that season. His mantle at Sevilla had been passed on to another club great: Pablo Blanco. A local boy who joined the club's youth system aged 15, Blanco spent the entirety of his professional career at Sevilla, with a club-record 415 competitive matches standing for 33 years and only being surpassed by winger Jesús Navas in 2017.

None of Blanco's appearances were gimmicks and he hung up his boots aged a relatively young 33, stating he had no desire to continue playing below his top level for Sevilla and opting not to join a rival club. He would go on to hold several secretarial positions across *Los Rojiblancos* and headed the recruitment of local youth players, like he had been, into the ranks. "Few like him symbolise the loyalty and the courage that define the Nervión club," read a press release from Sevilla's history department as they inducted him into their hall of fame in 2018. "This induction means everything to me," Blanco remarked. "I didn't expect to be at the club continuously for this amount of time. It makes me proud and emotional and I had a lump in my throat when they told me. When the president told me in his office, I felt incredibly honoured, speechless. I didn't know what to say or to do. I have been fortunate enough to be able to continue working with the club and watching its development since I retired, which I think has improved the level of Sevilla. With all the tough times that we have gone through over the years, we have reached where we are now and I have experienced it all first hand."

Blanco was one of the few talents who dedicated his entire career to the club, with many of its stars being auctioned off when attractive offers were received. It was within this context that Sevilla struggled to re-establish themselves back within Spain's leading clubs during the 1960s and 70s. Despite bouncing straight back from the 1968 relegation to finish third in 1970, they would only secure one more top-six finish across the following 19 seasons.

* * * * *

Sevilla are a club who are not only synonymous with nurturing some of the brightest talent from within Andalusia but also showing bravery in importing from overseas. This was as true for managerial staff and innovative coaching methods as for the playing squad. Between 1971 and 1974, two Austrians, a Greek, an Englishman and an Argentine would manage the club, along with four interim stints for Spaniards including the seemingly ever-returning Juan Arza.

This run of managerial changes began with the appointment of Max Merkel, who as a player had represented both Germany and Austria. The commencement of the Second World War coincided with Merkel turning professional, aged 21, but he managed to later win four titles with Rapid Vienna. His reputation was most clearly defined as a coach and he had already accumulated 15 years of management experience upon his Sevilla appointment in 1969. He had managed the Dutch national team and Borussia Dortmund before winning the Bundesliga title with both 1860 Munich and 1. FC Nürnberg.

Merkel was an authoritative figurehead who became famed for his dry wit and no-nonsense approach. At Sevilla, he became infamous for his exhaustive and demanding training sessions. He required the employment of translator José María Negrillo during his spell at the club but, according to the man himself, he believed props would be more useful in getting his message across to the players. This led to his 'Mr Whip' nickname, with players fearful of disobeying his strict orders in case of being reprimanded. This was an era when managers were synonymous with father figures, often giving liberties to star players and operating relaxed regimes. Merkel bucked the trend and there is little doubt that, in the short-term at least, it brought success.

It was under the Austrian that *Los Rojiblancos* secured their third-place finish in 1970, helped by the arrival of Paraguayan duo Herminio Toñánez and Bernardo 'Baby' Acosta. The latter would score 76 goals across six seasons in the Andalusian capital and was the first Sevilla forward namechecked by Betis goalkeeper José Ramón Esnaola years later: "He was very smart, very skilled. He got in front of you at corners and would not let you out – he knew how to maximise small advantages."

Sevilla secured a thrilling 3–2 league triumph at Real Madrid's Estadio Santiago Bernabéu in the process – the only visiting team to win there that season. But the success was short-lived with results deteriorating the following campaign, including a first-round exit in the UEFA Cup to Turkish club Eskişehirspor. It carried on a trend of underwhelming results in Europe for Sevilla, who lost all three ties in continental competition between the 1957/58 season debut and 1982. In 1962 they were eliminated from the Cup Winners' Cup by Scottish club Glasgow Rangers and four years later by Romanian side FC Argeș in the Inter-Cities Fairs Cup.

Merkel had been hired with a reputation of falling out with high-profile figures within clubs and it was no surprise when results stopped exceeding expectations that relations became frayed. It was rumoured that he was on borrowed time at the club and he was subsequently dismissed, with just one league game remaining of his second campaign, for signing a deal with Atlético de Madrid. *Los Colchoneros* won the Copa in Merkel's first season at the helm before securing the league title the following year. True to form, the success guaranteed by the manager was later followed by controversy. In an interview with German newspaper *Bild*, he said: "Spain would be so beautiful, if it wasn't for all the Spaniards." Atlético did not care much for the sarcasm and subsequently sacked Merkel, who would later successfully sue the club for an unfair termination of employment.

Sevilla could not come close to replicating Merkel's first season success; they turned to experienced Greek boss Dan Georgiadis but he failed to recover from a slow start and was replaced by highly rated English boss Vic Buckingham. Having enjoyed two coaching stints at Ajax Amsterdam and then Barcelona, Buckingham is credited with laying the foundations for the Total Football revolution at the Dutch giants. His blueprint of incisive short passing and possession-based football was later developed by Johan Cruyff, who played under his tutelage at Ajax, but he was unable to prevent the decline of results under Georgiadis and departed at the end of the campaign with Sevilla rooted to the foot of the table and relegated.

The club continued to try different approaches with little success. Another former Barça boss, Salvador Artigas, failed in his objective of promotion while Fernando Guillamón and Santos Bedoya – both promoted from their roles coaching the club's reserve side Sevilla Atletico – did not secure the posts permanently. They then turned to another Austrian, Ernst Happel. He had won the Dutch Cup for unfancied ADO Den Haag before domestic and European success with Feyenoord. Despite going on to win seven league titles across Belgium, Germany and Austria, alongside guiding the Netherlands to the 1978 World Cup final, his spell in Andalusia was a disaster. Tasked with winning promotion, the club finished ninth and managed to avoid relegation by a solitary point. To make matters worse, Real Betis lifted the Segunda title that campaign.

Below-par performances and results had been placed into perspective the previous year, when Sevilla forward Pedro Berruezo collapsed and died during a league match in Pontevedra. It was a first in Spanish football and sent shockwaves through the sport. Berruezo has been remembered in the club's Ramón Sánchez-Pizjuán home, with a bronze carving of his figure adorning the entrance hall while his outline is present as a tribute at Gate 10 – in honour of his shirt number – following the stadium's refurbishment in 2017.

A former Spain Under-23 international, Berruezo had arrived at Sevilla five years earlier from Málaga in a deal worth 4.2 million pesetas. Despite tough times for the club, the Melilla-born forward consistently impressed for *Los Rojiblancos* and netted a credible 38 goals across 135 matches. A month before Berruezo's death, the club had plunged into a constitutional crisis following the resignation of president José Ramón Cisneros Palacios. The head of a famous law firm in the city, Palacios bought and sold areas of land around the club's stadium to stabilise their financial position. This explains why the club's current training facilities are named Ciudad Deportiva José Ramón Cisneros Palacios with the 250,000m^2 area also home to Sevilla Atletico.

Palacios was succeeded by Eugenio Montes Cabeza, with the events of the opening weeks of his tenure proving far more difficult than any that followed in his 11-year stay in the role. It was not the first occasion when Berruezo had fallen ill during a match, having previously experienced difficulties against Alicante and Sabadell. The most serious complication had come the previous month, when he collapsed in a clash with Baracaldo CF. It was these series of prior incidents which still cast doubt upon the official report of a cardiac arrest, with others believing a cerebral infarction killed him. Despite medical diagnosis, no firm reasoning could be discovered for the player's continual fainting.

In 2003, on the 30th anniversary of Berruezo's passing, a highly emotive postcard which the player had sent home from Pontevedra to his pregnant wife Gloria Bernal and young daughter was published by *Diario AS* journalist José María García. Bought from the Parador hotel in the Galician city, where Sevilla were based for the match, Berruezo wrote:

"Hello chatillas!

Soon we will leave for the stadium because it's 2pm on Sunday afternoon and while I'm in the room, I will briefly join you with these sentences. How are you? And the little one? I am imagining how pretty and funny she will be with the little marmot suit and her stroller. And what about you? Take care to eat everything you need. I will call you tonight.

179

Well, I'm telling you this but you will be talking to me before you read this! I suppose your mother and sister are keeping well. Give kisses to the girl and the family, and one for you, from me who loves you so much, your Pedro."

Pontevedra led 1-0 at the break and shortly after the second half resumed, Berruezo's team-mates noticed he was in trouble. "We were going to move forward and Pedro tried to run forward, then just fell to the ground," recalled Pablo Blanco. "Some of us were petrified, unable to move and later, when [his death was] confirmed, we cried like children."

Goalkeeper Rodri recounted: "Pedro began to bend forward, as he did when he began to feel sick. I noticed straight away and he couldn't get straight up, so he looked towards the bench and then let out a great shriek. I will never forget that cry, it will stay with me forever. He collapsed to the ground and raised his right hand, so we ran to him. The Pontevedra team doctor jumped over the barrier and ran straight over while Manuel Bueno, who was closest to him, put his hand in his mouth so that he would not swallow his tongue. The Red Cross stretcher bearers transferred him to the changing rooms. Isabelo was on one side of him and me on the other."

Pontevedra doctor Díaz Lema and Antonio Gómez attended to the stricken Berruezo in the changing room, with Sevilla's club doctor Antonio Leal Graciani absent due to personal reasons. Speaking later in *La Actualidad Española*, Graciani revealed how he only found out about the death of the player directly from president Eugenio Montes Cabeza. A coramine injection did not work and it was decided immediately to transport the player to the local Dominguez Clinic, but Berruezo's life could not be saved. Pontevedra won the match 2-0 with Sevilla players not being told the fate of their deceased team-mate until the final whistle.

Over 25,000 turned up around the Ramón Sánchez-Pizjuán to welcome the player home on the Monday, with his body veiled by team-mates. The procession left for Málaga, where Berruezo was laid to rest. His widow received a total of almost 5 million pesetas from the club as Sevilla paid out the remainder of his contract. Three years later, Berruezo's widow brought a claim against the club placing blame for the fatal event on a work accident with Sevilla subsequently paying a total of 15,300 pesetas a month until each child came of age.

Chapter 19

Sevilla Stabilise, EuroBetis

THE year 1973 began in tragic circumstances for Sevilla but the summer arrival of Alhaji Momodo Njie, better known as Biri Biri, was to bring more joy to the club's fans than any other. The Gambian winger, who arrived from Danish club Boldklubben 1901, was the first-ever black player to play for Sevilla and became a cult figure. Indeed, the club's *Biris Norte* ultras – formed in the player's second season at the club – were named in his honour. Numbering over 1,000, the group sit in the Gol Norte of the Sánchez-Pizjuán – a part of the ground opened two years into the player's stint in Andalusia.

Biri Biri so endeared himself to the club's fans due to his combination of technical ability and supreme work rate. Across five seasons at Sevilla he netted 32 goals and built a strong rapport with the Sevilla support. However, the mercurial winger is said to have originally been destined to sign for Real Betis before a late intervention saw him join the red-and-white half of the city instead. His agent had struck a deal to sign for Betis but on his flight to Seville to complete the deal, he is said to have spoken to Juan Ramón Rodríguez – the coach of Danish side Randers, but originally from Huelva. Rodríguez was a fan of Sevilla and was aware of Biri Biri's talent, so he swiftly arranged for the two to meet and the rest is history.

Biri Biri is renowned as the greatest player Gambia has ever produced, while those who played alongside him go further: "I class Biri Biri even above Diego Maradona (who, ironically, would play for Sevilla two decades later) because he was a great goalscorer, dribbler and could play with both feet," former Gambian international Alhaji Babou Sowe told BBC Sport in 2005. "Biri Biri was superb, he was a complete footballer and he is the best by anybody's standard," Omar Sallah, another former international team-mate, told BBC Sport. "He used to save the day for Gambia when things were rough with his skills and without doubt he's the best player I have seen in my life."

Enjoying the prime of his career in the Andalusian capital, Biri Biri later said: "My best moment in my career was when I helped Sevilla to promotion to the Spanish first division in my second year with the club. I was so popular in Seville throughout my spell with them because I was delivering well and I was considered one of their best players."

In 2017, the former forward returned to Seville in a trip organised by the Federación de Peñas Sevillistas San Fernando supporters' group. Biri Biri watched his former side defeat Maribor in the Champions League before overcoming Málaga, and later told club media of his joy over returning to the city for the first time in eight years. "I'm happy because I haven't been here for many years," he said. "When I'm here I always think I'm in Gambia because the people love me so much and I love them too. The stadium and the city have changed a lot, but Sevillians are just as wonderful and the *Sevillistas* are the best fans in Spain."

With Biri Biri starring with 14 goals, Sevilla ended their three-year hiatus from the top flight in 1975 with a third-placed finish and automatic promotion. Appointed the previous summer, Argentine boss Roque Olsen produced a cohesive unit which was comprised of many Sevilla youth products. Olsen had been a famous player at Real Madrid during the 1950s before enjoying a 33-year coaching career in Spain.

Whilst the club's form following promotion was unspectacular – they finished 11th in their first season back in Primera – they swiftly stabilised with a relatively sound financial footing and clear direction off the pitch led by president Montes Cabeza. It was the beginning of an uninterrupted 22-year spell in the top flight for Sevilla and, over time, allowed the signings of notable players.

The two most important arrivals of the late 1970s were Argentinian duo Héctor Scotta and Daniel Bertoni. Sevilla spent 70 million pesetas to sign winger Bertoni from Independiente – a club-record signing at the time. He had won a remarkable eight titles at the Argentinian giants including three Copa Libertadores and starred for his nation at that summer's World Cup. "I was in Córdoba [the Argentinian city, rather than the Andalusian one] and Santos Bedoya, who I think was the sports director of Sevilla, came to see me along with Roberto Dale," Bertoni recalled in an *ABC* interview published in 2007. "They told me about Sevilla, about the new era they were entering into and it took them just a few minutes to convince me to sign. They really excited me and we fixed it that same day."

Bertoni added: "It was a few weeks before the World Cup, but no deal was announced. Then my performances ensured lots of attention and offers from other clubs, but I had given my word to Sevilla. Besides, I learned that the fans had put 1,000 pesetas each for me to play at Sevilla. Did you know that? I tell you, it is the greatest pride for a footballer. We may not have won many trophies but we were like a family and my memories are happy ones."

And what did the Argentine think of the city? "My daughter is named Macarena as she was conceived in Seville ... so yes, the city is very special to us. However, there were tougher moments. In my second season, we lost the derby 4–0 at Real Betis. It was awful, emotions are so high across the city that you get caught up in them. When I arrived home, my wife told me: 'Get ready quickly, Scotta will be here any moment'. I asked why, and she replied, 'He and his wife are collecting us to go to the *feria*'. I could not believe it, what would the fans have said? I let him go along with the wives because I could not have faced it!"

Striker Scotta had gained a reputation for his goalscoring exploits in South America as he netted a remarkable 60 goals in the 1975 calendar year (they all arrived within a 317-day period) while at San Lorenzo. From there he joined Brazilian side Grêmio, before joining Sevilla the following year. A native of Santa Fe, Scotta would transfer his goalscoring form to Andalusia with a total of 53 strikes in 101 top-flight appearances.

The Argentine's first appearance in a Sevilla shirt came in the 1976 Trofeo Ciudad de Sevilla – a summer friendly tournament which ran between 1972 and 1994. The majority of the tournament's editions featured both Seville clubs alongside other invited sides, with games held in both the Sánchez-Pizjuán and Benito Villamarín stadiums. The trophies were elaborate and celebrated the city's famous landmarks such as the Giralda and Torre del Oro.

Sevilla had won the first two editions before Real Betis struck back with victories in the 1974 and 1975 versions. Scotta arrived the following summer with his first game seeing the club defeat Brazilian side Cruzeiro on penalties before beating Betis 1–0 in the decider, with Scotta grabbing the decisive goal. The tournament would provide plenty of memorable moments including Betis winning 2–1 in the decider against Sevilla in 1980 – significant because it was the only victory for *Los Verdiblancos* at the Sánchez-Pizjuán between

December 1968 and September 1986. "It was my only victory in the stadium," legendary Real Betis goalkeeper José Ramón Esnaola later recalled. "It was very important regardless of the competition, I will never forget it."

The red-and-white half of Seville would triumph in a total of seven tournaments with Betis lifting the trophy on four occasions, while Brazilian club Vasco da Gama, West Bromwich Albion of England, Uruguay's CA Peñarol and Germany club VfB Stuttgart also lifted solitary titles. The 1992 version had the highest profile as the tournament returned after a seven-year absence to celebrate the Universal Exposition in the city that year. Porto defeated Betis in the showpiece in a version which also included Barcelona, Atlético de Madrid and Vasco da Gama.

"The trophy became a massive deal in Seville every summer," a local journalist, who reported on every one, but wished to retain anonymity, recalled when I spoke to him. "The problem was so many of the finals were Betis against Sevilla, there were five between 1975 and 1980! They were highly tense affairs and just as passionate as any of the other derbies, but it was too early in the season. Whoever lost suffered and season ticket sales might be impacted, while the money went to the Ayuntamiento de Sevilla [the city council]. That led to an ill-feeling between the parties and it was not sustainable. When Betis won in the Sánchez-Pizjuán in 1980, their first win at the ground in 12 years, Sevilla's president [Eugenio] Montes Cabeza pulled the club's support of it."

However, such tournaments were an insight for new arrivals into the city's passion for the sport and the rivalry which existed between its two leading clubs. Years later, on *La Colina Radio Show*, Scotta recalled the impact of the decisive strike against Betis: "It technically was not a competitive match but already the fans told me I had already achieved all I needed to!" Twenty-five years after that goal, Scotta's grandson Valentino Scotta was born and has subsequently progressed through the ranks of Sevilla's youth system.

* * * * *

Throughout their history, Real Betis have developed a reputation as an *equipo ascensor*, a yo-yo team who never stick around too long in any particular division. The club have never spent more than ten seasons in the same tier of Spanish football and the late 1960s signalled the start of a renewed period of flux. Relegation from the Primera in 1966 was followed by immediate promotion back to the top flight the following season, then subsequent demotion in 1968. Segunda titles were then secured in 1971 and again in 1974, with the club's constant rotation underlined by the three promotions being secured by three different men in the dugout – Luis Belló, Antonio Barrios and Ferenc Szusza.

However, Szusza's appointment acted as a steadying hand with five seasons at the helm and managing the club for 130 top-flight matches – a record at the time that has only since been surpassed by Lorenzo Serra Ferrer. The former striker was not well known outside his native Hungary but had a famed playing career at Újpest – netting 393 goals in 463 games and such was his popularity, the club's stadium later was named in his honour – while he was also part of the 'Magical Magyars' national side.

This new-found managerial stability was reflected too in the club's playing staff. To this day, the club's four record appearance holders made their Betis debuts between 1970 and 1976, while eight of the top ten represented the club during this time. It was an era which provided the platform for the club to enjoy success later in the decade. The year 1977 saw Betis lift their first-ever Copa del Rey trophy and subsequently qualify for the following season's Cup Winners' Cup, reviving 'EuroBetis' following a 14-year absence.

Szusza was forced to relinquish his post in 1976 – he would later briefly manage Atlético de Madrid – due to a visa issue. The Hungarian authorities had informed him that summer that he must return to the nation or risk never being allowed to re-enter. The ultimatum had to be decided upon by October and, after coaching the side for the first eight matchdays of the campaign, Szusza was eventually replaced by Rafael Iriondo.

The Basque had played in 15 top-flight seasons as a player, 13 of them with Athletic Club and two with Real Sociedad. His playing career at Athletic included winning one league title and lifting four Copa del Generalísimo trophies, a feat he repeated as their manager in 1969. The tournament changed its title to the Copa del Rey from the 1976/77 campaign onwards, following Franco's death, coinciding with Iriondo's debut season in the Betis hot seat.

The squad he inherited was Szusza's, with the recent inclusion of Dutch international midfielder Gerrie Mühren, known as 'the marshal of Ajax'. Mühren had won 12 trophies with the Amsterdam giants including three European Cups. He spent three seasons in Seville although he would not be available to play in the Copa for Betis due to the competition still forbidding foreign players to appear.

Another key figure of the Betis side ruled out by this technicality was forward Attila Ladinsky, who was originally from Hungary but was declared stateless after the authorities withdrew his citizenship due to his time abroad. In many ways, the Budapest native encapsulated the 70s culture of excess and gained a reputation as a keen drinker who regularly partied. Previously of Feyenoord and Anderlecht, Ladinsky later boasted in interviews that he "drank 45 beers" after scoring the winning penalty when Betis beat Sevilla 1–0 in 1976. "It was with Sevilla players too," he insisted in a 2013 interview with *ABC*. "We went out a lot with the likes of Sanjosé and Paco Gallego to drink beers and whisky. I still have lots of photos of that victory and the penalty, I waited until the last second for Paco [the Sevilla goalkeeper] to move then I shifted in the other direction." The forward's output did not appear to be greatly impacted by his drinking habits, netting 18 goals in 62 appearances for the club.

Ladinsky also spoke of his love for Betis, the city of Sevilla and the derby. "My heart is always going to be with Betis. I have lived unforgettable moments with García Soriano, Cardeñosa and the others, the people there are so wonderful. In my house in Budapest I eat Seville tapas, I like to speak Spanish and cook at home with food I remember from there and I still drink wine of course.

"I played in many derbies ... Vasas against Ferencváros, Standard against Anderlecht and Ajax against Feyenoord, but Betis playing Sevilla is special. When you score you feel so much joy that you feel like you are a flying monster, unstoppable."

The Betis team of the mid-1970s was littered with names who would establish themselves as club legends. Aside from their Copa del Rey triumph and European exploits, their league form was unremarkable (their fifth-place finish in 1977 was the outstanding domestic campaign) but, following the 1978/79 season outside the Primera, the period provided the foundations for a club-record 10-year stay in the top flight until 1989.

In 1977 one such iconic figure made his first-team debut for the club after emerging through their Triana Balompié (later renamed Betis Deportivo) youth system: Rafael Gordillo. El Gordo – his adopted nickname which is the same title as the prize in the famous Spanish Christmas lottery – was handed his debut by Rafael Iriondo on 30 January 1977 against Burgos and developed into not only one of the most adored players in the club's history but one of the most talented too. So good was El Gordo that he was named as the 15th-greatest footballer of the 20th century. The French weekly magazine

France-Football consulted their former Ballon d'Or winners in 2000 to elect the Football Player of the Century, with 30 of the winners voting and Gordillo ranking 15th – a place below George Best and one above Sir Bobby Charlton. The only Spaniard to rank higher on the list was Alfredo di Stéfano, who was voted fourth.

Gordillo was certainly distinctive; playing without shin pads and with his socks around his ankles, it was a peculiar image, like a street footballer. Born in the Extremaduran town of Almendralejo but raised in the Sevillian neighbourhood of Polígono San Pablo, where his parents originated, El Gordo joined the Betis youth ranks aged 15. He would go on to make over 500 top flight appearances across two spells for *Los Verdiblancos* and Real Madrid (forming part of their *La Quinta del Buitre* side) while he won 75 international caps, appearing in five major international tournaments for Spain. Of his three goals for the Spanish national team, just one arrived in Spain and fittingly it came at the Estadio Benito Villamarín against Iceland in September 1985, just months after the wing-back had joined Madrid.

By that stage, El Gordo had made just shy of 300 first-team appearances for Betis over the course of nine seasons and in his third, in 1980, he won the award of Best Spanish Player as run by the Spanish sports magazine *Don Balón*. His unrivalled technical ability and delivery with his left foot was combined with great agility and relentless work rate – he is said to have never stopped running throughout 90 minutes. He won the utmost respect among not only his peers but the fans too. Streets in the Andalusian towns of Guillena and Priego de Córdoba have been named in Gordillo's honour while a roundabout in his beloved Polígono San Pablo also bears his name. During his playing days, he was referred to as *El Vendaval del Polígono* – the gale of Polígono – who felt liberated without shin pads.

Seven years after leaving Betis, Gordillo returned, as he had always vowed he would. By 1992 the club had returned to form and were stuck in the second tier but by El Gordo's second campaign they were back up. After he annouced his retirement in 1995, Betis arranged a tribute match against Real Madrid in front of a packed-out Estadio Benito Villamarín in honour of El Gordo. The clash ended 2–2, with many of his former team-mates returning to action for the clash.

In 1995 he would temporarily emerge from retirement to join Andalusian club Écija Balompié in their heyday in the second tier, and for whom Gordillo later worked as a sporting director. He would then return to Betis as part of the club's technical team in 2000 and spent a year as president between 2010 and 2011. El Gordo proved somewhat of a lucky charm, earning a promotion in each of his stints as a player alongside his two roles off the pitch. "I have been through it all with this club, we have been relegated and there have been plenty of promotions too, but I hope this is the last," he acknowledged back in 2011. The following year, he was elected president of the Fundación del Real Betis and he has held a variety of roles since.

While Gordillo's place among the greats of Betis is without doubt, he was integrated into a side packed full of experience and knowhow. Among them was midfielder Javier López, who was signed from Racing de Santander in 1970 and would spend 12 seasons in the first-team squad. López will be etched into *Los Verdiblancos* legend for netting both goals in the 1977 Copa del Rey 2–2 tie with Athletic Club Bilbao before being capped by the Spanish national team.

López's 12-year stint in Seville was impressive but he was outlasted by two seasons by fellow 1970 summer signing Antonio Benítez. In their obituary published in the wake of Benítez's death in February 2014, *El País* described the versatile player as "introverted, superstitious and shy, with a giant heart." Signed from Xerez for a not inconsiderable sum of 2 million pesetas, Benítez would later captain the side to their 1977 Copa del Rey title. It was a particularly emotional game for Benítez whose mistake – a short back-pass – allowed Athletic's second goal in the Copa showpiece. With tears in his eyes as he realised the potential severity of his error, Benítez was the only one of the ten Betis players not to take a spot-kick in the decisive shootout.

Twenty-one years after Benítez's decision to opt out of striking a penalty, his son Pedro Antonio Benítez captained the Betis youth team that won the Youth Cup in 1998 against Alavés. The decisive penalty was, fittingly, struck by Benítez Jr. Perhaps some things are just meant to be.

The tenth and final penalty taker for Betis in that historic 1977 final was right-back Francisco Bizcocho, who had earned his debut in the Betis first team six years prior. Born in Coria del Río, Bizcocho had spent three years in the Triana Balompié youth team before spending the entirety of his 11-year professional career at Betis. In 2016, he was inducted into the club's Wall of Legends with president Ángel Haro stating: "Bizcocho represents fundamental values in a dressing room: honesty, effort, dedication, pride and love for our colours. He is an example for any Bético."

Central defender Antonio Biosca made his debut in the same year as Bizcocho and just like his team-mate, he would end his career at the Sevillian club. Signed from minnows Calvo Soleto after their demotion to the third tier, he would represent Betis on 285 occasions, scoring 19 goals. Biosca arrived in Seville as a left-back but he was soon converted centrally by boss Ferenc Szusza, with his true potential then realised. The Almería native was renowned for his aerial presence, being strong in the tackle, offering leadership and organisational qualities, while being able to play in several positions.

"The important thing for the side's success through those years was that we were all friends," Biosca recalled to *ABC*. "We were so close, and we still are to this day – we regularly keep in touch, lunch together and enjoy each other's company. We could have won a league title for sure; we know president Pepe Nuñez could not spend the necessary money as the club could not afford it. But we still achieved a lot."

Despite only having that solitary Copa title to show for their strong cohesion over the years, the capability of the individual players was recognised. Even though they were relegated in 1978, Biosca represented *La Roja* at that summer's World Cup along with midfielder Julio Cardeñosa – another cult hero at *Los Verdiblancos*.

Signed from Real Valladolid in 1974 following the club's ascension back to the top flight, Cardeñosa was a technically gifted creative midfielder – playing in the advanced number 10 role – with a wand of a left foot and tremendous vision for picking out a team-mate. His transfer to Betis was far from a formality and indeed the newly promoted club's signing was regarded as somewhat of a coup. Cardeñosa had long been linked to Barcelona, who held a purchase option for the playmaker meaning that anyone wishing to sign him must act swiftly and decisively. It had been reported he would join Sevilla but despite terms being agreed for a switch to *Los Rojiblancos*, they insisted his 13 million pesetas fee be paid in instalments, while Valladolid wanted a straight-up amount. Betis technical secretary José María de la Concha told president Pepe Nuñez he should have no reservations about paying the fee, which may have been considered outlandish, and the deal was done.

The photos of Cardeñosa's presentation displayed a Betis shirt with 17 on the back, to which the vice-president of Real Valladolid reportedly warned: "There has been a mistake, he likes to play with number 10." In response, Betis team attendant Alberto Tenorio (who had literally been born at the club's old Campo del Patronato home, as his dad Antonio, a former player, was then the groundsman) quipped: "He will have to earn it." And earn it Cardeñosa did, with 11 seasons of dedicated service.

Cardeñosa's finest hour – or 34 minutes to be precise – for Betis arguably arrived on 19 March 1978, as his side defeated Sevilla 3–2 in a pulsating derby at the Estadio Benito Villamarín. Entering the match, the hosts were without a win in six competitions; they were out of the Copa, out of Europe and relegation was an ever-increasing possibility. Sevilla, who had won the first derby of the season 1–0 thanks to Sanjosé's goal, were sitting comfortably in mid-table. The game came immediately after Betis's long trip home from the Russian capital after defeat to Dynamo Moscow, and they were underdogs. Yet Cardeñosa put in a virtuoso display to steal the show – he scored two direct free kicks either side of providing the perfect delivery for Javier López to head home. Sevilla had responded through the ever-dependable midfielder Enrique Montero and Biri Biri's penalty, but Betis held on for an unlikely victory, although, true to form, it ultimately was not enough to save them from the drop.

However, Cardeñosa's first goal for Betis had arrived in December 1974 as the Andalusians triumphed 1–0 at one of the cathedrals of Spanish football, Athletic Club's San Mamés. Future Betis boss Rafael Iriondo was in the home dugout but it was Cardeñosa who settled the game on the hour mark, scoring past Athletic's legendary shot-stopper José Ángel Iribar. Betis coach Ferenc Szusza did not make a single change the entire game and their three points were only secured late on thanks to goalkeeper José Ramón Esnaola, who thwarted Athletic's Ángel María Villar from the penalty spot. Three years later, Esnaola would be the penalty shoot-out hero – and not just from those efforts he saved – against Athletic to secure his status of adoration from *Béticos* everywhere.

It was somewhat ironic that Esnaola's most memorable moments came against the Bilbao giants; the goalkeeper was himself Basque but came from the Gipuzkoa province whose capital city is Donostia-San Sebastián, home of Real Sociedad. Indeed, Esnaola spent the first eight seasons of his professional career at La Real but it all could have been so different when, aged 19, he became severely ill when suffering a serious injury against Las Palmas. Spanish media reported he was in a "grave condition" after an accidental on-field collision and was subsequently rushed to hospital. It later emerged that he had shattered his pancreas and there were genuine fears that he would never play again. As it turned out, he would not only make a full recovery but establish himself as one of the nation's finest goalkeepers across the next two decades.

Esnaola joined Betis in the summer of 1973 in what was somewhat of a surprise move. *Los Verdiblancos* had just been relegated from the top flight while La Real had established themselves as a top-half side. Years later, the goalkeeper recalled how the move came about: "I was on honeymoon in Málaga and we passed through Utrera [a small town in the province of Seville], to see a relative of my wife. I could not stand the heat – it was 44 degrees – and said we must return to San Sebastián, and that I would only return to play football with La Real. But you never can tell what will happen in life, and later I signed for Betis."

It was just one piece of curiosity that meant that Esnaola – who remains the record appearance holder at Betis – was unlikely to ever sign for the club. Yet his eventual transfer to the Andalusians came with plenty of twists. He had initially agreed to join Atlético de Madrid while Real Sociedad had already signed his replacement, Francisco Urruti. Esnaola was then injured, ironically against Betis, which led to Atléti getting cold feet and cancelling the deal. The goalkeeper was left in limbo and that was when *Los Verdiblancos* made their move. The shot-stopper was also one of the figures for whom admiration crossed both sides of the football divide in the city, despite playing in 18 league derbies. "Even *Sevillistas* have told me that I was a fantastic goalkeeper and a good person. In the testimonial match for Pablo Blanco I gave him a gift and the Sevilla fans stood as one and gave me an ovation. I will never forget that."

On 25 June 1977, all these players would realise their potential and see their loyalty to Betis rewarded. Played at a full 70,000-capacity Vicente Calderón Stadium, home of Atléti, Betis faced Athletic Club in the Copa del Rey showpiece. It was an eagerly anticipated showdown but the Basques – who were aiming for their 23rd title having finished third in La Liga that campaign – were favourites against a team who, despite finishing a credible fifth that year, were in their first cup final since their 1931 defeat to the same opponents.

Betis lined up that day in Madrid as: Esnaola, Bizcocho, Biosca, Sabaté, Cobo, López, Alabanda, Cardeñosa, Soriano, Megido, Benítez. It took just 14 minutes for the Basques to take the lead as Carlos Ruiz Herrero opened the scoring but Francisco López hit back just before the break. The second half ended goalless to force extra time and when Spain international Dani restored Athletic Club's lead in the 97th minute, Betis feared the worst. However, with just four minutes remaining López – who had managed just 11 league goals in his first six seasons – struck again to send the Andalusians into euphoria and give them the momentum ahead of a nerve-ridden penalty shoot-out.

Both teams netted each of their first four penalties – Soriano, del Pozo, López and Biosca all successful for Betis, who were going first – but the great Julio Cardeñosa saw his effort blocked by the imposing José Ángel Iribar. It was match point for Athletic Club. Goalscorer Dani stepped up but saw his effort blocked by Esnaola, who later recounted: "I had never faced Dani from the spot before, but I knew he always went to the right. I had written down in a notebook how all their players preferred to go and that stayed in my mind."

As the shoot-out entered added time the tension was unbearable; defender Jaume Sabaté kept his head but after the Basques netted their effort, Sebastián Alabanda was thwarted by Iribar. Originating from Córdoba, the midfielder spent 11 years of his career at Betis including eight in the first-team squad and had been capped by Spain the previous year. Athletic, once again, stood on the verge but Esnaola, once again, was the hero for Betis as he got a hand to the penalty from Ángel María Villar, who decades later would be elected as FIFA vice-president. Esnaola himself then scored, as did Eulate and Bizcocho, who put Betis 8-7 up.

The epic penalty shoot-out was exhausting to watch and, by penalty 20, it was time for Athletic goalkeeper and captain Iribar to step up himself. His counterpart Esnaola stood firm once more and Betis landed their first Copa. "I don't remember much other than the hugs after it," laughed the shoot-out hero. His boss Irionda said in the aftermath: "I am extremely proud, and a little sorry." From the tiny town of Guernica, in the province of Bilbao, this victory had particular significance for the coach. Just as had been the case with their only major triumph prior to this victory, 42 years earlier, it was Basque heroes who dragged Betis over the line.

There was genuine hope that the Copa victory would prove to be the start of success rather than the pinnacle for this Betis side. They had recorded their first top-five Primera finish in 13 seasons and had won only the second major trophy in their history. Their triumph had guaranteed a spot in the following campaign's Cup Winners' Cup and this time 'EuroBetis' would live up to the expectation.

Coppa Italia holders Milan were first up but goals from Garcia Soriano and Eulate earned Betis a historic 2–0 victory at the Benito Villamarín. The Milanese giants improved considerably for the return leg and had levelled the tie thanks to strikes from Ugo Tossetto and

Fabio Capello but Francisco López continued his knack of scoring crucial goals as he netted the all-important away goal to seal progression. Next up were Lokomotiv Leipzig with López continuing his streak to give *Los Verdiblancos* the lead before Wilfried Gröbner sealed a draw for the hosts. A fortnight later, Garcia Soriano netted either side of Matthias Liebers's away goal in Seville to book a place in the quarter-finals.

There was a four-month break between November and March in the competition with Betis eyeing the possibility of going all the way. They returned with a home clash with USSR giants Dynamo Moscow but a frustrating encounter ended scoreless despite the hosts dominating and rattling the woodwork twice through Garcia Soriano.

The real controversy would surround the return leg two weeks later, when Betis flew to the Russian capital for the scheduled encounter before being informed that, due to heavy snow in Moscow, the game had been switched to Tbilisi. "It was a crazy situation," goalkeeper Esnaola recalled in a later interview. "Our coach, Iriondo, was absolutely furious, he was screaming and shouting. He told us all he wanted to see [Soviet political leader, Leonid] Brezhnev because of the scandal. We had to sleep at the airport, we did not have any food. Finally, a plane arrived to take us to Georgia but the impact was clear."

Iriondo's men were downed 3–0 in the city, now capital of Georgia, but reports at the time suggested their treatment throughout their stay was abominable, with no hot water in their showers or heating in their accommodation despite the freezing temperatures. It was a painful experience and appeared to derail the remainder of their campaign.

Despite winning their following match – Cardeñosa's virtuoso display in the 3–2 derby victory – Betis were relegated two months later. It was a demotion steeped in misfortune as Betis occupied the final relegation spot despite having a vastly superior goal difference to both Español and Hércules, who each retained their top-flight status due to the league's convoluted system of balancing points won at home compared to away. So tight was that season's league table that Betis finished within six points of Atlético de Madrid, ten positions above.

The quirk of the club being relegated in the same campaign in which they reached a European quarter-final is something in itself, but remarkably history would repeat itself in similar fashion 28 years later – a long European campaign being intertwined with relegation. In both instances, Betis bounced straight back to the top division at the first attempt and would remain there for a full decade, the most consistent runs in the club's history.

Chapter 20
Consistency Without Titles

SPAIN was infected with World Cup fever in the early 1980s as the nation fine-tuned their infrastructure ahead of hosting the 1982 edition. The tournament was a long time coming, having been awarded 18 years earlier when Franco's grip of power was seemingly stronger than ever. That was a time when the authoritarian regime was celebrating the 25th anniversary of their ascent to power and the conclusion of the Civil War. They were afforded the perfect PR foot-up as the national team lifted the European Championships in Madrid, defeating their ideological enemy the USSR in the showpiece. (see Chapter 2)

The 1980s were a very different time in Spain; Franco died on 20 November 1975 and the fascist regime was buried with him as the *Transición Española* began in earnest. In 1977, Spain held its first democratic elections in over four decades and a year later the Constitution of Spain was approved. The political situation remained particularly delicate but the failed Spanish coup d'état attempt in 1981 appeared to offer genuine consolidation of democracy in the nation. The socialist PSOE (Spanish Socialist Workers' Party) were elected the following year – under *Sevillano* and self-confessed *Bético* Felipe González – and remained in power for 14 years, allowing Spain to become a more self-assured, confident nation.

Yet González would not enter power until six months after the World Cup with the short-lived, and somewhat unsatisfactory coalition, Union of the Democratic Centre entering its final stretch of power. It was an uncertain time politically not only for Spain but globally, with the Falklands War still ongoing between two of the competition's participants – England and Argentina. There were strong signs of reconciliation on both fronts as the conflict in the

South Atlantic officially ended within 24 hours of the World Cup opening ceremony.

Held at Barcelona's Camp Nou stadium, Spanish Football Federation president Pablo Porta gave his inaugural speech in both Spanish and Catalan, the region in which he was born. "Barcelonans, Catalans, Spanish all, thank you, thank you very much for the welcome of our visitors," said Porta, following a ceremony preaching unity and peace. In the Camp Nou centre circle, a football opened from which a dove of peace was released in front of 2,216 children all dressed in white as inspired by artist Pablo Picasso's famous bird of peace. This was not so much asking for harmony as demanding it.

Seville would play a fundamental role throughout the tournament and indeed had been the birthplace of the tournament's emblematic image, Naranjito. The endearing mascot was the brainchild of Andalusian duo José María Martín Pacheco – a Sevilla fan from the region's capital – and the Cordobesa Dolores Salto Zamora. They created the image of the orange, in the offices of advertising company Publicidad Bellido in the heart of Seville, one of 586 drawings submitted by 200 agencies for the competition. José María, who had a strong background in advertising, was said to be the innovator of the idea while Dolores designed the shape and colour of the citrus fruit, adorned in a Spain kit and holding a football. "I saw oranges and wondered why not? I wanted to avoid the bull and the tambourine [the Spanish stereotypes] as mascot," José María later explained.

Initially, Naranjito's critical reception was particularly unfavourable. Many commentators called it a "monstrosity" and "public enemy number one", with suggestions that it would be better off drowned in the Guadalquivir. The offending item was even called "an infiltrated Francoist dwarf" – perhaps highlighting the delicate nature of Spanish nationalism at the time. The panel who decided that Naranjito was the winning design based their stance on how it accurately represented everything positive about Spain: colour, sunshine, happiness and fun. It is no coincidence that those who thought up the idea were from the middle of Andalusia. "Look, in Seville it smells of orange blossom and it's full of orange trees," José María told an interview with *El Mundo*. "We even export it to England because there they make bitter orange marmalade, it is famous. The mascot occurred to me walking the streets. As I said at the time, it was soft, sweet and pleasant. I wanted to break the stereotype of Spain."

A bone of contention emerged as the Spanish Federation bought the rights to the infamous image for 1 million pesetas before later selling it to a British company for 1,400 million pesetas. By that stage, opinion had shifted on Naranjito with plenty of merchandise adorned with his orange face and smiling, red cheeks. He was even the protagonist of TV series *Football in Action*, alongside his girlfriend Clementine and friends Citroni and the Imarchi robot, in which the writers inevitably had their creative juices flowing.

As it transpired, the legacy of Naranjito proved to be significantly more positive than that of Spain's wretched World Cup campaign. An opening game draw with lowly Honduras set the tone for an ill-fated tournament with Spain only scraping through their opening group; a win over Yugoslavia enough despite a shock defeat against 10-man Northern Ireland in Valencia. The second group would prove a bridge too far with defeat to West Germany and a draw with England seeing *La Roja* finish bottom of the group and being eliminated.

The visiting nations had not read the script and Spain were denied their spot in the semi-final at Sevilla's Ramón Sánchez-Pizjuán. Both stadiums in Seville had undergone a major remodelling ahead of the tournament, including a modernisation of facilities with emphasis on upgrades in lighting and ability to show night-time games on colour television.

Sevilla's stadium was also upgraded by a commemorative mosaic at its front, courtesy of Cordovan painter Santiago del Campo. The beautifully constructed and sizeable – standing at 470 square-metres – mosaic was built by 25 craftsmen with Sevilla's badge dominating the piece, surrounded by 58 other club shields. Real Betis are one of those included – although it is partially shadowed by that of French club Stade de Reims – while Real Madrid, Barcelona, Juventus, Bayern Munich, Arsenal, Santos and Independiente are among the eclectic mix of pennants. The city's delegate for the World Cup initially was Adolfo Cuéllar Contreras, a *Bético*, who was later replaced by *Sevillista* Ginés López-Cirera Villalba, then president of the Federación Andaluza (club affiliation for representation of the city was, predictably, a source of constant attention).

Seville became home to hordes of Brazil fans during the tournament, with the *Seleção's* opening group games against the USSR (held at the Ramón Sánchez-Pizjuán), Scotland and New Zealand (both at the Benito Villamarín) all taking place in the city. The toughest proposition for the pre-tournament favourites was their opening game against the imposing USSR whose renowned goalkeeper Rinat Dasayev – considered the second-best Russian goalkeeper ever behind Lev Yashin – would later spend the final three seasons of his career at Sevilla. The Eastern Europe side were unfortunate, having two strong penalty appeals turned down by Spanish official Lamo Castillo, and eventually falling to a 2–1 loss. While Spain having the opportunity, in the home of Sevilla, to reach their first World Cup final would no doubt have been a special occasion, the semi-final between West Germany and France would produce one of the tournament's all-time classic fixtures. France captain Michel Platini later recalled the fixture as his "most beautiful game", even if it is predominantly remembered for a brutal and callous incident.

With the game locked at 1–1 in the early stages of the second half, Platini played a defence-splitting pass to Patrick Battiston who had himself just taken to the field. Battiston comfortably beat the advancing German goalkeeper Harald Schumacher to the ball, before being knocked unconscious by a blatant shoulder smash. So serious were the Frenchman's injuries that he suffered cracked vertebra in his back, three broken ribs and permanently damaged teeth. Unbelievably, no foul was awarded by referee Charles Corver, who awarded West Germany the goal kick. Despite a lengthy stoppage in which Battiston lay prostrate on the floor and required substantial medical attention, Schumacher did not attend to his victim and instead showed his frustration at not being able to swiftly restart the action. The incident became known as the Tragedy of Seville, while the West German and French governments were forced into releasing a joint statement to calm tensions, such was the outrage. The game itself went to extra time, when France blew a 3–1 lead before eventually losing 5–4 on penalties. Days later, West Germany were defeated in Madrid's showpiece, losing 3–1 to Italy.

* * * * *

Two years prior to hosting football's most prestigious tournament, the sporting emphasis in the city was Sevilla FC celebrating their *Bodas de Platino* 75th anniversary (decades prior to the club reverting their foundation date from 1905 to 1890). The festivities began with a series of artistic performances at the Ramón Sánchez-Pizjuán with several local talents such as Naranjito de Triana, Pepa Montes, Paco Gandía, Ana María Bueno and María Jiménez performing live. The centrepiece of the celebrations focused on Sevilla's friendly with Brazilian club Santos three days later, although a 1–0 win for the visitors in front of just 15,000 spectators was not a memorable one. Indeed, the abiding memory of the clash was former Sevilla goalkeeper and two-time

Spain manager Guillermo Eizaguirre (See Chapter 2), now 71 years old, kicking off proceedings, ahead of a night of festivities at the city's luxury Hotel Alfonso XIII.

The links between Brazil and Seville were particularly prominent at the time, ahead of the South American nation making the city home for their World Cup ventures. Sevilla's best player of the time was midfielder Carlos Alberto Gomes Montero, better known as Pintinho. Signed from Vasco de Gama in 1981, the 26-year-old had already won three caps for the Seleção by the time he arrived in Andalusia. "It is true that at the time the team depended on me a lot and if things did not go well, then I was blamed," Pintinho explained to *ABC de Sevilla* decades later. "As soon as I arrived, teams put a defender on me for the entire game and it made things difficult."

It was not just on the pitch that the former Fluminense player struggled to adapt; Seville in the early 1980s did not enjoy the level of diversity that was to come in the decades that followed. "When I arrived, there was only one other black person in the city – a university student. I have seen him in the years since, he is a doctor now, and we often talk about it. It's great to see how things have changed but at the time we were just two kids and we were famous because of it … things are different now."

But Pintinho's memories of his time in Seville are overwhelmingly positive: "I still have all the headlines, written by the journalist José Manuel García, saved in my house: 'The king of Nervión', 'Samba has come', 'The black pearl'. We played 4-3-3, we were a very offensive team who liked to keep possession and play high up."

Manolo Cardo had been appointed manager at *Los Rojiblancos* shortly after Pintinho's Andalusian arrival and his offensive system allowed the Brazilian to net 23 league goals in his four seasons with Sevilla. Cardo had replaced Miguel Muñoz in the dugout and he would spend five years in the post – a club record since the formation of La Liga and one that has been matched only once in the years since, by Joaquín Caparrós in 2005. Cardo had been a squad player for *Los Rojiblancos* between 1962 and 1967 but gained prominence in coaching the club's youth sides, with a year in charge of Sevilla Atletico before his promotion to the first team.

Cardo's managerial debut came in the 15th round of La Liga matches that season – a testing trip to La Romareda to face Real Zaragoza. Pintinho was the star of the show for Sevilla; netting all four goals in a convincing 4–1 victory, with future Real Madrid legend Jorge Valdano responding for the hosts. Sevilla had started the match second from bottom in the 18-team league but a resurgence in form under the new boss resulted in a seventh-place finish, just one place and one point behind Real Betis – enough for both sides to qualify for Europe.

For *Los Verdiblancos* this was a third consecutive top six finish – their best sustained run of league finishes since their 1935 title. It was boss Luis Cid, known as Carriega, who had laid the foundations for this relative success, having taken the path less travelled and swapped the red half of Seville for Betis in 1979. The Galician had completed three full campaigns in charge at Sevilla but had been unable to guide his side into the top seven in these attempts. Out of work but remaining in Seville, newly promoted Betis dispensed with coach León Lasa after just two games the following season and turned to the experienced Carriega, who in 66 league games with the club won 29 and lost just 19.

By 1981, Carriega was snapped up by Atlético de Madrid and was replaced in Heliópolis by former player Luis Aragonés – who himself had spent the previous six seasons in charge at Atléti – but after just one game, a 2-1 defeat at Racing de Santander, he was gone. The symmetry between the two would continue as Carriega was sacked by the capital club after just 11 league games and three seasons later would return to Betis while by 1982 Aragonés had returned to Atléti. Returning Copa del Rey winning hero Rafael Iriondo replaced Aragonés in Seville and stabilised results. However, with five games of the season remaining and results stagnant, Iriondo was relieved of his duties with Betis believing European qualification remained in reach. They were right; club stalwart Pedro Buenaventura Gil (see Chapter 6) took charge of first-team affairs and secured three wins in his first four matches, before a final day draw in Barcelona clinched the club's place in continental competition.

Instability in the Betis dugout would continue into the following campaign with two new faces coming and going over the course of the year. First up was Hungarian Antal Dunai, aged just 39 and appointed following his success with Andalusian side Xerez, whom he guided to the second tier. Yet, as has been the case throughout their history, the bubble for Betis burst as soon as it began to properly take shape.

Dunai was beset with various problems right from the off, including with England international winger Peter Barnes who had been bought from Leeds United that summer. Speaking to *Diario AS* a month into the season, Dunai gave a frank interview explaining why the 25-year-old had not been involved more in early games: "The situation is not good, that's the truth. Of course, you need to take into account he is at a new club with a different style of play, a new climate and another language, but the truth is he has no understanding with the others. He needs to solve the language problem because we cannot play with no communication."

Barnes's stint in Seville was brief, lasting just one season in which he started only 12 times, but he outlasted Dunai who was gone by Christmas after just four wins in 18 games. The Hungarian had overseen the club's European exit too as they were eliminated by Benfica. It was the first appearance in the UEFA Cup for Betis – whose only previous European fixtures had come in the Cup Winners' Cup and its predecessor, the Fairs Cup – but the draw pitting them against the Portuguese giants presented a massive task.

Betis were edged out 2–1 in the first leg in Lisbon, which *ABC de Sevilla* headlined "A Result for Hope" ahead of the return in Seville. The away goal was netted by Paraguayan striker Carlos Diarte, whose struggles in domestic competition mirrored the decline for the team that campaign. Nicknamed *El Lobo*, the wolf, the South American had joined Valencia in 1976 in a landmark 60 million pesetas deal but despite netting 16 league goals in his debut season, there were fears he might never replicate these heights after tearing his knee ligaments. With just two league goals across the next two seasons, he spent a year with Salamanca before Betis gambled on his signing in 1980 and it proved to be a masterstroke.

Diarte formed a fantastic striking partnership with Enrique Morán, who had arrived from Sporting de Gijón the previous year. The two were devastating and when they clicked opposition defences could not handle them, as evidenced in the stunning 4–0 victory at Atlético de Madrid (then leaders of the Primera) in February 1981. By that summer, Morán was signed by Barcelona having hit 30 league goals across two seasons at Betis, leaving Diarte as the main goal threat. Despite netting 27 times in his opening two campaigns, the 1982/83 season saw him strike just twice in the league.

The Paraguayan would join French side Saint-Etienne at the end of the campaign but his strike in the Portuguese capital had given Betis hope of another memorable European result. A full house at the Benito Villamarín saw 5,000 travelling Benfica fans create a raucous atmosphere in Seville. The home fans exploded into life when a delightfully threaded through-ball from Julio Cardeñosa found Hipólito 'Poli' Rincón, who produced his typical masterful finish to give Betis the lead on away goals.

Rincón had arrived from Real Madrid the previous summer and had been earmarked as the long-term replacement for the outgoing Morán. Whilst the 1970s were about longevity for Betis, the 80s were shaped more so by inspired signings and Rincón topped the list. This was the season, his second at the club, when he would win the club's first and only Pichichi award courtesy of the 20 top-flight goals he netted throughout the campaign. It was an achievement made all the more remarkable by the club finishing 11th – their traditional dip whilst competing in Europe. Rincón would go on to net a total of 78 Primera goals for Betis – more than anyone else in the history of the club – while also scoring 10 goals in 22 caps for Spain.

Benfica took control of the game in the second half and late goals from Carlos Manuel and Nené saw Sven-Göran Eriksson's side progress, and they would go on to advance all the way to that season's final. It was an underwhelming return to European competition for Betis, as they celebrated their 75th anniversary. Events had begun in early September, coinciding with the birth date of the club, with a strong theme of Catholicism at its heart. Carlos Amigo Vallejo, the newly appointed Bishop of Seville, gave a mass of thanksgiving while the bells of the city's cathedrals rang in celebration. The centrepiece of the celebrations was a friendly game organised against Universidad Nacional de México, with a special plaque to honour the club's fans unveiled at the Benito Villamarín. Half-time saw a number of club legends paraded around the pitch as Betis ran out 2-1 victors thanks to goals from Rincón and Antonio Parra – a youth product who would later spend two seasons at both Atlético de Madrid and Real Madrid.

Yet one of the most famous matches in the history of the Benito Villamarín happened in December 1983 but it was not involving Betis, rather the national team. The Netherlands's 2–1 victory over Spain the previous month ensured their qualification group for the following summer's European Championships was going to the wire – both sides were level on points with one game to play, with an absence of scheduling sense ensuring both teams' one remaining game was at home to Malta.

The Netherlands defeated the minnows – whose captain was the appropriately named John Holland – 5–0 and having entered the round with a goal difference six goals superior to *La Roja.*, it meant Spain would need an 11-goal winning margin in Seville four days later to progress. Ahead of the match, the visiting goalkeeper John Bonello spectacularly tempted fate by telling reporters: "Spain couldn't even score 11 against a team of children."

There was no sign of a Spanish fairy tale at half-time despite a hat-trick from Real Madrid striker Santillana, as a Malta goal and missed penalty from Zaragoza's Juan Antonio Señor compounded the frustration. Rincón added a fourth in his home stadium a minute after the break and then scored his second nine minutes later. With just 30 minutes remaining, the hosts needed an unparalleled seven goals without conceding. In an unforeseen spell of craziness, Sporting de Gijón central defender Antonio Maceda netted two goals inside 90 seconds and barely had the game restarted when Rincón completed his hat-trick. Amid the euphoria, a comeback appeared possible but 12 minutes came and went with none of the required four goals being added. Then Santillana added his fourth and Spain's ninth while Rincón also made it a personal quadruple minutes later. Athletic Bilbao's Manuel Sarabia (whose son Eder would later be an assistant coach in the stadium with Real Betis) made it 11-1 before the hosts completed the scoring in the closing minutes, fittingly through Señor.

Netherlands boss Kees Rijvers somewhat magnanimously admitted "miracles can happen in football", but suspicions of foul play resurfaced in 2018 when two Maltese players along with boss Victor Scerri claimed they had been drugged at half-time. Scerri claimed on Spanish TV network Movistar that "whilst we have no proof", lemon wedges given to his side at half-time "by a man dressed in white" drugged his players. Silvio Demanuele – the scorer for the visitors that day – corroborated this information, claiming that he felt drunk during the second half. Another player, Carmel Busuttil, outlined how the training facilities and shabby accommodation had already raised suspicions among the group. Demanuele also claimed Spanish players were foaming at the mouth during the game and were drinking excessive amounts of water to compensate. The striker claimed that the symptoms were the same as steroids usage, citing his brother's bodybuilding career. It is important to clarify that, as at time of writing, none of these allegations or those surrounding match-fixing have ever been proven.

The match in Seville was one of the most significant for the Spanish national team throughout the 20th century and helped propel them to the final of the 1984 European Championships, before they fell to defeat against France. Betis could not replicate this success on the European stage despite returning to the UEFA Cup after an impressive fifth-place finish in the 1983/84 campaign. Under the guidance of Pepe Alzate, Betis were undefeated through their 17 home games that season, winning 15 and conceding just seven goals.

José Carlos Suárez, a goalscoring midfielder signed from Celta de Vigo in 1983, netted the only goal of the game as Betis defeated Romanian side Universitatea Craiova in Seville but there was a clear sense of frustration with *Los Verdiblancos* missing a number of clear opportunities; "Many opportunities but just one goal", as *ABC* wrote.

The Romanian side had reached the competition's semi-finals two years previously only to be knocked out on away goals by Benfica but this time round they progressed via the ruling at the expense of Betis. Austrian referee Heinz Fahnler was heavily criticised after the match which saw Diego Rodríguez sent off for Betis and an away goal controversially disallowed. "Eliminated by the referee", as *Marca* put it, with the hosts progressing after triumphing 5–3 in the penalty shoot-out. As was by now tradition for the club, their league form fell through the floor while they competed in Europe and they dropped nine places to 14th, avoiding relegation by a solitary point.

Concerns over such an alarming trait would dissipate with Heliópolis not seeing European football for another 11 seasons. Carriega had returned to the dugout to replace the outgoing Alzate in the closing stages of the 1984/85 campaign but he himself was replaced a year later by club legend Luis del Sol. Firmly established as one of the greatest players to have emerged not only from Seville, but the entirety of Spain, the former midfielder had spent time coaching the Betis youth sides before being elevated into the hot seat. Del Sol oversaw 50 matches at the helm but appeared to quickly fall out of love with the role – only managing 20 games at Recreativo de Huelva in 1990 before an interim return to Betis in 2001.

The club's league performances throughout the latter half of the 1980s were underwhelming but they did reach the final of the short-lived Copa de la Liga de España in 1986. In what were to prove the final matches of the competition, which had begun just four years earlier, del Sol's side faced Barcelona over two legs. They had beaten Osasuna, Valencia and fourth-placed Zaragoza to reach the showpiece. Betis defeated Barça 1–0 in the first leg in Seville and, fittingly for a team managed by del Sol, started with six youth products of the club: Diego Rodríguez, Al-Lal 'Alex' Mohamed, Antonio Parra, José 'Quico' Ruiz, José Ramón Romo and Perico Medina.

The game's only goalscorer was Argentine midfielder Gabriel Calderón, who would later join Paris Saint-Germain, in a 70 million peseta deal, and win 23 caps for his nation – one of which arrived as a substitute in the 1990 World Cup Final. He had been the marquee signing for Betis in 1983, aged 23, filling the foreigner spot vacated by fellow winger Peter Barnes, and enjoyed much greater influence than the Englishman. In his four seasons in Seville he netted 46 goals – an admirable return for a non-forward. Calderón's goal in Seville wasn't enough to secure the trophy for del Sol's men as Barça won the return leg at the Camp Nou 2–0.

Chapter 21

Betis Flounder as Sevilla Challenge

NOT since their debut European campaign in 1957 had Sevilla managed to progress in Europe but Manolo Cardo's team 25 years later replicated the feat, progressing past both Bulgarian side Levski Sofia and PAOK of Greece, before falling to defeat against German side Kaiserslautern in the round of 16. Unlike across the city at Betis, their European exploits did not have an adverse impact on their league form with Sevilla's fifth-place finish their highest in 13 years.

That was enough to secure a further season of European football but, like Betis the previous year, Sevilla fell by the wayside against Lisbon-based opponents. Enrique Magdaleno had given the Andalusians an 18th-minute lead in the first leg home clash against Sporting CP, but a second-half strike from Manuel Fernandes levelled the tie ahead of the return in Lisbon. It was a similar pattern for the second meeting as Enrique Montero and Francisco López twice gave Sevilla the advantage, but the hosts hit back twice before António Oliveira's decisive strike two minutes from time.

The end of that campaign brought about a key moment of change at *Los Rojiblancos* when Eugenio Montes Cabeza finished his 11-year presidency and was replaced by cattle businessman Gabriel Rojas. As vice-president, Rojas had made several improvements to the club's home including its modernisations and adaptation to an all-seater stadium. He was the individual accredited with the Sánchez-Pizjuán's awarding of the 1986 European Cup Final, when Barcelona famously failed to lift their first major European crown as Bobby Robson's side were defeated by Steaua Bucharest 2–0 on penalties.

Sevilla were still a long way from securing European glory themselves and Rojas lasted only two years in the presidency, when unsatisfactory results led to a change in management. Local businessman Luis Cuervas Vilches took the reins and remained in the post for nine years, but the first half of his presidency involved steering the club through choppy waters. From 1985 started a run of five consecutive seasons of underperformance as Sevilla failed to register a top-eight finish nor record so much as a quarter-final appearance in the Copa del Rey. Managers came and went and Manolo Cardo's five-year stint ended in acrimonious circumstances as he fell out with the club's hierarchy. Scotsman Jock Wallace was appointed in the hope of writing a new chapter linking Sevilla to the nation, but he lasted just one season in Andalusia.

Wallace had been appointed at the club months before Cuervas assumed his presidency and the talk at the time was that a change of management was inevitable barring an unforeseen run of strong form. Wallace had been sacked from his boyhood club Glasgow Rangers and was part of the mid-80s trend that brought British coaches to Spain, with Robson at Barcelona and John Toshack at Real Sociedad. A year after the Scot's arrival in Nervión, Englishman John Mortimore was appointed for a brief and unsuccessful stint across the city at Betis. The problem for Wallace was that he did not speak a word of Spanish, indeed he was only appointed after the owner of a Spanish restaurant in Leicester – which the Scot frequented when he coached the city's football team – acted as an interpreter in the negotiation process.

Perhaps it was unsurprising that the manager returned to raid Rangers for winger Ted McMinn, who had fallen out with Wallace's replacement Graeme Souness, and who had been brought to Glasgow from Queen of the South by the boss. McMinn later wrote his autobiography *The Tin Man*, in which he revealed that the language barrier the pair faced in Spain brought them closer than could have possibly been imagined.

"A couple of our favourite haunts lay on the other side of a notorious park called the Murillo Gardens," McMinn recalled. "During the day, it would be filled with families ... but after dark it became a hang-out for homosexuals, who were preyed on by local youths. Jock didn't scare easily and would walk straight through regardless of the danger. He believed they were less likely to attack couples so would take my hand and mince through as best he could. When we reached the other end he'd drop it like a stone, hoping no one had seen us. A keen-eyed photographer could have sold the story of 'Gay Football Manager and his Star Signing' for a fortune these days, but we always managed to get away with it."

It is unclear what drew Wallace to Sevilla initially – perhaps the fact that rivals Real Betis shared the green and white of Glasgow Celtic – but despite his dismissal at the end of the campaign, he wished to stay there. Unfortunately for him, president Cuervas had other ideas and sacked him the following August, despite allowing him to oversee pre-season. "This [decision] was due to the lack of progress with Wallace's Spanish," Cuervas said at the time. Apparently, there was a clause in his contract which said he must have mastered the language by the end of summer. Wallace was not perturbed, and he applied for the vacant job at Atlético de Madrid in 1988 but lost out to Ron Atkinson.

While Wallace's sole campaign yielded an unspectacular 10th-place finish, he had a profound impact on many of his players and he utilised the club's strong traditions of integrating youth players into the squad. Midfielders Jesús Choya and Rafael Paz Marín alongside forward Ramón Vázquez were all afforded prominent roles by Wallace, who was restricted by a lack of funds but was not afraid to give youth graduates their opportunities. Full-back Manuel 'Manolo' Jiménez, who would go on to become a Sevilla legend, was another youngster who, aged 22, was appointed vice-captain by the Scot.

"We had a very young squad at the time," Jiménez – who spent 13 years in Sevilla's first-team before spending a decade in a coaching capacity with the youth side and first team – recalled in an interview decades later: "Some of the players, like myself, had been promoted from the youth team, but Jock wasn't scared to use us. He made me vice-captain before I went on to captain Sevilla for 10 years.

"Jock's spell in Sevilla speaks for itself. Some coaches would never have had the same faith in the young home-grown players. But he stuck with us, he gave us confidence and became so influential in so many of our careers. Seven of the young players, including myself, went on to become Sevilla legends and play for Spain. The respect we earned throughout the years playing for Sevilla was all thanks to Jock. People still look at us as legends here and everybody knows that Jock was the man who made us believe in ourselves."

Fittingly, Jiménez was boss of Sevilla when they took on Rangers in the group stage of the 2009/10 Champions League. Sadly, Wallace had passed away 13 years earlier and prior to the game his former player spoke of how close their bond had been: "He came to see my debut for Spain in Sevilla against Argentina in 1988. It was a very special game for me because it was my international debut in front of all the Sevilla fans. I remember it very well because Jock had bought a house in Fuengirola and he had travelled back to Sevilla to watch me playing with Spain. I was honoured.

"Usually at the end of the game, players exchange jerseys with the opponents, but I didn't want to swap my jersey with an Argentinian player ... it had to be for Jock. It was a symbolic gesture towards him, but for me it was simply a very humble way to thank him for all the confidence and time he took to help me as a footballer. I still remember that moment with goosebumps and I'll always remember what Jock did for me. To be managing a game for Sevilla against Rangers is such a special moment for me."

Jiménez guided *Los Rojiblancos* to a convincing 4–1 victory in Glasgow that night, but whilst he was a player for the club those glorious European nights felt like a long way off. Primarily a left-back, he had formed part of a long-standing defensive unit, all of whom spent the majority of their careers at Sevilla, their local club. Right-back José Ramón Nimo had nine seasons in the first team until 1988, before spending the final season of his career at Betis. Central defender Antonio Álvarez Giráldez, another Seville native who would later spend eight years as assistant manager before briefly managing the side to the 2010 Copa del Rey title, made his debut aged 19 in 1974 and stayed in the first-team squad for 14 seasons until playing out the autumn of his career at Málaga. The year 1988 also saw the departure of Ricardo Jesús Serna who had debuted for *Los Rojiblancos* aged 18 and swiftly emerged as a star before spending the prime of his career at Barcelona, where he counted a European Cup title and Cup Winners' Cup trophy among his six honours in the Catalan capital.

Goalkeeper Francisco Buyo, signed from Deportivo de La Coruña in 1980, made 199 appearances in Sevilla's first team across six seasons and it would have been many more had he not signed for Real Madrid. Buyo spent a further 11 years in the Spanish capital, winning 12 major titles and by the time of announcing his retirement, he had appeared in 542 La Liga matches. Nicknamed 'the cat of Betanzos', after his Galician hometown, he earned international recognition whilst in Seville and is widely recognised as one of the greatest goalkeepers in the club's history.

Like Jiménez, midfielder Rafael 'Rafa' Paz made his first-team debut in the 1984/85 campaign and would remain in the first team until 1997, when he joined Mexican side Club Celaya for the final season of his career. Paz would become arguably the most recognisable Sevilla player between the 1980s and 90s, while he won seven caps for Spain including two at the 1990 World Cup in Italy, the only

Andalusian-based player to make the squad aside from club team-mate Jiménez.

Another Spanish international who was fundamental to Sevilla's identity during the 1980s was midfielder Francisco Javier López Alfaro. Born in the Sevillian town of Osuna, Francisco amassed over 250 first-team appearances across nine seasons with Sevilla and was capped 20 times by his nation – the most by any Spanish Nervionenses player at the time, and which has since been surpassed only by Jesús Navas.

However, Sevilla would not threaten the league's elite until the end of the decade, when Vicente Cantatore led the club to UEFA Cup qualification at the end of the 1989/90 campaign. Austrian striker Toni Polster, signed from Torino the previous year, hit a remarkable 33 goals in 35 league appearances to lead Sevilla to a sixth-place finish. Somehow, he missed out on that year's Pichichi award due to Real Madrid's Hugo Sánchez striking 38 times.

Polster predictably became a cult hero in Seville and even recorded the song 'Noche del Verano' for the club. "It was a truly beautiful experience in my career," he later recalled when reflecting upon his time in Seville. "Real Madrid were interested in me but, due to the numbers of foreign players back then, it was not possible. *Sevillanos* are hot-blooded and it was memorable for me."

Whilst the Austrian striker hogged the headlines, the mercurial Uruguayan playmaker Pablo Bengoechea was equally as important to Cantatore's side but his personality was somewhat less outgoing. "I never liked the attention, it's not in my character," he said years later. "Now my kids are back in Uruguay with a *Sevillano* accent. I got on well with everyone during my times there and I played with some great players: Francisco, Jiménez, Rafa Paz ... we should have won titles. We won twice away to Barcelona, but we dropped too many stupid points. The mentality of the club was not as strong back then."

One of those wins at the Camp Nou was a stunning 4–3 victory on 30 December 1989. The same day Real Betis defeated Espanyol 1–0 in the second division. It was the first time both Seville sides had beaten their Barcelona-based counterparts on a single day, and history would repeat itself on 11 November 2018, when Sevilla edged out Espanyol while Betis recorded a memorable triumph against Barça. The score? 3–4.

* * * * *

Between 1987 and 1990, eight different managers occupied the dugout at the Benito Villamarín as the club failed to find continuity on or off the pitch. Luis del Sol's exit – after recording a respectable top-half finish, ahead of Sevilla based on head-to-head record that season – took the club aback. Del Sol wanted to remain at the club but out of the limelight, moving 'upstairs' to oversee first-team affairs without actively training the first team. John Mortimore – a former Chelsea central defender – was appointed boss after concluding his second successful spell at Benfica.

The Englishman got off to the perfect start, leading his side to an opening day 2–1 victory at Sevilla to instantly make him a hit among *Verdiblancos* fans, with a follow-up 3–1 home victory over Espanyol continuing the good mood. But just four wins in the following 17 matches – with the penultimate game a 1–0 home reverse against their city rivals – saw Mortimore and del Sol both removed from their posts. The dissatisfaction with the management team went beyond mere results, which had left Betis in the relegation zone. They were also criticised for making too many personnel changes to the squad and 'removing the colour' from their style of play. Mortimore had also been accused of falling out with a number of key players, most notably star striker Rincón.

Just as he had done six years earlier, Pedro Buenaventura Gil stepped into the breach and met the club's objective of avoiding relegation, but only just. Two victories in three games had set up a crunch final-day meeting at the Estadio Insular in Las Palmas, with the hosts – coached by Roque Olsen, who had spent two seasons at Sevilla – needing a win to avoid automatic relegation while Betis needed a victory themselves to avoid a relegation play-off, or worse. It was quite a day for many *Sevillanos* because the date – 22 May 1988 – fell on Pentecost Sunday, a key day in the Catholic calendar and particularly so in Andalusia. Across the weekend, up to a million people prepare to start their pilgrimage to El Rocío to the south-west. So important is this date considered in Seville, that Betis public relations officer Gregorio Conejo ensured that each of the players received a White Dove medal which had been blessed the previous day at the Virgen del Rocío, the destination for the pilgrims. For Betis players and fans in Gran Canaria, this would be a true test of faith.

Furthermore, it was a huge day for Seville itself as Leonard Cohen was playing his first, and only, concert in the city. Held in the auditorium of Prado de San Sebastián as part of the annual Cita – a council-run event from 1984 to 1991 and the initiative of mayor

Manuel del Valle, which also involved household names such as The Kinks and James Brown – it was what Cohen would later call his "all-time most complete performance".

"The audience began waving white handkerchiefs and chanting, 'Torero'", he later recounted. "I don't know if we were any good that night, but somehow the hospitality of the audience was such that they awarded me the highest designation of the heart."

Béticos had been more focused on events earlier in the day as the league season concluded in the most nerve-shredding of fashions. The versatile Luis Miguel Gail had given Betis an early lead but Las Palmas struck back on the half-hour and the game remained in the balance for the following hour. With 17 minutes remaining and Betis heading for a relegation play-off spot, youth product Francisco Javier Zafra – who Buenaventura had handed a debut to earlier that month – entered the fray. With five minutes remaining, Zafra picked out defender José Díez Calleja who found the back of the net for only the third time in six seasons. Betis had their salvation, and the outpouring of relief began.

"Virgin, do not cry," chanted the Betis dressing room, led by boss Buenaventura and captured by TV cameras. "Tomorrow Betis will bring you flowers." An equally fitting piece may have been Cohen's 'Hallelujah', but unfortunately the cameras cut off after the religious acknowledgement. It was undoubtedly an emotional day, with Betis president Gerardo Martínez Retamero pictured in tears at the full-time whistle such was the relief of the late, late reprieve.

As it turned out, the seemingly inevitable had only been postponed rather than stopped altogether. Club legend Eusebio Ríos (see Chapter 16) took the reins in the summer of 1988 but after eight defeats and just two victories in 13 games, was replaced by Paraguayan Cayetano Ré. Despite an upturn in results (seven wins, six draws and 10 defeats) the club were facing up to the prospect of relegation in a typically competitive top flight. Again, the club turned to Buenaventura in the run-in but this time there was no miracle – despite the ever-returning coach no doubt issuing a few more Hail Marys. They won three games out of their final five, but Betis were back in the Segunda for the first time in a decade.

Juan Corbacho Troncoso was installed following relegation and an impressive first half of the campaign saw Betis clear at the top of the second tier, but a collapse in form and just one win in 12 – culminating in defeats to bottom-of-the-table Atlético Madrileño and Castilla, the B teams of Atlético de Madrid and Real Madrid respectively –

saw the club lose patience and turn to former midfield maestro Julio Cardeñosa, who had retired from playing five years earlier and had been coaching the Betis Deportivo team. Cardeñosa had six games to seal the deal but the return of three wins, two draws and a defeat was less a case of charging to promotion than limping over the line. Despite ascension back to the Primera, it was a frustrating campaign marked by underachievement with many signings failing to live up to their billing.

One such arrival was Sergei Neiman, who was incorporated from Dynamo Moscow in February, becoming only the third Soviet to appear in Spanish football (after Sevilla goalkeeper Rinat Dassaev and Espanyol's Vasili Rats), as the thawing of relations between West and East began to show in European football. Dynamo Moscow – the opponents when Betis controversially crashed out of the Cup Winners' Cup in 1978 – had been touring Andalusia in January 1990 in preparation for their own domestic league. Neiman's move to Betis was by chance; Chilean Patricio Yáñez suffered a slipped disc and his foreigner spot in the squad was freed up, coinciding with scouts watching Dynamo. Billed as a "technical and creative player, with offensive ability", Neiman was signed on a loan deal worth 15 million pesetas with an option to sign permanently for three seasons. The only non-native Spanish speaker in the squad, the midfielder made just seven first-team appearances and by the end of the season he was back in Moscow.

Betis secured promotion on the penultimate day of the campaign with a 1–1 draw at home to Sabadell with the goal fittingly scored by José 'Pepe' Mel, whose name would become synonymous with the club in the decades that followed. The striker arrived from Castellón and became an instant hit in Heliópolis, 22 of his 23 goals in his debut season were in league competition, earning him the Segunda's Pichichi award for the campaign. So regular were his goalscoring exploits, the expression "Do not say 'goal', say 'Mel'" became commonplace amongst the Betis support. The following season was the striker's sole campaign in the top flight but he made his mark – only four others, including his former Real Madrid youth team strike partner Emilio Butragueño netted more than his 14 league goals.

There was much more to Mel than just his ability to find the net – scoring 59 times in 133 first-team appearances for Betis. He was always credited as being a 'thinking footballer', questioning tactics and constantly displaying positional and tactical awareness. It is no surprise that he would later launch a managerial career which has spanned two decades and counting – including securing promotion in two separate spells at Betis and qualification for Europe – but more interestingly, he balanced his managerial career with that of a fiction writer. In June 2016 he published his third novel *La Prueba* (The Test), focusing on football-mad Pepito, following previous titles *El Mentiroso* (The Liar) and *El Camino al más All'* (The Road to the Afterlife).

Mel's goal led to the point which clinched promotion in 1990 and four days later, as was tradition, the club's players and staff laid a wreath at the Virgen de los Reyes in the city's cathedral. Just as had been the case two years prior, the religious tribute did not bring divine intervention the following season with chaos and instability once again engulfing Betis. Julio Cardeñosa was fired after seven matches with the team propping up the table with just two points and his fate was sealed by a comprehensive 3–0 reverse at home to Sevilla in matchday five. The match was all about Sevilla's new superstar striker, the Chilean Iván Zamorano, who netted twice in a comfortable victory for *Los Rojiblancos*.

José Luis Romero was appointed, poached from Logroñés – who were enjoying their first sustained period in the top flight – and despite Betis being restricted financially, the club's board backed their new man with several mid-season arrivals in an attempt to revive their struggling side.

Among the signings was 'El lobo de Bulgaria' – defender Trifon Ivanov earning the nickname due to his wolf-like, unshaven appearance and mullet hairstyle. Gaining prominence with CSKA Sofia and the Bulgarian national team, he quickly found favour among *Béticos* for his work rate and determination. However, he was less popular among coaches who did not approve of his ill-discipline and tendency to abandon his defensive positioning without instruction, commit senselessly rash challenges and inexplicably frequently shoot from upwards of 40 yards from goal. Ivanov became somewhat of a cult hero in Seville despite making just 60 appearances for the club, scoring 10 goals. He was to join Swiss club Neuchatel Xamax in 1993 and formed part of Bulgaria's famed run to the 1994 World Cup semi-finals before scoring the goal against Russia to clinch the nation's place in the 1998 tournament. Sadly, Ivanov passed away in 2016 with a heart attack, aged just 50.

Romero lasted for only 18 matches in the Betis dugout, securing only four wins and, with the club sitting second from bottom, he was fired. The penultimate game, unsurprisingly, was a 3–2 derby day loss across town in Nervión. Not only was he blamed for poor results but also for reported disharmony within the squad and his personal fallout with Pepe Mel – who insisted he would walk away from the club unless the boss was sacked – proved to be the final nail in his coffin. Legendary former goalkeeper José Ramón Esnaola was seen as the man capable of providing unity and was ushered in until the end of the campaign. Esnaola had impressed as coach of the club's B team and further represented the club's preference for an affordable, swift appointment. Despite winning two of his first four games, the situation proved irreversible and Betis were downed; no wins in their final nine matches saw them finish the campaign rooted to the foot of the table.

The summer appointment of Jozef Jarabinský led to the temporary 'ChecoBetis' nickname (even though Jarabinský himself was Slovak, his move to Seville came 18 months before Czechoslovakia divided into two). Czech forward Alois Grussmann also arrived that summer, and despite scoring only eight goals in 38 appearances he later said: "I cannot describe this well, but my heart will always be here in Betis." Despite the season not ending in promotion, it was Grussmann's sole season outside of his homeland, but he described the experience as "incredible". "What I remember most of all," he added, "were the fans. They always showed me support, they were always with me."

Six months prior to Grussmann's move, Czechoslovakia international midfielder Michal Bílek – who would later manage the Czech Republic between 2009 and 2013 – arrived at Betis from Sparta Prague. Bílek had starred in his nation's run to the 1990 World Cup last eight, he scored two goals at the tournament, and instantly became an integral figure at Betis. He played all 22 of the remaining league matches in his ill-fated debut campaign and missed only one match throughout the gruelling Segunda season. The trio of signings was completed in the winter of 1991 when forward Roman Kukleta joined from Sparta. As with his former team-mate Ivanov, Kukleta would die tragically young – passing away from organ failure in 2011, aged 46.

Less than a month after Kukleta's arrival, Jarabinský was gone – despite a solid start, a record of just one win in seven saw the boss fired by the end of January. Reports from the time occasionally cast doubt over how much power incoming coaches were able to exert on the Betis dressing room, not helped by the short-lived nature of the position. Mel, who remained at the club following José Luis Romero's dismissal, continued to take on an increasing level of responsibility. "He was a gentleman with us [Czech players]," Grussmann revealed.

"With all of us he behaved magnificently, no doubt sensing it was difficult for us. He frequently invited us to his house to eat and relax, it helped all of us."

Experienced Argentine Felipe Mesones was brought in to see out the campaign and results improved but not enough to clinch an automatic promotion – Betis falling one win short of second-placed Rayo Vallecano. They were forced into a tricky two-legged play-off against Deportivo de La Coruña, who had finished fourth from bottom in the top flight. Despite youth graduate José Luis Loreto's away goal at the Riazor, Depor triumphed 2–1 in the first leg and held out for a goalless draw in Seville to maintain their Primera status.

The following season saw Mesones replaced by fellow Argentine Jorge D'Alessandro in the Betis dugout, but it failed to drastically change their fortunes on the pitch. The former goalkeeper, who had spent the majority of both his playing and managerial career at Salamanca, was brought in from Figueres. The marquee summer arrival, however, was not the new boss – who brought American midfielder Tab Ramos with him from the Catalan minnows – but the returning Rafael Gordillo (see Chapter 19), back at *Los Verdiblancos* after seven years at Madrid.

But after six games the recurring feelings of negativity from inconsistency began to set in, with just two wins, two draws and two defeats in that time-frame. D'Alessandro warned "we need to act before things get out of hand" with the club keen to move on Kukleta due to a lack of fitness and the tactically ill-disciplined Ivanov, who were both occupying the coveted non-Spanish spots in the squad. Doubts were raised over the commitment of others too, with Gordillo playing on after sustaining an ankle injury in a 2–0 defeat at Real Valladolid.

As Real Betis historian Alfonso del Castillo highlights, the club had grand plans to explore foreign markets to rejuvenate their promotion campaign with a controlling midfielder and striker the two priority positions. The ever-loyal Pedro Buenaventura was tasked with exploring South America and recommended the club make approaches for São Paulo midfielder Raí and Müller, a striker who had returned from Torino the previous year. However, the Brazilian club's economic demands scuppered the possibility of any deals. Moving on to the seemingly more accessible Argentinian market, Buenaventura also picked out Vélez Sarsfield Alejandro Mancuso, a midfielder, and River Plate's Walter Silvani. Yet again, the club's restricted financial potential meant this was a dead end.

Attention was then turned to Eastern Europe, a market which had significantly opened up in the preceeding years with Hungarian and Yugoslavian football earmarked as offering particular value for money. Buenaventura and Rogelio Sosa were chiefly assigned to recommend the best players, with Partizan Belgrade duo Slavisa Jokanovic and Predrag Mijatovic along with Peter Dubovski, of Slovan Bratislava their targets. Betis had assumed their budget of 200 million pesetas would be enough to secure two of the players, yet it quickly transpired that any combination of the three would cost upwards of double that amount. "We do not have to sign these Yugoslavs," said Manuel Ruiz de Lopera, vice-president of *Los Verdiblancos* at the time. "We have cheaper and better players available, people who are even with their teams in European competitions."

At the time, de Lopera was relatively unknown having joined the club's board in September 1991 to serve under then president Hugo Galera Davidson. This was when Betis had been relegated from the top flight and this blow was worsened by the event coinciding with legislation passed the previous year forcing not-for-profit sports clubs throughout Spain to become public limited companies – *Sociedad Anónima Deportiva*, hence SAD being added to official club titles (Real Madrid, Barcelona, Athletic Club and Osasuna were granted exemption from this, later affording them advantages under corporation and property tax as well as preserving their not-for-profit status). The legislation was designed to increase the 'economic and legal transparency' of the clubs, but the reality for Betis was the restructuring forced them into raising a whopping 1,175 million pesetas – almost double the level of any other club across the top two divisions – or face a financial crisis. In three months, Betis fans raised 400 million pesetas, but despite a further 100 million being raised through larger investment packages, the club were still 680 million pesetas short. There was no interest from potential investors on the horizon and it was not until the summer of 1992 that de Lopera provided a package to get Betis over the line.

When he was elected president in 1996, de Lopera finally made shockwaves with his erratic style of leadership and insistence upon outlandish statements, often backed by eye-watering and unsustainable financial backing. Perhaps that was, in part, driven by his regret at not pushing the boat out to land the trio of original targets from Eastern Europe. Dubovsky joined Real Madrid in 1993, where Mijatovic moved in 1996 after spending three years at Valencia – making the club a profit of over 1,000 million pesestas in the process

– while Jokanovic spent seven years in Spanish football across Real Oviedo, Tenerife and de Deportivo La Coruña. Betis instead went further east to sign duo Andrey Kobelev and Vali Gasimov from Dynamo Moscow, but again their prudency cost them. Kobelev lasted just one campaign in Andalusia before returning to the Russian capital while striker Gasimov enjoyed marginally more success, netting 13 goals in 53 appearances.

The 1992/93 campaign saw Betis miss out on the top four and a shot at promotion via the play-offs with boss D'Alessandro replaced halfway through the campaign by the once again returning José Ramón Esnaola, who failed to generate any notable improvement. Croatian Sergije Krešić was installed in the summer of 1993 and made a strong start initially including eight wins from nine over the Christmas period, fueled by the form of summer signing Daniel Aquino. Nicknamed *El Toro* (the bull), Aquino had collected the second tier's Pichichi award for the top scorer with Mérida the previous year and would replicate the feat at Betis – hitting 26 goals across the season.

Two of the Argentine's goals arrived against his former club Mérida in the Copa del Rey round of 16 which ultimately propelled the club to a quarter-final double-header against Barcelona, reigning champions of Spain. Krešić's side were huge underdogs against a side gunning for the treble, led by the imperious Johan Cruyff, who possessed a team with a remarkable array of talent including Ronald Koeman, Pep Guardiola, Michael Laudrup, Romário and Hristo Stoichkov. The first leg saw Betis hold the Catalan giants to a scoreless draw in Seville before the return leg a week later on 3 February 1994.

The build-up to the second leg was dominated by Real Madrid's shock exit from the competition two days earlier, losing 3–0 at home to Tenerife. The Catalan media were gleeful and did not foresee any issues for the *Blaugrana*, coming up against opposition from the second tier. Such complacency was not limited to the media, with Cruyff himself totally dismissing the possibility of an upset. When quizzed after the first leg what chance he gave his side for progression he responded: "Are you serious?"

Yet half an hour into the clash a defensive mix-up between Koeman and Barça goalkeeper Carles Busquets allowed Juan Luis Amigo, better known as Juanito, to capitalise, rounding the goalkeeper before finishing into an unguarded net. It was Juanito's first start for the club and – whilst he would only score once more in his short stint in Andalusia – it ensured his cult status in the green-and-white half of the city. With the away goals rule in play, the *Blaugrana* needed two yet could not break down a stern defence. Koeman's nightmare match could have gotten worse yet he escaped a red card despite lashing out in frustration. A distracted Barça, wrote *El País*, "spent too much time revelling in the misfortunes of others, rather than focusing on their own virtues." The magnitude of the achievement should not be overlooked; Cruyff's side recovered to retain the Spanish league title and reached the European Cup Final. *Béticos* celebrated the result like a league title, with tens of thousands of fans gathering in the city's Plaza Nueva and mayor Alejandro Rojas Marcos joining in the celebrations.

Yet despite occupying an automatic promotion spot for most of the campaign and good Copa form, a run of five defeats from eight league games threatened to derail Betis hopes of a first return to the top flight in four seasons. Krešić was sacked and in came Lorenzo Serra Ferrer, who had spent nine years at the helm of Real Mallorca. Having lost 1–0 at home to Real Zaragoza in the first leg of the Copa semi-final, Serra Ferrer was not able to turn around the situation with a 3–1 loss in Aragon. That disappointment was swiftly forgotten, however, as Betis went undefeated through their remaining 12 league games, winning 10, to secure a return to the top flight. Serra Ferrer was just getting started.

Chapter 22

The Uncontrollable
Diego Maradona

THE early years of the 1990s for Sevilla were defined by arrivals who would go on to be – or in the case of Diego Maradona, had already established themselves as – household names within European football. Unfortunately for the club, none would be remembered for their stints in Andalusia but elsewhere within Spain. Maradona was a shadow of the emerging star who had shone for two years at Barcelona a decade prior while striking sensations Davor Šuker and Iván Zamorano – both prolific in Seville – would eventually complete their seemingly inevitable moves to Real Madrid. Sevilla were the first Spanish club of the tough-tackling, enigmatic midfielder Diego Simeone but the Argentine would become synonymous with Atlético de Madrid across two playing spells and a remarkable managerial stint.

'Bam Bam' Zamorano was the first significant arrival of the decade, joining from Swiss club St Gallen in the summer of 1990. Raised in a working-class family in the Chilean capital Santiago, the striker was encouraged to pursue a career in the sport by his supportive parents. "We struggled financially and I helped out by doing any jobs that would pay me – cleaning cars, windows, whatever," Zamorano said in an interview with *Marca*. "My dream was to play football; in the park, on the streets – wherever we could. It was always really competitive, and my father needed to come get me after dark as it wasn't safe. But it made me happy, my family were happy too – they encouraged me to pursue my talent."

Zamorano's boyhood team was Colo-Colo and he would fulfil a lifelong dream by finishing his career at the Chilean giants, but he enjoyed a remarkable 18-year career prior to that. Joining local side Cobresal aged 18, the striker moved to Europe three years later, becoming the first South American player at the unlikely outfit of St Gallen. A tally of 37 goals across 57 appearances displayed his natural goalscoring talent and he was sought by Sevilla to fill the foreigner spot vacated by outgoing Soviet goalkeeper Rinat Dasayev. The Chilean was often described as the 'complete centre-forward'; combining intelligence, physicality and technical ability, renowned for his movement, heading prowess and technique. His move to Seville may well have been influenced by then Sevilla coach Vicente Cantatore – a native of Argentina but who gained Chilean nationality due to his long service to football. Before a brief stint in charge of the Chile national team, Cantatore had led Cobreloa, based in the mining Atacama region of the South American country. His spell here overlapped with Zamorano's playing career at nearby Cobresal and, whilst it remains speculation, he may have used his contacts to engineer a future link-up. A constant throughout the striker's career was the need for a trusting manager, someone who could centre the attack around his talents and not become frustrated by his perceived lack of impact outside the penalty area.

The Chilean eventually completed his move to Spain in August 1990 in what was widely reported as a club record fee, although neither Sevilla nor St Gallen confirmed the details. Local media speculated that the total transfer fee added up to 300 million pesetas – roughly translating to €1.8m in modern terms – although the Andalusian club themselves denied this and *ABC* later suggested the sum total was closer to 250 million pesetas. What was obvious was that all parties viewed the deal as hugely significant and, whilst the Swiss league was no true gauge of an elite player, the excitement surrounding Zamorano's potential was palpable.

Zamorano's first goal for *Los Rojiblancos* came in his second match, at home to Real Madrid. 'Iván El Terrible' struck on the half-hour mark in a 2–0 victory for the hosts with Madrid's legendary Mexican marksman Hugo Sánchez unable to find the net. Less than two years later, Zamorano would be signed to replace Sánchez at the Bernabéu but there were still plenty of chapters to write in his short but goal-laden stint in Seville. Three weeks after defeating Madrid, Sevilla made the two-mile trip across the city to play Betis – the first derby in two seasons. Zamorano, then 23, was the star of the show – netting a brace in a convincing 3–0 victory for Cantatore's side.

However, the promising striker was not available for selection for Sevilla's UEFA Cup matches, which had been earned by their sixth-place finish the previous year. Their lack of goal threat was evidenced in their opening tie with Greek club PAOK – two scoreless draws were played out before Sevilla edged through on penalties. Just as had happened at Betis 14 seasons earlier, a European campaign was ended by a team from Russia's capital. Toni Polster's away goal was not enough as Sevilla crashed to a 3–1 defeat at Torpedo Moscow. The return leg in Seville saw Torpedo net an away goal in the ninth minute and despite a valiant comeback attempt – Pablo Bengoechea and Ramón Vázquez both on target – it was not enough for Sevilla.

Zamorano had been the only outfield arrival for the 1990/91 campaign but despite his scoring exploits, his legacy at Sevilla was outlasted by two goalkeepers who had joined the first-team squad: Juan Carlos Unzué and Ramón Rodríguez Verdejo, better known as Monchi. Unzué had been the backup goalkeeper at Barcelona behind Andoni Zubizarreta but he instantly became Sevilla's number one and accumulated over 200 top-flight appearances for the club over the next seven seasons. He was outlasted and eventually replaced by Monchi, who had been promoted from the club's Sevilla Atlético youth team at the same time as Unzué's arrival. Unbeknown to anyone at the time of Monchi's unremarkable playing career, he would later develop into the individual credited with the club's ascent to European greatness in the decades that followed (see Chapter 26).

Despite no significant downturn in form and a respectable eighth-place finish in 1991, boss Cantatore was gone from his role at the end of the campaign. Known as a strict disciplinarian, he was regarded as a man who could generate results but was a volatile figure who often fell out with players and club staff alike. He was replaced at the helm by Uruguayan Víctor Espárrago, who had spent two years as a player with Sevilla in the 1970s before enjoying long spells in Andalusia in the intervening years, playing and managing Recreativo de Huelva before moving on to Cádiz and then Valencia, who had pipped Sevilla to a top-seven spot the previous season.

Espárrago was to last just one season at the club – an average campaign concluding with just one point from the final seven fixtures – but he was credited with moulding the fearsome strike partnership of Zamorano and Davor Šuker. The Croat had signed from Dinamo Zagreb at the start of the season and left a lasting legacy at the club, netting 91 times across five seasons. The striker's departure from his native country came amidst its raging conflict with Serbian forces. The sobering background behind the move led the striker to comment to now extinct newspaper *Diario 16* upon moving to

Andalusia: "Imagine someone bombing Seville Cathedral. That's what is happening to my home."

Sevilla were later paired with the Croatian club in the 2016/17 Champions League, with Šuker telling *El País*: "I enjoyed an amazing career, playing in three World Cups and for clubs as big as Real Madrid, but Dinamo and Sevilla are my two loves. I have a torn heart; on one hand, Dinamo are the club who made me and on the other, Sevilla are the club where my career took off. The truth is Sevilla will always be special to me and I will always have great memories."

Šuker netted twice on his first start for Sevilla – whose fans quickly adopted the chant "Davor-Davor, Šuker-Šuker!" – against Real Sociedad, but just as Šukermania (as thought of by the local press) was gaining prominence and his partnership with Zamorano was getting started, the Chilean's exit from Andalusia was becoming increasingly inevitable. In March 1992, the striker told *El País*: "I've known for some time that Real Madrid are watching me and it [the move] is a very exciting possibility for me and I would love to play there. If things go wrong then I will stay at Sevilla, where I'm well." The previous summer, he had starred at the Copa América – and was second in the goalscoring charts behind only Gabriel Batistuta – and was entering the final two years of his deal in Seville.

Zamorano's contract contained a 1,000 million peseta clause that held up negotiations and with *Los Rojiblancos* unwilling to negotiate down on a star player – who had grabbed 21 goals in 59 leagues appearances – the move became protracted. Proceedings were complicated further by the situation of defender Nando Muñoz. A native of Seville, Nando debuted for the first team aged 20 and swiftly grew into a first-team regular. Three seasons later he was signed on a two-year deal by Barcelona, whom he helped to successive league titles and the club's inaugural European Cup in 1991. He played alongside former Sevilla defensive team-mate Ricardo Serna at the Camp Nou, continuing the pattern of the club's defensive youth products joining Barça that had been started by Paco Gallego in 1965 (see Chapter 18).

Sevilla exercised their option of returning Nando after two seasons, with Real Madrid promising to make them a healthy profit and the defender's move to the Spanish capital was inevitable. Eventually the double sale of Zamorano and Nando was processed as Sevilla landed a total fee cited by *ABC* as being 900 million pesetas. It was the transfer of Spain international Nando which generated further *morbo* between Spain's two biggest clubs, with Barcelona claiming the nature of the deal struck between Madrid and Sevilla contravened the rules.

Nando, like Ricardo Serna, landed multiple Spanish league titles and success in Europe – aspirations which at the time felt like a pipe dream in Seville. Whilst youth products transferring elsewhere generated big profits for *Los Rojiblancos*, the example of Zamorano showcased how scouting young talents in other leagues ultimately had similar potential for bringing invaluable revenue streams.

The Chilean blossomed into a true great at Madrid – netting a remarkable 101 goals across four seasons, before later starring for Italian giants Internazionale. Sevilla needed to find a new strike partner for Šuker and had a significant cash windfall to negotiate with. They would turn to one of the world's most prestigious ever players.

* * * * *

The summer of 1992 was one of significant change for Sevilla both on and off the pitch. Unsurprisingly, Espárrago was relieved of his managerial duties with the club appointing Carlos Bilardo in his place. The Argentine was the fourth successive South American to be handed the role and had earned prestige for landing the World Cup for his nation six years prior and taking them to the final of the 1990 edition. It was unsurprising that he emphasised the need to bring in players he could trust and who had played under him at international level.

Zamorano's departure left a striking vacancy while midfielder Pablo Bengoechea – the captain of the Uruguayan national team, known for his technical ability – departed Sevilla after five seasons, signing for Argentinian club Gimnasia La Plata. Yugoslavian Željko Petrović, who had arrived the previous summer as part of the deal which brought Davor Šuker to Andalusia, had failed to settle and was transferred to Den Bosch in the Netherlands. There was a need for reinforcements and Šuker was the only occupant of the four 'international' slots within the squad.

The first addition was central midfielder Diego Simeone, signed in July 1992 from Italian side Pisa on a four-year deal worth a reported 150 million pesetas. "I was interested in coming here from the beginning, to play for an institution like Sevilla under a manager I know very well," Simeone told reporters upon his unveiling. "I know Bilardo very well, I had other offers but my idea was to come here to a new team which I know can do great things. I want to win and I have been told of the spectacular atmosphere of this club, playing in front of 50,000 supporters. This is very important for me." There was an increasing sense, amplified by the exits of Nando and Zamorano to Madrid earlier that summer, that players were using clubs of Sevilla's stature to register on the radar of the nation's leading clubs. "I only think of the present," replied Simeone. "My principles are luck, faith and courage. I do not think of the future."

The move for Simeone was an exciting one; tipped as one of the world's most promising central midfielders, the deal was an opportunistic one following Pisa's relegation from the Italian top flight. Yet, considering strong rumours of another Argentine's possible arrival at the club, Simeone could not escape from the inevitable questions surrounding his international team-mate. "Maradona? Well, who wouldn't want to play with the best player in the world? It would be good for him, it would be good for football, it would be good for Sevilla."

At this point Maradona was stuck in an irreversible decline from his greatness and although this was not yet obvious, the warning signs were there. On 1 July 1992 – three months before his 32nd birthday – he completed a 15-month suspension from the sport after being tested positive for cocaine at a regulation anti-doping control test after a Coppa Italia match for Napoli. The Italian side wished to keep the mercurial playmaker on their books; he had been their talismanic captain, credited with de facto single-handedly leading the club to their only ever league titles, with two arriving in the space of four years. However, Maradona desired to leave Italy and head to another European club where the pressure upon his shoulders would not be so heavy. The seemingly perfect relationship had soured at the World Cup two summers prior, when the crowd in Napoli chanted: "The people love you, but Italy is our country." Two clubs emerged as leading candidates for his signature: Sevilla and Olympique de Marseille. There were similarities with Napoli – with all three clubs based in the south of their nation and holding a reputation for fiercely loyal and passionate fans.

A month after FIFA's confirmation of his ban, Maradona was arrested at his apartment in Caballito – the Buenos Aires suburb in which he resided – as part of an anti-drugs raid. "He didn't kill anyone, he didn't rape any one, he didn't rob anyone, he just hurt himself," Carlos Bilardo, who would play a fundamental role in bringing the player to join him in Seville, told *La Nación*. "He's a good boy, a simple person. He made a mistake." *Dieguito* remained a hugely popular figure both in Naples and Argentina, a rags-to-riches success story who had evolved into the greatest footballer of all time. This was an individual who in the eyes of many could do no wrong, and as the *New York Times* reported: "An estimated 400 people witnessed the arrest, shouting insults at the arresting officers and yelling to Maradona, 'We love you anyway.'"

Complications remained when his FIFA ban expired in the summer of 1992, with Napoli initially refusing to sanction any sale and the world's governing body intervening to process the move. Sevilla were the chosen destination and despite a number of administrative difficulties, Maradona completed his transfer to the Andalusian club on 28 September 1992. *Marca* led with the headline 'Today is the Day' and quoted Diego as declaring "Sevilla, I want you". Boss Bilardo reportedly told the player privately: "It is a great life here and you can play with no worries." It was an insight into Maradona's fragile state and Bilardo – his former mentor – realising he needed to step out of the limelight, into a less pressurised environment to thrive in a sporting sense. The boss had driven the sale and allegedly informed the club's board that should they not throw their full weight behind the deal, he would "be on the first plane back to Buenos Aires".

The signing had followed days of intense negotiations and lengthy meetings in FIFA's Zurich headquarters with the final discussion reportedly exceeding five hours in duration. The saga had lasted for 88 days. Sevilla president Luis Cuervas and his Napoli counterpart Corrado Ferliano were at loggerheads over how any deal could proceed. Sevilla had originally offered $4.5m while Napoli sought between $9–15m, with the final deal quoted by local media at $7.5 million. Spanish radio stations confirmed $3.5m would be paid immediately with the remainder divided up into four payments across the next two years.

Maradona remained at his hotel in Seville – where he had been present for a fortnight – waiting upon the outcome of the talks. With everything processed at his end, he only needed the green light. "Today I start to live again as I always have and as I only know how," a tearful Maradona told reporters. "I am eternally grateful to Sevilla and to my agent. I am going to do everything I can to be captain of the Argentine national squad again." Those closing words prophesied one strand of the breakdown in trust and understanding between the player and his club, fans and manager. He was not the only happy Argentine at the time, with then national team boss Alfio Basile saying he was "choked with emotion" and that he was excited to reinstate Maradona back into his Argentina side. It was quite a turnaround from the player vowing, 12 months previously, that he would never wear an Argentina shirt again.

Maradona wasted no further time dwelling in a hotel and began renting the house of famed local bullfighter Juan Antonio Ruiz, the Spartacus. There was a hint of humility at his unveiling by the club: "I'm not number one in the world anymore, I am down at 10,000 but I still hold the same dreams I had as a 15-year-old."

His first game for Sevilla was in a specially arranged friendly game against Bayern Munich. Such was the global excitement around Maradona's return to action, it was reported by Spanish media that 40 television stations had bought the rights to the match while Spain's Antena 3 station alone paid $1.5m to broadcast the game. This was the one truly successful element for the Andalusian giants throughout the entire ill-fated venture. "We will also be playing matches in other countries, including Japan and the United States, which should bring in reasonable sums," club president Cuervas commented. Maradona was a commercial cash cow, bringing unparalleled new-found attention to Sevilla and vastly expanding revenue streams. Maradona completed the 90 minutes and rattled the woodwork from a free kick before assisting Davor Šuker. The first of his 30 competitive games for the club came a week later at San Mamés against Athletic Club, but his involvement ended prematurely following an injury.

Maradona's understanding with Šuker was perhaps his biggest on-pitch success story of the season, with the Croatian later opening up about the relationship. "I had watched Diego when I was a child and, all of a sudden, we were eating breakfast together, training on the same pitch, sharing the same locker room ... it was incredible. He brought so much attention with him, there was one day that we were training but Diego was late. There was a big crowd watching us and then he eventually arrived in his Ferrari, and the crowds flocked to him.

"I hoped against hope he would speak to me personally and one day he called me to tell me just to run straight at the [opposition] goalkeeper and not to bother looking for him. He would find me, he said, and put the ball ready for me to finish and if you look at the goals that season – that is what happened." There were occasional reminders of Maradona's enduring genius throughout the campaign, as he pulled off outstanding pieces of technical skill. His greatest performance in a Sevilla kit arrived a week before Christmas, when he was instrumental in a famous 2–0 victory at home to Real Madrid –

Iván Zamorano's first return to Seville swiftly forgotten. His greatest individual moment was instant chest control, turn and finish in the second minute against Sporting de Gijón the following month. This was the old Maradona, he who had conquered the world. He was desperate to show his young children Diego Sinagra, Dalma and Gianinna that their father really was the superstar that they had been told all about. But these moments were notable for their infrequency and his outstanding natural talent quickly faded into the support act, rather than the main event.

In hindsight, the move was always destined to fail; Maradona's physical health was visibly deteriorating – he had piled on excess weight and never appeared to be operating at full fitness. Vice-president José María del Nido infamously felt the Argentine was "not fit to play golf" while he gained notoriety for frequenting nightclubs, prompting the club to privately track his movements away from the training grounds. Maradona was pushing the self-destruct button again, fraught with his own demons and inability to find a suitable off-pitch routine to complement his talent.

His psychological and mental state were suffering and his relationship with his new club was never going to reach such an unbreakable bond as he had enjoyed with Napoli and Argentina. Indeed, he prioritised representing his national side ahead of the wishes of Sevilla. The Argentine FA organised a centenary friendly against Brazil while they were to face Denmark in the 1993 Artemio Franchi Cup – a short-lived tournament which pitted the champions of Europe against those of South America. Sevilla requested that he played just one game to accommodate his selection in a tricky league tie at Logroñés. Yet Maradona typically ignored such instruction and played in all three and was non-existent in a limp 2–0 loss for his club.

Sevilla won just two of their final 11 league matches that season and missed out on European qualification, with Maradona's relationship breakdown with Bilardo and his club a running theme throughout the closing stages. He had lost the concentration and drive which had briefly returned in the opening half of the season. Sent off for dissent in a harrowing 3–0 league loss at Tenerife, he never regained his focus. Sevilla still had a shot at European qualification as they entertained Real Burgos – who had already been relegated – on the penultimate day of the campaign.

The situation going into the game was tense and there was a sense that the Maradona and Bilardo experiment was on a knife-edge. Weeks earlier, the boss had been said to be infuriated by the latest act of ill-discipline from the player and, upon finding him, had punched him straight in the face before the two engaged in an unseemly scuffle. Maradona's wife Claudia reportedly had to separate the pair, who then supposedly attempted to rebuild their relationship by going out drinking in the aftermath.

The house of cards was falling, as was Maradona's fitness. Sevilla led Burgos 1–0 at half-time in the crucial clash but the 32-year-old complained that a persistent knee injury – which had plagued him all season – was causing him too much discomfort and he could not play the second half. Bilardo was insistent that the star should play through the injury, due to the magnitude of the match and Maradona subsequently took three cortisone injections at the break. Yet eight minutes after the game recommenced, his number was up and youngster Francisco Pineda took his place. Maradona stormed off the pitch, launching an explicit avalanche of abuse in the direction of his manager on the way off before disappearing immediately down the tunnel.

The 32-year-old was said to have punched in lockers, breaking the skin on his knuckles before screaming at Bilardo later that he had played his final game for Sevilla. It was an unsavoury episode on a day that turned increasingly dark for the club as the underdogs hit a last-minute equaliser to kill off their European ambitions. Maradona was true to his word, there would be no redemption for him nor for Bilardo, who left the club that summer after failing to meet the objective of European qualification.

Luis Aragonés – who had previously been famed in Seville for his roles as player and boss in the green-and-white half of the city – was appointed in his place, having led Atlético de Madrid to third and sixth-place finishes respectively in the previous two campaigns. The Sage of Hortaleza would improve upon the previous season but despite a sixth-place finish, *Los Rojiblancos* once more missed out on European football by a solitary point. However, the improvement continued in the 1994/95 campaign and despite the sale of instrumental midfielder Diego Simeone to Atleti – kickstarting a chain of events in which the Argentine would bring the capital club kicking and screaming to the truly elite level of football – a fifth-place finish and European football was guaranteed by Aragonés.

The future boss of the Spanish national team was the seventh man at the helm of Seville between the years of 1984 and 1994, while 16 were in place across the city at Real Betis in the same period. Luis del

Sol was the only individual who both started and finished the season at *Los Verdiblancos*. But by the mid-1990s there was a palpable power shift in the city as Betis found success in stability while Sevilla were rocked by off-field chaos.

Chapter 23

Betis Surge as Sevilla
Engulfed in Chaos

UNDER Lorenzo Serra Ferrer, Betis had returned to the top flight in 1994 after a three-season absence. It had been eight seasons since Betis had finished ahead of their city rivals in the league standings but for six successive campaigns Seville turned green and white. Not that Sevilla's decline was at first apparent as Luis Aragonés landed them European football in 1995 in a season of huge significance for Sevillian football and one that ended chaotically, with the ramifications from off-field chaos impacting on the years that followed.

It was the first time in exactly 60 years – since the only league title for Real Betis – that both Seville clubs posted top-five finishes. The story of newly promoted Betis was remarkable, finishing above Barcelona on head-to-head record to secure a top-three finish. Both Seville derbies were defining moments in the campaign and ultimately were what separated the two clubs in the final league standings. Betis midfielder Alexis Trujillo decided the first clash between the sides in four seasons with his winning goal at the Ramón Sánchez-Pizjuán in January. The return match did not take place until 11 June – the penultimate day of a long campaign. Goals from Poland international Wojciech Kowalczyk and Juan Sabas – who had both arrived the previous summer from Legia Warsaw and Atlético de Madrid respectively, were enough to secure a 2–1 victory for Serra Ferrer's side. Coincidentally, this was only the third time Betis had achieved the 'league double' over their city rivals and the first since 1963.

That result had ensured *Los Verdiblancos* would return to European football but they still needed a win away to Real Madrid, who had already been crowned champions, on the final day of the campaign.

Sevilla fans were enduring a sense of déjà vu as they once again faced the possibility of missing out on a European spot by the slenderest of margins. It was a slice of fate that Aragonés needed at least a draw against former side Atlético on the final day of the campaign in Nervión to avoid another heartbreaking near miss. The final day brought joy for both Seville clubs. A double from Daniel Aquino saw Betis win 2–0 in Madrid and remarkably, bring up their 23rd clean sheet of the campaign. Sevilla recovered from going two goals down – the second coming from the boot of their former midfielder Diego Simeone, who upon realising what he had done, abruptly halted his celebration – to secure a 2–2 draw. Goals from Ramón Suárez 'Monchu' and Davor Šuker, his 60th league goal for the club, sealed a draw and their subsequent European qualification.

That was to prove only the beginning of the drama throughout those summer months in an unprecedented turn of events. Five years prior, Spain passed a law to ensure sports clubs became public limited companies and thus present finances to increase the 'economic and legal transparency' of sporting institutions – a move that almost led to Real Betis going into administration (for more details, see Chapter 21). In March 1995, an update to the law obliged clubs across the top two levels of Spanish football to submit to the governing body of the league a five per cent economic transfer, which would serve as a future provision against potential debts. A deadline had been put in place for 1 August 1995. Such changes to the bureaucratic structure of clubs had not come into the consciousness of the wider public.

A shock announcement from the league later that day ensured everyone was aware of just how severe the penalties would be. In a stunning press release, La Liga confirmed that both Sevilla and Celta de Vigo had not fulfilled their due payments – 85 million and 45 million pesetas respectively, five per cent of the respective budgets – and had subsequently been relegated out of the top two divisions, and into the third tier. Real Valladolid and Albacete, who had been relegated from the top flight, had been handed a reprieve in order to take up the two vacant spots, while Getafe and Leganés had their demotions from the second tier overturned too. As *El País* reported the following day: "First there was disbelief, then a sense of numbness. People began to congregate outside the stadiums, not knowing what to say. Finally, there was outrage in the streets of Seville and Vigo. Nobody believed that, for such small amounts, two clubs would suffer that sanction. From the initial surprise there came fear and indignation."

Sevilla insisted they had deposited a sum of 340 million pesetas in 1991 that had been valid for five years but were told the payments must be made every year. The league insisted that the ruling was 'inflexible' and all appeals must go to the nation's top sporting law court – the CSD. Such a decision was limited to Spanish football, meaning Sevilla would not lose their spot in European competition. Unsurprisingly, this information did little to quell the outrage from the club and its supporters. Mass rallies were held across Seville and in Vigo, in a bid to reverse the decision. Supporters' groups of Real Betis released statements ordering the decision to be reversed, so that their club and their city would not be robbed of their intense rivalry due to bureaucracy. One Sevilla fan even went on hunger strike.

It swiftly emerged Sevilla president Luis Cuervas, holder of 125 million pesetas of shares, had been preoccupied with visiting a sick relative while vice-president José María del Nido was on vacation visiting Disneyland Paris. José Álvarez Navarro – another club vice-president and holder of the second most important share package worth a reported 85 million pesetas – told reporters: "Someone will be held responsible for this."

Spanish football was facing an institutional crisis and was in disarray in the weeks that followed, with several clubs across the nation unsure of what level they would be competing at, severely impacting on any pre-season preparation. On 16 August the Spanish league held an emergency meeting between representatives of all 38 member clubs – excluding Sevilla and Celta – to discuss what action should be taken as a final decision. It was unanimously agreed that the decision for each club should be reversed. To solve the problem of Real Valladolid and Albacete, the league had agreed they should remain in the top flight, which temporarily expanded to 22 teams for two campaigns. It concluded an embarrassing period for authorities and signalled a further separation between the growing prominence of bureaucracy within the sport and the real life-blood of football: the fans. Ultimately, it was protests from the latter which won the day.

Sevilla's status within the top flight had been saved but the events inevitably led to mass institutional instability at the club. There had already been a change in the dugout that summer with Aragonés leaving his post to be replaced by Toni Oliveira, who had led Benfica to two Portuguese league titles and the 1988 European Cup final. However, Oliveira's appointment had been made by president Cuervas and it was he who ultimately paid the price for the summer administrational cock-up, leaving his role after nine years. José María del Nido temporarily took the reins to avoid a power vacuum before Francisco Escobar took office by October. In the dugout, Oliveira – who was associated with the former regime – was on shaky ground and, despite progressing past Bulgarian outfit Botev Plovdiv in Europe, just one win in eight league games and a painful 3–0 home defeat against Espanyol forced him to resign.

In need of a swift and affordable appointment, president Escobar turned to Juan Carlos Álvarez – a former midfielder who had spent seven seasons as a player at the club before coaching their B side Sevilla Atlético. Álvarez would last just three months at the helm, unable to stem the flow of mediocre league results. He did guide the club past Olympiakos in the UEFA Cup – Davor Šuker netting a vital away goal in extra time of the return leg in Greece – and into the round of 16, but a 4–2 aggregate elimination by Barcelona put an end to their European adventures.

The season was unravelling for *Los Rojiblancos* as Álvarez was dismissed and Uruguayan Victor Espárrago returned to the helm in January. That was the club's third coach of the campaign but a month later they would have a fourth president as Escobar left his position after just 127 days, ensuring he was the shortest-serving leader in the club's history. It was an alarming run of events for the club fuelled not only by poor results on the pitch but the deteriorating financial situation off it. Croatian Joško Jeličić was the only arrival on the playing staff and his impact was insignificant, certainly in comparison to his compatriot Šuker who would, it was announced, join Real Madrid at the end of the campaign. José María González de Caldas – an architect, promoter and bullfighting entrepreneur – was installed as club president.

There was no reversal of the situation under the guidance of González de Caldas, despite the summer of 1996 generating a genuine level of hope for *Sevillistas*. A 12th-place finish the previous campaign had signalled a significant regression from the Aragonés era and the departure of Šuker brought plenty of disappointment. There was an acknowledgement that funds needed to be injected into the playing squad and a series of summer arrivals raised expectations. Midfielder Matías Almeyda was instrumental in River Plate's domestic title and Copa Libertadores success, so Sevilla splashed out $9m on his signature – a record for an Argentine club player at the time. Greek set-piece specialist Vassilios Tsiartas, another midfielder, arrived from AEK Athens for 250 million pesetas. Croatian playmaker Robert Prosinečki, formerly of Real Madrid and Barcelona, arrived, as did his fellow Croat Ivica Mornar from Eintracht Frankfurt, along with Brazilian striker Bebeto, so famed at Deportivo de La Coruña. In the dugout, former Real Madrid defender José Antonio Camacho – highly regarded in Spanish coaching circles having promoted each of Rayo Vallecano and Espanyol to the top flight – was appointed.

It was a summer of wholesale change which represented a fresh start and a clean break from the instability which had preceded it. Yet it was the arrival of Argentine forward Cristian Colusso – another in the glut of summer signings – which summed up the disastrous season that *Sevillistas* were to endure. Signed as a 19-year-old after breaking through at Rosario Central, Colusso received the deeply unhelpful 'New Maradona' tag. His experience at Sevilla was so harrowing that he later admitted in an interview with *ABC* that it forced him to see a psychologist. "I went to play football but I lost everything," Colusso said. "I felt totally cheated. People know me just as 'the Colusso case'."

The Argentine played just six games for the club before it emerged that both he and the club had been swindled out of money. The signatures of Colusso and his parents were reportedly forged and the player laid the blame at the door of his representative, Roberto Rodríguez, whom he says "betrayed" him and who "never answered me again". He also reserved criticism for Sevilla president González de Caldas, who he alleges never informed him of the situation and who only ever spoke to him upon his arrival.

Colusso wasn't alone with his stint in Seville being short and not so sweet. Like the Argentine, striker Bebeto made just six appearances for the club and did not score. Such a short and unsuccessful stint is largely explained by Sevilla neither paying Flamengo the agreed transfer fee nor the player himself his wages – the latest sign of boardroom ineptitude. *Foro Sevillista*, a group of Sevilla members and shareholders, were forced into expressing their indignation at club president de Caldas after Barcelona released a statement in December claiming Sevilla's cheque for Prosinečki had bounced. The statement blamed de Caldas for portraying a "painful image" of Sevilla and called on the board of directors to act appropriately and dismiss him, or be held "equally responsible for the deterioration of the institution".

Ivica Mornar made just 14 appearances and both of his goals came in defeats. Almeyda would move on at the end of the campaign while boss Camacho could not recover from a horror start which brought just one victory and six defeats in the first nine games, with the club lodged in the relegation zone for virtually the entirety of the season. Davor Šuker's absence was being felt even harder than predicted –

a paltry five goals in their opening 10 league games demonstrated Sevilla's absence of killer instinct.

The writing was on the wall ahead of the mid-season Seville derby at the Ramón Sánchez-Pizjuán with Sevilla on a four-game losing streak in the league and with their city neighbours flying high, winning each of their last four outings. That third-place finish in 1995 had rocketed expectations in the green-and-white half of the city but history repeated itself the following year with the club struggling to cope with the twin demands of domestic and European football. Betis impressed in Europe, winning each leg of their ties with both Fenerbahçe and Kaiserslautern, before being edged out 3–2 by Bordeaux. They could not replicate their remarkable third-placed league finish from the previous campaign but recorded a respectable top-eight finish.

In many ways, Betis and Sevilla had switched roles in this period. While chaos reigned in Nervión, there was a clear sense of continuity and growth at Betis. Lorenzo Serra Ferrer was in his third full season in the dugout – making him the club's first manager to achieve such a feat since Ferenc Szusza, two decades earlier – while Manuel Ruiz de Lopera had assumed the position of president in the summer of 1996. A series of significant signings had been made to consolidate the club's growth, including goalkeeper Antoni Prats, Croatian full-back Robert Jarni from Juventus, Ajax winger and Nigerian international Finidi George and, perhaps most significantly of all, Spanish international striker Alfonso Pérez from Real Madrid.

Alfonso was the man who made the difference in the pre-Christmas showdown on 22 December. The main hallmarks of Serra Ferrer's side were defensive resilience, soaking up pressure and hitting the opposition on the counter-attack. Sevilla, possessing home advantage, felt the need to take the initiative and the opening 30 minutes were chaotic with fast-paced, frenetic attacking play from Camacho's side. Yet Betis never looked vulnerable and there was an increasing sense that Sevilla were playing more with their hearts than their heads. Such suspicions were fuelled by home defender José Miguel Prieto needlessly felling Alfonso inside the penalty area. Alexis Trujillo made no mistake from the spot for 1–0. From that moment onwards, there was little doubt over the destination of the points as Sevilla looked unsure of themselves, with the players devoid of confidence and cohesion. Alfonso doubled the lead nine minutes after the break before defender Tomás Olías added a third. The second half was played to the backdrop of *olés* from the visiting fans, revelling in their new-found superiority over their fiercest rivals. The win matched Betis's biggest-ever victory in the derby and their first three-goal triumph in Nervión since their 1935 title-winning campaign.

"Today everything has gone very wrong," Camacho said after the game. The club's vice-president Francisco Escobar added, not entirely convincingly: "The coach will continue with us, we have confidence in him." The Sevilla misery was in contrast to Betis joy, with Serra Ferrer – a measured individual who rarely got caught up in the extremes of victory or defeat – surmising: "My joy is the product of everything that has been done throughout this league." Meanwhile Betis vice-president Ángel Martín revelled: "We have been eating cake this season, we had been missing the icing and today we got it."

There was no immediate upturn in results for Sevilla and the final straw for Camacho arrived six weeks later. His side led sixth-placed Real Sociedad 2–0 in the 84th minute and were on course for just their second league triumph in three months. Yet such was the fragility and nervous energy within the stadium, the Basque side scored three quickfire goals to steal the points. Camacho was gone and Carlos Bilardo was restored, four seasons after his sole campaign at the helm. Yet three defeats in four games saw the Argentine concede that he could not turn around the club's predicament.

Former midfielder Julián Rubio – who played for *Los Rojiblancos* between 1972 and 1979 – was promoted from the club's youth setup. Rubio's task was simple: salvage the club's two-decade long top-flight status in 17 games and prevent only the third relegation in their history. With just one victory in nine games, the situation was bleak. There was a late rally as Sevilla won their fourth game of the season and took a point in the chaotic return derby at Real Betis. Helped by a red card to *Los Verdiblancos* defender Roberto Ríos in the 27th minute, a bad-tempered affair had been marked positively by two Croats: Robert Jarni netting twice for Betis and Robert Prosinečki's penalty giving Sevilla hope. Substitute Juan José Cañas netted four minutes from time to seemingly wrap up a victory for the 10 men but there was a final twist as two of the visitors' second-half introductions, Salva and Jesús Galván, rescued a remarkable point with two goals inside the final two minutes. This was a hugely significant few minutes of play. Firstly, it was three different academy products scoring in the most important game of their lives and, arguably more significantly, whilst it would not be enough to save Sevilla from their fate, it prevented Betis from securing a third-placed finish for the second time in three seasons. Serra Ferrer's men missed out on a top-three finish courtesy of their inferior head-to-head record against Deportivo de La Coruña.

As is so often the case in football, underperforming arrivals from abroad and a tightening of club finances are not exclusively a negative. For Sevilla it continued to afford a pathway to the first-team squad from the youth ranks. Despite all the furore over the flood of summer arrivals, the two most exciting players were two forwards who had been nurtured by the club: José Mari and Salvador 'Salva' Ballesta.

José Mari was the star of the club's B side and earned his first-team debut less than two months after celebrating his 18th birthday – José Antonio Camacho's fateful final game in charge, the harrowing late collapse against Real Sociedad. He swiftly established himself as a regular in the starting line-up and netted seven goals in the second half of the season. A quick, skilful forward with notable self-assuredness and energy, the local boy had the potential to establish himself as a true Sevilla club legend. Yet circumstances, many of which were beyond his control, handed him a different path. The team's relegation meant all their star assets were vulnerable and the player himself had not penned a long-term deal at the club. Sevilla president González de Caldas was blamed for a lack of foresight and sporting organisation and was himself replaced at the end of the relegation campaign by Rafael Carrión Moreno – six months after fan groups had demanded a change of direction.

José Mari subsequently joined Atlético de Madrid – ending months of speculation that a deal had been agreed – after his 150 million pesetas release clause (around €900k) was activated (Atléti youth team players David Cordón and Míchel were included in the deal). Two years later, the forward's transfer fee had multiplied more than 20 times over as he joined Milan in a landmark deal worth a reported €19m. His career didn't quite the reach the potential it had once promised and after a four-year stint at Villarreal, he joined Real Betis for a season in 2007, but he never reached the heights of his opening campaigns.

Salva Ballesta – a native of Zaragoza, but who emerged through Sevilla's youth ranks – was another young forward with big potential and, like José Mari, he would go on to win four caps for Spain. Three years older than his fellow forward, Salva had already spent three seasons in the club's B team and had a loan stint at Écija to ensure he was a more rounded player, offering more consistency and assurance. He hit an impressive 12 goals in just 29 starts in his debut campaign, despite the team's poor performances. Salva remained with Sevilla through relegation but injury problems restricted him to just three goals in 14 appearances in the Segunda and with the team missing out on promotion, he departed in 1998 for Racing de Santander.

Salva's playing career was a sparkling one and not only did he fulfil his early potential but in many aspects he exceeded it. He won the Pichichi Trophy in the 1999/00 season, netting a remarkable 27 La Liga goals for Racing before a further goal-filled spell with Atlético de Madrid and stints at other clubs, most notably Valencia and Málaga. However, the forward is remembered most of all not for anything he did on the pitch but the views which he expressed off it.

Raised in a military family – his father was a military pilot and he became a qualified fighter pilot himself, before opting for football – Salva never shied away from comments to promote his self-described "patriotism", which would later compromise his own career. The Spanish flag was sewn on to his boots and the inscription 'Arriba España' – the Francoist slogan – was etched into the soles. Salva, who insisted multiple times he would never represent a regional team, described representing Spain as "the greatest pride". When asked about the war in Iraq, Salva replied: "I would go first. All soldiers would be happy to defend their nation, if they were real military." He is on record declaring his admiration for leading Francoist aviator Joaquin Garcia-Morato and the infamous Nazi pilot Hans Rudel, while he declared in 2006 he would like to meet Antonio Tejero, the leader of an attempted coup d'état in 1981 which sought to overthrow Spain's fledgling democracy.

Salva's views often compromised his playing career. While at Málaga, he was rebuked by some fans of Osasuna (the club based in the region of Navarre, with views overlapping with the Basque Country) at their El Sadar home and after being shown a red card was caught on cameras shouting at the fans: "Long live Spain, you sons of bitches!" Whilst playing at Real Sociedad, a group of the Basque club's fans brought a banner simply reading: 'Salva, die!' Ahead of playing for Levante against Barcelona, he declared "he had more respect for a dog's turd" than Barça defender Olegeur Presas, who had written a lengthy blog post questioning the fairness of the treatment of Catalan separatists. The situation came to a head in February 2013 when Celta de Vigo cancelled their agreement to appoint him as their assistant coach, after succumbing to protests from the club's fanbase.

Back in 1997, Sevilla's problems did not end with their summer relegation. A host of star names were sold, and affordable replacements signed. Greek midfielder Vasilis Tsartas – who netted 49 goals across four campaigns at the club, including many from set-pieces – became the club's standout player but results on the pitch remained dire. They could only muster a seventh-place finish in the Segunda in 1998, a whopping 11 points off the top four and a coveted promotion play-off spot. Julián Rubio was dismissed after six games and Vicente Miera, Juan Carlos Álvarez and Fernando Castro Santos failed to bring about a change in fortunes. It would not be until the following season, the second half of which was under the stewardship of Marcos Alonso Peña, that promotion would be achieved. An underwhelming fourth place was followed by victory in both legs over Villarreal in the promotion/relegation play-off.

Chapter 24

Near Misses and Heartbreak

CHAOS had engulfed Sevilla – instability in the boardroom, in the dugout and on the pitch. Just as so often had been the case at Real Betis, they were finding out that volatility off the field led to vulnerability on it. Yet just as something very unSevilla-like was happening, in Heliópolis they were riding the crest of a wave.

Betis qualified for Europe three times in the latter half of the 1990s, recording four successive top-eight finishes including third and fourth, while in 1997 they reached their first Copa del Rey showpiece in two decades. It was the culmination of a season which promised so much for Lorenzo Serra Ferrer's side – they had led the table after four weeks, were second in February and were in a top-three spot for 15 consecutive weeks in the second half of the campaign. A six-game winless run ahead of the final day saw them agonisingly miss out on third for the second time in three seasons as Deportivo edged them out with a superior head-to-head record.

Yet there was still the final of the Copa to come against Barcelona – who had missed out on that season's league title to Real Madrid by two points. Betis had reached the showpiece thanks to victories in both legs of their ties with Tenerife and Rayo Vallecano, before overcoming Celta de Vigo in the semis. After a 1–0 victory in Seville, the situation had threatened to unravel in Vigo as the hosts levelled the tie and both sides were reduced to 10 men – defender Juan Ureña seeing red for Betis as a bad-tempered tie spilled over. With three minutes remaining and extra time looming, captain Alexis Trujillo struck the decisive leveller.

Trujillo became a player of true significance for the club, spending seven seasons as a first-team regular after joining from Las Palmas when they were in the second tier in 1993. The central midfielder was already aged 28 and had a decade of professional football under his belt but just like many of the region's fine wines, Trujillo improved with age in Seville. His brother Blas is a prominent PSOE politician back in his Gran Canaria home and while Alexis spent the majority of his career on the Canary Islands – including a four-year stint at the now extinct Universidad de Las Palmas at the end of his career – he became synonymous with Betis. Upon his departure from Betis in July 2000, *ABC*'s tribute included the words: "All moves passed through him, and when they did, the ball almost always went where it was desired to go. He had hard workers around him to obey his thoughtful orders." Captaining the team under Serra Ferrer, he would a decade later be the boss's number two before going on to work for the club in technical roles and as a chief scout. Indeed, he oversaw first-team affairs for their final two games of the 2016/17 campaign following Víctor Sánchez del Amo's dismissal.

Of his 22 goals in a Betis shirt, his late strike at Celta's Balaídos was arguably the most significant. The hosts needed two in two minutes but they were flattened and Betis were through. After 20 years they were going back to the Spanish capital although this time it would be to Real Madrid's Santiago Bernabéu and not the Vicente Calderón, home of Atlético de Madrid, as it had been back in 1977.

Narrowly missing out on the league title was not the only reason Barcelona were so focused for the match. It was only three seasons earlier that they had been eliminated from the Copa by Betis, then in the Segunda, at the Camp Nou. A victory would also ensure their 23rd title in the competition to equal the record set by Athletic Club Bilbao. Bobby Robson's star-studded side were undoubted favourites but were without the devastating striker Ronaldo Nazário, who had hit an eye-watering 47 goals that campaign and was developing into one of the finest strikers ever to grace a football pitch. Fellow Brazilian forward Giovanni was also unavailable, but this was a side containing Luís Figo, Luis Enrique, Hristo Stoichkov and Argentine striker Juan Antonio Pizzi, a team who had scored 102 league goals in 42 matches – 17 more than champions Real Madrid.

The pattern of the game was always likely to be Barcelona dominating possession and territory with Betis happy to soak up pressure and maximise counter-attacking opportunities. Trujillo, alongside his two central midfield partners Albert Naɗ and Juan Cañas, would attempt to stifle the controlling influence of Barça captain Pep Guardiola and Iván de la Peña, while the collective and individual performances of the Betis front three of Robert Jarni, Finidi George and Alfonso Pérez would be vital to their hopes of an upset.

For Alfonso this was a particularly significant stage. He had joined Real Madrid as a 14-year-old and spent nine years at the club, making 88 first-team appearances – heavily limited due to competing against club legend Emilio Butragueño and then former *Sevillista* Iván Zamorano – before joining Betis. From the capital's Getafe suburb, the local team named their stadium the Coliseum Alfonso Pérez in his honour, despite him never playing for the club or indeed in the facility. Alfonso joined Betis in 1995 and while his 12-goal return during his debut campaign was respectable, his 25 strikes in the 1996/97 season saw his status elevated to among the nation's elite. Standing out in the era for wearing white boots, he was equally effective while alongside Italian-born striker Pier or at the head of a three-pronged attack, with Finidi and Jarni proving to be equally troublesome for opponents.

Finidi had arrived at Betis a year after Alfonso but unlike the striker, the Nigerian winger's talents had already been showcased to the wider football public. He starred for his nation in the 1994 World Cup and was instrumental in Ajax's European Cup triumph in 1995 before helping them to the following year's final. His signature was a massive coup for *Los Verdiblancos*, who were beginning to loosen the purse strings under the stewardship of president Manuel Ruiz de Lopera. "Several of the great clubs wanted me, including Manchester United and Real Madrid, who almost signed me," Finidi later explained. "My agent had a pre-agreement with Madrid but Ajax found out and the deal broke down, so I ended up at Betis." He was a nimble winger who gave opposition full-backs nightmares, not only for his capability of beating a man and delivering a cross, but also for his ability to hustle them.

The Nigerian also became famed for his goal celebrations, when he would wear a green Cordovan hat – hugely popular throughout Andalusia, due to their origins in Córdoba – which had been thrown on to the field of play each time he scored. The tradition had begun back in 1973 with the club's Argentine midfielder Eduardo Anzarda, when fan Gabino Varilla – a Betis *socio* since 1957 – brought the item to the games and threw it on in celebration. It is a tradition which has been carried on through the decades since and Finidi became synonymous with the ritual, donning the garment in each of his 38 goal celebrations across his 130 games at the club. His celebrations were also Matador-like with suggestions this had been inspired by visits to the city's Maestranza bullring, with the winger emulating the moves of Curro Romero or Emilio Muñoz. "I often feel like a bullfighter," he later admitted.

On the other side of the Betis front-line was Croatian Robert Jarni, who had joined from Juventus in 1995. Playing the majority of his career as a forward-thinking full-back, Jarni starred in a more advanced role in Seville and was a key component of Serra Ferrer's successful side. Despite his slight frame, his trickery and pace meant he was a huge offensive weapon and added balance to the side. His departure in 1998 was a controversial one riddled with conspiracy theories, after the player had starred for Croatia at that summer's World Cup.

Real Madrid had reportedly held a long-term interest in Jarni but their approaches were turned down by Betis, who sold the Croat to Coventry City in August 1998 for £2.6m. However, Jarni never played for the English club and just ten days later joined Madrid for £3.4m, with widespread suggestions that had been the plan all along, which the full-back later denied: "Coventry wanted to sign me following my displays with Betis and in the World Cup but when Real Madrid came, I had no choice. It was a family decision – they did not want to go to England, our children were in Spanish schools. Coventry understood the situation."

Despite a sprinkling of stars from abroad to help propel Betis to their success in the late nineties, there were similarities to the legendary team of two decades earlier. Four of the players who featured in the 1997 final came through the club's youth system and between them amassed over 1,000 games for the club: central defenders Juan Antonio Ureña and Roberto Ríos (son of club legend Eusebio, see Chapter 16), left-back Juan Merino and midfielder Juan Cañas (whose nephew José would play for the club a decade later). Just as with their captain Trujillo, all four would continue their associations with the club after their playing days with the long-serving Merino – who would also become a real estate business partner of Trujillo – most prominent. He would take charge of first-team affairs on an interim basis on several occasions and would have stints as number two to Pepe Mel, his old team-mate.

The 1997 Copa del Rey final was held in late June, with the soaring Madrid temperatures doing little to quell a tense day in the capital. *El País* reported over 80 arrests were made throughout the day due to various outbreaks of disturbances among rival sets of fans not only of the participating clubs but of those based in the host city. The Spanish capital was a sea of green and white in the build-up to the game with a reported 85,000 *Béticos* descending upon the city for the event.

The game itself lived up to the billing and it took Betis just 11 minutes to take a shock lead through the in-form Alfonso – "the great *Verdiblanca* star of the game", as the subsequent Catalan-based *El Mundo Deportivo* match report stressed. He ran on to an angled Finidi pass and his shot could only be parried by the Barça goalkeeper back into the striker's path, with the ball fortunately ricocheting into the net. Lorenzo Serra Ferrer's tactics were working and an early goal suited the reactionary style they often deployed against the biggest clubs. Barça were typically enjoying plenty of the ball but were not forging clear-cut opportunities, not helped by the below-par display of forward Hristo Stoichkov who, as *El País* described, "appeared outrageously disinterested". However, a minute before the break Luís Figo levelled the score with a dazzling individual run and long-range effort, and it was the Portuguese winger who would be instrumental in the game's outcome.

The longer the second half progressed, the more each side tired and notably Betis were flagging the most. Barça were creating the game's clear-cut opportunities but with eight minutes remaining and the game increasingly open, Finidi found space on the right side of the Catalan team's penalty area and slammed home to restore the Betis advantage. However, with the Andalusian side five minutes away from lifting the trophy, Pizzi drifted into their penalty area unmarked to head home a Barça equaliser. The game went to a gruelling extra time, unwanted by both sets of players, and in the 114th minute Figo decided the outcome with his second of the game. Like the Betis opener, it had a large element of fortune – a mishit Barça pass deflecting off a Betis defender leaving goalkeeper Pedro Jaro's instinctive reaction only to parry to Figo, who duly accepted the close-range finish.

The Copa title was not the only thing Barça took from Betis that summer, with boss Serra Ferrer bringing an end to his remarkably successful three-year stint in the dugout to take up a directorial position in the Camp Nou. It was a new-look Barcelona for the 1997/98 campaign, led by Louis van Gaal, whom Serra Ferrer would replace three years later.

* * * * *

Luis Aragonés was back as Betis boss in the summer of 1997, 16 years after managing the club for just one match before accepting a return to Atlético de Madrid. His popularity at the club had waned following his two-year stint across the city at Sevilla but his credentials were not in question, having led Valencia to a second-place finish in

1996. Outside of defender Roberto Ríos joining Athletic Club for a club record 2,000 million pesetas (€12m), there were no significant departures from the playing staff with the most notable arrival that of Real Oviedo striker Oli, who would win his only two caps for the Spanish national side that season. His strike partnership with Alonso brought a combined return of 27 goals, five of which arrived in European competition.

Betis were in the Cup Winners' Cup due to their exploits the previous year and just as they had done in 1978, they progressed all the way to the quarter-final stage before failing. Hungarian side Budapesti VSC were defeated 4–0 on aggregate before FC Copenhagen of Denmark were seen off. However, *Los Verdiblancos* received their worst possible draw in the quarter-finals. They would have viewed any of Roda, Sparta Prague, Vicenza, Stuttgart, AEK Athens or Lokomotiv Moscow as beatable and a path to the final appeared to be opening up. The one side who Betis wanted to avoid at all costs was Chelsea and it was the Blues, who predictably went on to lift the trophy, who they were paired with.

Visiting striker Tore André Flo netted two superb individual goals for Chelsea within the opening 12 minutes of the first leg in Seville, putting a major dampener on the vociferous atmosphere. Alfonso pulled a goal back after the break to reduce the arrears and offer hope of a miracle back in London. Those dreams were multiplied when Finidi opened the scoring at Stamford Bridge in the 20th minute, but the hosts hit three successive goals to seal their progress. The home defeat to Chelsea was the only one of 14 European home matches Betis failed to win between 1984 and the Champions League group stage in 2005, with the club securing 11 clean sheets in the process.

Domestically, 1997/98 was only the third campaign since the Civil War when Real Betis were competing in the top flight without their city rivals. Their eighth-place finish that season was deceptive; Betis finished just four points from a top-three finish and just six points from a runners-up spot.

Their standout result of the season came in the run-in for a European finish when they travelled to Barcelona, who had already wrapped up the league title with three games to spare. Betis had only ever won at the Camp Nou on three previous occasions – all in the 1980s – and had a poor record in the stadium, including 12 consecutive defeats between 1933 and 1964. However, they managed to exert a small element of revenge from the Copa final loss the previous year. Winston Bogarde headed Barça in front before Alfonso and Finidi – who netted twice – again featured on the scoresheet to land a memorable victory.

The real storyline of the season for Betis was off the field, when the club made global headlines for their signing of a talented Brazilian winger. The timeline of events began in the summer of 1997 with Le Tournoi competition in France – a four-team warm-up tournament for the World Cup the following year. Brazil were one of the four participants and among the household names in their line-up was a relatively unknown winger: Denílson de Oliveira. Then aged 19, he had debuted for hometown club São Paulo as a 17-year-old and would go on to net 58 goals in 110 appearances, while the first of his 61 international caps was won in 1996. He showed incredible skill and trickery in France, mixing a scary turn of pace with dribbling, directness and unpredictability. He was already drawing comparisons to some of the finest Brazilians to have ever graced the game.

By the end of the mini-tournament, Denílson was boarding a plane back home but a bidding war had commenced among Europe's elite clubs for his signature. This was at a time when Europe's giants considered Brazil's internationals to be the true elite of football. Ronaldo had jointed Inter in a world record deal, while Barcelona replaced him with two other Brazilian attacking stars – Rivaldo, of Deportivo de La Coruña and Monaco striker Sonny Anderson. Atlético de Madrid signed playmaker Juninho Paulista from Middlesbrough, while the previous year Valencia had landed former Barça hitman Romario. As *El Tiempo* wrote at the time: "Without the Brazilian dynamite, Spanish clubs are left fearing disaster. Brazilians are considered the best architects of offensive play, inborn scorers, skilful and dangerous when they enter the final third." To sign a Brazilian attacking star was seen as the ultimate statement of intent.

Real Madrid, Manchester United and PSV Eindhoven were all linked to Denílson, as were Lazio and Barcelona. Indeed, the Catalans had appeared to finalise the deal before a late rise in São Paulo's quoted price held up the formalities. It was at this juncture that Betis president Manuel Ruiz de Lopera, the property tycoon and devout Catholic, sensed the ultimate statement of intent to challenge Spain's established football order. The story goes that Lopera spent over an hour praying at Salesians Holy Trinity church in the Trinidad district of Seville, before making his approach to the Brazilian club.

The full details of the deal were extraordinary, just as the Betis president had hoped. The club had struck a £21.5m agreement with São Paulo for Denílson, surpassing the previous record of £19m set by Ronaldo's move to Inter earlier that summer. The quoted release clause was a hefty £261m (the previous record was thought to be Clarence Seedorf's £91m at Real Madrid) while the length of contract was set at 11 years – taking the winger up to his 30th birthday. The one condition was that he would remain in Brazil for one more year before joining Betis after the World Cup. "We worked very hard to get it, but now we can give all the Betis fans something to celebrate," Lopera beamed to reporters when concluding the move. The player himself appeared somewhat less celebratory when later discussing the move with weekly sports magazine *Don Balón*: "I'd gone to bed believing I'd signed for Barcelona but when I woke up, I realised that it would actually be Betis. Their offer was one they [São Paulo] could not reject and economically it suited me, so I gratefully accepted it."

The deal was remarkable on almost every level and while it was an attempt to place Betis – traditionally the perennial underachievers in Spanish football – on the global football map, it was part of a sustained project of self-adulation by their president. Three years after the deal for Denílson and coinciding with the club's descent back to the second tier, he decided to rename the club's Estadio Benito Villamarín after himself (the name change was reversed a decade later) as well as the club's training facilities. Football agent Michel Basiljevich, acting on behalf of his client, Nigerian international Sunday Oliseh, told Spanish media he would not negotiate the midfielder's proposed move to Betis because Lopera was "an imbecile running a dictatorship". Oliseh never moved to Seville.

Spanish football writer Sid Lowe dubbed Lopera – nicknamed locally as Don Manué (the thick Andalusian accent leading to the dropping of the final syllable) – as "the Prince of Darkness", describing him as "Real Betis's evil overlord and all-round oddball" and summing up his background in a column for *The Guardian* newspaper, wrote: "Lopera is a man who made his millions selling second-hand tellies secured on houses with huge rates of interest collected by big men in dark suits; who drives round Seville picking up stray dogs; who carries huge wodges of cash in black bin-bags; whose sexual predilections are best left alone; whose business partner mysteriously disappeared back in 1975; and who likes nothing more than winding up Sevilla." In *Morbo*, Phil Ball described the Betis president as an "unbalanced man despite the chips on both shoulders".

Indeed, in due course Sevilla would be presided over by Lopera's nemesis, José María del Nido. The two shared many similarities including their fanatical Catholicism, shady business backgrounds, outlandish statements and lust for controversy. But before all that, the Denílson experiment had already started to unravel. He was unveiled in front of over 20,000 Betis fans upon his long-awaited arrival in the summer of 1998, but all did not go as planned.

The winger did not find the net in any of his first 26 appearances for the club and scored only twice that season. "I'm giving my all to prove I'm the best in the world," he said in December, having not yet found the net. "But the reality is I'm only the most expensive ... now I need to score to improve things in my head." Whilst his huge reserves of natural talent were obvious, his play became predictable, he was obviously uncomfortable using his right foot and opposition teams nullified his threat. He had thrived in Brazil with less pressure on the ball and more time to show his tricks but in Spain he was not afforded such luxury. There were doubts that he had settled culturally too, rarely seen outsides the confines of his deluxe villa on the outskirts of the city.

The performances were not all Denílson's fault of course. That summer had seen Betis secure the appointment of António Oliveira, who had just landed consecutive league titles for FC Porto. However, not wholly unpredictably, he had an early disagreement with Lopera and was on his way before overseeing a game. Vicente Cantatore arrived but was gone after just seven games with the club rooted to the foot of the table. In true Betis fashion, their one victory under the Argentine came in a 1–0 victory at Real Madrid, secured with a strike from Finidi.

It was becoming increasingly apparent that Denílson's price tag was weighing him down. "Betis are a great club who want to win trophies, but that is the reason behind my transfer fee, not anything else. Of course, I think about the price tag a lot, there is plenty of coverage. People thought I would come to Spain and be the top scorer in the division. It did not help me one bit."

The pragmatic, conservative Javier Clemente arrived and his style of play was not much liked by *Béticos* (see Chapter 1) nor by the players. His insistence on tactical discipline and rigidity did little to help the individualistic Denílson flourish, even if it did see Betis recover to record a comfortable mid-table finish. That was the year Sevilla restored their top-flight status and the rivalry would be renewed at Spanish football's top table. It was to be all too brief, but the controversy and fallout reached new heights as tempers reached boiling point.

Chapter 25

Presidents Go to War

FANS of Real Betis and Sevilla are often like competitive siblings. They love provoking one another, winding each other up – they cannot help themselves. Fuelled by a prominent concept in Andalusia –*guasa*, having a sense of humour and a lot of banter, being deliberately silly and trying to having a laugh, often with a dash of wickedness–point-scoring and one-upmanship are among their favourite pastimes. Sometimes it is funny, often it is engaging but occasionally it goes too far. The rivalry enjoys such distinction in large part due to its insistent, never-ending need for one set of fans to assert their authority over the other. To show they are the city's number one. Their dad is bigger than your dad. At their core is an outward showing of a superiority complex yet equally the deepest fears of both are being outdone by their city rivals. Such combativeness is all well and good for an incomparable spectacle but without leadership from those at the top of the clubs, it has the potential to boil over.

Manuel Ruiz de Lopera's presidency at Betis had added fuel to a rivalry that had been interrupted throughout the 1990s due to the fluctuating fortunes of both clubs. Of the eight seasons between 1991 and 1999, only three contained Seville derbies. Lopera's insistence on signing Denílson was one element of a prolonged vanity project, allowing Betis fans to boast that they – for so many years viewed as the city's poorer relations – were now the club with the financial might. Of course, the signings of Alfonso and Finidi, among others, earlier in the decade were not cheap and allowed the club to fight for major domestic honours but they did not catch global headlines. Lopera believed statement signings were a show of strength and, not incorrectly, would prove enough for him to garner the adoration of the club's fans, who would continually vote him back into the role come election time.

At the turn of the century, Sevilla were led by the popular Roberto Alés who had helped steer the club back into the top flight whilst reducing debts and helping lay the sporting structures for future successes – not that it was apparent at the time. Alés was replaced in 2002 by his vice-president José María del Nido, who was assuming the permanent role as leader of the club for the first time. Like Lopera across the city, his popularity grew with on-field success mixed with hugely successful additions and an upturn in investment in the playing staff. Like Lopera, del Nido would hold office for over a decade and, like his Betis counterpart, would end his career mired in controversy and finally criminal proceedings, leading to jail terms. Sid Lowe described the Sevilla president as "a classic Andalusian snob with polished head and overbearing arrogance."

The personal feud between Lopera and del Nido, based almost entirely on a rampant sense of self-importance, developed into a virus that engulfed the rivalry and led to clashes between the two throughout the 2000s and beyond being labelled as high risk by police, with unsavoury incidents and violence becoming increasingly regular. *Diario AS* editor Alfredo Relaño, writing in a column in 2007, was moved to focus blame to the very top of both of Seville's clubs: "Betis and Sevilla is a flammable mix. And the worst thing is, it is one that's in the hands of pyromaniacs." Real Betis fan and historian Alfonso del Castillo told me that the duo "exacerbated the rivalry in a very dangerous way."

A sign of things to come arrived a fortnight before the turn of the millennium when a group of Sevilla players were involved in an assault outside the Birdie nightclub, a 10-minute walk from the club's Ramón Sánchez-Pizjuán stadium. The incident occurred after 4am on 17 December 1999 with three players – Marcelo Otero, Marcelo Zalayeta and Nico Olivera – later standing trial for their actions. They were at the establishment alongside their team-mate and fellow Uruguayan Tabaré Silva, who reportedly attempted to calm tensions.

The players claimed a group of young men had approached them inside the nightclub and "began to insult and provoke" them, while Zalayeta added that abuse was also shouted at his wife. The day after the attack, one of the victims, who worked as a lawyer in the city, denied these allegations and told *Cadena Ser* that there was "a strong possibility" that the assault was due to the fact it emerged they were Betis fans. They insisted there was no abuse and were leaving the club when the attack took place, with Olivera allegedly asking them "what are you laughing about", before adding he was going to "break his head".

The players followed the three men out of the club and subsequently began to punch and kick them. According to a witness, the attack was so brutal he thought the men "were going to be killed" and that the players were "extremely drunk", adding that Olivera "was totally out of his mind"!

One of the victims suffered a dislocated jaw and a broken leg, with the physical injuries taking almost six months to heal. Tabaré Silva, who was not involved in the altercation, reportedly told the victims: "Excuse me, they are intoxicated," before returning a wallet to one of the men and hastily taking off. The following day, Otero, Zalayeta and Olivera were arrested but, following a lengthy legal process, they all avoided jail time, although they were each ordered to pay a fine of €2,700.

It was not only Sevilla players who made the headlines for their late-night antics but at least when Real Betis players held a Halloween party in 2001, the ending to the evening was a rather more comical one. Midfielder Benjamín Zarandona was the host of the event at his home in Simón Verde – about a 20-minute drive from the club's stadium. "The evening had gotten a little out hand," he later admitted. "We had expected 30 people to come but it was a lot more." Indeed, rising star Joaquín Sánchez, aged 20 at the time, estimated there were 200 in attendance: "It had begun as a dinner and just kept going."

And going and going. That was until 4.30 in the morning, when an unexpected and uninvited visitor turned up. "I thought it was a lie, but I needed to find out," Betis president Lopera reflected. An anonymous tip-off, presumably from an uninvited team-mate, had alerted the supremo to the activities. Lopera phoned the team's coach Juande Ramos and, in the middle of the night, they intended to give the players the Halloween fright of their lives.

"I saw a car pull up outside and then I saw Lopera climb out of it ... I got really scared," admitted Benjamín. You could tell Lopera, whose obsession with control and authority rarely subsided, was secretly loving it. "When Benjamin saw me, he went white and disappeared from sight," the president continued, with a chuckle. "All of a sudden I heard screams and glass shattering, then they began trying to climb out of windows, Denílson got stuck halfway, while others hid behind curtains." It is important to remind ourselves at this point that this account, unlike many others from Lopera, is entirely accurate.

Joaquín, who would later become famed for being football's ultimate practical joker, was not laughing on that evening. "I saw Benjamín bounding up the stairs, looking extremely dishevelled, screaming about who had invited Lopera," he added. "Then Lopera began to pick us up, one by one. Denílson had run towards the window and wanted to jump, but it was a big drop. 'Where are you going?', I asked him. 'You are going to kill yourself! Just let him say what he wants.' But he was already halfway out the window."

Betis had made a strong start to that league campaign in 2001/02 with five wins in their opening seven, having won promotion the previous year. But form had nosedived in October with the Halloween antics coming in the midst of a six-game winless run. Lopera was (or at least wanted to appear to be) a hard taskmaster and would not tolerate such ill-discipline at 'his' club, which would have been understandable had the fallout from the event been handled in-house and away from the prying eyes of news reporters. Conversely, Lopera saw this as an ideal opportunity to brief journalists about the details of the event with the players involved predictably becoming a target for angry fans.

Benjamín, the protagonist, saw his house the target of bricks and graffiti while Denílson was harassed at the club's training facilities by 'supporters', who loudly insisted the Brazilian did not possess the *cojones* to represent their team. Four days later, Betis were loudly booed as they took to the pitch against Real Zaragoza before unsurprisingly falling to a limp 1–0 defeat, their first home loss of the season. Lopera had activated the ultimate demotivating approach and, realising his error, changed tack to one of forgiveness. Well, on one condition: defeat Sevilla in the upcoming derby. The result was a scoreless draw so dull that *ABC* coined it "The Great Yawn" with the match report musing if the encounter was the most anticlimactic in the fixture's history. Not that too many were concerned this would present a long-term trend, with events 18 months previous still fresh in the memory.

The 1999/00 season was arguably the most memorable in the distinguished history of the Spanish top flight. Shock results were a weekly occurrence, there was a power vacuum across the division and it was undoubtedly the year of the underdog. The league title went to Galicia for the first time ever as Deportivo de La Coruña finally landed the title that had eluded them in the 1990s (and making them just the second Spanish team, after Real Betis, to win each of the top three divisions in Spain), while the Pichichi award went to Racing de

Santander's Salva Ballesta (see Chapter 24) and the Zamora trophy to goalkeeper Martín Herrera of Alavés, who were back in the top flight for the first time in 43 years. The three clubs to be relegated? Real Betis, Atlético de Madrid, Sevilla.

It was Sevilla's first campaign back in the top flight, but they could muster just five league victories all season. An early 3–0 thrashing of Betis had provided hope for a promising season, but it was the only success in their opening 16 matches in all competitions. Despite a memorable 3–2 victory at home to Barcelona in December, boss Marcos Alonso was unable to stop the rot of results and was replaced by B team boss Juan Carlos, who could not halt their inevitable descent.

The fate of *Los Rojiblancos* was painfully clear with months of the season remaining but an incredibly competitive battle was unfolding immediately above them in the standings in the race to maintain top-flight status. The second Seville derby saw Betis hoping to extract revenge for their heavy defeat earlier in the campaign and, despite sitting 14th, they were strong favourites against a Sevilla side who would not win on the road all season. When Denílson converted a fourth-minute penalty the hosts appeared to be on course for victory but the ever-reliable Vassilios Tsiartas levelled things up with 15 minutes remaining with a spot-kick of his own. Substitute Jesuli even managed to rattle the post late on for the visitors but neither side could find a winner. "Both sides lost" ran the headline in *ABC*, recognising both teams' desperate need for points.

That was Alonso's penultimate game at the helm of Sevilla while Guus Hiddink was the man in the dugout for Betis. The Dutchman had replaced Carlos Timoteo Griguol in early February but just one win in 13 games saw him replaced at the end of April, with Betis perched in the midst of a relegation fight. Bosnian Faruk Hadžibegić came in to oversee the final few weeks of a traumatic campaign – the club's sixth permanent appointment since Lorenzo Serra Ferrer had departed for Barcelona less than two years earlier.

Hadžibegić would win two of his three matches in charge but Betis would join their city rivals in demotion to the second tier, as they finished three points below Real Oviedo. The latter's three points gained at Sevilla in matchday 34 proved to be of particular interest to Betis. Throughout the match, Sevilla players appeared to be putting in a minimal effort and did not seem bothered by any of the three goals they conceded. The possible exception was Norwegian goalkeeper Frode Olsen, who was substituted off at half-time with the score at 1–0 to Oviedo, for having the temerity to be making a wilful effort to save shots at his goal, much to the disapproval of the Sevilla fans inside the stadium. Ironically, Luis Aragonés – who had coached both Seville clubs – was in the dugout for the Asturian side that day and, despite Sevilla scoring two consolation goals late on to give the 3–2 scoreline a semblance of respectability, the match was the clearest case of *morbo* between the city rivals for many years.

Not that allegations of match-fixing were anything new. Many *Sevillistas* point to suggestions – which have never been proven – that Lopera had been offering Sevilla's opponents extra incentives throughout his presidency, even at times when the club were languishing a division below Betis. Lopera denied the allegations of course but added, with a wry smile, that he did not understand the fuss even if he did. Quite what the benefit of this approach would be to Betis was unclear, because no Seville derby robbed both clubs of their biggest payday of the season, but it underlined Lopera's hardened anti-Sevilla approach. So strong were the convictions of fans that such underhand activity was rife that an anonymous Sevilla fan even sent Lopera a death threat, while many *Béticos*, toeing the party line, defended the murky allegations. Neither club could sincerely take the moral high-ground but at least both sets of fans did not hide their tacit approval of such 'tactics'. The sorry chain of events underlined a cultural problem within Spanish sport; often an absence of morality and authenticity fuelled by a deep sense of mistrust.

It was the beginning of the deterioration in Lopera's public image, which took a further hit in 2002 when his side's home clash with Real Madrid was abandoned before half-time following a power cut inside the stadium. The magnificently named local boy Jesús Capitán Prada, better known as Capi, fired Betis into the lead in the 35th minute but eight minutes later, and with all the momentum with the hosts, the stadium was engulfed in total darkness. This was primetime Saturday night viewing in Spain and there had already been an element of irritation as kick-off had been delayed due to a failure of the main power supply. The club kickstarted the backup system, providing a strange lighting for the opening half, but that then failed entirely too, with the game subsequently postponed.

Lopera later posed for photos with the generator at the stadium, insisting that this was "top of the range" equipment that he personally had bought for €360m. "Even Madrid and Barcelona do not have this level of equipment," he quipped. His declaration that refunds would not be available for the match only worsened the situation before electricity company Sevillana Endesa compounded the situation. "We could have fixed this issue, we have specialist teams to deal with these moments," a spokesman told the national press. "But Lopera would not let our technicians into the stadium unless they paid an entrance fee, he was insistent nobody can watch the game for free." It was ironic that Lopera was allegedly so het up over freeloaders, as he himself blagged the club a free replacement generator as a result of the sorry incident.

There was a debate played out as to how the game should proceed, with some within the Madrid media suggesting the game should be restarted from scratch while Betis cried foul, saying that their 1–0 advantage in the 43rd minute should hold. In the end, probably the correct conclusion was reached, and *Los Verdiblancos* got their way, but as Madrid full-back Míchel Salgado surmised: "We would rather start a goal behind than have to tolerate Lopera's complaints." The surreal return game was started with a drop-ball by the corner flag where it had been postponed the previous month, with striker Ronaldo Nazário returned to Madrid's team due to the expiry of his suspension. The entire flow of the game had changed and the visitors deservedly equalised five minutes after half-time with the game ending 1–1.

Both Seville clubs had returned to La Liga in 2001 and fixtures were played to a typically passionate and ferocious background but there was now an extra edge that had not always been prevalent in previous decades. Things once again came to a head in a league meeting between the two at the Ramón Sánchez-Pizjuán in October 2002. In the warm-up before the match, five young Sevilla fans were spotted trying to steal balls being used by Real Betis goalkeeper Antonio Prats. A security guard tried to intervene and so bad was his beating that he was left hospitalised with broken ribs. In a separate incident, a Sevilla fan ran on to the pitch behind Prats and attempted to punch him in the back of the head, but thankfully did not land his effort.

The culprit was soon confirmed to be 29-year-old Francisco Chincoa Pino, who had been sitting in the Gol Norte stand, fuelling speculation that he was a member of Sevilla's *Biris Norte* group, which he denied. "I want to apologise to Prats, Sevilla and Betis for what I did," he said days later during court proceedings. "I am not from any violent group or from *Biris*, to whom I also apologise. I'm sorry. My intention was not to attack Prats and that's why I'm going to apologise to him in front of my lawyers. I do not want to hurt Sevilla because the club would be hit financially. The culprit is me and I have to pay."

Chincoa's apology was welcome, as was Sevilla's decision to revoke his membership but the culture of fear that such incidents would continue was now clear.

"I did not expect it at any time, although you get a scare," Prats admitted in the aftermath. "I realised he was drunk, and when you have 100,000 fans of course there will be a handful who are capable of barbarity. But I saw what happened to the security guard, I could not get it out of my mind. He was just 20 metres from me. I had never felt intimidated before, I have played here many times."

Perhaps Lopera's character requires deeper evaluation. He was born in 1944 as Manuel Ruiz Ávalos, but reports citing police sources say he changed his name to Manuel Ruiz de Lopera aged 30. This name alteration came when he became a warehouse manager of a company distributing home appliances which subsequently was declared bankrupt. He allegedly sold the remaining produce to working-class neighbourhoods in Seville on short-term loans with high interest rates, which were required to be met within days. He developed a real estate business partnership with José Luna Gázquez in the early 1970s but in 1975 Gázquez took a trip to Portugal and never returned. Lopera made millions through his business dealings, often shady and containing more than initially met the eye and translated this approach into his running of Betis.

There was a steady build-up of opposition to the Betis chief inside the club and by the mid-2000s his position became increasingly untenable. In 2006 he gave a bloated press conference full of self-praise and reminiscing over his "actions to save the club" from the abyss 14 years earlier, before declaring: "To those who want my death I will make them happy," and announced he would be leaving the post that summer. His departure would presumably give Lopera more time to spend on his hobbies, which genuinely included collecting stray dogs around Seville.

Olive businessman José León filled the presidential position that summer but Lopera never really disappeared from the presidential box, because he had ensured a huge bust of himself had been erected in the middle of the facility. It was inevitably, and some may conclude deliberately, going to stir up trouble and the first post-Lopera derby at the Betis stadium (at this point still named in honour of their former supremo) did not disappoint. Held in February 2007, it was the year in which Betis were celebrating their 100th anniversary and it was customary for all visiting dignitaries to be presented with a monument honouring the celebrations. Which is when the fun and games started.

Sevilla president del Nido had declined the offer of paying homage to the stadium's tribute – unsurprisingly, as he routinely refused to refer to the stadium by its official Manuel Ruiz de Lopera title – and, in an inexplicably reckless decision, the Betis stadium announcer decided to broadcast this development to the 50,000 home fans. As Sid Lowe detailed in the aftermath, del Nido was told he could not sit in the front row of the directors' box to watch proceedings due to his actions and would instead be placed beside the bust of his long-standing adversary. An unseemly fracas then broke out, with Lopera's nephew Javier Páez reportedly pushing del Nido. But that was justified, insisted Betis director Gregorio Conejo, because the Sevilla president had insulted Páez. Lowe described how the fractious atmosphere led to "missiles from the stands, with coins, bottles, lighters, sandwiches and papers raining down. One fan had even raided the minibar of his hotel, sending a tiny and hideously overpriced bottle of whisky sailing towards Sevilla keeper Andrés Palop."

These events were the culmination of a long-running personal feud between the presidents. Years earlier, Lopera had promised he would make it his "duty to stir up the derby," while his supreme self-confidence had been challenged by del Nido, who had himself proclaimed: "I'm the most important man in Seville after the Pope." That comment had come during the city's annual *feria* event, a week-long celebration within the Andalusian capital (see Chapter 3). In 2005, the spiralling levels of *morbo* between the sides spilled over into the festivities, when a Betis fan sneakily had placed the club's badge on the Portrait of King San Fernando, overlooking the grand entrance to the event. The upshot was a typically disproportionate level of offence from some *Sevillistas*, with one section complaining it was an "affront" as the entrance had been "soiled". It was no coincidence this happened during Sevilla's original centenary celebrations (before the foundation date was adjusted from 1905 to 1890). Lopera lapped up the event and teased that he knew the "Betis hero" who had added the badge but would not compromise his anonymity and give "Benavente" (Del Nido's unused second surname) the satisfaction. Del Nido's retort referred to his own "university education", with the implicit implication that Lopera did not possess one.

At the time of the *feria* incident, the two clubs were neck-and-neck in the league, but Sevilla had begun to establish an advantage and had appeared to consolidate a top four position. That would have guaranteed a Champions League spot and offered the prize of Sevilla being the first-ever Andalusian club to qualify for the competition (although they had previously competed in its predecessor, the European Cup, 47 years prior). "It is fantastic for the city of Seville to have a club in the Champions League for the first time," cooed del Nido. But Betis surged past their rivals in the closing few weeks of the city and it was they who secured that honour. "Del Nido was correct, it sure is fantastic," de Lopera said with a smile on his face the width of the Guadalquivir river. (It is important to note at this point that Sevilla's 'demotion' into a UEFA Cup spot began a sequence of events that saw them lift the honour the following year.)

Lowe observed: "If they had any shame, they would be ashamed of themselves, but these two just can't help it." Some of the incidents and faux outrage had a distinctive comical quality but they were increasingly fused with violence and disturbances between supporters. Fireworks were launched at rival sets of fans; seats were ripped up at both stadiums and thrown across barriers and towards those seated below them. Police began to advise away fans against going to matches as their safety could not be guaranteed. The derby had become a tinderbox and 'arsonists' were almost being egged on by those in positions of authority.

The fallout after the 2007 league clash carried on after the full-time whistle, with Betis threatening to ban del Nido from future derbies at the stadium. "That would be illegal, they cannot ban a president," the Sevilla chief raged afterwards. "I'll be here again, let's see them try and stop me."

As fate would have it, del Nido did not have long to wait in keeping his promise as Sevilla returned to Heliópolis for the return leg of their Copa del Rey quarter-final later that month. The build-up to the game predictably centred around the off-field issues rather than any huge expectation for a fascinating spectacle on it. The league meeting between the two had finished scoreless, as had the first leg of the Copa clash. Indeed, Betis were stuck in a rut and had scored just once in their previous six games. This was partly the reason why Lopera was not masquerading in public; he was blamed for failing to reinvest properly in the first-team squad and whilst he insisted he had deep pockets, the fans retorted this was irrelevant if he had short arms. This came in the midst of a golden spell for Sevilla both domestically and in Europe, which also played into the frustration of Betis fans with their underperforming outfit and, according to cynics, speeded up Lopera's departure.

Betis did not ban del Nido on the one condition that he sat beside Lopera's ridiculous bust in the directors' box, but tensions were high and something had to give. This was a knockout tie, one side had to lose. In the end, the derby itself was the ultimate loser. Three minutes before the hour mark, Sevilla's prolific Malian striker Frédéric Kanouté fired the visitors into the lead and broke the fixture's goalscoring drought. One-time Betis boss Juande Ramos was now in the opposing dugout and was establishing himself as a *Sevillista* hero. When Kanouté's strike hit the back of the net, Ramos maintained his typically composed demeanour as the rest of the visiting bench erupted in celebration. One bottle came down from the stands, then another. Both landed in Sevilla's dugout and one hit the celebrating Sevilla full-back Dani Alves, who was on the floor. Then another bottle flew through the air, and this one made a full connection – with the back of Ramos's head. The coach reached to the back of his head in pain before stumbling forward on to the pitch and collapsing unconscious. It emerged that there was logic behind the high velocity of the bottle's movement through the air: it was frozen.

Panicked, several Sevilla officials surrounded the stricken coach and minutes later he was stretchered off without moving a muscle. As one, the visiting team and staff followed the medics down the tunnel and the match was swiftly abandoned. "Die Ramos, die," was reportedly chanted by a section of the home support. It was a dark day for Betis, for Sevilla and for Spanish football. This was not one moron, there were multiple bottles thrown in this one game alone. A coin hit del Nido as he assumed his position in the directors' box. A multitude of lighters, coins and screws were regularly pelted towards the field of play. Rival flags and emblems were burned inside the stadium while, for the second time in a month, Sevilla fans' entrance into the stadium was delayed until after kick-off leading to further disorder in the streets outside the ground, with bins being set on fire.

The Spanish sports minister also weighed in on the incidents and did not hold back in his criticism for the leadership of both clubs: "It was a shameful incident, we will now have to act with the utmost rigour," Jaime Lissavetzky told Radio Marca, before adding: "We warned before the game that there were many actions that could have led to what eventually happened. The one who sows winds gathers storms. Certain individuals from the clubs generated a climate that meant the game could not take place in a normal atmosphere."

But what was a 'normal atmosphere' at a Spanish football match? Objects regularly being pelted on to the playing field? Displays of outright and unashamed racism? Earlier that month, Betis won 2–1 in Bilbao against Athletic Club but the assistant referee was struck by an object thrown from the home fans while the previous season Sevilla goalkeeper Andrés Palop was struck by a beer can. The infamous pig's head thrown at Real Madrid's Luís Figo upon his return to the Camp Nou generated headlines but the practice of throwing objects at officials, opposing players, managers, presidents and fans was a pandemic throughout Spain. Then there was the audible racism and monkey chants directed towards black players which was so regular that few batted an eyelid. Clubs were not leading by example, yet neither were Spanish authorities; club fines for all these incidents were a mere drop in the ocean.

Betis president José Leon issued an apology, but the club were fined a (typically paltry) €2,700 while they were struck by a three-game stadium ban – with the club temporarily forced to relocate to the multi-purpose Estadio de La Cartuja across the city (indeed, the frosty relations at boardroom level had impacted on neither club coming to a satisfactory agreement on how to best utilise the stadium). Ramos spent the night in hospital and was closely monitored but there was a widespread acknowledgement that this could have been worse, much worse. A 30-year-old man was subsequently arrested and charged. The final 33 minutes of the match were played out three weeks later but was in Madrid and behind closed doors. No further goals were scored in Getafe's Coliseum Alfonso Pérez stadium, and Sevilla advanced to the semi-finals. And then the final, which they won.

And that was the thing – the explosive nature of the off-field antics, the violence and various unsavoury incidents did not lead to the club's successes on the pitch but threatened to detract from them. The 2000s were a decade when Sevilla enjoyed an unprecedented level of success and in which Betis won only their third-ever major trophy. Following the bottle incident, Sevilla president del Nido declared: "Both clubs must now exercise responsibility. I do not want to add fuel to the fire, only water."

Regardless of the sincerity of these words – and it must be remembered del Nido had regularly dabbled in fanning the flames – the rivalry in Seville was to fundamentally change after the Copa del Rey debacle. Not coincidentally, it was also to be the final derby match played by Sevilla's academy product Antonio Puerta, who appeared destined for stardom. Fears of violence leading to tragedy would soon be replaced by unity in the most heartbreaking of scenarios. But it's important to remember the good times for both clubs in the years leading up to the summer of 2007, and there was plenty to celebrate.

Chapter 26

Monchi – Sevilla's Genius

*"We should not look to Betis; our objectives must
be more ambitious" – Monchi*

IN 1948, Sevilla lifted their fourth Copa del Rey title having won the league crown two seasons earlier. The club were a relentless winning machine, the powerhouse of Andalusia – lifting 18 of the 21 regional titles up to 1940. No other major trophy arrived during the remaining 52 years of the century, with the club's Segunda title in 1969 their only piece of silverware. Sevilla's relegation back to the second tier in 2000 signalled the continuation of a sporting crisis with genuine fears over the club's economic future.

As has been the case throughout their history, particular appointments and moments marked tangible turning points for the club. Roberto Alés was selected as club president in the summer of 2000 and he subsequently brought in the relatively unknown coach, Joaquín Caparrós. Born in the Sevillian town of Utrera, Caparrós had spent three seasons in charge of Recreativo, whom he guided to the second tier. Such were the financial restrictions upon Sevilla at the time, it was little surprise that they moved for a coach with a low profile but few could have envisaged he would spend five full league seasons at the helm in Nervión – the only man in the club's history to do so (Manolo Cardo was only in situ for four and a half campaigns).

Caparrós helped the team to the Segunda title at the first attempt and proceeded to guide the club to four consecutive top-half La Liga finishes along with two qualifications for the UEFA Cup. Under Caparrós, Sevilla developed a reputation of playing with intensity and directness. He acted as a father figure for many of his players, yet his demands were relentless, asking that they push themselves to their limits. The departure of Caparrós was not in correlation to any decline in results but rather to an alleged fallout with the club's new president José María del Nido. Whilst it would be remiss to overlook the achievements of Caparrós at *Los Rojiblancos*, he was not the most significant appointment at the turn of the century.

Ramón Rodríguez Verdejo, 'Monchi', was a man who had been in the background at Sevilla throughout the 1990s. The goalkeeper had come through the club's youth system and spent the entirety of his professional career with them but featured just 109 times in the first team. Always in the background, always undervalued. Yet at the turn of the millennium he was appointed the club's sporting director, tasked with two fundamental objectives by the board: developing the club's youth system and implementing a vast scouting policy both inside and outside Spain. Essentially, he was responsible for maximising profits at the club and ensuring that incomings outstripped outgoings.

Monchi was undoubtedly the most influential individual in transforming Sevilla from an underachieving entity steeped in mediocrity into arguably the most vibrant, progressive club in European football. Earning the nickname *El Lobo de Sevilla* – the Wolf of Seville – he was a visionary whose fresh ideas cut through and made a real, tangible impact. The magnitude of his successes can be measured on two fronts: the mass profits his business generated the club and the continued on-pitch success which Sevilla enjoyed.

From the Cádiz town of San Fernando, Monchi developed a worldwide system of over 700 scouts to closely monitor the performance of players. Modern, innovative data measures were compiled – sprints per game, endurance levels, range of passing, positional discipline and flexibility; essentially, the qualities and measurements not evident without thorough research. A team of analysts monitored continents, nations and divisions with ideal monthly XIs produced based on a series of specific measurements. After a period of months, players who frequently scored highly in specific qualities were then monitored more closely and the club subsequently began negotiations with those who ticked the required boxes.

One of the fundamental pillars of Monchi's approach was that no player was unsellable, based on pragmatism relating to the club's financial situation. No matter how slick their business programme and sporting successes, Sevilla would never be able to compete in the same financial stratosphere as Barcelona or Real Madrid, nor with clubs who benefitted from significant investment such as those in England's Premier League. "The board of directors bet, even with money from our own pockets, to sign important players," explained club president José Castro, who assumed the role in 2013 after years of vice-presidency. "Above all, we were not afraid to sell any of them." Across Monchi's 17-year stint as sporting director, the club generated €93m in the sales of five star youth players: José Antonio Reyes, Sergio Ramos, Jesús Navas, Alberto Moreno, Luis Alberto. Furthermore the following list of 25 players was signed for a combined outlay of €116m, while their eventual sales totalled €477m: Júlio Baptista, Dani Alves, Álvaro Negredo, Ivan Rakitić, Grzegorz Krychowiak, Carlos Bacca, Kevin Gameiro, Clément Lenglet, Steven Nzonzi, Christian Poulsen, Vicente Iborra, Aleix Vidal, Vitolo, Luís Fabiano, Federico Fazio, Martín Cáceres, Adriano, Seydou Keita, Gary Medel, Geoffrey Kondogbia, Yehven Konoplyanka, Alexander Kerzhakov, Timothée Kolodziejczak, Adil Rami, Fernando Llorente.

That cast of 30 players made Sevilla a remarkable profit of €454m in transfer revenue and does not even come close to telling the true value of their transfer model. Goalkeeper Andrés Palop arrived on a free transfer from Valencia, where he had been a back-up shot-stopper, in the summer of 2005 and spent eight seasons as a virtual ever-present for the club, winning six trophies. Brazilian midfielder Renato arrived as a free agent in 2004 from Santos and made 282 first-team appearances. The following year, Enzo Maresca – another midfielder – joined from Juventus for just €2.5m and became a valuable asset during Sevilla's trophy-laden years. The Italian's crowning moment came in the 2006 UEFA Cup Final when he netted twice in the 4–0 demolition of Middlesbrough and was named man of the match. Maresca's popularity in the city rocketed further when he donated his €10k prize money for the award to Seville's San Juan de Dios hospital.

Then there were the fearsome strikers. Frédéric Kanouté joined from Tottenham for €6.5m in the same summer as Maresca, in a deal which raised eyebrows. The Malian had netted only 19 goals across his previous three seasons in the Premier League and the fee was seen as somewhat of a risk, yet he turned into one of the most priceless arrivals in Sevilla's history. He scored 136 goals across seven seasons in Andalusia, becoming the club's highest-scoring non-Spanish player and building a fearsome striking partnership with Luís Fabiano. Kanouté's playing style was distinctive too; possessing supreme chest control and elegance, contrasting to his physical and battling predecessor Baptista, who was nicknamed 'The Beast'. Alongside his playing exploits, Kanouté's Islamic faith was also significant in his stint with the club. For a while, Sevilla's shirt sponsor 888.com was taped over on the Malian's shirt because he claimed his religion forbade the promotion of gambling. In 2007, the striker also paid €500k to buy the only mosque in Seville as the private premises had been put up for sale, thus allowing Muslims within the city to continue to honour their faith.

Instrumental central defender Javi Navarro, known for his no-nonsense approach and being somewhat of a 'tough bastard', joined on a free in 2001 and spent eight seasons in the heart of defence before retiring following a series of knee problems. Navarro's initial defensive partner was the equally fearsome Pablo Alfaro who was eventually replaced by Julien Escudé in 2006 from Ajax. Escudé, who cost just €1.5m, spent six seasons as a regular at *Los Rojiblancos* and earned prominence in the France national side for the first time, winning 13 caps.

Palop, Renato, Escudé and Kanouté were all allowed to depart on free transfers at the end of their stints at the club while Maresca joined Olympiakos for a token €1.5m. These are players whose importance to the club cannot be measured solely within Monchi's remarkable profit margins – although they all represented excellent market value in deals that no other club could spot – but by their on-pitch successes, remarkable consistency and integration into *Sevillismo*. Whilst there are numerous pieces of data and economics underpinning Sevilla's triumphs under Monchi, the most impressive element of all was something far less tangible. Escudé, a Frenchman signed from a Dutch club, was describing the derby against Real Betis as "like going to war" within a year of moving to the city. The single most important strand for the success of players at the club was buying into the Sevilla ethos, building an emotional link with their fanbase and transmitting their passion on the pitch. It is tricky to categorise this into real terms, but there is a palpable sense of sentiment and feeling in Seville's population and Sevilla found a way of channelling this energy into the club and its staff.

This was an idea built upon with the release of the club's 'Himno Centenario' in 2005 – the original 100-year anniversary of its birth before the revision to 1890. Penned by Francisco Javier Labandón Pérez, known as *El Arrebato*, the chant is played before each Sevilla home game and has become one of European football's most famed melodies. It replaced the original anthem, written in 1983, and quickly became a massive hit – reaching number one in Spain's singles chart and being the second-highest selling single of 2006. As ever, this wound up those across the city at Real Betis (who have an infectiously beguiling and passionate club anthem of their own), with president Manuel Ruiz de Lopera typically weighing in with the information that *El Arrebato* was in fact a Betis fan – which is denied by the artist himself, who played in Sevilla's youth team. Capturing the mood of futile oneupmanship, Lopera's Sevilla counterpart José María del Nido claimed that it was nice for Juande Ramos – then Sevilla boss, formerly of Betis – to "finally be working at a big club".

Sevilla's anthem is belted out with passion, with the "oooooo" rising and falling, singing of "a heart that beats screaming Sevilla … And Sevilla, Sevilla, Sevilla, here we are with you Sevilla," before explaining, "And that's why I've come here to see you today." The entire lyrics, which include referencing the city's Giralda bell tower, are now on display around the redeveloped Ramon Sánchez-Pizjuán stadium, including the club's motto: 'It is said that they never surrender.'

Sevilla's 'Himno Centenario', an English translation

The story goes, that on 14 October a dream was born,
Her mother was Seville, she gave her name and a support to defend her.
A great example of Seville, the red-and-white family of the Sánchez Pizjuán,
A heart that beats shouting Sevilla, lifting the team to victory.

Chorus
And that's why I've come to watch you today,
I'll be a Sevillista until I die,
The Giralda looks proudly on Sevilla in the Sánchez Pizjuán,
And Sevilla, Sevilla, Sevilla, here we are with you Sevilla,
Sharing the glory in your badge, the footballing pride of our city.

It is said that they never surrender, and that your football art has no rival,
My team's been fighting for 100 years, flying the flag of the city.
A great example of Seville, the red-and-white family of the Sánchez Pizjuán,
A heart that beats shouting Sevilla, lifting the team to victory.

Unai Emery – Sevilla's coach between 2013 and 2016, who helped them to win the Europa League title in each of his three seasons at the helm – was so enraptured by the chant that he insisted new signings learn the lyrics word by word and it became tradition for it to be played on the team bus before games. He explained during his time that the "perfect combination" for the club was "to transmit emotion, to compete, to win." Full-back Jorge Andújar Moreno, known as 'Coke', was captain for the 2015 and 2016 Europa League titles: "Some of our signings do not understand Spanish but they still sing half of the anthem because it's so catchy. It's something very special when all the fans stand up with their scarves and sing this."

Antonio Álvarez, a former Sevilla player and boss, current member of the club's hall of fame, and now director of the Antonio Puerta School of Football, said: "When you go out on to that pitch you feel like you are trapped. Feeling that stadium singing the anthem is something mystical." Joaquín Caparrós, who returned to the Ramón Sánchez-Pizjuán in 2018, explained: "The players of the youth team want to reach the first team and their desire is to hear the Sevilla anthem on the pitch."

This emotional element should not be downplayed and, whilst there are tangible factors – led by Monchi's sporting vision and excellent planning – that were the bedrock of success, it is not entirely coincidental that the release of the 'Himno Centenario' led to a period of unprecedented success for Sevilla. In their 115-year history up to 2005, they had won just four major titles and none in 57 years. In the 13 seasons since, they have won nine major honours and have lost a further nine finals (figures include European Super Cups and Spanish Supercopas). In the 2004/05 campaign, they qualified for European football for just the ninth time in their history but that sparked a run of 15 seasons in Europe from a possible 16.

The club developed a relentless lust for winning trophies, often prioritising cup successes ahead of league positions, which remained excellent regardless. "When I arrived here, the first thing I was told by the club was that whilst playing in the Champions League is great, nothing can compare to winning trophies," Unai Emery explained. "Now I have felt it, this is the greatest feeling there is."

And that is perhaps the most striking aspect of Monchi's Sevilla: the successes. Landing the UEFA Cup title in 2006 – secured with a 4–0 triumph over Middlesbrough – was a remarkable achievement, but its significance to the club and the city has been downplayed by history due to it becoming the norm. The following year was, as is the consensus, the best in the distinguished history of the club. They began the campaign with a 3–0 demolition of European champions Barcelona in the European Super Cup and went on to retain their Europa League crown, defeating Espanyol on penalties after a 2–2 final draw. Then they added the Copa del Rey, their first in six decades, and narrowly missed out on the league title – with it often cited that the fatigue of their heavy schedule throughout the season eventually took its toll in the decisive final two rounds of games.

All this was achieved under experienced coach Juande Ramos. He led Sevilla to 75 victories in his 133 matches at the helm across two seasons, landing an unprecedented five titles in the process. Ramos had tweaked the intense nature of play developed under Joaquín Caparrós into a slightly more restrained and nuanced style. He insisted on a 4-4-2 formation, utilising width, focusing on overlapping full-backs and carrying out relatively straightforward tactical ideas to the letter. His Sevilla side were also notable for their physical condition, with fitness coach Marcos Alvarez somewhat of a pioneer in dietary requirements and conditioning. Indeed, much of Ramos's success at Sevilla was credited to Alvarez's rigorous methods but equally they were later questioned at Tottenham and Real Madrid, where Ramos was less successful. In many ways, the managerial career of Ramos was largely unspectacular outside of his spell at Sevilla for whom the coach – who did not possess great charisma, nor did he regularly get swept up in emotional moments – was very much the right man, at the right club, at the right time. But while his guidance from the sidelines was clearly significant, the real stars of this period were the players.

"Sevilla has two sides to its history, and the turning point came in 2006," Mateo González, head of sport at *ABC de Sevilla* explained. "Before this time, it is clear that Juan Arza [legendary striker of the 1940s and 50s] is of course their best player ever. After 2006, the starring role could be for Frédéric Kanouté, Luís Fabiano, Jesús Navas or Daniel Alves."

It was at this juncture that stars began to depart, tempted by greater finances and promises of prolonged and sustained success at the true giants of European football. Selling to Barcelona, Real Madrid and the superpowers in other leagues became an annual occurrence for Sevilla. Not that this would cause any need for panic. In the summer of 2005, the club's best players Sergio Ramos and Júlio Baptista – scorer of 50 goals in his two campaigns with the Andalusians – were sold to Real Madrid. The club proceeded to win the UEFA Cup the following season and again the year after that. Sales were normalised and accepted by fans, which largely explains why most former players are not disliked for leaving but appreciated for playing their role at the club and, more often than not, enjoying successes and leaving upon amicable terms.

Genuine doubts would later develop that Monchi had lost his Midas touch. The club broke their transfer record to land Ivorian striker Arouna Koné for €12m in the summer of 2007, yet he scored just twice in 41 appearances. Not every player is the right fit for the club and when Koné later joined Levante on a free transfer, he hit 17 goals in his debut campaign. Colombian defender Aquivaldo Mosquera had arrived the same summer for €8m yet was sold for half that price two underwhelming seasons later. Javier Chevantón was also signed for €8m in 2006 from Monaco but only scored eight La Liga goals across three seasons while Didier Zokora, who joined from Tottenham in 2009, also did not enjoy a memorable spell in Seville. The club now had more money to spend but, in a quirk of the intricacies of football's market, this proved almost a disadvantage.

Another Copa del Rey title arrived in 2010 and for eight consecutive seasons, Sevilla's final league position never dipped below sixth. There were also two occasions on which they progressed to the last 16 of the Champions League. Two consecutive ninth-place finishes in 2012 and 2013 brought concerns that this remarkable run of success was over, that Sevilla's innovation and invention in the transfer market could no longer create the same impact.

The policy had shifted following the breakup of the club's greatest-ever squad with greater focus on signing established players or those who were already desired elsewhere. At the time, this had appeared the logical step following Sevilla's ascension to be a club who were regulars on the European scene and challenging for trophies. But often football is without logic and with a stagnation in results, combined with the global economic downturn hitting Spanish football hard, Monchi once more changed tack.

In 2014, the sporting director gave an enlightening account: "We had two disastrous seasons in an economic sense and there was a debt of €22m, so we needed to sell. If our size of club is not managed intelligently or it allows itself to build up a debt, it could be sunk altogether. We know how to sell well, but clubs now know this and in turn charge us higher fees for players. That does not take into account the fact that we pay good salaries – this is part of our project to ensure we are an attractive proposition. Our sales recently have not allowed us to reinvest in the squad, but it is to service the debts and our salary budget. In the past, we brought in and renewed Dani Alaves, Luís Fabiano and Frédéric Kanouté, now our situation is different. We have to reinvent ourselves."

And reinvent themselves is what they did. Monchi reverted to signing young, developing players and those whose careers had appeared to stagnate, thus offering value. The pressing economic situation and mounting debts around this time were not unique to Sevilla. Banks were the main creditors of clubs across the nation, but the European Union took issue with why so many clubs had been allowed to build up mass debts and take on investment projects beyond their means, without having to repay the taxes owed. Spanish tax authorities were forced to act with the fostering situation seen as unfair to other taxpayers in the nation and to other European clubs.

Many historic names were hit particularly hard including Deportivo de La Coruña, Celta de Vigo, Osasuna, Real Zaragoza, Real Oviedo, Real Mallorca, Racing de Santander, Albacete and Real Betis. Others, such as Valencia, were temporarily passed into public ownership after failing to return payment on a loan guaranteed by the regional government. It was under the ownership of Bankia bank, who became nationalised because of their own debts meaning the club went into public ownership. Subsequently, Valencia were forced into abandoning their Nou Mestalla project – leaving a half-built stadium in the city.

It was a particularly precarious time for a multitude of Spanish clubs who, if they could not balance their financial sheets with their sporting ambitions, would be staring into the abyss. But this was a situation with which Sevilla and Monchi had previous experience, with the Andalusian club having faced a myriad of off-field problems less than two decades earlier, with the sporting director helping to steer them back on track with consistent financial returns alongside, crucially, sustainable and progressive results on the pitch.

In 2014, they won the Europa League (as it was now called) for a third time, defeating Portuguese champions Benfica in the showpiece's penalty shoot-out. As became the pattern, stars departed; club captain Ivan Rakitić joined Barcelona (Sevilla made a €17.5m profit on the midfielder who had signed three years earlier from Schalke), while full-back Alberto Moreno joined Liverpool. In 2015, they won the tournament again – their fourth success making them the competition's most successful ever side, as they defeated Dnipro Dnipropetrovsk in the final. Star striker Carlos Bacca, who netted twice in the final, joined Milan while full-back Aleix Vidal was snapped up by Barcelona. The following year, remarkably, Sevilla retained the trophy with a 3–1 victory over Liverpool in the final (and became the first team since Bayern Munich, 1974–76, to win three consecutive European titles). Éver Banega joined Inter, Grzegorz Krychowiak moved to Paris Saint-Germain while Atlético de Madrid signed Kevin Gameiro, and Coke, the two-goal hero of the final, signed for Schalke.

Antonio Cano, president of the *Peña Sevillista Macarena* has explained: "I had never seen a title in my life, we'd only ever celebrated promotion to the top flight. But the more titles you win the greater the demand becomes and the more you want to continue winning."

The key behind the success was to have a sustainable method of recruitment and squad reinvention. Álvaro Negredo's exit was offset by the arrival of Carlos Bacca, who himself was replaced by Kevin Gameiro and then Wissam Ben Yedder. Monchi worked on the premise that all players were expendable, whether in terms of bringing in a financial windfall or due to their careers having already peaked.

As with most walks of life, luck plays a huge role in the difference between success and failure. Arouna Koné enjoyed great successes in his career both before and after Sevilla but could never find his feet at *Los Rojiblancos*. Plenty of future greats escaped the clutches of Monchi, including Uruguayan striker Luis Suárez and Robin van Persie when both were based in the Netherlands. "I went to Rotterdam to finalise the deal for Robin [then at Feyenoord] but during my stay he got a call from Arsenal whose offer was bigger and he went there," Monchi revealed in 2017. "Marcelo [the roaming Brazilian left full-back] was a near miss too – we were in advanced negotiations, but he ended up at Real Madrid." And there were plenty more besides. "Nigel de Jong was in Seville and familiarising himself with the city, and his representatives were telling me how keen he was to sign, but when I turned up for the meeting, I was told they had already agreed to go to Hamburg."

Yet luck was not always against the sporting director, such as with the signing of Ivan Rakitić. The Croatian midfielder arrived in Seville without speaking a word of Spanish but before agreeing terms with the club, he received an offer to sign for another European giant. He went for a drink at the hotel bar to mull over his options, but instantly became enchanted with the waitress. Sceptical of a footballer's nomadic career, Rakitić reassured her and within two years he and Raquel Mauri were married. Had she not been working that first night, Rakitić may never have met his future wife nor would he have signed for Sevilla.

Throughout Monchi's tenure in Seville he became increasingly linked with a move away. There was constant speculation that he would move to Real Madrid, while he temporarily resided in London to improve his English and spoke frequently of a desire to work in Italy. His departure became a matter of *if* and not *when*, before an announcement in April 2017 that he had agreed a four-year contract with Roma. Rakitić described the sporting director's move as akin to "buying ten new players", such was his significance. But despite his first season in the Italian capital seeing Roma reach their first semi-final appearance in the Champions League since 1984 (when it was then titled the European Cup), an underwhelming second campaign saw Monchi exit the club in March 2019. Confirmation arrived soon after that he would return to Sevilla, the club of his life, from 1 April 2019.

Across his 17 years at the helm of Sevilla's sporting direction, he oversaw 151 new signings and during a subsequent interview with Radio Marca, he revealed what he thought was his strongest XI of signings during that tenure: Andrés Palop; Dani Alves, Javi Navarro, Julien Escudé, Adriano; Christian Poulsen, Renato, Ivan Rakitić, Éver Banega; Luís Fabiano, Frédéric Kanouté.

Monchi was the man responsible for constructing what is widely believed to be Sevilla's strongest-ever team between the years of 2005 and 2008, unearthing stars and generating unparalleled profit margins. He navigated through two periods of financial uncertainty before building another team of multiple European title winners, this time based on a model of annual renewal and with greater financial disparity with the national and continental elite.

There is no sure-fire way of predicting if Sevilla's remarkable ability of winning trophies and admirers can continue in the long term despite Monchi's return. However, the structure and mindset which he helped instil have established the club in a position of supreme relevance within both Spain and Europe. "We are an ambitious club, we have never conformed," explained El Arrebato, who wrote the club's 'Himno'. "We do not accept being second best. It is not necessary to always win, but it is necessary to compete. Whoever fights to the end never really loses."

Expectations have been massively elevated and perhaps the younger generation of Sevilla fans are not aware of just how good they have had it in recent years. If Sevilla have learnt anything from the Monchi years, it should be the need for constant reinvention and not to be afraid of doing things differently.

Chapter 27

Local Heroes Lead Cup Triumphs

FOR the first five years of the new century, there was scant evidence of a decisive power shift in the city. Both Real Betis and Sevilla achieved promotion in 2001 and both recorded a top-half finish in each of the next four seasons in the top flight. Indeed, for three of those four campaigns it was Betis who edged out their city neighbours in the standings and, in 2005, they recorded a top-four finish – enough to become the first Andalusian side to qualify for the Champions League in its current format – and to secure Seville's first major trophy of the century, the Copa del Rey.

Up until that point, the two Sevillian clubs were on a similar footing with little to separate them. There was no clear indication of the worrying decline for Betis which was to come in the second half of the decade, nor that Sevilla were building towards the greatest side in their history. Under the guidance of Víctor Fernández, Betis qualified for the UEFA Cup in 2002 but despite winning all four matches in aggregate victories over Zimbru Chișinău and Viktoria Žižkov, they were edged out by French club Auxerre 2–1 in the third round.

Across the city at Sevilla, only long-serving central defender Javi Navarro would play any significant role in their European title three seasons later. Dani Alves would arrive in 2003 accompanied by the emergence of four huge talents from the club's youth system. José Antonio Reyes was the eldest of the quartet, a year older than Antonio Puerta and two ahead of Jesús Navas, with Sergio Ramos the youngest. Indeed, Reyes had debuted as a 16-year-old in January 2000 – the youngest player in the top flight at the time – and offered a rare ray of optimism during a campaign otherwise mired in negativity and eventual relegation.

The significance of Reyes was that he was the first star to emerge from a newly revamped youth system, offering a clear pathway from the *Cantera* to the first team. He only became a regular in the starting line-up in the 2001/02 campaign, Sevilla's return to the Primera, and scored 25 goals across four seasons. A versatile attacker, his reputation grew and grew, rising through the international youth teams before making his debut for Spain's senior team five days after celebrating his 20th birthday.

Reyes was a footballer whose significance should not be measured in his goals return but in those aspects of the sport which are less tangible. He was loved by *Sevillistas* not only because he was a local (from the Sevillian town of Utrera) but because he expressed his personality on the pitch. He was daring, possessing the ability to unlock opposition defences either with a burst of pace or through his supreme technical ability. Reyes was being linked to a host of Europe's leading clubs but his starring role in Sevilla's 4–1 victory at home to Real Madrid in November 2003 hastened his inevitable departure, which eventually came two months later when Arsenal paid €26m for his services.

Sevilla president José María del Nido described the sale as "the saddest thing we have ever had to do," but insisted the fee "was out of this world ... more than Real Madrid paid [Manchester United] for David Beckham." Reyes was not the first Sevilla star to be sold; four years earlier, central defender Carlos Marchena, then aged 21, who would go on to win 69 caps for Spain, was sold to Benfica. That sale had been out of necessity and acknowledgement of Sevilla's precarious financial position, but by early 2004 the club had stabilised. They were now a regular in La Liga's top half and Reyes himself had penned a long-term contract through to 2010. His sale demonstrated two things: firstly, that Sevilla were not afraid to sell their stars and, moreover, they could now drive a hard bargain.

"I'm both the happiest and saddest man in the world at the moment," Reyes said following his move. "I'm leaving the best team in Spain to join the best team in England. This is a step forward in my career but I will not forget the club that I am leaving, who I love with all my heart."

The attacker was never held dear in England as he had been in his native Andalusia, but his talent was never in question. He subsequently enjoyed stints at Real Madrid, Atlético de Madrid and Benfica before returning to Sevilla in 2012. Reyes made up for his lack of medals in his first stint at the club by his role in the three successive Europa

League titles, before joining Espanyol in 2016 following the expiration of his contract. "The first time I left in tears but at the same time I was happy because I knew I was financially improving the club, and I knew I would always return," Reyes said. "But now I cannot hold back the tears because this is my last time here and I want to be remembered as someone who fought for this badge."

Upon confirmation of Reyes's move to Arsenal, fans gathered outside the Ramón Sánchez-Pizjuán stadium to voice their displeasure at the sale of their hero. His long-term contract and the club's greatly improved financial stability had appeared to afford them significantly more power in retaining their stars. Performances and results were building year upon year and the consensus at the time was that individuals at the head of the club were showing greed. Sevilla fans need not have fretted, with a series of future stars on the cusp of making their mark in their first team.

* * * * *

At Real Betis, another attacking star was emerging. Joaquín Sánchez Rodríguez, simply known as Joaquín, would come to define *Los Verdiblancos* in the 21st century and establish himself as arguably the most emblematic player in the club's distinguished history. The winger was not a Sevillian by birth, but instead came from the *pueblo* of El Puerto de Santa María, in the province of Cádiz – that part of Spain most famed for its wicked sense of humour and sense of fun. And boy, does Joaquín embody these values.

It is unquestionable that Joaquín was one of the most talented players ever to represent Betis and for a period was one of the most sought-after talents in world football. A star for both club and country, the one question mark over his career was if he ever truly fulfilled his potential. He has spent a decade and counting in the first-team squad at Betis across two spells, separated by five seasons at Valencia and two apiece at Málaga and Fiorentina. Yet he has only two pieces of silverware to show for his career – both successes in the Copa del Rey. Typically, each comes with a fantastically distinctive story in true Joaquín style, but this was a winger who was one of the finest players of a generation.

There was also a very clear sense of something unfulfilled at national level too – all 51 of the winger's caps came by the age of 26, with his last arriving just before *La Roja's* period of unprecedented success – lifting two European Championship titles either side of the 2010 World Cup.

The 2002 World Cup saw Joaquín's popularity truly explode on a national scale; he was Spain's star player of the tournament, but it was the manner of the side's exit which truly won him fame. Eliminated at the quarter-final stage by tournament co-hosts South Korea, Joaquín had provided the cross for Fernando Morientes to head home what appeared to be the game's only goal. Yet the officials judged that the ball had gone out of play before the cross. It had not. In fact, it was not even close. *La Roja* were left furious as it was their second goal of the game which had been contentiously ruled out. The game went to penalties and, as fate would have it, Joaquín's penalty was decisively saved by Korean goalkeeper Lee Woon-Jae. Such moments have the potential to ruin young players, but upon their return to Spain, hundreds of fans turned up and chanted the winger's name.

Back at Betis, Joaquín was rapidly becoming the star of a team who were establishing themselves in the top half of the divisions and showing themselves to be capable of downing the league's giants. In September 2002, the winger put in a virtuoso performance in a landmark 3–0 victory at home to Barcelona, scoring a goal and running riot against the Catalan giants. The match itself was remarkable but the report of the proceedings in Madrid-based *Diario AS* was even more astonishing. In what appeared to be praise of the Joaquín-inspired hosts, the report read: "Betis enjoyed a night of easy sex at the expense of Barcelona." They described the winger's goal – to make the scoreline 2–0 midway through the second half – as the "pre-climax" before defender Fernando Varela added a third for "the glorious climax itself." Whilst such reporting indulged in a hefty chunk of hyperbole, Joaquín was a player and Betis were a team who were making a lot of people sit up and take notice.

Four years later and Joaquín's connection with national team boss Luis Aragonés – previously player and coach of Betis – broke down, with the player later describing the relationship as "love-hate". The crucial moment in the winger's international career came in the wake of a 3–2 defeat to Northern Ireland in the qualification campaign for the 2008 European Championship. "Right now, the national team is a mess," an emotional Joaquín told reporters. "We are in chaos and Luis doesn't know how to handle it in these difficult moments." He later admitted he had "paid the price" for speaking out of turn.

It was a difficult period in Joaquín's career, not because of his form on the pitch but the decisions he took off it. It was inevitable that one day his talent would outgrow what Betis could offer both in a financial and sporting sense, with the winger linked to a number of Europe's leading clubs. Sir Alex Ferguson was said to be a long-term admirer while in 2006 Joaquín vetoed the opportunity to join Chelsea after a mammoth €36m fee had been agreed. His father Aurelio Sánchez explained years later: "I told him to come to Seville immediately to sign the contract. It would be a five-year contract at €6m per season. He could have made a fortune, but he never thought about the money. Manuel Ruiz de Lopera [Betis president] called me crazy. He had been raffled to all of Europe and this led to him losing his love for Betis."

The Spanish press were enchanted with Joaquín and regularly touted him as the successor to Luís Figo on the right flank at Real Madrid, to become the 'Andalusian Galáctico'. A protracted summer of confusion, claims and counterclaims followed. Betis chairman José León had resigned himself to the player's departure before announcing a U-turn. "I met him in a bid to convince him to stay, but remarkably he ended up convincing me," León told a press conference.

The summer of farce continued when halfway through August the player had an apparent change of heart again, declaring his intention to leave the club. Surprisingly, it was Valencia who agreed an €18m fee plus the transfer of Mario Regueiro, but the move had several twists remaining. The Uruguayan player had no desire to leave the Mestalla and the move was held up, before the adjusted straight transfer of €25m was agreed. But the player was entitled to a percentage of the fee, leading to a vengeful Lopera playing another negotiating trick. Betis held a contractual clause to send the player to a club on loan should they wish, leading to a bizarre episode in which Joaquín was loaned, against his will, to second tier Albacete Balompié (at least it wasn't to Siberia, as had initially been suggested, prompting Joaquín to retort, "I'll need to buy a new woolly hat."). The player, highlighting the ridiculousness of the episode, posted photos of himself making the journey before he was swiftly recalled to Betis and his move to *Los Che* was processed for just €25m.

It was a defining period in the winger's career – he impressed in patches for Valencia without ever hitting the heights he had done at *Los Verdiblancos*. His sense of mischief was not as widely appreciated at his new club and particularly under boss Ronald Koeman. "I am a player who needs to be in a good state both psychologically and physically," Joaquín later said. "I need to have a fun day to play good football." Koeman was later replaced by Unai Emery, another coach who insisted on hard work, discipline and relentless preparation – qualities which would later serve him so well at Sevilla. But this was not compatible with Joaquín, who confessed, "These days it is hard to smile. I need to keep quiet and work hard."

A regular over five seasons at Valencia, it would be incorrect to call it an unhappy spell for the player but there can be little doubt that, at such a pivotal point in his career, it was not the right environment for him. The club were in chaos behind the scenes and the fractures began to translate into the performances with Valencia failing to reach their potential. Neither was Joaquín, who was rarely viewed as one of the club's most important players despite staying there during a player's typical 'peak' years – the latter half of his 20s. He did fewer interviews, appearing more serious as he attempted to gain an equal footing alongside David Villa, David Silva and Juan Mata at the club. He completed just eight full matches in the 2009/10 campaign but a raft of player sales saw him promoted to vice-captain the following year – evidence of his relentless work ethic paying off.

But Valencia was never Joaquín's natural environment and having to suppress his personality was never going to be a long-term solution for his career. The year 2011 brought about a move to Málaga, an Andalusian rival of Betis who had benefitted from substantial financial backing from new Qatari owners. Joaquín would call the Costa del Sol side his "second home" with the decision to make a joke at his presentation ceremony ultimately paying off.

"It is the Champions League Final," Joaquín began, after taking the microphone, "and a man turns up late at the stadium, looking for somewhere to sit but it is full. Suddenly, he spots a free seat, and, as he approaches, the woman beside it says: 'You can sit here if you want.' The man is glad but he can't understand why the seat was empty. 'It's my husband's,' explains the woman. But where is he? 'He died', the woman continues. 'Oh, I'm sorry,' says the slightly befuddled man. 'Was there not anybody else who could fill it?' The woman insisted, 'No, they're all at the funeral'." The Malaguistas broke into laughter, as did Joaquín. He was back.

Fans love him, the media love him, team-mates love him. And at Málaga, he struck up a successful understanding with boss Manuel Pellegrini. He helped the Andalusian club reach a remarkable Champions League quarter-final in 2013, where they were only denied by controversial late strikes from Borussia Dortmund. But the most memorable moments for Joaquín came away from the pitch. In a TV interview conducted at the club's training ground, the reporter asked him what his hobbies were. "Tennis," the winger replied, before team-mate Júlio Baptista, standing nearby, began to guffaw with laughter. "He says tennis," responded former Sevilla star Baptista, doubling over. "He has never played tennis in his life!" To which Joaquín, all seriousness now gone from his face, replied: "I don't even know how to pick up a racket, Húlio!"

Baptista is Brazilian and Júlio is pronounced with a 'J' in his native Portuguese, but in Spanish the pronunciation is an English-sounding 'H'. So Joaquín became referred to as Húlio in his native country, a nickname he is fond of and he even requested that the name be placed on the back of his shirt, although rather sadly, La Liga declined. *Marca* ran the headline 'Húliazo' when the winger netted the only goal in the Seville derby in September 2018 and referenced his nickname throughout the report.

The list of anecdotes for Húlio is endless. There was the time he claimed he could hypnotise a chicken, so during a studio TV appearance that theory was put to the test. He was once asked what he liked most about being Álvaro Cejudo's roommate at Real Betis, to which he replied: "Waking up to a good morning kiss." Spanish referee Eduardo Iturralde González once recalled how, during a game, the winger asked him if he was planning on getting married. When an on-guard Iturralde replied that he was, Joaquín responded: "You're making a mistake." After Betis won the Copa del Rey in 2005, the trophy had pride of place at the altar of his wedding. Three years later when he tasted similar success at Valencia, he posed for a photo in the dressing room afterwards wearing only his trademark cheeky grin.

None of this is an act, it is not put on. This is Joaquín's authentic personality and has earned him widespread fame. *ABC de Sevilla* head of sport Mateo González told me: "Joaquín is special. He is a light in the dark of football. He is happy, funny, a great player ... a legend for Betis of course, but he receives applause at every stadium in Spain. Maybe Sevilla's fans don't love him so much but they recognise he is an honest boy who shows his best in every game." And could he be set for a career in entertainment when he retires? "Without doubt," González replied. "He will be a star. He is representative of the happiness of Andalusians." *Estadio Deportivo* journalist Carlos Pérez added: "It is impossible for Joaquín to be viewed in a negative light by anyone. He is someone with an overwhelming personality and an enviable sense of humour."

Yet maybe the jokes overshadow, or at least slightly detract from, the impact of his performances. From the dazzling young star of Spanish football to the enduring brilliance of a winger who, in his late

30s, is not out of place at the top end of La Liga. "Behind the character hides an excellent professional," Pérez continued. "He cares so much, he has bought shares in the club."

Joaquín spent two seasons in Italy with Fiorentina but just 29 league starts across two seasons, coupled with him celebrating his 34th birthday in the summer of 2015, meant his desire to return to Betis – who had just returned to the top flight – was inevitable. "I want to return home," was the caption of a social media post by the player, who appeared sombre in the photo attached. A banner at Fiorentina's training ground read: 'Matador, non ci lasciare. Con la pelota ci hai fatto innamorare' ('Matador do not leave us. With the ball at your feet you have made us love you.') The agreed fee for his transfer was €2m, but the true value of the deal can be measured in the 2,000 extra Betis season tickets sold in the 24 hours following the announcement.

"Joaquín is Betis and Betis is Joaquín," said Pepe Mel, who was back in the dugout at *Los Verdiblancos*. "I'm like a little boy in a toy store," Joaquín proclaimed during his unveiling back at the club. "I spent nine years away from the club but I have always been Joaquín of Betis. This club has given me everything." Over 19,000 *Béticos* turned up at the Benito Villamarín for the event (a higher number than five of the ten La Liga attendances that weekend), which saw the player's right arm secured in a plaster cast – reportedly due to him hitting a wall when it appeared the deal would fall through. "I enjoyed many beautiful moments during my first spell at Betis, but now I am really living out my dream. This is the happiest moment in my career." Eduardo Macía, the club's sporting director described the move as "Betis welcoming its soul back into our body."

Joaquín's longevity in the sport is remarkable, making over 800 senior appearances for club and country with no signs of age catching up with him. As *El País* described: "Joaquín provides the art", and in this light it is not wholly unsurprising that his ambition from a young boy had not been to play football but rather to be a bullfighter. He even joked in an interview with the same newspaper that he was breastfed until the age of six: "When we were younger and played football outside, the other guys would get thirsty and go to the water fountain, but I ran to my mum."

Yet it was Joaquín's uncle, nicknamed *El Chino*, who had the greatest influence on his early career. The player would later refer to him as his mentor and as "one of those people who rarely exist. He believed in me as a footballer." He drove his teenage nephew from his

Cádiz hometown to Seville for training sessions and matches when he was in the youth system. *El Chino* died in 2002, with the winger often dedicating goals to him by raising his fingers to heaven. Joaquín was one of eight children in his family and his brothers Lucas (for Cádiz) and Ricardo (a Betis youth team player) also were keen footballers. "Anyone who saw Ricardo when he played knows he is more technical than me," Joaquín later said. "What I have is more speed, I always focused on the things that Figo did on the right flank."

Whenever he finally decides to hang up his boots, he will have no shortage of options. He has already personally invested €1m in Betis shares "because it's my life," and as journalist Carlos Pérez told me: "He will one day be president of Betis." When asked directly about this by Spanish TV station La Sexta in 2018, Joaquín responded, without hesitation: "It would be a dream come true!" There will always be question marks over his medal haul, and how it is not befitting a player with such enduring quality. "Perhaps I could have done more," the player has reflected. "But I could have done a lot less too."

Joaquín is an artist, combining supreme technical ability, tactical awareness and total dedication but, above all, he is a great person. And football would be a much more endearing sport if more of its stars followed his lead.

* * * * *

Back in 2004 at Sevilla, the jeers would soon turn to cheers with the club recording successive top six finishes in the immediate aftermath of Reyes's transfer, followed by their greatest season of the modern era. While Reyes had departed, his best friend Jesús Navas was at the heart of the club's successes. Fleet of foot, the wafer-thin winger became known for his fearsome speed, directness and an ability to beat his opponent with ease. Navas debuted for the club two days after his 18th birthday in November 2003 and, 15 years later, the club named their main pitch at their Ciudad Deportiva training ground in his honour: Estadio Jesús Navas.

Hailing from the Sevillian town of Los Palacios, a half-hour drive south of the Andalusian capital, Navas was one of many Andalusians descended from Gitano population – Spain's Romani people. One of five children, he was even temporarily replaced in Sevilla's first-team squad by elder brother Marco, who later explained: "Jesús was very skinny and struggling to adapt, so I was chosen ahead of him." The only concern over Jesús was his slight frame, so the club's dieticians decided that he should be afforded more liberty with his calorie intake to bulk up. This was a player who was clocked at running 100 metres in 10.8 seconds and who was so fast that, when tested on one of the club's treadmills at their training facilities, broke the machine.

Navas would become a Sevilla icon and by the time of the training pitch name change, he had already amassed more first-team appearances than any other player, surpassing the great Juan Arza and closing in on a remarkable 500 matches. Sevilla president José Castro stated upon the name unveiling: "We believe that for your values, your work, your way of being, your *Sevillismo* and for everything you have given us in these years, it is only right we give this stadium your name and immortalise it."

Sevilla's official club media branded him a "living legend" and during an interview with *The Guardian*, Alberto Moreno – another future Spain international who had graduated through Sevilla's markedly improved youth academy – described Navas as his idol and said he possesses a photo of himself, aged 11, alongside Navas. He spent a decade at the club before joining Manchester City in 2013, but by that stage he had played in more cup finals and won more trophies than any other player in the Andalusian club's history. He won two UEFA Cups, two Copa del Rey titles, a European Super Cup and a Spanish Supercopa. Navas has also earned 35 international caps for Spain – more than any other *Sevillista* – and lifted both the World Cup (where he began the sequence of events leading to Andrés Iniesta's winning strike) in 2010 and the European Championships two years later. After four seasons in England, he rejected the offer of a contract extension at City to return to Sevilla. By any definition, this was a club legend.

Yet Jesús Navas was not a typical footballer, with his personality a world away from that of Joaquín Sánchez across the city, as he did not enjoy being in the spotlight. A year after making his first-team debut, he suffered what the club described as a "panic attack" which, it emerged, was due to chronic homesickness. It was reported he was uncomfortable being away from his "closed environment" and so severe were the symptoms they led to depression and seizures. A proposed 2006 transfer to Chelsea broke down over his unwillingness to leave Seville and he even rejected international call-ups based on the distance from his home city. It was only after special arrangements were made, including assurances that Navas would always be close to former Sevilla team-mate and close friend Sergio Ramos, that he agreed to go on duty with Spain. After assistance from therapy, Navas convinced himself to join Sevilla on a pre-season tour of the United

States but had it not been for his early misgivings, his career would undoubtedly have gone down a different path. His eventual move to Manchester – a city whose weather system sharply contrasts with that of Seville – was helped in part by brother Marco joining nearby lower league club Bury and bringing his young family to the north-west of England.

The boy may have been taken out of Seville but it was unquestionable that Jesús Navas – who predictably returned to *Los Rojiblancos* four years later on a free transfer – never forgot his roots. He ensured new houses were built in his Los Palacios hometown and that the project employed as many unemployed labourers as possible.

By the time of the winger's transfer to England, he had already achieved cult hero status at his boyhood club. He starred in Sevilla's run to the 2006 UEFA Cup title, playing in all 12 matches. It was the start of a run of eight campaigns when Navas averaged 45 matches per season and while he rarely stood out as a star performer – he netted just 46 goals in his first 650 official club appearances – he was vital to the success of his club and country. Navas was a reliable performer; a team player with an admirable work ethic with tactical understanding and flexibility, illustrated by a later switch from out-and-out winger to wing-back or full-back.

Navas produced big moments too, including netting the decisive second goal in stoppage time of the 2010 Copa del Rey final victory over Atlético de Madrid at Barcelona's Camp Nou stadium. Sevilla led 1–0 as the bad-tempered encounter ticked into injury time. Atlético had won the Europa League trophy the previous week but had suffered a disappointing league campaign, finishing 16 points and five places off Sevilla in fourth. The game was littered with narratives including Navas being pitted against his best friend, with José Antonio Reyes now starring in Atléti's attack.

It was Jesús Navas who had the last laugh. With Atlético desperate for an equaliser, the winger opportunistically pounced on a tired, misplaced pass in the opposition defence on the halfway line. He evaded two desperate, lunging challenges to find himself one-on-one with goalkeeper David de Gea, whom he rounded before producing a composed finish to settle the tie. It ensured Antonio Álvarez – appointed only two months earlier to replace his former long-serving Sevilla team-mate Manolo Jiménez – was the winning manager, in just his 10th match at the helm. Jiménez was a key figure in the cup run, including masterminding the elimination of Barcelona, and it was fitting that he and Álvarez – who amassed a combined total just shy of 700 first-team appearances for Sevilla without winning silverware (see Chapter 21) – shared the success. It was the club's fifth Copa title and second in four seasons, with the Spanish FA later deciding that the club could keep the title due to Spain's World Cup success later that summer.

* * * * *

There was no doubt about it, this was a golden age for Sevilla. A mix of underappreciated signings mixed with youth-team graduates moulded into a side a with a relentless winning spirit and unshakable self-belief. That Copa title followed on from the success fours years earlier, when Frédéric Kanouté's goal had been enough to defeat Getafe 1-0 in the 2007 decider (the culmination of an eventful cup run which had seen Juande Ramos knocked unconscious with a bottle thrown in the tense quarter-final against Real Betis, see Chapter 26).

However, it was not only Sevilla who had built their titles on a new-found identity, with their youth products as the building blocks to success. Over at Betis the ideas were very similar with a focus on developing their own players ahead of strong investment in transfers. Both clubs were closely intertwined during this period – both had been relegated in 2000, both had financial pressures and restraints upon them, and both had won immediate promotion, with the inclusion of a number of young Sevillians in their sides.

While Sevilla's greatest-ever campaign occurred in 2006/07, two years earlier their city neighbours had enjoyed a season which, if not their greatest ever, was their most significant. Their fourth-placed finish had ensured they were the first Andalusian club ever to qualify for the Champions League in its current format and weeks later they landed the second Copa del Rey title in their history.

Boss Lorenzo Serra Ferrer had returned to the club at the start of the campaign after seven years away – his final season in his first stint culminated in a heartbreaking Copa final loss against Barcelona, but upon his return he was to go one step better. It was a wide open tournament with Barça stunned in the round of 32 by minnows UDA Gramenet and Real Madrid eliminated in the round of 16 by Real Valladolid.

Betis overcame a trio of lower-division sides, Cádiz CF, CD Mirandés and giantkillers Gramenet, to set up a semi-final with Athletic Club de Bilbao. Just as they had famously done 28 years earlier, *Los Verdiblancos* emerged victorious on penalties, this time after two scoreless draws. Osasuna were waiting in the final; the Pamplona-based club had never previously reached the Copa showpiece but surprise triumphs over Sevilla and Atlético de Madrid earned their rightful place. The omens were all in place for Betis with the final held in Atlético's Vicente Calderón stadium, the scene of their 1977 triumph.

Five of the Betis starting XI in the 2005 decider had graduated through the club's youth system while three of their substitutes were also graduates of the club. Not counted in those figures was captain and domineering central defender Juan Gutiérrez Moreno – commonly known as Juanito. Betis had signed the defender, then aged 21, from Cádiz's B side eight seasons earlier and he would be one of the savviest pieces of business by the club, appearing in over 250 league matches and winning 26 caps for the Spanish national side.

Juanito played in front of goalkeeper Antonio 'Toni' Doblas, from the Seville district of Bellavista, who was in his first of four seasons as the Betis number one. Central defender David Rivas was born in Seville's neighbouring city of Dos Hermanas and would spend a decade in the Betis first team, while right-back Meli was another who had come through the club's youth system. Like Joaquín in front of him on the right flank, he was born in Cádiz. Holding midfielder Arturo García Muñoz, 'Arzu', was another from Dos Hermanas and, also like Rivas, would spend ten years of his professional career representing Betis. Experienced midfielder Juan José Cañas was then in his 15th season at the club and was an unused substitute, although two further local boys were used from the bench. Fernando Varela was primarily a right-winger although the brilliance of Joaquín saw him mainly deployed at right-back, and then there was Dani. (Midfielder Capi, another Seville local who made over 300 appearances for Betis and won four caps for Spain, was absent due to injury.)

Daniel Martín Alexandre was born in Triana and was a *Bético* to the core. He had grown up playing football on the streets and this was evident in his style of play. The forward had a low centre of gravity, would hassle and harry opponents and was not averse to the dark arts of the game, often going to ground easily and attempting to manipulate the officials. A highly promising attacking talent who had his career restricted by several serious injuries, his decisive moment in the 2005 Copa final would forever write him into Betis folklore.

Dani's winning strike had nothing to do with histrionics and instead, as described by *El País*, he "showed only precision and no theatre". It was a match with plenty of passion and emotion but without a lot of free-flowing football as the fear of making a mistake trumped the freedom to create. Tensions were high, perhaps too high.

The game was littered with errors and yellow cards, there were nine of them shown throughout the encounter with Osasuna's Pablo García sent off late in stoppage time.

Striker Ricardo Oliveira opened the scoring for Betis in the 74th minute, capitalising on a defensive error by Osasuna captain César Cruchaga. Oliveira was one of three Brazilians in the starting line-up for Betis although, somewhat bizarrely, there were four in the pre-match team photo. Winger Denílson, the one-time world record transfer who was that day named as a substitute, knew this was the end for him at the club so he joined in the photo. This was to be the former São Paulo man's seventh and final season in Seville before joining French club Bordeaux that summer.

But there were several twists still lying in wait. Eight minutes after Oliveira had scored what had looked to be the winning goal, Osasuna struck back. The Navarrese club have a long-standing reputation of physicality, aerial strength and intensity in their play, so it was no surprise that 6ft-tall striker John Aloisi – who had been brought on as a substitute just three minutes earlier – headed home an equaliser.

While the qualities of Osasuna were closely associated with a typically British brand of football, Betis under Lorenzo Serra Ferrer could be more closely compared to an Italian side. Just as they had been in Serra Ferrer's first spell, they took pride in their defensive organisation, knowing when to absorb pressure and constructing incisive counter-attacking play. And so it proved once again in their decisive, winning sequence of play in the 114th minute. An Osasuna cross into the box was repelled by the Betis defence and four short passes from *Los Verdiblancos* sprung the high press, leaving them with a three-on-three break. One threaded pass released Dani, who took one touch before unleashing a left-footed drive across the goal and into the bottom corner, in front of where the instantly delirious Betis fans were housed.

The shaven-headed striker's celebration was pure, unbridled joy as he pelted off behind the goal, open-mouthed and screaming with delight before eventually being mobbed by his team-mates. The Copa was decked in Betis colours, 28 years on. Less than a month after the trophy was secured, it was still adorned in green and white ribbons as it sat proudly on the altar of Joaquín's wedding. The winger was tying the knot with wife Susana and the entire Betis squad was in attendance, alongside their title. This was Joaquín, after all.

There were great moments still to come in the calendar year for Betis. They recorded a creditable if ultimately unsuccessful campaign in their inaugural Champions League outing. A win at Anderlecht and scoreless draw at Liverpool were impressive, but the crowning moment was a 1–0 home victory over José Mourinho's Chelsea in Seville. Dani was once again decisive from close-range (and once again a substitute, replacing the injured Oliveira), evading challenges from both John Terry and William Gallas before slotting past Petr Čech. A third-placed group finish saw Betis handed a UEFA Cup spot and despite eliminating AZ Alkmaar, they were ousted by Steaua Bucureşti in the round of 16 stage.

This was to prove a false dawn for Betis. It would be eight years before they returned to European football. The next decade would see them record just one top-half finish in La Liga while spending three campaigns in the Segunda as financial problems bit hard. Boss Lorenzo Serra Ferrer's uneasy relationship with president Manuel Ruiz de Lopera quickly unravelled. After the Copa success, the coach sent a message to Lopera: "Betis will be what you want them to be, Don Manuel." Unsurprisingly, Serra Ferrer was gone the following year and would not return to the club until 2017, when he was appointed as head of the club's sporting direction. Following Serra Ferrer's exit, Lopera was accused of directing finances in the region of €30m away from the club in order to pursue his own business interests and the internal ructions within the club, in the absence of on-pitch success, rumbled on and on.

Just as with Sevilla in 2010, the key theme of the Betis 2005 Copa success was the prominent role of their local heroes. The core of their side hailed from the provinces of Cádiz and Seville. In the red-and-white half of the city, coaches Manolo Jiménez or Antonio Álvarez were installed in the dugout and then there were the decisive scorers in the final. It was Jesús Navas who netted the crucial breakaway goal in 2010 but the other goal of the encounter was scored by another youth graduate on the opposite flank: Diego Capel. Three years younger than Navas, the Almería native would make 173 first-team appearances for Sevilla, before joining Portuguese club Sporting CP in 2011, and won three caps for the Spanish national team.

Capel was only on the fringes of the first-team squad for the back-to-back UEFA Cup successes, when he played second fiddle to another Sevilla youth-team graduate who appeared destined for greatness. The story of Antonio Puerta is a tragedy that transcended the sport and quelled one of football's fiercest and increasingly dangerous rivalries, leaving the entirety of Spanish football and the city of Seville in deep mourning.

Chapter 28

Antonio Puerta Heals a City

ANTONIO Puerta was always destined to play a special role in the city's football scene. His father, Añoño, had played across the city for Real Betis even if his first-team action was limited to 18 minutes of a Copa del Generalísimo tie against Villarreal in 1973, although he played frequently for their Triana Balompié reserve side. Antonio, however, was *Sevillista* to the core, growing up in the Nervión district and a stone's throw away from the Ramón Sánchez-Pizjuán stadium. He joined the club aged nine having started his career at AD Nervión and progressed through each age range with increasing prominence.

Future first-team boss Manolo Jiménez was Puerta's coach at Sevilla's B side (now named Sevilla Atlético) and described the versatile left-sided player as "A captain without an armband". Puerta's first-team debut arrived when he was a 19-year-old in March 2004, as boss Joaquín Caparrós started him in a 1–0 home defeat against Málaga, while his first goal came eight months later against Numancia. However, he would need to wait until the second half of the 2005/06 campaign before finding a regular run of games in the first team.

Also comfortable in the left-back slot, Puerta was most at home on the left flank of Sevilla's midfield in their 4-4-2 formation and began to compete with Brazilian Adriano for the position. A late winner in a league victory at Atlético de Madrid gained him instant recognition within the club's fanbase but it was during the UEFA Cup semi-final against Schalke that Puerta delivered his defining moment.

He appeared as a 77th-minute substitute in the second leg, and the tie went to extra time after two scoreless encounters. This was a match etched with tension as Sevilla battled to win a place in their first-ever European final. Indeed, the second leg was played on the *Jueves de Feria*, the Thursday of the city's festival, and the anticipation was huge. At the time, this was thought to be the club's 100th season of football and it was fitting that as the scoreboard ticked just past minute 100, the deadlock was finally broken. Puerta's close friend Jesús Navas broke free down the right wing and delivered a cross right across the box, which evaded everyone and ran through to the unmarked Puerta. The substitute had the time to shape his body for a first-time effort, unleashing a rasping left-footed drive which appeared to be flying wide of goal before curling inwards and going in via the post. The power and placement of the shot explained Puerta's *La Zurda de Diamante*, 'Diamond Left Foot' nickname.

Two weeks later, Sevilla lifted the UEFA Cup after overcoming Middlesbrough 4–0 in the decider – Puerta appeared as a substitute in the 85th minute – as they ended a run of six decades without a major title. For the Andalusian club, winning trophies was like getting tomato sauce out of a bottle – sometimes it takes a while to come out but when it does, it all comes at once. The UEFA Cup was the first of five trophies in the space of 15 months. There are many moments which can be pinpointed as being particularly critical in the most successful period in the club's history but Puerta's strike against Schalke was the one that started it all.

Sevilla followed the 2006 UEFA Cup title with their greatest-ever campaign. Not only did they add their first Copa del Rey title in 59 years, but they retained their UEFA Cup – defeating Espanyol in a penalty shoot-out in Glasgow. The undoubted star of that European success was goalkeeper Andrés Palop, who remarkably netted an equaliser at Shakhtar Donetsk in the fourth minute of added time in the round of 16. The placed header from a Dani Alves corner forced extra time and *Los Rojiblancos* subsequently marched on in their European travels. Palop also scooped the man of the match award in the Glasgow showpiece – stopping three of Espanyol's four penalties.

It was a truly memorable season for Sevilla, beginning with a scarcely believable 3–0 demolition of European champions Barcelona in the UEFA Super Cup. Taking apart a side containing Ronaldinho, Lionel Messi, Xavier Hernández and Samuel Eto'o in such convincing fashion was a statement of what was to come. Antonio Puerta took to the field with nine minutes remaining but single-handedly was involved in two special sequences of play. With Sevilla leading 2–0, Barça were stretched and Puerta collected the ball on the halfway line and ran. And ran. And ran. Evading three defensive challenges with breathtaking changes of speed and direction, he was only denied what would have been one of the all-time iconic goals by the outstretched hand of goalkeeper Victor Valdes. Puerta's other moment of genius did put the icing on the cake, though. With the ball on the left byline, he outmuscled and outpaced the great Carles Puyol, who hauled him down for a clear penalty which was duly converted by Enzo Maresca.

Puerta was involved in 48 matches that season, starting 35. For large parts of the campaign it appeared that Sevilla could become the champions of Spain for the first time in 61 years. Journalist Sid Lowe's best XI of the season from La Liga featured four of the club's players: Andrés Palop, Dani Alves, Javi Navarro and Christian Poulsen (*Sevillista* youth graduate Sergio Ramos, now at Real Madrid, was also included). It was an exhausting campaign which totalled 63 matches – a whopping 13 more than eventual champions Real Madrid – and it is not unfair to say Sevilla's success in cup competitions denied them the league title that year. Of the 17 league games which they failed to win, 11 came within four days of a midweek cup game.

One of those critical results came with just six rounds of league games remaining when Sevilla travelled to Real Madrid. Juande Ramos's side were firmly in the mix for the league title, just one point behind leaders Barcelona and one clear of Madrid, in third. Enzo Maresca gave Sevilla a deserved lead five minutes before half-time and even though Ruud van Nistelrooy levelled the scores on the hour-mark, it was the visitors who continued to be in the ascendancy. Dani Alves somehow missed a sitter from just two yards out and had that gone in, it would have killed Madrid in the title race and allowed the Andalusian side to put one hand on the trophy. As it was, *Los Blancos* scored twice in the final 13 minutes while Sevilla defender Aitor Ocio was sent off. Javier Chevantón pulled a goal back in stoppage time but an equaliser was one step too far and the title race was set to go to the wire.

Sevilla won each of their next three games to place themselves firmly back in the race, netting two goals in the final 15 minutes at Deportivo de La Coruña to rescue victory from the jaws of defeat. They also had city neighbours Betis and striker Rafael Sóbis to thank for scoring a last-minute equaliser at the Camp Nou as the league leaders stumbled. With two matches remaining Sevilla were third and two points behind both Barça and Madrid, with the penultimate day of the season bringing scarcely believable drama.

Madrid had the toughest assignment – a trip to European-chasing Real Zaragoza, with Barcelona hosting mid-table Espanyol and Sevilla travelling to Real Mallorca. None of the three title hopefuls were victorious. Van Nistelrooy netted a last-minute equaliser for Madrid to rescue a draw at virtually the same time as Raúl Tamudo scored a dramatic leveller for Espanyol in the Catalan derby (the second time in the run-in when Barça were denied at the death). Sevilla were closing in on the door to success, but they could not find the key.

"That Mallorca game will never be forgotten, if only we'd have won ... but we fought until the end," Jesús Navas reflected years later to *ABC*. There was a tangible sense of regret over what had really felt like a once-in-a-lifetime opportunity. Not that Navas himself could be blamed, as he was injured in the warm-up. Frédéric Kanouté was not involved in the matchday squad due to exhaustion and Adriano went off injured in the opening 10 minutes. Sevilla had no luck – they had several strong penalty appeals waved away while defender Ivica Dragutinović was dismissed late in the second half. It was Sevilla's sixth scoreless away draw of the league campaign and it blew their opportunity of jointly leading the table going into the final day of the season, as their title hopes went up in smoke. They lost 1–0 at home to Villarreal on the final day of the campaign, but it was the draw in the Balearic Islands which proved decisive as Madrid, who were certainly not the best team in Spain that season, lifted the league title thanks to a superior head-to-head record against Barcelona. The sporting pain felt by Sevilla across the final two league games was a tough pill to swallow but was a drop in the ocean in comparison to the agony felt two months later.

* * * * *

The 2007/08 campaign had initially appeared to be a continuation of Sevilla's remarkable rise into the elite of Spanish and European football. They became the first Andalusian team to win the Supercopa de España and did so emphatically, defeating Real Madrid 1–0 in Seville before embarrassing the Spanish champions 5–3 in the Santiago Bernabéu with Frédéric Kanouté grabbing a hat-trick. With one trophy secured straight away, the club were also on course to participate in the Champions League group stages for the first time ever. A 2–0 victory at home to AEK Athens in the qualification round put Juande Ramos's side on course for a new adventure.

Their first La Liga task of the campaign was a home clash against Getafe, whom they had overcome months earlier in the Copa del Rey final. The pre-match build-up had centred around the future of Dani Alves. The Brazilian international, who was blossoming into one of world football's greatest full-backs, had received two bids from Chelsea which were knocked back by Sevilla. Alves had claimed he "could not turn down" such an opportunity and publicly spoke of his dismay at how club chairman José María del Nido had handled the situation. Ahead of kick-off, a banner by Sevilla's *Biris Norte* ultras read: "Alves, you came here as a child, you'll leave as a mercenary." The situation appeared irreparable but a few hours later nobody was concerned with the defender's future, not least the player himself.

Pablo Hernández's free kick had given Getafe a first-minute lead, dampening an atmosphere which had just seen the recently attained Supercopa paraded around the pitch. Sevilla could not get into their rhythm and on the half-hour mark a Getafe attack petered out with the ball drifting out of play for a goal kick. Goalkeeper Andrés Palop had attempted to restart play swiftly but his attention was diverted by team-mate Ivica Dragutinović – the Serbian defender was rushing back towards the byline where Antonio Puerta had initially collapsed to his knees before lying down on the pitch. Medics sprinted on, with Puerta appearing to be writhing on the ground in agony. Puerta had twice previously been forced to withdraw from matches when suffering dizzy spells but there had been no previous concern about his health or well-being.

A sense of anxiety was replaced with relief as Puerta, with the help of medical staff, was helped to his feet and walked gingerly off the pitch, replaced by Duda. Sevilla won the game 4–1 but, unbeknown to those on the pitch, Puerta had collapsed again in the dressing room and was rushed to the city's Virgen del Rocío hospital. Dramatic televised footage showed the resuscitated player being rushed out of the stadium and into an ambulance by medics, with the news reporting later that evening that he had suffered five cardio-respiratory stoppages.

There was grave concern for the 22-year-old, who had been scouted extensively by Manchester United and Arsenal while Real Madrid had also been strongly linked with him. A local boy, he had not only won the hearts of Sevilla fans but was deeply admired by rivals too. In hospital, it was not only his club team-mates who rushed to see him but many from Real Betis too, alongside former colleagues José Antonio Reyes and Julio Baptista, and close friend Sergio Ramos. His condition was described as stable but critical.

The Spain international spent 36 hours in an induced coma connected to a ventilator but his condition worsened to 'extremely critical'. On 28 August 2007, at 1.30pm, Puerta passed away. It emerged that he possessed a hereditary and incurable heart disease which brought on prolonged heart attacks, resulting in multiple organ failure and irreversible brain damage. An interrogation over how this had gone undetected would follow but the initial reaction was one of deep, painful mourning. The club, the city, the league and the nation were reduced to harrowed disbelief. For the second time in Sevilla's history, a player had passed away as a result of his playing career. The similarities to Pedro Berruezo's death (see Chapter 18) were remarkable, but that had been 34 years prior and there had been huge advancements in medical science since.

The first-team squad immediately returned to the city from Athens as their return match had been postponed due to the tragedy. Tens of thousands lined the streets as Puerta's coffin was returned to the Ramón Sánchez-Pizjuán, where he had represented his boyhood club just four days earlier. Spontaneous applause and chants of "Puerta amigo, Sevilla esta contigo" (Puerta friend, Sevilla is with you) were audible, but most people simply broke down in tears.

An official delegation from Real Betis made their way to Nervión to pay tribute, with the entire *Los Verdiblancos* first-team squad attending both the vigil and funeral of a player who embodied their eternal rivals. This symbolism itself was powerful but was nothing compared with what was to follow – a red-eyed and visibly emotional Manuel Ruiz de Lopera embracing his sworn enemy José María del Nido. Mourning and sorrow had given way to unity, humanity and hope. "Betis and Sevilla are brothers," Lopera told *Canal Sur* that night. "Antonio Puerta has sent us a message of unity from heaven."

Cynicism about Lopera's actions would have been appropriate under any other circumstances but this message was both powerful and enduring. The following month, Betis celebrated their centenary year with a special event at the Royal Alcázar in the heart of Seville. Del Nido and several Sevilla officials attended the event without incident, while earlier that year he would not countenance sitting alongside the ludicrous bust of Lopera in the Betis directors' box. Two years earlier, no Betis officials had been present at Sevilla's celebrations due to the frictional relationship which was manifesting itself at all levels. Now, the most popular name to be printed on Betis shirts was that of Puerta and a new, mature approach from Lopera had helped steer the city and its rivalry back on to the right track. "When Puerta passed away, Sevilla and Betis were in an awful situation of war between the boards and the fans from both sides," Mateo González, head of sport at *ABC de Sevilla* explained to me. "That horrible death made everybody change their minds and face the rivalry in a better way."

Puerta's girlfriend, Mar Roldan, was heavily pregnant at the time of his death, and two months later Aitor Antonio Puerta Roldan was born and was instantly made a life member of Sevilla.

In the immediate aftermath of the player's passing, Sevilla retired Puerta's 16 shirt but were forced to reinstate it by jobsworths at the Spanish FA, whose rules stipulated that players must fill numbers 1–23. Puerta's friend David Prieto subsequently took the shirt, describing the number as "a responsibility, a proud moment, and an honour." Jesús Navas inherited the number upon his return to Sevilla in 2017 and said: "This is an important number; I know what it represents. Antonio will always be in my memory. He had incredible values and it is our duty to carry these on."

Sevilla have done plenty to ensure their former winger is never forgotten, because anything else would not be an option. The Antonio Puerta Trophy match is annually played at their stadium and a football school was set up in the player's name to give local young players their chance to develop and play alongside their heroes, just as Puerta had done. Chants ring out in his honour in the 16th minute of every home game and, in 2012, a street was named after him, with Calle Antonio Puerta replacing Calle Palacio Valdés just a few minutes' walk from the club's stadium.

However, in May 2008 Puerta's parents Antonio Puerta García and Dolores Pérez Castaño published a letter which represented a stunning attack on the club's handling of their son's death, with particular criticism directed at president del Nido. Puerta's image had been used by the club to promote a fundraising 'Champions for Africa' friendly encounter, a decision which proved too much for his grieving family. In addition to clarifying how the image had not been requested through them, the letter added:

"Neither president del Nido, nor any member of his Board of Directors, has had the decency to contact this family, either by phone or in person, to express some form of condolence.

"Neither del Nido, nor any member of his Board of Directors, neither by telephone nor personally has invited us so if we want to attend, we would have to buy the relevant tickets. Since the death of our son Antonio, we have had to listen to del Nido, in numerous media outlets, use the name of Antonio Puerta and his death to praise the feelings of the Sevilla fans and to pretend to be in pain. This is for his own benefit, hiding the fact that in more than eight months, he has not even been able to make a single phone call to this family.

"Our family doubts any initiative of del Nido as we believe his expressed feelings of pain due to the death of our son are exclusively to reinforce his image of president before the fans of Sevilla FC, as evidenced by the behaviour he has had with us to this day."

The letter closed with expressed gratitude to fans of all clubs who had expressed grief for their son. Just as with Berruezo's death in 1973, the family of the bereaved sued Sevilla – this time for €240k – to accept responsibility for the passing and acknowledge the player had assisted them financially before his death.

How del Nido and Sevilla's board conducted themselves is clearly worthy of question, but renewed feelings of togetherness and harmony within the city were not up for debate. In June 2012, tragedy rocked the green-and-white half of Seville as Miguel 'Miki' Roqué Farrero passed away from pelvic cancer, aged 23. He had been diagnosed with the condition 16 months prior after a check-up for continual back pains and underwent surgery the following day to remove the malignant tumour.

Roqué had joined Betis on a four-year deal from Liverpool in 2009 but would play just 14 games for the club before his condition came to light. The central defender had immediately announced his retirement from the game and withdrew to his Catalan hometown of La Pobla de Segur to undergo his treatment. This was also the birthplace of then-Barcelona skipper Carles Puyol, who underwent surgery for serious and prolonged knee injuries throughout Roqué's illness and the two became close friends. Puyol even donated €30k to his fellow defender's treatment but despite this and a vast fundraising initiative – of which both Betis and Sevilla, as clubs and fanbases, contributed significantly – Roqué tragically passed away soon after. He would become affectionately known as 'The Eternal 26' within the Betis support, with applause in the 26th minute of every home game in his memory.

Pepe Mel was the manager of Betis at the time and whilst he combined coaching with writing crime novels, the most significant words he ever penned were in letters directly to Roqué during his final weeks. "You always cheered me up when we were going through our tough times, I know you'll remember this," Mel wrote. "You were fighting a life-or-death battle, but you found the time to cheer me up about football. You made me a better person. I want to thank you."

Sevilla fan Guillermo Tinoco admitted that the reaction from Real Betis to the death of Antonio Puerta and subsequent passing of Miki Roqué fundamentally changed his view on the rivalry between the clubs: "The derbies have been softened by these incidents, although you still sometimes have violence between the ultras due to politics. But I went from being anti-Betis to wanting to see them win against teams from Madrid."

Dos Hermanas – the neighbouring city to Seville, located within its province – translates directly into English as 'two sisters'. Perhaps Lopera's words back in 2007 were the most apt when describing the footballing relationship within the city of Seville: "Dos Hermanos" [two brothers]. Brothers are competitive and sometimes combative, they squabble over superiority and status, but conversely, they share a lot more than they care to admit and when the going gets tough, they are there for each other. [1]

1 Following the competition of this book, former Sevilla captain José Antonio Reyes tragically passed away in a car crash on 1 June 2019. Reyes, who had joined second tier Extremadura five months prior, had been travelling between his hometown of Utrera and Seville when the accident occurred. As with the passing of Antonio Puerta 12 years earlier, it left the city and the world of football in mourning.

Chapter 29

Corruption, Regression and Charges

SEVILLA'S European successes continued after their successive Europa League crowns. Despite carrying the trauma of Antonio Puerta's death, they qualified for the Champions League group stages for the first time in their history with a 4–1 win in the rearranged tie at AEK Athens in 2007. They stormed the group stages too, winning five of their six matches and topping the group courtesy of a 3–1 home win over Arsenal – inflicting the Gunners's first defeat in seven months. The Andalusians were favourites for their round of 16 tie against Turkish side Fenerbahçe, but the tie went all the way to penalties after two 3–2 home victories. Memories of Glasgow nine months previously were not enough for Sevilla as the oft-reliable trio of Julien Escudé, Enzo Maresca and Dani Alves all saw their spot-kicks stopped, and the Istanbul giants progressed.

It became increasingly evident that despite a hugely gifted squad, Sevilla were a side who were drained mentally as well as physically. They had enjoyed the highest highs and endured the lowest lows while their group of players, the most talented and successful in the club's history, was beginning to disintegrate. Despite finishing just three points behind Barcelona in the 2007/08 campaign, they ranked fifth and slipped back into the UEFA Cup, where they finished fourth in their five-team group.

The core of the team from the initial European success remained in place from 2006 until 2010 (or beyond): Andrés Palop, Ivica Dragutinović, Fernando Navarro, Julien Escudé, Renato, Adriano, Jesús Navas, Luís Fabiano and Frédéric Kanouté. Under boss Manolo Jiménez they regrouped and recorded a third-place finish in 2009 alongside reaching the semi-finals of the Copa del Rey. Had it not been for their absurd level of recent success this would have been viewed through a different lens, but so normalised had this winning machine become that expectations were now elevated almost unrecognisably. This in part explains Jiménez's departure in the 2009/10 campaign, despite success in the Copa and another Champions League last 16 appearance. The flip side of this was a 36-point deficit to the league champions and their European exit coming against CSKA Moscow. For the second time in three seasons, Sevilla had topped their group and been handed a 'winnable' knockout tie but had failed to deliver when it mattered most. This was a club who did not suffer fools gladly and for whom winning was the only option.

Antonio Álvarez, the man who led Sevilla in their 2010 Copa del Rey final success, lasted just 21 games and was dismissed in September 2010 – with just three wins from the opening 10 games of the season. They threw away a 3–1 Supercopa de España first leg lead against Barcelona to go down 4–0 in the Camp Nou and, more pertinently, lost both legs of their Champions League qualification tie against Braga. Elimination by Porto in the last 32 of the Europa League and a fifth-place finish in La Liga – and more significantly, now 38 points from the league's summit – saw Gregorio Manzano last just eight months in the role.

It was telling that Sevilla had just three coaches between 2000 and 2010, but then six in the 34 months between March 2010 and January 2013, when Unai Emery was appointed. The two full seasons in between brought successive ninth-place finishes – their lowest league finishes since 2003. Their only European appearance was a Europa League aggregate defeat to Hannover 96. It would be a stretch to describe this as a crisis period for the club, but it certainly marked a regression to normality.

But the instability stretched beyond the first-team squad and management, as president José María del Nido was sentenced to a seven-and-a-half-year prison term by a Málaga court in December 2011 for his part in the embezzlement of public funds in the so-called Minutas case. Del Nido, who was also a high-ranking lawyer, presented €6.73m worth of bills to the Marbella town authorities for legal work between 1999 and 2003 that was never carried out. He was sentenced for crimes of fraud, corruption and embezzlement and ordered to pay €2.7m to Marbella Town Hall. He had acted as a lawyer for former Marbella mayor Julián Muñoz who was implicated in the Malaya case – the largest corruption investigation ever launched in Spain. Del Nido, who was found to be in a 'hardcore group of decision-makers' in the criminality, was barred from practice for 44 years and from holding any sort of office for 15 years.

Sevilla vice-president José Castro reacted to the news by offering his support: "We wish to give our president all the greatest support possible. It is a tremendously unjust sentence that will not serve to remove del Nido from the presidency of Sevilla because it is not a firm sentence but one that can be appealed." Marcelino García Toral added: "I hope he continues to be president of Sevilla for a long time and continues achieving success." Del Nido had a long association with the club, having first joined the board as vice-secretary in 1986 – a position his father had held 15 years earlier. He had been the club president for over a decade and had helped wipe €40m of debt off the club's books and was still held in high esteem in the stands of the Ramón Sánchez-Pizjuán.

An appeal was launched which went to the High Court which ultimately saw the fraud charge dropped and six months shaved off del Nido's sentence, but he was ordered to serve seven years behind bars. Such a decision forced his removal from power at Sevilla with José Castro – who built his business in the construction industry – stepping into the breach in December 2013.

* * * * *

Sevilla's lean spell was nothing compared to that of Betis, who followed up their top-four ranking and Copa del Rey title in 2005 with four successive lower-half finishes and eventual, inevitable relegation. Just as with Manolo Jiménez's later dismissal at Sevilla, the second exit of Lorenzo Serra Ferrer – known as 'Don Lorenzo' in Heliópolis – from the Betis hot seat led, somewhat predictably, to a revolving door. Eight different coaches were in the hot seat between July 2006 and July 2010.

A 1–1 draw at home to Real Valladolid on the final day on 31 May 2009 confirmed a painful relegation with Betis going down courtesy of their head-to-head record against Getafe, who survived thanks to away goals. Club debts were mounting and the demotion to the second tier sharpened feelings of dissatisfaction with Manuel Ruiz de Lopera – who remained a majority shareholder (owning 54 per cent of shares) and was influential in the club's management despite not officially holding the presidency.

A crowd of 65,000 *Béticos* took to the streets two weeks later in a famed protest against Lopera referred to as 15-J (15 June). The mass movement ground the centre of Seville to a standstill, marching from the Plaza Virgen de los Reyes – adjacent to the city's cathedral – to the Plaza Nueva, where the Town Hall is located and where Betis fans congregate to celebrate successes. Emilio Soto, one of the organisers of the protests, reflected upon its significance: "The enemies of Betis now know many *Béticos* are waiting to kill them. Us *Béticos*, with firm dignity, can finish whoever is holding the club back, no matter how powerful they are. There are values to this club which a *Bético* can never lose."

With the slogan '15-J Yo Voy Betis', a number of club legends including Rafael Gordillo, Luis del Sol, Hipólito Rincón and Julio Cardeñosa joined the fans in an attempt to initiate real, meaningful change at the top of Betis. The feeling of animosity towards Lopera had been built over years with continued claims and evidence coming to light of his shady handling of the club and active siphoning of funds towards his own business interests.

Three years before the march, Lopera stood accused of not paying corporation tax between 1996 and 1997 with an inspection finding "a series of fiscal irregularities in the professional relationship between Betis and several companies belonging to its president and maximum shareholder." The prosecutor's office claimed Lopera had drained funds from Betis via his Encadesa business which had been given exclusive rights to administer the earnings produced by the club. In a statement, the prosecutor remarked that Lopera had "abused his position for his own or a third-party benefit and prejudiced the interests of the club," adding that Encadesa's accounts "lacked transparency." Betis accounts showed losses of over €11m with the club owing a further €8.3m to the tax office.

Despite the significance of the 15-J march, no upper management changes were made during the season, which would ultimately see Betis fail to gain promotion back to the top level. Betis finished fourth and just two points off the Segunda title, missing out on ascension due to a convoluted inferior head-to-head record in a three-way tie with Levante and Hércules – who both won promotion. Yet it was off-field matters which were once again more significant as Seville judge Mercedes Alaya began investigating the relationship between Betis and businesses owned by Lopera, which led to the former president being formally charged with fraud. A week ahead of the commencement of preliminary court proceedings, Lopera sold 94 per cent of his Betis shares (and a decisive 51 per cent ruling stake in the club) to Bitton Sport, headed by Luis Oliver.

There was significant suspicion around the entire deal; Oliver had previously been involved with Spanish clubs Cartagena and Xerez –

who subsequently encountered significant financial difficulties – and the sale was processed for a notably cheap €16m (although this was, in part, due to the club carrying an estimated €85m of debts). However, before this could be formally sanctioned, judge Alaya froze the shares and left Oliver with nothing, despite already placing a €1m non-refundable deposit. Lopera still held significant influence within the Betis boardroom and when Oliver's attempts to buy further nominal shares were approved by the club's hierarchy, the judge was once more forced to respond. The underlying suspicion was that Lopera was reinventing his control of the club through different fronts and Betis playing legend Rafael Gordillo – one of the most vocal critics of Lopera's operation – was granted the power to administrate Lopera's shares, and subsequently become acting president.

In October 2010, lawyer Jaime Rodríguez-Sacristán Cascajo was installed as new president after predecessor José León Gómez's official resignation. How much power anyone really held at this stage was unclear due to the institutional chaos which had engulfed the club. Later that month, Lopera criticised the decision by the judge to suspend his sale of shares, commenting that it was "causing serious and substantial economic damage to different people and the club itself." As a defence of his own action, he reiterated that he remained "a Bético at heart."

But Lopera's influence was dwindling both in reality and symbolism. A vote among 9,926 Betis members was held to initiate a name change of the club's stadium, which had been named after Manuel Ruiz de Lopera since the turn of the millennium. Only 160 voted to retain the former president's name, while a convincing 6,107 votes went towards reinstating the former title of Benito Villamarín – the club's former chairman. (2,786 voted for the stadium to carry the name of its barrio Heliópolis, as it had been between 1939 and 1961, while just 655 votes opted for Ciudad del Betis – the city of Betis.) The club's training facilities were also cleansed of Lopera's name and instead named in honour of club legend Luis del Sol.

The results of legal investigations were damning for Lopera. It was estimated that between 1993 and 2008, €24.9m of the club's money was directed from the club towards Farusa, Tegasa and Encadesa – businesses to which the former president was linked. In 2012 there were complaints by 17 Betis shareholders that Lopera's purchase of shares 20 years earlier was irregular. In 2017, a Seville court declared void Lopera's purchase of 31.38 per cent of the club by his Farusa company in June 1992 – essentially, Lopera never paid for the shares which made him the majority holder at the club. Local media responded to the findings by claiming this was "the big lie of Betis."

However, Lopera was acquitted of the alleged crimes relating to misappropriation and unfair administration. Proceedings had lasted for a decade and culminated in a nine-month trial. "In some way the unfair damage to my person and my heritage must be repaired," Lopera bemoaned to reporters outside the court. "With the successes and errors in which, as is normal, I will have committed during my long term, you can never say, in any way, that a president of yours, Ruiz de Lopera, used the office in an ignominious way to rob and enrich myself." The former president pointed to the "extensive, solid, rigorous and equitable foundations" upon which the judgement had been made. "Ten years have been necessary to make the truth prevail that I never took over the club's resources and that, on the contrary, during my fifteen years in office I gave the club all the financial support that was within my reach."

But by this stage Betis had moved on. No longer are they a club run dictatorially and intertwined with outside business interests. *Los Verdiblancos* are a club whose majority shareholder is their fanbase: 14,000 of them.

Chapter 30

Betis, the Club of Art

HAVING narrowly missed out on promotion in 2010, Betis managed to bring several significant figures to the club despite being engulfed in off-field chaos due to the ongoing legal issues surrounding their ownership. Former striker Pepe Mel was appointed manager having spent four seasons in Rayo Vallecano's dugout and two strikers were signed: Rubén Castro and Jorge Molina.

Castro initially had excelled at hometown club Las Palmas and was prolific at under-21 level for Spain but a move to Deportivo de La Coruña in 2004 stalled his progress. He was loaned out on five different occasions, but he had netted 14 goals the previous campaign at Rayo, under Mel. The €1.7m move to Betis would instantly be recognised as supreme value as the striker netted 32 goals in his debut season.

Molina had arrived from Elche and weighed in with 22 strikes that year. Cameroonian midfielder Achille Emaná netted 14, with Betis topping the table with 85 goals and 12 points clear of Barcelona B, in third. The impact of both forwards lasted far beyond their debut season – Castro netted a remarkable 148 goals across his seven full seasons at Betis, over 20 per campaign. This ensured he became the club's all-time leading goalscorer, comfortably surpassing the great Francisco González 'Paquirri' (see Chapter 13) whose goals led Betis to the 1935 league title. Molina, meanwhile, scored 77 times across six seasons – seventh on the club's all-time list.

Despite the excellent longevity of their forwards, this was an era for Betis marked by instability, underachievement and mismanagement. Betis managed to finish seventh in 2012/13, their second campaign back in the top flight, two places and six points clear of Sevilla. Each of the Seville derbies would be among the most notable in the fixture's distinguished history. José Antonio Reyes, in his second season in his second spell at Sevilla, opened the scoring in the first minute in the derby at the Ramón Sánchez-Pizjuán. Reyes added another after the half-hour mark while central defender Federico Fazio also netted a brace before the break. The ever-reliable Castro pulled one back for Betis but upcoming star midfielder Ivan Rakitić completed the misery in the final minute. Sevilla had completed a *manita* against their neighbours – a little hand, with all five fingers raised in jubilation.

In the April return at the Benito Villamarín, it appeared *Los Rojiblancos* were well on course for a similar triumph. Rakitić had scored twice before Álvaro Negredo added a third. It was still the 32nd minute. The natives were mutinous and whilst Colombian forward Dorlan Pabón added respectability to the scoreline before the break, few foresaw what was to come. Castro netted a penalty and in the 55th minute, Gary Medel was sent off for Sevilla. Thirty minutes of relentless Betis pressure finally told in the 88th minute when Nigerian substitute Nosa Igiebor, who many had expected not to play for the club again due to disciplinary issues, found the net. The Villamarín erupted. Bedlam. *El País* cited the match as "frenetic" while *Diario AS* opted for "epic" and *Marca* noted it was "extreme". It was Nosa's first goal in the Primera, it was the first time Sevilla had blown a three-goal lead in the top flight and it happened as the city was preparing for its annual *feria*, which defines the year for many *Sevillanos*. It would lead to *Los Verdiblancos* finishing above their city neighbours for the first time in eight years, but the bragging rights were short-lived.

The following season, Betis were relegated in last place with a pitiful six wins across the entire campaign – a whopping 15 points adrift of safety. Nothing could have made the season worse, right? Wrong. Betis progressed to the Europa League round of 16, only to suffer an exit in the most painful possible manner. Mel had been sacked earlier in a disastrous season which was defined as much by painful defeats to their city rivals as by mass ineptitude which had engulfed the club. The week which saw October turn into November summed up a catastrophic campaign. It started on a Saturday with a 5–0 defeat at Atlético de Madrid – who scored after 13 seconds – and on Monday Mel held a press conference to insist he would stay. The following day, ultras turned up at the club's training facilities to question the players before holding a private meeting with Mel himself. That led the manager to hold a further press conference on Wednesday to distance himself from the event, saying he had no other choice in the circumstances. That did little to convince the club hierarchy, who on Friday issued a statement blaming Mel for the entire episode. On the pitch, they missed two penalties in a scoreless draw with Levante on Thursday before slipping to a last-minute defeat at Málaga on Sunday – the winning goal deflecting off the goalkeeper before looping into the net via the post. If Betis did not have bad luck, they would have no luck at all.

A month later Mel was gone and replaced by Juan Carlos Garrido, who enjoyed just one victory and lasted only 47 days before he was sacked. A run of three consecutive losses, including a five-goal reverse at home to Real Madrid saw Betis cut their losses and turn to Gabriel Calderón. The Argentine had played for the club between 1983 and 1987, and while there was no great expectation that he would halt their inevitable slide back towards the second tier, there was optimism he could lead a European run. Calderón guided his side into the round of 16 with a 3–1 aggregate win over Rubin Kazan – a 2–0 win in Russia sealing an encouraging start to his reign.

Then they were paired with Sevilla in the last 16 of the Europa League. By certain measures this was the most significant Seville derby, and it was certainly unique – the first of its kind on the European stage. Sevilla were clear favourites due to the discrepancy in domestic form but they fell to a shock 2–0 home defeat in the first leg thanks to goals from Leo Baptistão and the aptly named Salva Sevilla (from the Almería province and who had previously played for Sevilla Atlético). "Betis take advantage," announced *ABC de Sevilla* who continued that the hosts were "not right" with Betis goalkeeper Antonio Adán lauded for his fine performance.

The return leg at the Benito Villamarín the following week was seemingly destined for Betis to land a knockout blow but instead they shot themselves in the foot. Reyes netted in the 20th minute while 15 minutes before the break, Carlos Bacca restored aggregate parity and the game went to penalties. Betis midfielder José Antonio Delgado was nicknamed *Nono* and that was exactly what Betis fans were lamenting when he missed the decisive spot-kick. Sevilla's celebrations were so jubilant that they broke the roof of the dressing room after the game, which the club subsequently paid to fix.

Throughout their history, Betis often conspired to rescue defeat from the jaws of victory and when things began to go badly, they imploded. After their Europa League elimination, Calderón's side lost seven of their next eight league games. They were going down without a fight. The situation was all too much for central defender Paulão, in his second season at the club. The Brazilian was sent off in the 4–0 league defeat at Sevilla earlier in the campaign and never refound his confidence. In the 14th minute of a league game at Rayo Vallecano, he played a drastically under-hit back-pass to goalkeeper Adán, allowing Rayo's Rubén Rochina to score. Then, 12 minutes later, Paulão scored an own goal. He sunk to his knees and was unable to carry on. "He couldn't cope with feeling responsible; he couldn't carry on after the mistake," Betis boss Calderón explained. *Diario AS* journalist José Antonio Espiná accused the defender of "pissing on the manquepierda philosophy." It signaled the sorry surrender of a season. Players could not cope, managers could not survive and the club was in administration, with little hope for the future.

* * * * *

Six months after Betis were relegated from the top flight, industrial engineer Ángel Haro and José Miguel López Catalán, an economist, both joined the Real Betis board. The club were under an ongoing judicial investigation into former president Manuel Ruiz de Lopera and they were bankrupt. "I did not know Ángel until we both came on the board," López Catalán explained to *El País*. "Immediately we got along and we were clear that in order to renovate the club you had to buy more shares, even risk your assets, to have a voice and vote and undertake a project of change."

Haro won the Betis presidency in February 2016 – in the club's first season back in La Liga following promotion the previous summer – to become its sixth incumbent in five years, with López Catalán elected as his vice-president. The two Sevillian businessmen – who were aged just 41 and 45 respectively at the time of their appointments – each bought 10 per cent of the shares of the club with the decision taken to leave the club's future primarily in the hands of the fanbase. This was a rather unusual model for Spanish Public Limited Companies (SAD), with only Real Sociedad and Eibar in Spain's top flight using a similar model. "After a healthy agreement on all sides, we wanted a model where *Béticos* would hold the final decision," Haro told *El País*. "The moment things go wrong, we want others to come and take the decisions. We alone are not saviours."

The duo won on a ticket of delivering Betis back to the fans. The first section of shares was sold in 2017 at a price of €120 each – deemed to be affordable. The initial idea was to limit this to 10 shares per fan, but such was the unexpected demand this was reduced to five per person. The second tier cost four times the price of the first and was targeted at more affluent fans who could help pay off the arrangement with the previous shareholders. The supporters now own 55 per cent of the club's shares.

Romualdo Bautista, president of the Betis Peña San Bernardo in the city, spoke of a "moral obligation" on his behalf to buy shares. "I am a worker who has a normal salary, but I must support the club as much as I can," Bautista was cited as saying by *El País*. "Almost all of our members are doing the same thing, all the fans I know have bought shares." He continued that "we do not expect our team to always win, but we expect them to compete and give their all. We want to help."

Haro joined the club's board when it was in financial ruin and he is passionate about the need for sustainable growth. "The economic control of La Liga is the best thing that could have happened, because before then clubs were allowed to spend beyond their means. We have a system in place which gives sustainability both in the medium and long term, while also achieving maximum results on the pitch."

Betis captain Joaquín personally bought two per cent of the club's shares and explained: "I feel part of this family and I am only trying to return everything that I have received here." Lorenzo Serra Ferrer, the former boss who was the club's director of football at the time, owns one per cent of Betis. "I did it because of the opportunity this institution has given me to perform professionally," he explained. "The warmth of Betis fans is unique; I feel at home here. I want to remain linked to this club for as long as possible."

Joaquín and Serra Ferrer are the two figures most strongly associated with the club in the 21st century, while both have drawn on similar ideas of why they fell in love with the club. "The fans demand bold, attacking play," Serra Ferrer analysed. "To play with art. That idea is very pronounced here and it is a factor we take when choosing who our coaching staff and players will consist of." Joaquín added: "At every club it is important to create a good atmosphere and positive feelings but at Betis it is different. Expression and joy are the hallmarks of this club, and it undoubtedly has an impact on the team."

In recent years, Betis have matched success on the pitch with significant strides off it. In the 2017/18 campaign, they recorded their first top-six finish since the 2004/05 season under coach Quique Setién. "We admit the success came a little more quickly than our initial anticipation," Haro confessed, whilst revelling in his side's qualification for the Europa League. This marked the first season of the club's redeveloped Benito Villamarín home, which not only increased its capacity from 52,000 to 60,000 – due to redevelopment of the Gol Sur, the stand in which the atmosphere within the stadium is generated – but underwent a long overdue facelift befitting a club who are one of Spain's biggest.

For the 2017/18 season, Betis broke the 50,000 barrier of season ticket sales for the first time in their history and increased this to over 55,000 the following year. In 2018, Betis had the fourth-largest volume of 'interactions' across its social media pages (a key measurement for attracting sponsorship) in Spain, behind only Barcelona, Real Madrid and Atlético de Madrid. Notably, they had over twice the numbers generated of the side next on the list: Valencia. On YouTube their presence was even more significant – they were third in video views behind only Barça and Madrid. "Football is just an actor in the entertainment industry and content must be generated," explained Haro. "This is very important for the club; it modernises us and helps us grow our fanbase and revenue streams."

"It's complicated to describe Betis; you have to be born a Betis fan to understand," former playing legend and one-time acting president Rafael Gordillo explained in an interview with *The National*. "I represented Real Madrid but playing for Betis is the greatest when you are born a *Bético*. We have a history of suffering; we are the team of the barrio." Yet in 2018, Betis were the fourth-best supported club in Spain despite having won just one major honour in the previous four decades. "There are a lot of things that for me as a northern [Spanish] person are difficult to understand," Quique Setién, appointed Betis boss in 2017, explained. "I understand the passion for the club, the patience of the fans and the rivalry in this city with the other team but it's difficult to explain that to newcomers because it's irrational."

So how do the fans explain it? "There is a Sevillian nature ... a particular way of living and facing life," Javier Guerra Lamos of the Peña Bética Escocesa explained to me. "When bad moments come in, we face them with humour and Betis fans translate this into supporting our team. The fans are crucial, not only for the squad to feel strong and motivated, but in order to understand the club itself. You have to think of it in terms of the passion. The average Sevillian is passionate about life and shall express themselves in this way to transmit what they love."

As Gordillo stated, Betis are a club who are hard to define and difficult to measure in terms of their scope. In the middle of the 20th century, large numbers of Andalusians travelled north to find work with many settling in the Basque Country and Catalonia. There are over 30 Betis *Peñas* in the Catalan region alone and the club regularly hold open training sessions there, such is the demand from the Andalusian diaspora. When playing against Barcelona B in the second tier in March 2015, over 12,000 *Béticos* packed into the Mini Estadi in the Catalan capital.

Real Betis go beyond Seville, beyond the surrounding barrios and beyond Andalusia. Many non-Spaniards may reply 'Real who?' when their name is mentioned but within Spain Betis are a fundamental part of the nation's football fabric. Often underachieving and suffering more heartache than they care to imagine, they are a club who tend to attract sympathy from neutrals. As Lorenzo Serra Ferrer described, it's all about the art. "Betis is a way of living," the former boss added. Players have to understand that here, everything in life involves Betis. People here live with a lot of passion and that is passed down through the generations. You have to understand it and embrace it."

You cannot run a football club on emotion alone but combined with savvy business direction and those with the club's best interests at heart having a final say, it is indisputable that there is a base for Betis to become a leading club in Spain and make a lasting, meaningful impact in European competition. After all, this has already been achieved by their neighbours across the city.

Chapter 31

Sevilla, the Club of Europe

"We've already got used to winning. You have to go to win always. The more you get, the more you have and the more demand there will be." – Antonio Cano, president of Peña Sevillista Macarena

SEVILLA had won five trophies in the 15 months between May 2006 and August 2007 with their greatest-ever squad. Their 2010 Copa del Rey triumph was their only piece of silverware in the six years that followed. Unai Emery became the club's sixth manager in the space of 34 months following his appointment in January 2013 and brought much-needed stability. Emery enjoyed moderate success in his playing career and came from a strong sporting background. His father Juan spent 15 years across the top two tiers of Spanish football, his uncle Román played for Málaga, while his grandfather Antonio, a former goalkeeper of Real Unión Club, conceded the first-ever goal in Spain's Primera division.

Emery had built his early coaching reputation on his success with Andalusian club Almería, whom he guided to the top flight for the first time in their history in 2007 and subsequently recorded an impressive top-eight finish. At Valencia, his teams were ranked sixth, then third three times in La Liga despite a series of star exits and budget restrictions. His managerial style was based on intensity, both in the manner of his side's play and their meticulous preparation for matches. Winger Joaquín, who played under Emery at Valencia, once joked of the overload of information the boss subjected them to: "There were so many videos I ran out of popcorn." Players were given individual discs to bring home and analyse after training but Emery suspected defender Jeremy Mathieu, who later joined Barcelona, was not watching them. One day, the Frenchman was given a blank copy and the following day, Emery asked if he had learnt a lot from the recording. "Yes, it was really insightful," came the reply.

After leaving the Mestalla, Emery spent an unsuccessful eight months at Spartak Moscow before returning to Sevilla. He was now a more rounded coach, possessing the self-awareness to adapt his relentless methods to his playing staff. Instead of giving players homework, he would spend five minutes with them individually following training to clarify what he thought they needed to focus on. "The best thing would be one day you don't show them [a video]," Emery described. "Then they come to say: 'You haven't shown me the video today.' Then you know for sure it is working for them."

Despite the mass upheavals on the pitch (stars Jesús Navas, Álvaro Negredo, Geoffrey Kondogbia and Gary Medel were all sold), the coaching team remained united and consistent. Juan Carlos Carcedo was Emery's long-term number two, following him to each new club even when the opportunity was presented to him to be Almería's number one. It was indicative of the spirit which Emery attempted to instill in his squad. The personality of his players was very important – those who were prepared to learn and adapt but equally as important, those prepared to battle and fight. "In key moments, my players never fail," Emery told reporters ahead of the 2016 Europa League final against Liverpool. "My goal is bringing together all the positive energy and I have complete faith in my players and in this club. Sevilla do not fail when we are focused. We are winners, we are the champions."

Under Emery, Sevilla had won the Europa League in 2014 and 2015. They found themselves a goal down against Liverpool at half-time in the 2016 showpiece, but the manager's pre-match comments were justified by their second-half showing. Kevin Gameiro levelled the score before Jorge Andújar Moreno, known as Coke, netted twice. Coke, who was also the captain, was a right-back but played in a more advanced role for the final due to injuries – as part of a three-man attack behind lone striker Gameiro. His leading part in his side's victory personified Emery's words. This was a team of winners, with a true champion mentality.

This was not a squad with the same level of depth nor talent as the one from a decade previously. Sevilla were not equipped for a title challenge, but this was as much to do with Barcelona, Real Madrid and Atlético de Madrid upping their standards to truly become Europe's elite trio. Sevilla prioritised cup competitions like no other club and made winning trophies a habit. The 2014 Europa League title set the tone – coming from two goals down from the first leg to edge out Real Betis on penalties (see Chapter 30). Remarkably, that was arguably not the most dramatic moment of their run. They were pitted against Valencia in the semi-finals and whilst they won the first leg 2–0 in Seville, they found themselves 3–0 down in the return, deep into stoppage time. With just seconds left, Coke hurled a long throw into the box, flicked on by Federico Fazio, and Stéphane M'Bia – on loan from English second-tier club Queen's Park Rangers – headed home. The camera cut to the Sevilla bench, showing Emery sprinting on to the pitch, tie askew, before changing direction and sprinting down the touchline, hugging all those around him. This unshakable self-belief in victory was evident at every turn and manifested itself once more in the showpiece against Benfica. The Portuguese giants enjoyed the better of the opportunities, but the game went to penalties and Sevilla – just as they had done seven years earlier against Espanyol – held their nerve for victory.

Ivan Rakitić won the man of the match award against Benfica, but he was sold to Barcelona that summer. The following year, Carlos Bacca's double defeated Ukrainian side Dnipro in the final, and he was sold to Milan in the months that followed, while wing-back Aleix Vidal left for Barça. Gameiro and Coke – the two heroes of the 2016 victory – left in the close-season, as did star midfield duo Grzegorz Krychowiak and Éver Banega. Club captain Reyes left too, while the following summer Mariano, Adil Rami, Vicente Iborra and Vitolo – all regular starters in the 2016 success – departed. Of the team who lifted the 2014 Europa League title, only defenders Nicolás Pareja and Daniel Carriço remained by September 2016.

By that stage, Emery had departed too – appointed at Paris Saint-Germain – but his legacy at Sevilla will remain forever. He expertly coached a consistently changing side to success within Europe, winning the Europa League in each of his three full campaigns at the helm. Like Ramos's success in Europe years earlier, Emery's game was based upon directness, intensity and pragmatism. He preferred a 4-2-3-1 system and did not suffer fools gladly. When players did not buy into his ideas, they were sidelined and swiftly dispensed with, such as attacking trio Gerard Deulofeu, Ciro Immobile and Marko Marin. Sevilla never recorded a top-four finish under Emery – they were one point shy in the 2014/15 campaign but the following season they slipped to seventh and, somewhat remarkably, failed to record an away victory in the entirety of the league campaign. They required reinvention.

It came that summer with the appointment of Argentine coach Jorge Sampaoli, who arrived with a reputation of high-tempo, frenetic, attacking football over a 25-year managerial career in South America, and who had won the Copa América with Chile the previous year. With 12 incomings and an equally high volume of departures that summer, a new-look Sevilla sprinted out of the blocks and accumulated 55 points in their opening 25 games (three more than the entirety of the previous campaign, with 13 matches remaining).

Sevilla were in a title race for the first time in a decade and the excitement went beyond just that of their domestic form. They progressed through a Champions League group (their spot attained via the Europa League title) containing both Juventus and Lyon. Paired with Leicester City – who had stunned English football by winning the Premier League title nine months earlier, but who were now badly out of form – it appeared *Los Rojiblancos* had been presented with their best chance yet of a sustained run in the Champions League. They had suffered disappointing round of 16 exits at the hands of Fenerbahçe and CSKA Moscow in the past decade but were overwhelming favourites for this tie.

Sampaoli's side dominated the first leg with goals from Pablo Sarabia and Joaquín Correa giving them a two-goal lead, but they should have been further ahead. Correa was thwarted from the penalty spot, while both Vitolo and Rami struck the woodwork and Sevilla enjoyed over 70 per cent of possession. But Jamie Vardy's away goal put the tie in the balance and ultimately proved to be the point at which Sevilla's season unravelled as a true car crash.

Leicester won the return leg 2–0 with a limp showing from the Andalusian side culminating in Samir Nasri's red card. The French midfielder had excelled in the first half of the campaign, but his form subsequently nosedived, in line with his team-mates. Sevilla won just four of their remaining 13 league games and slid to fourth – a whopping 21 points off the title pace, although enough to qualify for the Champions League the following year. Sampaoli's ongoing flirtation with the Argentine FA, who eventually appointed him as their national team boss at the end of the campaign, was closely linked to Sevilla's late-season slump.

Sampaoli's fellow countryman Eduardo Berizzo was appointed that summer, having led Celta de Vigo to successive Copa del Rey semi-finals and to the Europa League last four just months earlier. Despite a respectable return of 25 points from their opening 13 league games, alongside sealing progression to the Champions

League round of 16, Sevilla's form plummeted when Berizzo was diagnosed with prostate cancer. Assistant Ernesto Marcucci stepped into the breach while the boss received treatment and oversaw a 5–0 loss at Real Madrid. Berizzo returned to the dugout after three weeks but two games and one point later he was sacked, three days before Christmas.

Vincenzo Montella, who had been sacked by Milan the previous month, was appointed on an 18-month contract of which he would only serve four months. The Italian's first league game in charge was a harrowing derby humiliation at home to Real Betis, from which he never really recovered. It had all the ingredients to be a thriller, played on the night of Dia De Los Reyes, when Spain celebrate the Three Kings bringing presents. The derby itself was the perfect gift for *Béticos*, particularly the 600 who stayed in the Ramón Sánchez-Pizjuán long after the full-time whistle was blown.

Their party had started early, with 13,000 turning out to watch the Betis training session that morning. Their side were buoyed and star midfielder Fabián Ruiz – from the Sevillian town Los Palacios y Villafranca – rifled home an opening goal for Betis after 21 seconds; only José Antonio Reyes has ever netted a faster goal. One record had almost been broken, but others would fall. The last of the eight goals hit the back of the net 94 minutes and 34 seconds after the first when Cristian Tello's strike flew past Sevilla goalkeeper Sergio Rico. It was the first time the two clubs had played out a top-flight fixture with eight goals and it was the first time the fixture had produced as many strikes since a 1961/62 Copa del Generalísimo fixture at the same stadium. That time Sevilla had been 5–3 victors but now it was the green-and-white half of the city who celebrated.

There was a distinct sense of significance surrounding the result. It ended Sevilla's unbeaten home record, which had stretched back 14 months and 29 matches – their previous loss had been against Juventus in the Champions League. Sevilla had also been unbeaten in the previous eight derbies, of which they'd won six, scored 19 and conceded just two. *Diario de Sevilla* noted that it was only the fifth Betis victory in the fixture since the newspaper began publishing, 19 years prior. *Marca* and *Diario AS* both spoke of Betis "making history", not surprisingly, given that this was the first time they had scored five goals or more against their fiercest rivals. *El País* wrote that they had "burned" Sevilla, while *ABC* called it a "magical day". Betis captain Joaquín Sánchez warned his team-mates after the match: "Anyone who gets home before five in the morning will be fined."

The derby loss was not the only harrowing defeat of the campaign for Sevilla and it was just one of six games in which they shipped five goals, of which four came in Montella's 28-match rein. There were also 4–0 league defeats at Valencia and Celta de Vigo. It was a tough season, but it was an odd one, spiked with fantastic moments. There was their run to the Copa del Rey Final, including a memorable quarter-final victory over Atlético de Madrid in which they won both legs. The 5–0 reverse to Barcelona highlighted the need for change both in the dugout and within the squad. Yet, somewhat oddly, this miserable run of form was interjected with one of the club's finest achievements.

Sevilla defeated Manchester United in the Champions League round of 16 to reach the quarter-final of the competition for the first time in 60 years. A scoreless draw in the first leg in Seville was followed by a memorable 2–1 victory at Old Trafford. French forward Wissam Ben Yedder was brought on in the 72nd minute. In the 74th minute he slammed the opening goal of the tie into the bottom corner and in the 78th minute he headed home from a corner. United pulled a goal back late on but the Andalusian club were deserving victors.

The club's previous quarter-final in the competition in 1958 had seen an 8–0 first leg defeat away to Real Madrid, but the 2018 edition against Bayern Munich was to prove much more competitive. Pablo Sarabia opened the scoring for Sevilla in the first leg in the Andalusian capital, atoning for his earlier glaring close-range miss. But Bayern levelled the score just before the break with a slice of good fortune, Jesús Navas inadvertently diverting Franck Ribéry's cross into his own net. Spain international Thiago Alcántara won the game for Bayern and, despite a credible scoreless draw in Munich, Sevilla were out. The two fixtures came in the midst of a nine-game winless run which led to Montella's dismissal, although he will always be remembered for the triumph at Old Trafford.

Joaquín Caparrós returned to the club after 13 years to oversee the final four league games of the season, collecting 10 points – including a win over Real Madrid and 2–2 draw with Betis – to confirm the club's qualification for Europe the following season. Caparrós, who insisted he did not want payment from the club due to "eternally being in their debt", was retained by the club and appointed director of football that summer. One of his first actions was to snatch Girona's Pablo Machín as the long-term manager.

* * * * *

Since the turn of the millennium, Sevilla have evolved from a club struggling both in a sporting and economic sense into a side regularly challenging for major trophies. A top-half finish is no longer the barometer for accomplishment, having been achieved in 18 consecutive seasons. "When I look back, qualifying for Europe used to be a success for us," Victor Perea, of the Peña Sevillista El Origen, told me. "But now we must win a title for the season to be considered a triumph."

European football writer Andy Mitten has described the scarcely believable cup victories for Sevilla as the "new normal" for their fans. "They went from winning nothing to winning major cups year after year," he told me. "They found their place in the sun and that became the new normal, even if their gates have remained usually consistent."

Such glory may conversely lead to a tricky situation for Sevilla, who have now set a standard for themselves which is beyond any reasonable expectation. "Nowadays, we have so little time to reflect on victories that it's difficult to fully appreciate them," Andy Brassell analysed. "Also – a bit like with Barcelona under Frank Rijkaard and the era under Pep Guardiola – the two spells of Sevilla dominance in the Europa League are so close together that it's difficult for many to see the seam. Only when it's in the past, in a prolonged fallow period, will people start to fully absorb this era."

Sevilla do not possess the resources for regularly challenging Real Madrid, Barcelona or Atlético de Madrid for the highest honours, but it is not through the lack of trying. Strong sports management has been fundamental to the club's rise, but a strong identity has been equally significant and both aspects will play a fundamental role in their future.

Whilst a large part of the club's resurgence has, quite correctly, been attributed to their ability to navigate the transfer market expertly, the fundamental success has been their incorporation of young, local talent. The definition of *Sevillismo* is felt most strongly in the heart of the city itself. "Ninety per cent of the players who have progressed through our academy were born in Seville," Pablo Blanco, a former local player himself who is now tasked with heading the club's youth recruitment, has explained. "It has always been the case, since I was in the academy many years ago, that the ultimate dream is to make your first-team debut with this club."

The appointment of former boss Joaquín Caparrós, from the Sevillian town of Utrera, to the position of director of football has been "sensational", according to the long-serving Antonio Álvarez, also involved with the club's youth academy. "A training day is organised once a week within all the different levels at the club to understand what it is like to be part of this club." Former youth products such as Francisco López Alfaro, Carlos Marchena and Paco Gallardo regularly attend the sessions, explaining to the youngsters what it requires to follow in their footsteps, and how high the rewards can be. "In our training complex, there are always crowds and former players who come to watch the youth teams," Álvarez continued. "There is a lot of excitement around this process."

Caparrós himself stressed the importance of this: "It's exactly what we want, this policy is a necessity and policy of the club. In recent times we have not had as many homegrown players in the first team, and that is not in keeping with the traditions of the club." President of the Peña Sevillista Macarena, Antonio Cano, has said: "He [Caparrós] started everything." This relates to Caparrós's first spell in charge of the club, between 2000 and 2005. José Antonio Reyes, Sergio Ramos, Jesús Navas and Antonio Puerta were among the stars to come through Sevilla's academy.

"I'm optimistic about the future," Caparrós insisted. "We are constantly improving our youth facilities and we have state-of-the-art equipment. The brand of Sevilla is now known on a global scale – our colours and our badge are famed. We all know how many people have made great sacrifices for us to be where we are now, and we try and repay that whenever we take to the field."

Sevilla's president José Castro first joined the club's board in 1997 and took up the vice-presidency two years later. He is a man who has experienced first-hand their rise to the summit both domestically and in Europe. "The club's stagnation had to change, and from an innovative thought process we have evolved," Castro told *El País*. "Before we did what we could and we tried to get by, but board members have invested money from our own pockets to sign important players. Crucially, we have never been afraid to sell them and grow again."

Castro speaks of a '*Sevillista* faith' – an unshakable belief that they can defeat illustrious opponents, that they never admit defeat and believe in the most improbable of comebacks. "Faith is what has made us win," Castro explained. "To never give up and try to give everything until the last second. When we start competitions, we give everything, everything, everything until we cannot give any more." Director of football Caparrós has added to this idea: "That faith is what makes all of us inside not relax and think about Sevilla every time we start our day."

Cano, the head of the Peña Sevillista Macarena, echoed similar sentiments. "We have achieved many titles with this pure faith," he explained. "I have attended all the finals of Sevilla, that is what my club has given me." Sevilla fans have enjoyed a lot of success in recent years; perhaps they do not realise just how good these times have been. Or perhaps this level of expectation generates a sense of self-assuredness and, in turn, leads to further success. If they remain true to their principles of believing in youth and believing in themselves, their century-long tradition of lifting trophies remains in safe hands.

Bibliography

Select Bibliography

Álvarez Rey, Leandro and Braojos Garrido, Alfonso: *Sevilla en el siglo XX, Volume 1* Braojos Garrido, Alfonso (Universidad de Sevilla, 1990)

Anderson, Peter and del Arco Blanco, Miguel Ángel: *Mass Killings and Violence in Spain, 1936–1952: Grappling with the Past* (Routledge, 2014)

Ashton, Timothy J: *Soccer in Spain: Politics, Literature and Film* (Scarecrow Press, 2013)

Ball, Phil: *Morbo: The Story of Spanish Football* (WSC Books Limited, 2011)

Burns, Jimmy: *La Roja: A Journey Through Spanish Football* (Simon & Schuster UK, 2012)

Carmona Rodríguez, Manuel: *Enciclopedia del Real Betis Balompié* (Solís Márquez, 2013)

Castro Juan, Rodríguez Agustín and Romero, Carlos: *Breve Historia del Sevilla FC, desde tablada a mejor equipo del mundo* (Punto Rojo Libros, 2010)

Castro Prieto, Juan: *Primeros pasos del foot-ball Sevillano, 1890–1915* (Autor-Editor, 2004)

Chavez, Christopher and Goss, Brian Michael: *Identity: Beyond Tradition and McWorld Neoliberalism* (Cambridge, 2013)

Del Arco, César: *Medio Siglo de Fútbol Sevillano – Victorias, Anecdotas y Venturas del Real Betis Balompié* (Selecciones Graficas; Sevilla, 1958)

Franco, Juan Luis: *La Copa del 39, Sevilla Football Club, Campeón de España* (Red Love Ediciones, 2018)

Goig, Ramón Llopis: *Identity, nation-state and football in Spain. the evolution of nationalist feelings in Spanish Football in Soccer & Society*, Volume 9, 2008 – Issue 1

Lee, Laurie: *A Rose for Winter: Travels in Andalusia* (Hogarth, 1955)

Martínez Calatrava, Vicente: *Historia y estadística del fútbol español* (Fundación Zerumuga, 2002)

Matute Y Gaviria, Justino: *Aparato para describir la historia de Triana y de su iglesia parroquial* (The British Library, 2010)

Rodríguez López, Manolo: *Historia del Real Betis Balompié* (Biblioteca de Ediciones Andaluzas, 1982)

Romero, Carlos: *Mentiras del Futbol Sevillano* (Punto Rojo Libros, 2014)

Salas, Nicolás: *El tranvía, crónica de costumbres de la ciudad de Sevilla* (Almuzara, 2008)

Thomas, Hugh: *Rivers of Gold: The Rise of the Spanish Empire* (Penguin, 2010)

Urbano, Carlos: *La Decada Perdida* (Alfar, 2017)

Select Webography

https://www.bdfutbol.com/
http://betisstats.blogspot.com/
http://www.cihefe.es
http://eldesmarque.com
https://espanaestadios.com/
http://lafutbolteca.com
http://www.lapalanganamecanica.com/
http://lastablasverdes.blogspot.com/
http://www.manquepierda.com
http://www.rsssf.com
https://www.sefutbol.com
https://www.uefa.com
Official club websites of Real Betis Balompié and Sevilla Fútbol Club

Select Newspapers/Magazines

ABC de Sevilla
Diario AS
Diario de Sevilla
Dundee Courier
El Correo de Andalucía
El Liberal
El Mundo
El Mundo Deportivo
El Noticiero Sevillano
El País
El Porvenir
Estadio Deportivo
Faro de Vigo
La Vanguardia
Madrid Sport

Marca
Panenka
Revista Líbero
Sevilla
The Guardian